THE NEXT LIBERATION STRUGGLE

# Other books by John S. Saul

Socialism in Tanzania: Politics and Policies, co-edited with Lionel Cliffe (in two volumes, 1972-73)

Essays on the Political Economy of Africa, co-edited with Giovanni Arrighi (1973)

Socialism and Participation: Tanzania's 1970 National Election, co-edited with the Electoral Studies Committee, University of Dar es Salaam (1974)

Canada and Mozambique (1974)

Rural Cooperation in Tanzania, co-edited with Lionel Cliffe and others (1975)

Words and Deeds: Canada, Portugal and Africa, co-authored with the Toronto Committee for the Liberation of Southern Africa, (1976)

The State and Revolution in Eastern Africa (1979)

The Crisis in South Africa, co-authored with Stephen Gelb (1981 and 1986, revised edition)

O Marxismo-Leninismo no Contexto Mocambicano (1983)

A Difficult Road: The Transition to Socialism in Mozambique (1985)

Socialist Ideology and the Struggle for Southern Africa (1990)

Recolonization and Resistance: Southern Africa in the 1990s (1994)

Namibia's Liberation Struggle: The Two-Edged Sword, co-edited with Colin Leys (1995)

Millennial Africa: Capitalism, Socialism, Democracy (2001)

Development after Globalization: Theory and Practice for the Embattled South in a New Imperial Age (2005)

# THE NEXT LIBERATION STRUGGLE

## CAPITALISM, SOCIALISM, AND DEMOCRACY IN SOUTHERN AFRICA

## JOHN S. SAUL

BETWEEN THE LINES · UNIVERSITY OF KWAZULU-NATAL PRESS · MONTHLY REVIEW PRESS · THE MERLIN PRESS
Toronto · Scottsville · New York · London

The Next Liberation Struggle

© 2005 by John S. Saul

First published in Canada in 2005 by
Between the Lines
720 Bathurst Street, Suite #404, Toronto, Ontario, M5S 2R4      1-800-718-7201
www.btlbooks.com
ISBN  1-897071-00-0
Library and Archives Canada Catloguing-in-Publication data are available from the publisher.

Published in Africa 2005 by
University of KwaZulu-Natal Press
Private Bag X01, Scottsville 3209, South Africa
www.uknzpress.co.za
ISBN  1-86914-076-1

Published in the U.S.A. 2005 by
Monthly Review Press
122 West 27th Street, New York, NY 10001, U.S.A.
www.monthlyreview.org
ISBN  1-58367-125-0 paperback
ISBN  1-58367-126-9 cloth
Library of Congress Cataloging-in-Publication Data are available from the publisher.

Published in Europe and Australia 2005 by
The Merlin Press Ltd
P.O. Box 30705, London WC2E 8QD, UK
www.merlinpress.co.uk
ISBN  0-85036-568-6
British Library Cataloguing-in-Publication Data are available from the British Library.

All rights reserved. No part of this publication may be photocopied, reproduced, stored in a retrieval system, or transmitted in any form or by any means, electronic, mechanical, recording, or otherwise, without the written permission of Between the Lines, or (for photocopying in Canada only) Access Copyright, 1 Yonge Street, Suite 1900, Toronto, Ontario, M5E 1E5.

Every reasonable effort has been made to identify copyright holders. Between the Lines would be pleased to have any errors or omissions brought to its attention.

Front cover photograph: David Hartman
Cover and text design by Margie Adam, ArtWork
Printed in Canada

Between the Lines gratefully acknowledges assistance for its publishing activities from the Canada Council for the Arts, the Ontario Arts Council, the Government of Ontario through the Ontario Book Publishers Tax Credit program and through the Ontario Book Initiative, and the Government of Canada through the Book Publishing Industry Development Program.

THE CANADA COUNCIL   LE CONSEIL DES ARTS
FOR THE ARTS         DU CANADA
SINCE 1957           DEPUIS 1957

Canadä

ONTARIO ARTS COUNCIL
CONSEIL DES ARTS DE L'ONTARIO

In memory of

## Otto Roesch

(1951-1994)

fellow scholar activist and dear comrade

who died far too young

# CONTENTS

PREFACE .... ix

INTRODUCTION: Liberation, and After .... 1

## PART I — CONTINENTAL CONSIDERATIONS

Capitalism, Socialism, Democracy .... 15

1. Sub-Saharan Africa in Global Capitalism (with Colin Leys) .... 17

2. "What Is to Be Learned? The Failure of African Socialisms and Their Future .... 32

3. Liberal Democracy vs. Popular Democracy in Sub-Saharan Africa .... 54

## PART II — SOUTHERN AFRICA: A RANGE OF VARIATION

Peace and Reconciliation, Authoritarianism, and "African Socialism" .... 87

4. On War and Peace in Africa: The Mozambican Case .... 94

5. Lubango and After: "Forgotten History" as Politics in Contemporary Namibia (with Colin Leys) .... 107

6. Mugabe, Gramsci, and Zimbabwe at Twenty-Five (with Richard Saunders) .... 129

7. Julius Nyerere's Socialism: Learning from Tanzania .... 146

## PART III — SOUTH AFRICA: DEBATING THE TRANSITION

South Africa in Transition .... 167

8. The Transition .... 173

9. The Post-Apartheid Denouement .... 195

10. Starting from Scratch? A Debate .... 229

11. The Hares, the Hounds, and the ANC: On Joining the Third World in Post-Apartheid South Africa .... 242

PART IV — CONCLUSION

12. Africa: The Next Liberation Struggle .... 257

APPENDIX: A Class Act: Canada's Anti-Apartheid Record .... 269

NOTES .... 279

INDEX .... 342

# PREFACE

To begin, let me indicate my own pleasure with how this book has come into being. Each of the articles that provided the initial drafts of the following chapters was produced under the most compatible of personal and political circumstances and developed in conjunction with the most sympathetic of editors and publications; the details of those origins are specified at the beginning of the notes for each chapter. Moreover, earlier versions of a few of these essays were first brought together in a book of limited circulation published by Africa World Press under the title of *Millennial Africa*; they find fuller and more cohesive expression when linked, as they are here, with other essays and developed within a fresh overall editorial format.

I should also add that there is for me a particularly comfortable fit with the four publishers that have now stepped forward to make the present book a reality and to get it out to as wide a range of readers as possible. It is, for example, a privilege to work with one of Canada's most exemplary progressive publishers, Between the Lines, with whom I have had the honour of collaborating on a joint project previously. Let me mention specifically in this regard BTL's editorial co-ordinator, Paul Eprile, so encouraging and supportive throughout the process of bringing this book to publication, and Robert Clarke, the editor of my text at BTL, and very much more than a "copy editor."

Equally appropriate is the link with Monthly Review Press in New York, not least because it was with Monthly Review Press that my book *Essays on the Political Economy of Africa* (co-written with Giovanni Arrighi) was first published more than three decades ago. The present book is the sixth that I have produced through Monthly Review as part of my continuing Africanist odyssey; I remain in profound debt to my friend Susan Lowes, formerly of that press, for her gracious and committed assistance on my earlier volumes and to Andrew Nash, the current director of Monthly Review Press, for his support of the present one.

With Merlin Press I share a similar long-time connection, as a regular contributor since the 1960s to Merlin's annual volume *The Socialist Register*, once edited by my friend the late Ralph Miliband, and now by two other close comrades, Leo Panitch and Colin Leys. The *Register* has been an invaluable outlet for my Africanist production over the years, and I want to thank Merlin's director, Tony Zurbrugg, for the opportunity now to publish a volume of my own with his press.

Finally, one of my principle intentions in seeking to publish this book in the present form was to ensure that an edition of it, appropriately priced and distributed, would be available to potential readers in Southern Africa itself. I am particularly grateful that Glenn Cowley and the University of KwaZulu-Natal Press have joined with the other three publishers to make this happen.

Let me merely add, as I have had occasion to note of an earlier book of my writings, that there are not only benefits but also risks attendant upon presenting this kind of collection. I have drawn together essays linked thematically, essays that mark a distinctive, if also valedictory, moment in my own intellectual and political development. Moreover, they all circle around certain common issues, germane to Africa at the turn of the millennium. There is, for example, the fallout from "the age of structural adjustment" (as Bill Freund has referred to the recent period in Africa), with the recolonization and stark retrogression in many parts of the continent that has been attendant upon it. There are the reinvigorated claims for democratization and more humane outcomes present in Africa, as well as the record of aspirations and efforts to realize such outcomes that have often fallen far short of their presumed goals. And there is also the abandonment of much of what once passed for progressive African Studies and the production, in many cases, of merely a defeated academic echo of the thoughts of key power-wielders in this brave new world of unalloyed capitalist globalization.

At the same time these chapters were each originally prepared as essays for distinct forums and occasions. I have had to edit them together carefully in the interests of readability and cumulative coherence of argument. Inevitably, however, my preoccupation with a select band of central concerns pulses through the separate essays and even led in these essays' original iterations (as I have found in reworking them for publication here) to some overlap of issue, citation, and phrasing. I have done my best to eliminate the risk of repetition where it has seemed both necessary and possible to do so. Nonetheless, the careful reader may still discern certain favoured licks and familiar riffs reappearing from time to time within the choruses that the diverse chapters of this book represent — just like those recurring thematic motifs that give unity and texture to a good jazz solo, I choose to think. But, of course, the reader will be the best judge of my success in realizing my intentions in this and other particulars.

The analogy breaks down right from the start in any case. For this book is very far from being a solo performance: I have just too many personal debts to acknowledge for that to be true. First, the deepest thanks is to my extended family: Patty (especially), Jo and Nick, Andi and Dave (and now Ben, Clare, and Quinn), who have stood by me through some difficult times (especially during the aftermath of my recent serious accident and long course of recovery) while also, always, encouraging me in my work. Special thanks, too, to my great friend Colin Leys, himself a great support at every turn, who also shared in the writing of two of the chapters of this book (chapters 1 and 5) as well as in the generation of most of the ideas contained in the book as a whole. Thanks, as well, to Richard Saunders, now my valued colleague at York University, with whom it was a pleasure to work on chapter 6. My fellow members of the editorial working group of the now late and much-lamented *Southern Africa Report* (especially my long-time comrade in arms, Joe Vise) helped sustain my attempt to be both scholar and activist over many years, as did the numerous dedicated contributors to the magazine's pages (I think, in particular, of Jonathan Barker, Patrick Bond, Linda Freeman, Judith Marshall, and Eddie Webster, friends and interlocutors in other venues as well as collaborators with SAR).

A number of my students became co-conspirators at SAR but also comrades, friends, and mentors, especially, from early on, David Pottie, Marlea Clarke, and Carolyn Bassett, and later Marnie Lucas, Sabine Neidhardt, and George Niksic, as did older comrades (and former Mozambique hands) such as Lois Brown and David Cooke. Those, both in Southern Africa (in Mozambique, Namibia, South Africa, and elsewhere) and in progressive Africanist circles (academic and/or activist) around the world who have offered me friendship, hospitality, and enlightenment comprise a group far too numerous to mention, but I trust they know who they are and appreciate how very much I feel myself to be beholden to them. Nonetheless, I must specifically thank Professor Jackie Cock and her colleagues in the Sociology Department at the University of the Witwatersrand for providing me, in Johannesburg, with a stimulating environment in which I could develop further some of the ideas now to be found in chapters 8 and 9, and the same could be said, more generally, for a host of "scholarly comrades" at Toronto's York University over the years. As for the dedication, once again it speaks for itself. *A luta continua, caro Otto.*

# LIBERATION, AND AFTER

The essays in this book, written over the past decade, mark the end of white minority rule, especially in the southern cone of the continent — a change that was the result of a first, successful, liberation struggle carried out by the people and movements of those territories that were thus freed. But as we shall see they also mark the difficult birth pangs of a new struggle, a second liberation struggle, against the global structures and domestic elites that have come to inherit much of the power and many of the privileges of the erstwhile beneficiaries of the old colonial and settler-dominated orders.

For me personally the book represents both an ending and a beginning. It is an ending in the sense that it pulls together the most evolved reflections that I have been able to draw from the intellectual and political engagement with developments in Africa, which I embarked upon almost forty years ago. Moreover, it also brings into focus a series of my publications, comprising some fifteen volumes written or edited, that found their first expression in book form more than thirty years ago — in my two-volume work *Socialism in Tanzania* (1972-73), edited for the East African Publishing House with Lionel Cliffe, and in *Essays on the Political Economy of Africa* (1973), co-authored with Giovanni Arrighi for publication by Monthly Review Press.[1] From the mid-1960s onwards I attempted to understand the realities of an Africa that was only recently coming to independence from colonial rule, an Africa that, when I first went to teach and to learn there, basked in the nationalist victories achieved but had also begun to show clear signs of the contradictions and setbacks that would haunt the continent to the present day. During seven years spent in Tanzania, and in subsequent periods of teaching in post-liberation Mozambique and post-apartheid South Africa, as well as the many years spent since the 1960s in researching, writing, and acting politically around Africa-related issues in Canada, I was to bear witness to both victories and contradictions.

For the Tanzania years provided me with more than the opportunity to witness at first-hand some of the initial moments of the politics of independence. The country's capital, Dar es Salaam, had also become, by the 1960s, the central base for movements that were being forced to fight for their national liberation in new and more confrontational ways: the decades in which victorious nationalist regimes north of the Zambezi River first sought to find their feet in the brave new world of formal independence were thus paralleled, for many years, by a quite distinct process — a war, in fact — in Southern Africa. In that region — in Mozambique and Angola, in Rhodesia (Zimbabwe), South-West Africa (Namibia), and South Africa itself — intransigent white minority regimes were not prepared to enter into any negotiations whatsoever concerning a transition to majority rule, thus posing a different kind of challenge for nationalists and democrats than had been true, for the most part, for their counterparts elsewhere on the continent.

In Dar es Salaam I was able to make close contact with members of Southern African liberation movements, notably with those of the Front for the Liberation of Mozambique (FRELIMO, later Frelimo), and to learn of their struggles to overcome the obstacles before them. As a direct result, and even while retaining an interest in and involvement with Africa more broadly considered, much of my adult life became devoted to the cause of Southern African liberation — to analyzing it and, working with others, seeking to help facilitate it. My work in this regard was prin-cipally within the Toronto Committee for the Liberation of Portugal's African Colonies/TCLPAC, soon to be the Toronto Committee for the Liberation of Southern Africa/TCLSAC, of which I was member for the almost three decades of its existence. It is therefore no accident that much of the empirical evidence that is closest to the surface in the chapters that follow is — as this book's subtitle suggests — drawn from the countries of Southern Africa.

I began here by speaking of this book as both an ending . . . and a beginning. For the Thirty Years War for Southern African liberation, 1960-90, which parallels much of my own experience of the continent, has more recently become the pri-mary focus of my ongoing intellectual work. I am, in effect, shifting my job description from that of a political scientist to that of historian, and am now also working on a book that will, when completed, examine that war and its aftermath as a region-wide moment of both considerable significance and great global import. The essays before us now thus become, amongst other things, a contemporary benchmark against which to track the history that has produced them. At the same time, some understanding of that historical process (in diachronic terms) becomes a necessary backdrop to understanding (synchronically) the complexities of the present.[2]

## The Thirty Years War for Southern African Liberation (1960-90) and Its Aftermath

In the 1950s and 1960s, as the British, the French, and even the Belgians felt con-strained (albeit from continued bargaining positions of relative economic strength) to enter into negotiations with rising nationalist elites in their several colonies, it was crucial to the fate of Southern Africa that the decolonization process that

2

unfolded in sub-Saharan Africa found no echo there.[3] In fact, it came to a screeching halt when African aspirations confronted the established power of intransigent white minorities in Southern Africa. Portugal remained in a belligerent and unapologetic colonial occupation of Angola and Mozambique, and the white settlers of Southern Rhodesia would soon consolidate their own control over that land through the 1965 Unilateral Declaration of Independence (UDI) from Britain.

Most centrally, South Africa's apartheid government stood firm in its illegal possession of South-West Africa (which would eventually become Namibia) and confident that it could sustain its own racist premises and practices inside South Africa itself. Such regimes were not prepared to yield to the nationalist and democratic claims of the majority. In Africa south of the Zambezi revolutionary action and ever more effective forms of mass struggle would be necessary to defeat white minority rule, colonial and quasi-colonial — which was the case only infrequently north of the Zambezi and not at all required in the British-controlled High Commission Territories within the region, independent from the mid-1960s as Botswana, Lesotho, and Swaziland. In consequence the "overthrow of colonialism" that ultimately did occur in this region has come to stand as one of the most dramatic and heroic moments in all of recent history.

Between 1960 and 1990, then, Southern Africa became a theatre of war. This was a period bounded, in its beginnings, by a number of events: by the 1960 banning of the African National Congress (ANC) and Pan-Africanist Congress (PAC), which precipitated attempts by these movements to launch armed struggles in South Africa; by a further buildup in Angola of the pressures that erupted into violent confrontation there in 1961; and by Dar es Salaam's emergence as the central staging ground for liberation movements in Angola, Mozambique, Zimbabwe, Namibia, and South Africa. The period spanned the ensuing conflicts that brought independence to both Angola and Mozambique in 1975 and the establishment of majority rule in Zimbabwe in 1980. And it closed, in 1990, with the liberation of Africa's last colony, Namibia, and with the release, in South Africa, of Nelson Mandela and the unbanning of the ANC, which set the stage for a period of negotiations (1990-94) towards establishment of a democratic constitution there and the holding of the "freedom elections" of 1994 that brought the ANC to power.

This regional war of liberation has held a deep significance. As early as 1902 W.E.B. Du Bois asserted, remarkably, that the chief issue facing the twentieth century would be "the colour bar," the "world movement of freedom for coloured races." In this respect, the Thirty Years War in Southern Africa had produced, by the turn of the century, the overthrow of the last (and most intransigent) expression of institutionalized and unapologetic racist rule in the world. In continental terms, too, the liberation of Southern Africa was the final act in the continent-wide drama of nationalist-driven decolonization that was at the centre of African history in the post-World War II period.

The nationalist assertions in Southern Africa in the 1960s and 1970s also partook in the anti-imperialist radicalization of the time that seemed to promise, at least momentarily, a socialist advance in many parts of the Third World. For various reasons — perhaps, above all, because of the growing hegemony of global neoliberalism by the end of the period and the flawed practices of the movements themselves — this aspiration has been the most difficult to bring to fruition: neither the guerrilla-based "people's wars" nor (in South Africa) a genuine mass mobilization produced, with "liberation," sustainable socialist projects or even, in many cases, markedly democratic ones (see chapter 3). Moreover, given the importance of Eastern military support for the liberation wars, Southern African nationalism intersected with Cold War rivalries (the u.s. preoccupation with Cuban assistance to the newly installed regime in Angola offers one especially negative case in point) and with Sino-Soviet tensions that also compromised radical outcomes.

The diverse territorial theatres of war — Angola, Mozambique, Zimbabwe, Namibia, South Africa — had their own concrete and specific histories and dynamics; but the war of liberation carried out across the subcontinent also had its distinctly regional dimensions. Military relations established between liberation movements ranged from the abortive joint military campaign of the ANC and Zimbabwean African People's Union (ZAPU) in Rhodesia in the 1960s to the far more effective links forged between the Front for the Liberation of Mozambique and the Zimbabwe African National Union (ZANU) in northern Mozambique and eastern Zimbabwe during the 1970s.

Political ties also developed among Frelimo, Angola's MPLA (Popular Movement for the Liberation of Angola), and the PAIGC (African Party for the Liberation of Guinea and Cape Verde) in Portugal's West African colony of Guinea-Bissau, all of them co-operating to establish an alternative voice internationally to pit against Portugal's own posturing. Indeed, the liberation movements more broadly shared in the work of projecting the importance of the Southern African struggle: in Africa; in international forums; in the "socialist countries"; and together with their supporters in the non-governmental organizations (NGOS), churches, trade unions, and even some governments (notably in Scandinavia) of Western countries. Nor should the pan-regional symbolism of shared struggle be underestimated: the successes of Frelimo and the MPLA were potent and often-cited points of reference for activists inside South Africa as the popular movement revived there in the 1970s and 1980s.

The various liberation movements were also forced to take cognizance of the regional nature of the resistance to their claims. Significant links — economic, political, and military — were established by Portugal, Rhodesia, and the apartheid regime in South Africa in defence of white minority rule. Equally significantly, the victories in the region did not occur simultaneously. This meant, for example, that Mozambique and Angola, coming to independence in the mid-1970s a full fifteen years before Mandela's release, became targets of ruthless wars of destabilization (see chapter 4) waged by a South Africa anxious to retain a protected perimeter against the precedent of liberation and the establishment of ANC rear bases. Hence South Africa's invasion of independent Angola, and its creation of and/or support for such markedly destructive counter-revolutionary forces there as UNITA (Union for the Total Independence of Angola) and, in Mozambique, Renamo (Mozambican National Resistance), which was itself first created by the Rhodesian regime. Such aggression was also backed, both tacitly and overtly, by various Western interests, notably the United States under President Ronald Reagan, who was both well dis- posed towards apartheid South Africa and, driven by counter-socialist and Cold War considerations, quite willing to target Angola and Mozambique for "rollback" and to delay Namibian independence.

The liberation of Southern Africa also became a focus of a continental politi- cal endeavour. Despite differences amongst themselves in concrete political priori- ties and the levels of commitment of resources that each was prepared to offer, the already independent African states did assume, through the Organization of African Unity (OAU), a significant responsibility for the waging of the struggle. Central in this regard was the OAU's Liberation Committee, itself successor to the Pan-African Freedom Movement of East, Central and Southern Africa (PAFMECSA). Moreover, the front-line states — Tanzania and Zambia and, once they had achieved their own freedom from Portuguese rule, Angola and Mozambique — played a notable role in advancing the struggle further to the south.

The establishment of the Southern African Development Coordination Conference (SADCC) was also noteworthy as a move, however modest, to provide countries within the region with an institutional counterweight to South Africa's overbearing economic power. Indeed, despite very real shortcomings, the role of the rest of Africa in contributing to the struggle for the liberation of Southern Africa stands as the most significant expression of Pan-Africanism in practice yet witnessed on the continent. To repeat: no amount of concern as to the deeply compromised nature of the outcome of the war for Southern African liberation should blind us to just what was achieved, both within the region and by Africa as a whole, in real- izing the basic precondition — that is, the removal of white minority rule — of any meaningful freedom there. However much it was a historical anomaly, such rule would not have disappeared of its own accord and without a fight.

Nonetheless, the outcome of the Thirty Years War remains contradictory. Indeed, in the more sustained analysis of the history of that war that I am now writing, I have tentatively entitled the last chapter "Who Won?" For, alongside the general victory of the war lies the devastation inflicted across the region during the long campaign. This devastation was, in my own direct experience, vast in Mozambique in both material and human terms (especially during the years after the winning of formal independence in 1975 and owing especially to the contin- ued depredations of a South Africa still dominated by apartheid); moreover, the price to be paid there with respect to undermining the once noble aspirations of Frelimo was also very high indeed (see chapter 4). In Angola, even more desper-

5

ately, the war (at once a civil war and a proxy war waged by apartheid South Africa and the United States) ground on relentlessly well beyond any 1990 cut-off date, with cruel import for that country. In South Africa, too, 1990 was as much the beginning of a new struggle for justice as the ending of an old one. The negotiations over the realization of a successor regime to apartheid continued for another four bloody years — until, that is, the election that finally brought the ANC, and Nelson Mandela, to power in 1994.

Even more importantly (as we shall see in Part III, below), the socio-economic compromises embedded in those negotiations and in the ANC's own post-apartheid project have continued to undermine positive prospects for South Africa's poor. Meanwhile, the unresolved question of land, a crucial issue in the liberation struggle itself, has remained a pawn in post-war Zimbabwean politics, with grim consequences (including the manipulation of it by Robert Mugabe in the interests of his own continuing authoritarian control of that country) right up to the present (see chapter 6).[4] And in Namibia (see the introduction to Part II and also chapter 5) the negative inheritances of its otherwise successful liberation struggle have also significantly compromised the moral integrity of the successor state there.

In the end, then, the positive implications of the removal of formal white minority rule have been muted for most people in the region: extreme socio-economic inequality, desperate poverty, and disease (AIDS most notably) remain the lot of the vast majority of the population. Unfortunately too, the broader goals that emerged in the course of the liberation struggles — defined around the proposed empowerment and projected transformation of the impoverished state of the mass of the population of the region — have proven extremely difficult to realize. Even the sense of a common regional identity that might have been expected to surface from the shared region-wide struggle that was once the war for Southern Africa liberation has been offset, if not entirely effaced, by many of the same kinds of xenophobia and inter-state rivalries that mark the rest of the continent. In now writing of the Thirty Years War for Southern African liberation I hope that a greater consciousness of the shared war will help to remind Southern Africans of its heroic dimensions and help rekindle some sense of their joint accomplishment — and that this will provide a positive point of reference from which they can work to once again fire the flames of joint resistance in the new millennium.

Nonetheless, Southern Africans, in realizing their "liberation," now find themselves moved to join the ranks of Africans further north in the search for a way out of the corner into which they have been driven by both the continent's broader history and the inhospitable state of the global economy. They become, in short, potential recruits for "the next liberation struggle" — a struggle against the savage terms of Africa's present incorporation into the global economy and of the wounding domestic social and political patterns accompanying it — that alone can be expected to free them.

## Africa: The Capitalist Cul-de-sac and the Socialist Alternative

Beyond the opportunity that I have had to observe at close hand both the Southern African liberation struggle and its aftermath, my writing here also embodies another kind of history, once again both personal and public. In fact, its composition really began over thirty years ago, in Dar es Salaam and at the university there. In the heat of debates over the theory and practice of Tanzania's vibrant and challenging radical initiatives of the time, many of us, teachers and students, expatriates and locals alike, first cut our political teeth on the question of Africa's contemporary circumstances and possible futures. As I round off, in this book, a series of more recent writings on the African continent, it may seem that we have come a long way from those Tanzanian debates; but there is a strong note of continuity as well.

My central intellectual preoccupation remains now, as it was in the 1960s, the revolutionary prospect in Africa. Indeed, it continues to take as a starting point the premise that a "revolution" — both in post-apartheid Southern Africa and in the rest of Africa — is both necessary and possible on that continent. Note, then, that my books from the early 1970s — the Tanzania "readers" co-edited with Cliffe and the volume of essays co-authored with Arrighi — shared the premise that, as we phrased it then, "socialist construction is a necessary means to the end of development in Africa." Indeed, despite the considerable passage of time since those words were written, I personally see no reason to change this premise now.

It was, of course, with that premise in mind that many of us took seriously the struggle in Tanzania in the 1960s and 1970s. We were not, I think, as naive in our hopes for progressive outcomes there as some of our latter-day critics would like to think. After all, the kind of fine-grained research that so many of us did there demonstrated the complexity of the situation on the ground.[5] The materials published in our readers, and also much else published in and about Tanzania at the time, offer proof of our understanding of that complexity. And there was also our saying of the period, when confronted during our own long stay in the country with the deluge of visiting, primarily American, scholars who floated through post-Arusha Declaration Tanzania: "If you came to Tanzania for six weeks you could write a book; if you stayed for six months you could write an article; but if you stayed for six years you didn't know what the hell was going on!"

What, as expatriates, we did seek to do — alongside Tanzanians similarly inclined — was to help tease out, even reinforce, socialist possibilities from within the contradictory reality of the Tanzania of the time. Perhaps we did overestimate just how much might be accomplished along these lines (a certain "optimism of the will" was certainly at play). But it is significant that in the introduction to our reader Cliffe and I cited Tanzanian president Julius Nyerere's own cautionary injunction that "we are NOT a socialist society. Our work has only just begun." And I don't know how many times during that period I recited like a mantra the warning of Roger Murray, a prominent analyst of African development — if only

in an attempt to keep the full import of its possible implications at arm's length —
that "the starting-point for a lucid understanding of contemporary counter-revolutionary dynamics is a recognition that the historically necessary [socialism] should
not be confounded with the historically possible."[6] It is a warning that haunts me
to this day. But so, too, does a more recent, more generalized, and even more chill-
ing utterance by the U.S.-based Polish writer Adam Przeworski: "Capitalism is irrational, socialism is unfeasible, in the real world people starve — the conclusions
we have reached are not encouraging ones."[7] Nonetheless, even if it would be
unwise to ignore the kind of Greek Chorus represented by these sobering thoughts
from Murray and Przeworski, it would be even more inappropriate to yield to any
such pessimism as Przeworski's.

Writing over three decades ago Arrighi and I came to the same negative conclusions as did other of our colleagues at the time as to the impossibility of a newly
emergent post-colonial Africa realizing either economic growth or (still less) a
meaningful advance towards human development from within the then-present
terms of its framing by global capitalism. Instead, we argued, "the key trend" is
"towards increased subservience vis-à-vis a rationalizing international capitalism"
— with development "effectively constrained by such a continental pattern" and
with, in consequence, a "Latin Americanization of independent Africa . . . well
underway."[8] It was on this basis that we then suggested the "necessity" of a socialist break by Africa from the global capitalist system. Were we guilty — as writers
of the dependency school with whom our work was sometimes lumped were also
said to be — of underestimating just what capitalism was capable of providing?
Obviously, global capitalism has proven to be a rather more flexible and heteroge-
neous target than some within the dependency school imagined at the time. Yet
any such flexibility and growth potential on the part of global capitalism have not
been much in evidence with respect to the African case.[9] Indeed, as Manfred
Bienefeld was to write many years later of the now much maligned "dependency
approach" to Africa:

> Both those on the right and the left would do well to remember that the pres-
> ent African crisis was most clearly foreseen by those looking at Africa from a
> dependency perspective in the 1960s. After all it was their contention that a
> continuation of a "neo-colonial" pattern of development would lead to disas-
> ter because it would produce a highly import and skill dependent economic
> structure that would depend critically on external markets and external
> investors and decision makers; that dependence would eventually become dis-
> astrous in its implications because the long term prospects for Africa's terms of
> trade were almost certainly poor; moreover, that dependence would be further
> reinforced because it would also create within African countries a degree of
> social and political polarization that would lay the foundations for an increas-
> ingly repressive response once those contradictions became critical. Finally, that

view was also very clear as to the fact that this entire edifice was essentially constructed on the back of the peasantry who would have to pay for it eventually. This describes exactly the present circumstances of Africa.[10]

There is, I hasten to add, no need here to debate the historical merits of the dependency school per se or to discuss whether Arrighi or myself or others writing at the time are now or ever have been card-carrying members of that school — even though I personally would continue to profess a strong inclination towards it.[11] For even though the current African crisis certainly has its roots in the nature of colonialism's impact on Africa and in the kind of transition to independence that had been occurring there during the period that we were chronicling in the 1960s, it is the present situation on the continent that concerns me more centrally here. And as regards this present situation I will continue to argue, on the basis of recent research, that Africa — given the specific nature of its insertion into the global capitalist economy — remains entirely unlikely, without a dramatic change away from a capitalist trajectory, to register significant progress. I advance this position most strongly in chapter 1, where I assert (together with my co-author Colin Leys) that the plight of Africa "is relegation to the margins of the global economy, with no visible prospect of continental development along capitalist lines" and that, in sum, "the dream of a transformative capitalism in Africa remains just that: a dream." Moreover, this is the underlying premise on which this entire book is based.

Of course, writing in the late 1960s, Arrighi and I quite specifically cited Murray's warning, registering the counter-revolutionary potential of the new bureaucratic elites, the numerical weakness of the working class (and even the co-optability of some of its members), and the lack of ready availability of "the peasantry" for revolutionary purposes. We noted the limitations of the victorious "nationalisms" of the 1950s and 1960s, which seemed the crystallization of an effective challenge to imperialism, but must now be generally reinterpreted, in light of independent Africa's "false decolonization" (in Fanon's suggestive phrase), as no real defence, but instead as "so many myths designed to legitimate the dominant position of the new ruling classes."[12]

In addition, we marked the way in which this brand of nationalism had transformed pan-Africanism, which had, we said, originally drawn "upon a living tradition of racial and cultural themes and a sense of shared grievance" and had moved "from a radical force seemingly capable of offering real resistance to the further subordination of Africa to Western capitalism, into a conservative alliance guaranteeing the stability of existing neo-colonial structures." Domestically we also acknowledged that class contradictions in independent Africa were "blurred by racial, ethnic and nationalist dimensions which hamper the development of subjective conditions favourable to radical change." We concluded, "For some time to come class antagonisms are unlikely to contribute in a determinant way to the internal dynamics of contemporary Africa." Finally, we analyzed the dismal failure to find either appropriate economic strategies or non-authoritarian political formulas within such early quasi-socialist experiments of the time as Nkrumah's Ghana and Touré's Guiné.[13]

Even so, against any temptation towards total pessimism we also set some store by certain aspects of post-Arusha Declaration developments in Tanzania (see chapter 7). Even more crucially, we located a promise of continued radical advance in that part of Africa that had yet to be transformed by anti-colonial nationalism: "Hopes must instead be focussed upon the liberation struggle in Southern Africa, the implications of which are bound to have truly continental dimensions."[14] Of course, we now know (as documented in chapter 2) that the project of socialism has thus far proven to be a failure in Africa even beyond those first attempts in Ghana and Guiné (and in Tanzania itself). We also know that the liberation of Southern Africa has fulfilled little of the promise of negating the counter-developmental hegemony of global capitalism that revolutionary nationalism in the ex-Portuguese colonies and Zimbabwe and a working-class-driven transformation in South Africa seemed possibly to portend.

For some, these more recent negative developments will merely provide a capstone to their sense of the economic and political defeat suffered by radical Africa and further underscore their sense that the continent's continuing economic crisis intersects with social, political, and cultural realities that yield only limited promise of any likely amelioration of Africa's crisis.[15] But need our "pessimism of the intellect" really run so deep? This is a question that will stalk the chapters that follow.[16] And it is one to which I will return in the conclusion (chapter 12) in evoking, in light of the findings in the first three parts of the book, the processes that might yet give rise to the "next liberation struggle" in Africa.

Each of the following three parts has a brief introduction of its own, which I hope helps to build the overall logic of the book. The preoccupations of these sections move successively from the most general to the most concrete in order to reach the conclusions of the final chapter. Thus Part I (chapters 1-3) sets out the broad themes of the book's argument. Part II (chapters 4-7) then investigates the resonance of several additional themes linked to debates about the past, present, and future of the region, with case studies in particular of Mozambique, Namibia, Zimbabwe, and Tanzania. Part III (chapters 8-11) focuses, in turn, specifically on South Africa, on my own evolving understanding of the nature of the transition away from apartheid in that much scrutinized country, and on my own growing scepticism as to the wisdom and viability of the socio-economic outcomes, largely neo-liberal and inegalitarian, that the ANC's post-apartheid political hegemony has brought to that country. My conclusions, including my positive identification of the significant forces now emerging to challenge the project of the existing ANC leadership, have proven to be controversial ones in South Africa itself, as the discussion (in chapter 10) of the criticisms that these views have evoked makes clear. Nonetheless, it is my own strong sense that a new stage of revolutionary activity is slowly but surely being born in post-apartheid South Africa itself as elsewhere on the continent — a sense that drives most powerfully the argument of my concluding chapter as to the possible imperatives and implications of Africa's next liberation struggle.

# PART I

# CONTINENTAL CONSIDERATIONS

# CAPITALISM, SOCIALISM, DEMOCRACY

In this first part of the book, with its broad themes, we move from an assessment — largely negative — of the prospects for capitalist development in Africa to considerations of what is to be learned for the future — not only from the tangled record of previous socialist assertions but also from the mixed success of democratic aspirations on the continent. All three chapters evoke the central argument of this book: that the problems of Africa (including those of Southern Africa) in the new millennium are sharply defined by the particular mode of the continent's insertion into the wider global capitalist system and, further, that African countries are most unlikely to realize either substantial economic growth or a significant measure of humane development along the lines defined by such a circumstance.

By highlighting capitalism as part of the problem, I am also emphasizing that socialism is — must be — part of the solution. To say this is, unfortunately, to run against the grain of most of the analyses offered up by the African studies establishment. Indeed, it was one of this establishment's leading figures, Richard Sklar, who threw down the gauntlet against the left almost two decades ago in what now seem to be especially symptomatic terms. In a celebrated 1988 essay, "Beyond Capitalism and Socialism in Africa," Sklar notes, as if it were self-evident, that "few sophisticated socialists today rate the 'developmental merits' of socialism above those of capitalism; fewer still would dispute the short-term advantages of capitalism for early stages of industrial development."[1] Advantages? In Africa, almost certainly not — if the argument presented in chapter 1 here has any merit. And yet, by so finessing the growth question, Sklar seeks at a stroke to confine socialists to the terrain of an almost exclusively "moral" critique, to merely an admirable, if limited, unease at capitalism's tendency (in his words) to "marginalize concern for human need" even as "the factors of production are being combined to form efficient organizations." Some redress of this negative tendency, and just enough state intervention to cover society-wide infrastructure costs and to mildly regulate capital in the interests of its own more effective functioning: this is Sklar's prescription.

But what can this mild aspiration regarding state regulation mean in practice? Unfortunately the story of the present crisis of the left does not stop with the surrender of much that passes for African studies to the grim illogic of the global marketplace. For this ignoble, if also contested, surrender has been paralleled by a much more fundamental process: the weakening of the drive for socialist endeavour in the realms of political practice and applied ideology in Africa. This is, of course, a failure that analysts like Sklar can be entirely sanguine about in building their case for an improbably developmental and humanized capitalism. But for those who take left preoccupations more seriously the fact remains that socialist assertions on the ground have indeed been routed across the continent, especially in the two countries, once beacons of progressive possibility, that serve as litmus tests for much of our discussion in the later chapters of this book: Mozambique and South Africa. As a result, and more than ever, the road towards grounding a practice in Africa that could serve to effectively challenge capitalism's cancerous hegemony seems a long one. Nor can these pages pretend to offer an entirely convincing map for such a journey (a theme to which I return, in any case, in the book's conclusion). What readers will find, however, is an insistence that global capitalism cannot meet the real needs of most Africans and an affirmation of the crucial necessity to develop an imaginary that seeks not to go "beyond capitalism and socialism" but instead to continue to juxtapose their rival claims.

This is not to say that emphasizing the requirement of a sustained focus on, first, the weaknesses of capitalism (chapter 1) and, second, the conflicted, but essential, journey towards a revival of self-consciously socialist theory and practice (chapter 2) is adequate to the task of fully understanding each and every issue faced by Africa. The discussion of the contemporary struggle for democracy in Africa (chapter 3) — written several years ago but still absolutely relevant in light of South Africa's most recent (2004) national election and other such exercises elsewhere — acknowledges that the challenges specific to the political realm cannot be reduced to mere reflexes of the pattern of capitalist development, worldwide and local. Those challenges include the work of establishing democratic sensibilities and institutions appropriate to the tasks of disciplining autocrats, both actual and potential and including those "on the left"; reconciling differences (particularly those turned murderous through the mobilization of "identity politics"); and helping to restore some measure of "peace" in deeply conflicted settings. Nonetheless, the tendency to narrow the connotations of "democracy" to its merely "liberal" version reveals a weakness of theory and practice (the absence of an honest and effective political economy of African underdevelopment, for example). For such an approach blurs the necessity for the kind of revolutionary transformation in the economic and social, in addition to political, structures of Africa (and beyond) that alone can give meaning to democracy — a genuine popular democracy — there.

These first chapters, then, seek to locate Southern Africa not only in a continental perspective but also, more broadly, with reference to the overall trajectory of the global, capitalist-dominated economic and political system. They thus provide a necessary backdrop to the chapters that follow. Indeed, such an approach has been a crucial dimension of my own work from its outset, as in, for example, the two central chapters, co-written with Giovanni Arrighi, of my early book *Essays on the Political Economy of Africa*.[2] For the push to generalize outward from Southern Africa has from the first sparked much of my broader writing on both the nature of capitalism and the struggle to overcome it.[3] And this approach remains a crucial aspect of my most recent work of a more general character.[4] Nonetheless, my emphasis here is on the subcontinent that I know best and where, as I also know very well, the struggle continues.

CHAPTER 1

# SUB-SAHARAN AFRICA IN GLOBAL CAPITALISM
(with Colin Leys)

If we define sub-Saharan Africa as excluding north Africa but also bracket off, for the moment, the continent's southern cone, dominated by South Africa, the key fact about the rest — the greater part of the continent — is thrown sharply into relief: after eighty years of colonial rule and almost four decades of independence, in most of it there is some capital but not a lot of capitalism. The predominant social relations are still not capitalist, nor is the prevailing logic of production. Africa south of the Sahara exists in a capitalist world, which marks and constrains the lives of its inhabitants at every turn, but is not of it. This is the fundamental truth from which any honest analysis must begin. This is what explains why sub-Saharan Africa, with some 650 million people, over 10 per cent of the world's population, has just 3 per cent of its trade and — only 1 per cent of its GDP; and why income per head — averaging $460 by the 1990s — has steadily fallen, relative to the industrialized world, and is now less than a fiftieth of what it is in the OECD countries.[1]

It also explains why sub-Saharan Africa's economies have not responded well to the market-oriented development policies urged on it by the World Bank and other outside agencies since the 1980s. Now the aid flow is declining, while population growth is still racing, it was said, towards a barely imaginable 1-1.2 billion in the year 2020.[2] Indeed, by 2003-4 the World Bank could still admit that, despite the much touted (but, in fact, "sputtering") global recovery, the situation is "unlikely to produce growth rates strong enough to cut sharply into unemployment" and that, in particular, Africa's extremely slow growth "is far short of the pace necessary to make significant dents in the poverty headcount or to achieve the Millennium Development Goals in health and education."[3]

As we shall see, some forms of capital see plenty of profitable opportunities in sub-Saharan Africa, but the likelihood that the region is going to be developed by capitalism seems smaller than ever. On a continent of household-based agrarian economies with very limited long-distance trade, colonialism imposed mineral extraction and cash-crop production for export, with manufacturing supposed to come later. Today, however, world demand is weakening for the export crops that

African farmers produce — coffee, cocoa, tea, cotton, sugar, tobacco — and competition from much more productive capitalist agriculture in Asia and Latin America is intensifying; while the dependence of industrial countries on Africa's minerals and metals is also declining (by about 2 per cent a year).[4] And takeoff into manufacturing for internal consumption is blocked by an inability to compete with imports and by tiny domestic markets; meanwhile collapsing infrastructures, political risk, and poorly trained workforces tend to make manufacturing for export uncompetitive, even at very low wages.[5] As the Economic Commission for Africa has stated, in most of Africa industrial expansion faces "impossible difficulties."[6] South Africa is, of course, the big exception, with a diversified and relatively sophisticated economy and a population growth rate well below that of the rest of sub-Saharan Africa: if we include all of Southern Africa in our definition of sub-Saharan Africa (the more usual definition), South Africa alone accounts for about two-fifths of its total GDP.

## Africa in Global Capitalism: Two Perspectives

There are two ways of picturing Africa in the context of global capitalism. One is from the point of view of the people living and hoping to improve their lot in sub-Saharan Africa's forty-eight nation-states with a considerable variety of kinds of "insertion" into the global capitalist economy and a corresponding range of experiences of development (or the lack of development).[7] The other is from the point of view of capital, for which Africa is not so much a system of states, still less a continent of people in need of a better life, as simply a geographic — or geological — terrain, offering this or that opportunity to make money.

On the first view, what stands out are two general features. First, besides South Africa, the one large industrialized country in the subcontinent, there are just six other countries with over twenty million inhabitants each — Congo/DRC, Ethiopia, Kenya, Sudan, Tanzania, and Uganda — and one super-large country, Nigeria. Between them, these eight countries account for 61 per cent of all Africans south of the Sahara (and Nigeria, with an estimated 120 million inhabitants by the turn of the millennium, contains almost one in five of them); the other forty countries are small, including twelve mini-states with populations of less than two million.

The second general feature is that, in terms of income per head, size and wealth do not go together: Nigeria is one of the poorest African countries, despite its formidable oil production, with a per capita income of only $240 in 1996. The so-called "middle-income" African countries are Senegal, Zimbabwe, Swaziland, Côte d'Ivoire, Congo PR, Cameroon, Botswana, Gabon, and South Africa. Yet with the exception of South Africa and its near neighbours, and the partial exception of Côte d'Ivoire, most of the citizens of these countries are often no better off than their apparently poorer neighbours: most of the "middle-income" countries are mineral exporters; their per capita income figures are boosted by the value of the oil and other minerals that the big transnational corporations extract and export from them.

In most of Africa, even in countries with major mineral exports, economic life still largely revolves around an agricultural cycle that remains acutely dependent on capricious weather conditions. Growing pressure of population means a constantly expanding landless labour force, partly working for subsistence wages on other people's land, partly unemployed or underemployed in the cities, sometimes migrating to neighbouring countries (for example, from Burkina Faso to Côte d'Ivoire), living on marginal incomes and with minimal state services, including education and health. This situation seems set to persist, or get worse. After a moment of optimism in the mid-1990s, no one now expects to see the 5 per cent growth in GDP per annum that is agreed to be necessary for any significant reduction in poverty (given average population growth in the subcontinent of 2.7 per cent per annum). Few people hold out any hope that the region will even begin to close the gap with the industrialized (or post-industrial) world.[8] As the United Nations' Economic Commission for Africa (ECA) put it in 1998:

> According to current estimates, close to 50 per cent of the population [of Africa] live in absolute poverty. This percentage is expected to increase at the beginning of the next millennium and to prevent that, African countries will need . . . to create 17 million new jobs each year [merely] to stabilize the unemployment rate at the current level.

The Commission did not see this as a likely prospect.[9]

Indeed, there was a similar story to tell in 2004, when, in May, the ECA stated publicly that "poverty levels on the continent had increased by 43 percent over the last 10 years."[10] The Commission argued, "If the number of people living in extreme poverty is to be halved by 2015, as called for in the millennial development goals (MDGs), not only would economies need substantial growth of at least seven percent, but incomes would have to be distributed more equitably."[11] And yet, as ECA senior economist Shamika Sirimanne put it, "The share of commodities in export earnings of HIPC [highly indebted poor countries] countries averages about 84 percent, making them extremely vulnerable to short-run volatility and secular downward trends in world prices."[12] Moreover, the later reports of the even more market-oriented African Development Bank continue to have, despite every effort to identify bright spots, a similarly sombre tone overall, and understandably so. In sum, in the foreseeable future there are simply no good reasons to think that capitalist development is going to transform the situation.

## Africa through Capital's Eyes

On the other hand, from a corporate viewpoint, in which the aim is not to develop countries but to exploit profitable opportunities, the prospects can still appear bright enough. Above all in the oil, natural gas, and minerals industries there is optimism, even excitement. Africa's resources are still substantially untapped, with many existing discoveries yet to be developed and many new ones still to be made. The "investment climate" has been made easier, thanks, as we will see, to a decade and a half of aid "conditionality," and the returns can be spectacular; the rates of return on U.S. direct investments in Africa have been, for example, the highest of any region in the world (25.3 per cent in 1997).[13] Under World Bank-IMF prompting, stock exchanges have been established in fourteen African countries with another six in prospect, with brokers in London and New York beginning to take an interest in speculating on them; the Economist Intelligence Unit notes that some of these stock exchanges have "generated" annual returns "in excess of 100 per cent."

An economic profile of Africa drawn from this perspective would pay relatively little attention to countries or states, except as regards the physical security of fixed investments and the availability of communications and transport facilities. Instead it would highlight a group of large transnational corporations, especially mining companies, and a pattern of mineral deposits, coded according to their estimated size and value and the costs of exploiting them (costs that technical advances are constantly reducing) — and a few associated African stock exchanges worth gambling on.

This map would also include numerous agricultural opportunities, such as the plantation or outgrower production of tea, coffee, cocoa, cotton, sugar, and the like; some low-tech manufacturing for local markets, such as beer and soft drinks, plastics, and cement; and a very limited amount of export manufacturing (of textiles, for example) by subsidiaries of foreign firms, especially under the Lomé Convention, which gave African countries special access to European markets. A larger-scale version of this map, for smaller capitalists, would show many more modest-scale opportunities for the making of individual fortunes, ranging from construction to transportation, import-export businesses, and hotels. And on no actual map, but existing in reality, are the illegal business opportunities, from diamond smuggling to gun-running and drug trafficking, that corruption and the collapse of state authority increasingly open up. In short, the profile is one of "crude, neo-imperialist" capitalism, exploiting people and resources, but often not needing — and usually incapable of building — the wider social, economic, and political structures required for the development of capitalist production relations and sustained, broad-based capital accumulation.

These two perspectives — of the African people themselves, and of capital — raise a familiar question. Is Africa a victim of exploitation or of marginalization? The short answer must be that it is both. In the popular meaning of exploitation, Africa suffers acutely from exploitation: every packet of cheap Kenyan tea sold in New York, every overpriced tractor exported to Nigeria, every dollar of interest on ill-conceived and negligently supervised loans to African governments (interest that accrues to Western banks) — not to mention every diamond illegally purchased from warlords in Sierra Leone or Angola — benefits people in the West at the

expense of Africa's impoverished populations. Yet, as Geoffrey Kay once provocatively suggested, in the Marxian sense of the term Africa has "suffered" not from
being exploited, but from not being exploited enough.[14] Not enough capital has
been invested; too few Africans have ever been employed productively enough to
create relative surplus value; the reinvested surplus has been too small.

Either way the result is relegation to the margins of the global economy, with
no visible prospect of continental development along capitalist lines. Population
growth has outstripped production growth; the chances of significantly raising per
capita output are falling, not rising; the infrastructure is increasingly inadequate;
the market for high-value-added goods is minuscule. Global capital, in its constant
search for new investment opportunities, finds them less and less in Africa.[15] Which
does not mean that nothing is happening, let alone that no alternative is possible.
It simply means that Africa's development, and the dynamics of global capitalism,
are no longer convergent, if they ever were.

## Disciplining Africa

This lack of convergence is not what was supposed to happen. During the period
of independence — between 1955 and 1965 — the structural weaknesses of
Africa's economic position were generally recognized and it was assumed on all
sides that active state intervention would be necessary to overcome them. Although
Africa would still be expected to earn its way by playing its traditional role of pri-
mary-product exporter, the "developmental state" was to accumulate surpluses
from the agricultural sector and apply them to the infrastructural and other requirements of import-substitution-driven industrialization. Some left variants of the
developmental state sought, in the name of various brands of socialism, to press
this interventionist model even further.

For various reasons, internal and external, this project was not notably successful, even in mineral-rich countries. Globally, by the 1970s, the terms of trade had
turned significantly against African agricultural products while rising oil prices also
hit most of them hard. Loans, both public and private, advanced in the heyday of
African optimism, became crippling burdens as the era of high interest rates set in,
while Africa's own economic backwardness discouraged any great influx of private
capital from abroad. Internally, as well, the class basis was too weak for either a
real capitalist or a real socialist project; under these circumstances the "developmental state" became primarily a site for opportunist elements to pursue spoils and lock
themselves into power. The result: a stagnant Africa that became "the most indebted area in the world." On the continent total external debt, as a percentage of GNP,
rose "from 39.6 percent in 1980 to 78.7 percent in 1994; and as a percentage of
the value of exports it went up from 97 percent in 1980 to 324 percent in 1990."[16]

Fatefully for Africa, this debt came due, in the 1980s, just as the premises of
the dominant players in the development game were changing. The Western
Keynesian consensus that had sanctioned the agricultural levies, the industrialization

21

dream, the social services sensibility, and the activist state of the immediate post-independence decades — and lent money to support all this — was replaced by "neo-liberalism." For Africa this meant the winding down of any remnant of the developmental state. The new driving premise was and continues to be a withdrawal of the state from the economy and the removal of all barriers, including exchange controls, protective tariffs, and public ownership (and with such moves to be linked as well to massive social service cutbacks), to the operation of global market forces. Agriculture became key: free markets, low taxes, and the abolition of urban food subsidies were now to stimulate a reassertion of the "comparative advantage" of rural Africa's cash crops within the global division of labour.[17] States in Africa were compelled to comply: they were debtors, after all, and, with the decline of the Eastern bloc, were also fast losing whatever limited leverage this alternative source of support had given them.

Enter then, crucially, "the age of structural adjustment"[18] in which the neo-liberal reorientation of economic policy became required medicine for virtually all sub-Saharan African economies. Given that most of Africa's debt was to the World Bank and other multilateral agencies, the Bank and the International Monetary Fund (IMF) emerged as particularly central to the process of dictating global capitalism's new terms to Africa. As manifested in their aggressive administering of Structural Adjustment Programs (SAPS), the invasive impact of the international financial institutions (IFIS) on the national sovereignty of target countries cannot be overstated. "What has emerged in Accra," Eboe Hutchful once wrote of the Ghanaian SAP experience, "is a parallel government controlled (if not created) by the international lender agencies," while "the other side of the external appropriation of policy-making powers is the deliberate de-politicalization that has occurred under the ERP [Economic Reconstruction Program], and the displacement of popular participation and mobilization by a narrowly-based bureaucratic management."[19]

Of course, as this process has proceeded the IFIS have come, in theory at least, to modify somewhat the more hard-boiled dictates of the 1981 document, the Berg Report, that first codified this approach. Subsequent reports have emphasized the need not only to better protect the poorest of the poor against the "transitional" costs of adjustment, but also to permit a more active role for a transformed ("market-friendly") state. Yet such fine-tuning changes little that is essential to the overall project: the sustained downgrading of the claims of the social vis-à-vis the counterclaims of the market — alongside the loss of any sense of what a genuinely democratic state (as distinct from an "enabling" state, "insulated" from popular pressures) might hope to accomplish.

What has been the upshot of this kind of structural adjustment even when measured in strictly economic terms? Certainly the economic weaknesses of Africa have not been overcome. As one leading academic commentator, John Ravenhill, concluded, "Any expectations that adjustment would bring a swift turnaround in the continent's economic conditions have been dashed — despite the occasional claims of the World Bank to the contrary." Indeed, he continued:

> Looking back on Africa's first decade of structural adjustment and looking for-
> ward to the end of the century, there are few grounds for optimism. Few
> countries have been able to sustain a multi-sector program of adjustment,
> while, in those that have, several key economic indicators give cause for con-
> cern — especially the increasing levels of indebtedness and the failure of
> investment to revive.[20]

That is also the considered judgment of many African experts. "During the past
decade and a half, African countries have gone through the phase of adjusting their
economies with the support of the World Bank and the IMF," writes the Economic
Commission for Africa, but "an authoritative and candid evaluation of the ESAF
[structural adjustment facility agreements] programmes shows that the results were
disappointing compared to the programme targets and to the performance of non-
ESAF countries."[21]

Indeed, as the United Nations confirmed in 2004, "An increase in international
trade for the world's poorest has not led to any real reduction in poverty in these
countries." The UN also noted that while "many of least developed countries ["particularly the 34 in sub-Saharan Africa"] were more integrated into the world
economy than their rich counterparts," they had nonetheless "seen trade balances
worsen as they have liberalized trading" — and it predicted that the number of
those "living in absolute poverty" would continue to rise exponentially.[22] Others
have been even more critical/pessimistic: Africa's "crisis and the IMF and World
Bank Stabilization and Structural Adjustment Programmes," stated Nigerian economist Bade Onimode, "have generated and exacerbated a serious decline in the
African economy, and created the catastrophe of suffering facing the rural and
urban poor, women, children, workers, peasants and other vulnerable social
groups."[23] In an important article about Mozambique, David Plank echoes Onimode
in defining the current phase of Africa's positioning within the global capitalist system as "recolonization," a situation that, in his view, is more, not less, confining
than the phase of formal colonialism itself. "Recent developments in Mozambique
and elsewhere," he writes, "suggest that the most likely successor to post-colonial
sovereignty will be neo-colonial vassalage, in which the Western powers assume
direct and open-ended control over the administration, security and economic policies of 'deteriorated' states under the banner of the U.N. and various donors."[24]

To be sure, even with Plank's suggestive elaboration in his text, the term
"recolonization" may remain more evocative metaphor than scientific concept.
Nonetheless, it does capture much of the reality of contemporary Africa. Formal
colonialism, sometimes consciously, sometimes not, subordinated sub-Saharan
Africa's development to the needs of stronger economic centres. Nothing now on
the official agenda significantly changes this. The situation in which Africa finds

itself, shaped both by its long-established weaknesses and by the terms of its current subordination, makes it a mere taker of global capitalist signals, forced at least for the moment merely to slot into the role that has been defined for it by capital and capital's functionaries beyond the continent's borders.

## The Politics of Marginalization

What accounts for the degeneration of Africa's erstwhile "developmental states"? A sad story of inexperience, incompetence, corruption, ethnic competition, decline, indebtedness; then structural adjustment, state contraction, state breakdown, war; further decline, further war: such is the consistently overgeneralized media account tinged, all too often, with a barely concealed element of racism.[25] But, as Perry Anderson puts it, "It is merely in the night of our ignorance that all alien shapes take on the same hue."[26] In fact, several quite different trajectories are discernible in the histories of African states, with different potentials for the future.

To understand this we must backtrack briefly to the 1960s. The newly independent African states inherited the colonial state structures, geared to expanding export production of taxable primary crops and minerals. For political support the new leaders had to rely not on urban working classes or middle classes, which mostly barely existed, but on rural notables, whose allegiance they secured through chains of patronage stretching from the ministers' offices to the villages. By the mid-1970s — sooner in many places — this system had become unstable. There was not enough patronage to go round, and those excluded from it mobilized their districts and ethnic groups in increasingly unmanageable opposition. In response to this, "centralized bureaucratic" regimes were created in which an all-powerful president controlled the patronage system with the help of a centralized bureaucracy and army.[27] The best-known examples are Nyerere's Tanzania, Kenyatta's (and Moi's) Kenya, and Mobutu's Zaire, but there were others. Where this kind of system was not created, "clientelism" persisted without central control and degenerated into ever more unstable "spoils" systems — Nigeria, Ghana, Uganda, Sierra Leone, Somalia, amongst others — in which everything was eventually up for plunder.

Economic decline tended to be faster and worse in spoils systems, but virtually no regime was immune from the economic regression of the early 1980s. The impact of the structural adjustment that followed was severe on both kinds of regime. Shorn of patronage by cuts in state spending and jobs, and under pressure to "democratize" — really, to liberalize — even the centralized bureaucratic regimes weakened, while the spoils systems staggered towards terminal crisis. At this point, however, significant differences emerged in the capacity of African states of both kinds to survive, due to important differences in their underlying economic and social structures.

States that relied on peasant export production for revenue and growth had needed to build robust links with the rural areas, and these links proved surprisingly resilient even in face of the acute stresses of structural adjustment, especially when centralized bureaucratism had maintained a degree of prudential control over inequality and injustice in the deployment of state patronage.[28] States that depended on mineral exports from foreign-run mining enclaves, however, had not needed to develop such widespread networks of support, and this lack of support proved a crucial weakness in the new situation. Moreover, mineral exports offered extremely rich and vulnerable pickings to well-armed gangs, and armies were less and less able or willing to combat these gangs; indeed, in many cases the new warlords were former military officers who had struck out on their own as army pay and privileges dried up and armies disintegrated in the wake of coups, counter-coups, and civil wars. It is therefore in mineral-rich countries such as Angola and Congo/DRC, with their less developed political links to the rural areas — and especially where extreme "spoils politics" had already ruined the state (as in Sierra Leone and Liberia) — that warlordism, fuelled by oil and diamonds, has threatened to become endemic.[29]

In this region of Africa, says defence specialist Dale Grant, "What is left of the old Belgian Congo has become a vast pipeline for African rebel movements to smuggle gems and minerals out of their own nations and into the world market." He adds:

> Even the promise of concessions before a victory is won is a marketable com-modity, a sort of futures' market in African outcomes. In early 1997, [Laurent] Kabila sent a representative to Toronto to talk to the mining companies about "investment opportunities." This man may have raised as much as $50 million to support Kabila's march on the capital of Kinshasa. A few months later, the Canadian mining industry was reading announcements like this May 1997 press release: "Vancouver, BC. Tenke Mining Corp . . . is pleased to announce that the Alliance of Democratic Forces for the liberation of Congo-Zaire has signed an agreement . . ." Kabila was not in power when this statement was made. The AFDL is a political fig leaf for his personal rule. His final push to power was spearheaded by fresh troops with new uniforms, weapons and vehicles.[30]

Of course export crop economies are not immune to the risk of warlordism, which can spill over from neighbouring countries (from the Congo and Sudan to northern and western Uganda, for example) or arise from other causes. The originally ethno-religious conflict in southern Sudan, a tragic case in point, illustrates the way in which humanitarian aid to the victims of warlordism can become another source of funding for warlordism, with rival forces extracting a large share for themselves as the price of allowing any of it to reach sick and starving civilians.[31] But in the long run warlordism probably does need a source of revenues greater than peasant export crop production can provide, and by no means all African countries are doomed to undergo it. Still, small-scale production of export crops alone spells continuing economic marginalization. It is hardly credible that

successive generations of young Africans will be content to accept this, and political networks of rural notables held together by patronage, as the last word in
African economic and political development.

## Socialism and South Africa

There was, of course, another trajectory to African politics. Some states — Ghana,
Tanzania, and Mozambique, among others — professed to bend the logic of global
capitalism in favour of more progressive outcomes. The earliest of these attempts,
most often instigated from the top down and perhaps more populist than socialist
("African Socialism"), foundered in both developmental and democratic terms,
although not in the long run any more noticeably than did its African capitalist
counterparts. Still, the absence of self-conscious class action from below, the
administrative and ideological weaknesses of the leaderships, and the severe challenge of finding space for autonomous manouevre within the global economy
proved intractable. Better sited, in Chris Allen's view, were socialist attempts of
more Marxist provenance that grew out of some of the liberation struggles in
Southern Africa, most notably in Mozambique.[32] In such cases it remains difficult
to extract the morals to be drawn from their ultimate failure because, due to the
vicious destabilization that they experienced at the hands of apartheid South Africa
and various hostile Western interests (Reagan-inspired rollback, for example), they
were given so little scope to learn from their initial mistakes.

Still, certain characteristic weaknesses of their socialist practice are discernible,
contributing at least in part to the often grim outcome — including resubordination to the most overbearing of demands from global capitalism — of the projects
mounted in such countries as Mozambique and Angola: far too many instances of
overweening industrial plans and of forced villagization in the countryside, far too
little democratic sensibility towards the complex values and demands of their presumed popular constituencies. Future attempts to develop counter-hegemonic projects in Africa will have to learn lessons from such experiences and also determine
how to disentangle, for purposes of popular mobilization, the all too discredited
notion of socialism from this troubled past.

In this respect the overthrow of apartheid in South Africa was once thought to
hold special promise. In the mid-1980s, for instance, Harry Magdoff and Paul
Sweezy argued:

> [South Africa's] system of racial segregation and repression is a veritable para-
> digm of capitalist super-exploitation. It has a white monopoly capitalist ruling
> class and an advanced black proletariat. It is so far the only country with a well
> developed, modern capitalist structure which is not only "objectively" ripe for
> revolution but has actually entered a stage of overt and seemingly irreversible
> revolutionary struggle.[33]

Magdoff and Sweezy did leave open the possibility of other, less palatable outcomes, but noted, by way of summary of what was at stake, that "a victory for counter-revolution — the stabilization of capitalist relations in South Africa even if in somewhat altered form" would be a "stunning defeat for the world revolution." Unfortunately, if measured against such a standard, defeat would seem to be an appropriate description of what has transpired during the last ten years or so in South Africa. For "the stabilization of capitalist relations" is, by any measure, one clear attribute of that country's transition.[34]

True, there have been many other devastating defeats for the cause of "world revolution" since those words were written, but the implications for Africa of the taming of South Africa's promise in this respect may serve to reinforce the gloomy mood. At the same time others may see a different kind of promise in South Africa's size and relatively high level of economic development. As Manuel Castells reminds us, "South Africa accounts for 44 percent of the total GDP of all sub-Saharan Africa, and 52 percent of its industrial output." In consequence, he suggests, "the end of apartheid in South Africa, and the potential linkage between a democratic, black majority-ruled South Africa and African countries, at least those in eastern/southern Africa, allows us to examine the hypothesis of the incorporation of Africa into global capitalism under new, more favourable conditions via the South African connection."[35]

No doubt (as Castells himself soon concedes) South Africa's continental importance in this respect can be overstated. After all, it occupies only the southern tip of what is a vast continent. Even more to the point, the ANC's decision to abandon the more directive and mobilizational "growth through redistribution" model that initially drove its project in favour of a market-driven, export-competitive, neo-liberal strategy, *pace* Castells, has limited promise of growth and even less promise of delivering substantial returns to the vast mass of South Africa's own impoverished population.[36] Not only have possible alternatives been abandoned, then, but, as even Castells concludes, "The real problem for South Africa is how to avoid being pushed aside itself from the harsh competition in the new global economy, once its economy is open."[37] That, and the question of just what the fallout from hopes denied in South Africa will ultimately be: political decay, heightened criminality, increased authoritarianism — or reactivation of the popular struggle to realize humane and genuinely developmental socio-economic outcomes?

## Alternatives?

The destiny of Africa under actually existing global capitalism is, then, stark; not even the World Bank's experts pretend otherwise.[38] Without a change in World Bank/IMF policy on debt relief, without the end of dogmatic market liberalism as a condition of aid, without a clampdown on predatory outside forces, without protection of all sorts, Africa is doomed to stay marginalized. Without such changes all independent African initiatives seem to be painfully vulnerable. Yet U.S. policy remains blindly market-oriented, as witness the U.S. Congress's own Africa trade bill, which has sought to make market-oriented policies obligatory for African states seeking free trade with the United States. What chance is there of change in this external context?

In the short run not much, perhaps. In the medium run, however, a lot seems likely to change. First, African countries will present increasing dangers to the rest of the world: leading exporters of AIDS and other diseases, happy hunting grounds for mafiosi and mercenaries, anomic black markets for money, weapons, unlicensed drugs, untested blood, dangerous food additives. As these dangers become clearer, Africa will gradually move back towards the head of the aid queue. Second, the climate of opinion is changing in the countries of the North as the social costs of global deregulation become more and more evident. The hegemony of the "Washington consensus" is in decline. As a new generation of Africans is forced by worsening conditions to go beyond the all too understandable political cynicism that tends to prevail now, and to spearhead new movements for reform and development based once more on collective goals and traditions, it will find new sympathy abroad. Third, global capitalism is unquestionably coming up against the limits of the environment; within a few decades continued broad-based growth will be increasingly impossible and market logic will be in question on all sides.

What role can Africans — and African states — themselves be expected to play at this global level in any attempts to transform the capitalist structures that frame the continent's prospects in such a negative way? Africans have certainly been participants in debates about the possibilities of debt relief, both in the assertions of "global civil society" around this issue (the church-driven Jubilee 2000 initiative, for example) and, through their states, in attempts to extract such adjustments as the IFIs are prepared to grant, for example, in the recent (and extremely limited) Highly Indebted Poor Countries initiative. African states have also sought, since the 1980s, to formulate continental terms of reference for modifying global imperatives through such initiatives as the Lagos Plan of Action and the All-African Alternative Framework.[39] And they have attempted regional undertakings — the Economic Community of West African States (ECOWAS) and the Southern African Development Community (SADC), for example — that, in various stages of gestation, seek in proposed common markets (and modest regional planning mechanisms) the kind of scale that might make greater global leverage possible.

However, these diverse initiatives must remain limited since such actions of African states to roll back the debt and/or secure the benefits of larger-scale units are premised precisely on vulnerable quasi-capitalist national economies. Insofar as these economies remain unlikely to generate investment of a more productive and transformative variety — whether from (still extremely weak) domestic bourgeoisies, from international capital, or from complementary state initiatives — investment of the hit-and-run variety is likely to remain the commonest kind, with predictable lack of developmental results continentally, regionally, and nationally.

In sum, the dream of a transformative capitalism in Africa remains just that: a dream.

But what are the signs that Africans can generate the will and the resources to go further? For one thing, multiple developmental assertions do exist at the very local level, and they demand to be chronicled. Thus Jonathan Barker speaks of the existence, in Africa and beyond, of "thousands of activist groups addressing the issues of conserving jobs and livelihoods, community health, power of women, provision of housing, functioning of local markets, availability of local social services, provision and standard of education, and abusive and damaging working conditions."[40] There are also resistances directed more broadly and self-consciously against the kind of parasitic governments that attempt to ride the African crisis to their own advantage. What is more, IFI-induced austerity has rendered such governments even more vulnerable to challenge from below. In response to economic adjustment measures, write Stephen P. Riley and Trevor W. Parfitt, "African peoples have adopted many diverse strategies to challenge, deflect, or avoid bearing the costs of austerity involved and to seek a political alternative to the politicians they hold responsible." Riley and Parfitt document an impressive range of (primarily urban) actors — "lawyers, students, copper miners, organizations of rural women, urban workers and the unemployed, journalists, clergymen and others" — whose direct action has shaken numerous African governments in recent years.[41]

Such resistances — what Célestin Monga refers to as the "collective insubordination" of Africa[42] — have been one factor driving the renewed saliency of democratic demands on the continent. True, democracy of a sort has also been high on the agenda of Western interests, which see some limited form of "liberal democracy" as both a possible means for helping legitimize their broader agenda and a possible check upon state elites that have become just too corrupt to stabilize a viable business climate. To the extent, however, that the project of liberal democracy takes hold in some countries it will achieve little more than the stabilization of property-threatening situations by a momentary recirculation of elites. The class and productive bases for a stable hegemonic bourgeois democracy are just not there, making likely a "persistent domestic unrest over further austerity," as Riley and Parfitt argue. "In Africa, as perhaps globally, 'democracy cannot sustain the debt; the debt cannot sustain democracy.'"[43]

But to what extent might this climate of democratization also open up space for popular initiatives that could prove more transformative? For, in the end, the greatest obstacles confronting the mounting of an African alternative remain as much internal as external: how to act collectively when the mass of the society is still grounded in precapitalist production relations, and already under growing economic and social stress? It is still easier to mobilize people in terms of ethnicity, or religion, than in terms of a social and economic project beyond the local level. Moreover, those with the education and experience to develop a project for radical change are often cut off from the majority by language and distance. Well over a quarter of a million African professionals — a very significant proportion of the continent's intelligentsia — are now living outside Africa altogether. For those who remain, the natural desire to live like a "normal" (Western) person tugs constantly against the poverty, insecurity and constant setbacks of a life dedicated to the struggle for radical change; and the old problems of democratic and accountable leadership that have dogged all popular movements in history reappear.

Yet more dramatic possibilities are indeed in the air, and even beginning to take organizational form. Crude predatory capitalism is already being confronted, in Ogoniland and elsewhere, most often in the name of democracy but also with a redistributive thrust that the imaginary of "democracy" cannot in the end entirely encompass. As the need to attach the demand for socio-economic rights more self-consciously to the demand for political rights becomes even more widely felt, so too can the popular critique of power be expected to expand its focus beyond local abuses of office to confront global injustices (from the abusive Nigerian state, in the Ogoni case, via Shell Oil to a fresh perspective on the workings of the global system, perhaps). In Zambia, for example, the broad trade union-led democratic movement that brought down the autocratic Kaunda government resulted only in the far more IFI-dominated, austerity-driven, and authoritarian Chiluba regime. Can we expect to find Zambians asking much more searching questions about the nature of power, national and global, next time round — while also beginning to imagine struggles that could narrow the sweeping prerogatives of capital that now serve to frame their negative circumstances? When merely "democratic" challenges to power in a country such as Kenya collapse into squabbling, often cast in ethnic terms, between rival opposition leaders — entirely to the electoral advantage of the ruling Moi clique — a younger generation of political activists seems likely to draw lessons relevant to crafting more progressive political practices in the future.

In Zimbabwe, for example, a strong trade union movement has driven a dramatic strike wave in recent years, arguing (alongside other popular organizations) for the formation of a new party to challenge the rancid Mugabe regime from the left: as Patrick Bond wrote (perhaps too hopefully) of this initiative, "What is crucial is that the opposition's political orientation is potentially both post-nationalist and post-neoliberal, perhaps for the first time in African history."[44] No doubt moves such as this — towards creating the broader united fronts capable of pulling together politically both very local and diffuse national resistances — are required. In continental terms they are still in their infancy, however. For one thing, finding a language of "popular democracy"[45] that is both unifying and empowering enough to link together the very diverse realities of urban and rural Africa will be a challenge, as Mahmood Mamdani has emphasized in recent writings.[46] It will be even more challenging to link that language, in turn, to the kind of socialist discourse — still to be rescued from the debris of recent socialist practice, worldwide and African — that could be expected to illuminate the capitalist underpinnings of Africans' problems. And yet, in some circles of African intellectuals this task of recuperation has begun: reaching all the way from the deliberations of Codesria, the prominent Dakar-based progressive research organization (home base at one point to Samir Amin, for example),[47] to the assertions of the National Union of Mine-Workers of South Africa, which regularly evoke just such socialist premises to critique the neo-liberal predilections of the ANC government.

The odds being so long, and the alternative so hard to see, it might be thought that this projection of a renewed socialist thrust in Africa is pure fantasy. Yet it is hardly realistic to imagine that nothing radical is going to happen. What the prominent South African historian Colin Bundy wrote several years ago of the struggle to retain a radical vision in his own country seems equally true of the continent as a whole. "There will be many who remain unconvinced," he noted. "They believe that would-be socialists in South Africa are doomed to defeat: epochally quixotic, tilting forlornly at windmills driven for the rest of history by capitalist energies. To speak of 'prospects' for socialism, they say, requires a leap of faith."

And "perhaps it does," Bundy concedes. At the very least it "requires stamina, creativity and collective resourcefulness." And yet, as he continues, "to imagine that a milder mannered capitalist order can secure a decent future for the majority of South Africans . . . or that South Africa can somehow be absolved its economic history and enter a future like that of Sweden or Taiwan: now that *really* requires a leap of faith."[48]

# CHAPTER 2

# "WHAT IS TO BE LEARNED?" THE FAILURE OF AFRICAN SOCIALISMS AND THEIR FUTURE

The current situation in Africa is a bleak one, then. In the context of the failure of capitalism in Africa, and alongside whatever else may come to be asserted politically on the continent, it seems likely that some revival of socialist discourse and socialist aspiration will also, almost inevitably, have to occur. In this I am reminded of Roger Murray's warning, made after surveying the wreckage of failed quasi-socialist hopes in Nkrumah's Ghana, that "the historically possible" should not be confused with "the historically necessary," by which he meant socialism.[1] Now, as the new millennium proceeds, Africans will again have to face the challenge epitomized in this formulation — and we will debate in this chapter the extent of the truth it may still contain.

But Africans will also have to face this challenge (as to the very plausibility of renewed socialist assertion on the continent) in the additional light of the experience of the socialist endeavour that has actually occurred in the four decades since those first heady days of independence that witnessed Kwame Nkrumah's ascent to a key role on the African left. For, unfortunately, these decades have seen the failure (or is it the defeat?) of all of the various attempts to build socialism that have, from time to time, flared up across the continent. The fact that capitalism as a socio-economic system has itself done nothing more to transform in positive ways the lot of the vast majority of Africans can offer only cold comfort to socialists in Africa in light of this failure. True, such socialists will learn something useful to their purposes from the current bankruptcy of capitalism in Africa, but they will have to explore carefully the record of these failed socialisms as well. What is to be learned from such a study? And just what is it possible for Africans to reclaim, for present purposes and in a changed context, from the devastation of socialist-inspired hopes and efforts both on their own continent and further afield? These questions, too, will be explored in the following pages, both in general terms and by means of thumbnail sketches of three of the experiences in Africa that have seemed to many to have offered most in the way of socialist experimentation and/or aspiration: Tanzania, Mozambique, and South Africa — all three of which are countries in which I have lived and worked for extended periods.

# Socialism(s) in Africa

## Continental perspectives

In the immediate post-colonial period the language of socialism was attractive to nationalist elites and emergent intellectuals in Africa as a means of further distancing themselves from the colonial powers (and the "imperialist system") from which they had won their independence. Often this reflected the sincere belief that a socialist system promised a more just and humane society than any other likely alternative.[2] Socialism could also seem, in light of the apparent strength and rising ascendancy of the Soviet and Chinese models, to offer an effective growth strategy and a convincing rationale for the kind of "developmental state" thought necessary on the left (but even, at the time, on the right) to realize socio-economic transformation.

In many of its earliest expressions the goal of socialism in Africa intersected with the ideological discourse of "African Socialism."[3] This term came to summarize a claim — now much discredited — that there is a "socialism" distinctive to Africa, one that springs, quite spontaneously, from egalitarian cultural predispositions and communal social practices antedating the European penetration of Africa. These predispositions and practices were said to have survived the impact of colonialism and to provide the basis for giving a promisingly collectivist tilt to the policies of post-colonial governments. Sometimes these notions reflected the cultural-nationalist preoccupations of certain members of the first generation of successful African nationalists, less eager to advance a deeply critical analysis of their own societies than to develop an indigenous alternative to left-wing discourses (Marxism, for example) that they considered too Eurocentric or too potentially divisive. Léopold Senghor of Senegal best exemplified such a tendency, perhaps — although it should also be noted that this perspective was, from the very earliest days of African independence, viewed with suspicion by other putatively socialist leaders such as Kwame Nkrumah of Ghana and Sekou Touré of Guinea. These leaders employed a rather more universalistic, if still hazily defined, "progressive" discourse in outlining their own (ultimately unrealized) left-populist and "anti-imperialist" goals.

More often the rhetoric of African Socialism was adopted quite cynically by opportunist elites, on the rise everywhere in Africa, to give a veneer of progressiveness and apparent concern for popular aspirations to their otherwise self-interested and increasingly capitalist policies. By means of this ideological rationale these elites sought to mask the workings of new class structures and continuing imperial linkages that a more rigorous socialist discourse might have more readily revealed to popular scrutiny. A particularly notorious example of this manipulative use of the concept was the Kenyan government's "Sessional Paper no.10" on "African

Socialism and Its Application to Planning in Kenya" (1965), which, substantively, had almost nothing to do with any recognizably socialist intention. It was not long before the Kenyan leadership itself began to rationalize its policies in much more straightforwardly capitalist terms. And certain other much touted variants on "African Socialist" themes — the "Humanism" of Zambia's Kenneth Kaunda, for example — also proved to have little or no genuine socialist content.

In Tanzania, the most sincere and well developed of all variants of African Socialism — and the African experiment perhaps most often discussed and debated in the late 1960s and early 1970s — the experience of socialism was driven by the philosophy and practice of *ujamaa* ("familyhood") as generated in that country by Julius Nyerere. In Mozambique in the late 1970s and, briefly, into the 1980s, a Marxist socialist current had grounded itself more prominently than ever against the pull of African Socialism. This current grew, in particular, out of the experience of the liberation struggles of Southern Africa and found its most advanced expression in the practices of the Frelimo movement and its subsequent government in Mozambique. And, finally, South Africa: in the late 1980s and early 1990s many eyes were focused there, and particularly upon the principal liberation movement, the African National Congress. The ANC was linked both to the South African Communist Party and to a highly mobilized and radicalized network of mass organizations on the ground (including the country's vibrant trade union movement); it seemed to many to promise, in a relatively economically well-developed setting, a much clearer socialist possibility than elsewhere.

Not that the examination of these three cases will exhaust the range of continental experience. Thus, a truly adequate survey of socialist theory and practice on the continent in the decades since the heyday of Nkrumah and Senghor would also have to highlight the theoretical contributions of the likes of Guinea-Bissau's Amilcar Cabral and Burkina Faso's Thomas Sankara; the false dawn of hopes for the ongoing transformation of an Eritrea finally liberated from Ethiopian overlordship; the Stalinoid excesses of that same Ethiopia and of Angola; the shallow, but momentarily enticing (at least to the more credulous of observers) chimeras of socialism in such countries as Somalia and Zimbabwe; and much else. Although I do not intend to go into these other cases here in any depth, I will draw on the full breadth of this continental experience when presenting, in the second part of this chapter, a preliminary summary of the problems and preoccupations that students of socialisms (past and future) in Africa — as well as would-be practitioners there — should keep uppermost in their minds.

## Tanzania

Julius Nyerere and his colleagues in the Tanzania African National Union (TANU) mounted in the late 1960s and early 1970s what was probably the most sincere and well developed of all variants of African Socialism.[4] Suspicious, in part on religious grounds, of Marxism and "class struggle," Nyerere nonetheless evinced, though his ujamaa approach, a high moral tone, a certain scepticism as to the bona fides of Western economic interests and strategies, and a genuine concern for the fate of the mass of the population in his impoverished country.

Nyerere first exemplified his position in a seminal essay, "Ujamaa: The Basis of African Socialism." He wrote that socialism "is an attitude of mind" and that "We in Africa have no . . . need of being 'converted' to socialism. . . . [It is] rooted in our own past — in the traditional society which produced us."[5] At the same time Nyerere sought to balance this (rather romantic) perspective against his own deepening awareness of the profound contradictions inherent in modern African society, producing a series of widely quoted analyses of rural questions, education, leadership, and democracy. Few were the African leaders, for example, who could utter to the mass of their fellow countrymen a statement like the following (summarized in The Nationalist newspaper):

President Nyerere has called on the people of Tanzania to have great confidence in themselves and safeguard the nation's hard-won freedom. He has warned the people against pinning their hopes on the leadership who are apt to sell the people's freedom to meet their lusts. Mwalimu [i.e. Nyerere] warned that the people should not allow their freedom to be pawned as most of the leaders were purchasable. He warned further that in running the affairs of the nation the people should not look on their leaders as "saints or prophets."

The President stated that the attainment of freedom in many cases resulted merely in the change of colours, white to black faces without ending exploitation and injustices, and above all without the betterment of the life of the masses. He said that while struggling for freedom the objective was clear but it was another thing when you have to remove your own people from the position of exploiters.[6]

And he wrote equally bitingly about the kind of class polarization that was being produced both by class penetration of the countryside and by the elitist logic of post-colonial education systems. He also spoke eloquently about the economic choices open to his people:

The question is not whether nations control their economy, but how they do so. The real ideological choice is between controlling the economy through domestic private enterprise or doing so through some state or collective institution. But although this is an ideological choice, it is extremely doubtful whether it is a practical choice for an African nationalist. The pragmatist in Africa . . . will find that the choice is a different one. He will find that the choice is between foreign private ownership on the one hand, and local collective ownership on the other. For I do not think that there is a free state in Africa where there is sufficient local capital, or a sufficient number of local entrepreneurs, for locally based capitalism to dominate the economy. Private investment in Africa means overwhelming foreign private investment. A capitalist economy means a foreign-dominated economy. These are the facts of the African situation. The only way in which national control of the economy can be achieved is through the economic institution of socialism.[7]

In consequence of these perspectives, Nyerere moved his party, TANU, to adopt policies that sought to curb elite aggrandizement and encourage equality, to make foreign investment serve positive social ends, and to facilitate a new pattern of collective life for rural dwellers, about whose materially backward existence he seemed to care deeply. However, even though Nyerere was to sustain his eloquent critique of capitalist-induced global inequalities until his death in 1999, in Tanzania itself his project was not successful, either economically or in terms of realizing socialist ideals. Yet despite this failure, so sophisticated an economist as Manfred Bienefeld has been able (against the grain of some alternative perspectives) to draw positive lessons from the economic policies of Nyerere's Tanzania, seeing the Tanzania of the 1960s and 1970s in this respect as being far more "model" than "anti-model":

The Arusha Declaration, with its nationalization of the commanding heights of industry and finance, its granting of greater priority to agriculture, its leadership code and restriction of TANU membership to those who supported its new strategy, did not automatically increase the resources of the country nor the incomes of its people. It did not even reduce the contribution which foreign capital and technology could objectively make to development, nor the need for hard work, nor the need to make wages and incomes commensurate with production and effort. What it did do was to give the Tanzanian state greater control over the investible surplus being produced in the country. It also further reduced private capital's direct influence within the Party and its indirect influence through its command over resources. As a result, it achieved greater freedom for determining a wide range of economic, social and political policies, including the country's foreign policy. . . . The primary objective of the new strategy was to permit a less uncertain, a more domestic needs-oriented and a more socially responsive utilization of investible resources. It was thought that it could elicit greater effort and commitment from those engaged in production, and that it could eventually capture dynamic external economies, through a greater freedom to direct investment towards nationally defined, long-term objectives.[8]

Of course, one can quarrel, from the left, with various aspects of Nyerere's actual "socialist" practice within the frame of these economic objectives — while also noting the decline in terms of trade and the rise in oil prices and interests rates

that marked the hostile global circumstances within which Tanzania lost its footing. Interestingly, on the negative side, it is the high costs to socialist intentions of
Nyerere's undemocratic propensities (not least vis-à-vis the rural sector, where
forced villagization became the final stage of his experiment in rural communal-
ism) that Bienefeld himself tends to emphasize, and I would agree with him. There
is a certain irony here since Nyerere's model of a democratic one-party state has
some times been praised as offering precisely the kind of institutionalization of a
judicious dialectic between leadership and mass action that could overcome divisive tendencies (ethnic and other challenges to a nascent national consciousness)
while keeping leaders honest. And, indeed, there is something to be said for the
view that this system (with its system of intra-party elections and the Leadership
Code, which sought to control the potential corruption of leaders) successfully
avoided some of the intra-elite political opportunism and consequent mobilization
of ethnic politics that has often scarred politics elsewhere in Africa. But it is also
easy to underestimate the formidable costs that accompanied the kind of "guided-
democracy by philosopher king" (in this case, by "Mwalimu" — "the Teacher" —
as Nyerere was called), costs to be measured principally in terms of the authoritarian manner in which progressive popular mobilization at the left edge of TANU's
own agreed policies was smashed.

In this regard I would mention the crushing of the workers at the Mount
Carmel Rubber Factory and beyond in the early 1970s (this being, in any case,
merely the most recent stage in the enforced establishment, from quite early on,
of a bloodless, state-dominated union movement in the country), and I would
underscore the importance of the crushing of the irreverent spontaneity of the peasants of the Ruvuma Development Association (RDA) and the subsequent collapse of
the project of ujamaa villages into a forced march towards collectivization. Indeed,
I suggest these to be much the most revealing political moments of the Nyerere
years. And I note the extent to which it concentrated the mind to see, as I had
done, one of my own students, a duly elected student leader, being dragged from
the offices of the university's vice-chancellor (where he had gone voluntarily for a
meeting) and viciously bumped down the concrete stairs of the administration
building by members of the Tanzanian Field Force Unit brandishing automatic
weapons — this for his daring, on behalf of his fellow students, to interrogate university administrative practices from the perspective of the new TANU Guidelines.
Such developments were at least as exemplary of the true meaning of "One-Party
Democracy" for many ordinary Tanzanians as were the "democratic one-party elections" they were being encouraged to participate in — while also giving the lie to
claims that Tanzania's socialism was actually empowering ordinary people in their
struggle against nascent class formation in the country.

Of course, the developments at Mount Carmel, in Ruvuma, and at the university all suggest that a democratic transformation from below of the one-party state
was not going to be allowed to happen in Tanzania, whatever some of us may have

hoped to the contrary at the time. As it happens this was a lesson that would have to be taught again, in Mozambique, where the claim to "democratic substitutionism" made by the Frelimo leadership there also helped choke off any drive to sustain from below the initial revolutionary gestures and quasi-socialist breakthroughs being made from above by that leadership. In sum, as regards socialism in Africa, the challenge of democracy, of the dialectic between leadership and mass action, quite simply would not go away.

## Mozambique

There had always co-existed in post-colonial Africa a more Marxist socialist current. This sensibility had surfaced at the edges of Nkrumah's own project, for example, and also contributed to the leftward inflection of radical populism in Algeria, where an interesting form of collectivism and auto-determination was briefly attempted in the rural areas. But it was to resurface most prominently in the rejection of Nyerere's ideas by a later generation of socialists, many of them linked to the liberation movements and post-liberation governments of Southern Africa.

Mozambique's Frelimo movement (and subsequent party of government), led first by Eduardo Mondlane and then, after his assassination in exile by the Portuguese, by Samora Machel, housed probably the most serious of these critics.[9] Deeply suspicious of Western capitalist dictates and anxious to address the needs of its impoverished population, Frelimo found in Marxism an alternative to the vague nostrums of African Socialism and a possible guide to realization of the collectivist aspirations that had developed in the course of the movement's armed struggle against the Portuguese. As Mondlane said shortly before his death:

> I am now convinced that Frelimo has a clearer political line than ever before. . . . The common basis that we had when we formed Frelimo was hatred of colonialism and the belief in the necessity to destroy the colonial structure and to establish a new social structure. But what type of social structure, what type of organization we would have, no-one knew. No, some did know, some did have ideas, but they had rather theoretical notions that were themselves transformed in the struggle. Now, however, there is a qualitative transformation in thinking that has emerged during the past six years which permits me to conclude that at present Frelimo is much more socialist, revolutionary and progressive than ever and that the line, the tendency, is now more and more in the direction of socialism of the Marxist-Leninist variety. Why? Because the conditions of life in Mozambique, the type of enemy which we have, does not give us any other alternative. I do think, without compromising Frelimo, which still has not made an official announcement declaring itself Marxist-Leninist, I can say that Frelimo is inclining itself more and more in this direction because the conditions in which we struggle and work demand it.[10]

Once Frelimo was in power (now under the presidency of Machel) this sensibility led to a heightened role for the state in the economy and an attempted practice of egalitarianism in class, gender, and racial terms. Unfortunately the experience of Mozambique exemplifies above all else the pitiless circumstances under which socialist endeavour has most often been launched in Africa: the legacy of a backward colonialism that locked into place a particularly dependent economy (dependent not least on its apartheid neighbour, South Africa) and, thanks in part to the backwardness of Portugal itself, a systematically undertrained and marginalized indigenous population. Moreover, the hostility of the external environment was intensified because independent Mozambique — as well as the socialist project of its victorious liberation movement, Frelimo — came onto the historical stage in the very epicentre of the ongoing Thirty Years War for Southern African liberation. Choosing, once in power, to support liberation struggles in neighbouring territories, Frelimo found itself the target of Rhodesian and South African counterrevolutionary wars of destabilization, with these wars in turn eventually being sanctioned by the Reagan White House as part of its policy of rollback of left-leaning states. A debate continues in the literature as to the precise weight of these situating factors in dictating the failure/defeat of Mozambican socialism: I have myself argued that the external variable was crucial; the intensity of escalating destabilization deprived Frelimo of any space within which to learn from its mistakes and correct certain of the negative features of its socialist practice.

Still, the fact remains that when holding power (after 1975) Frelimo failed to avoid the authoritarian and vanguardist practices, the stiff intolerance towards cultural diversity, and the economic strategies, top-down and technocratic, that had come to characterize the Marxist-Leninist brand of Marxism elsewhere. Indeed it could be argued that Frelimo's domestic policies — exemplifying clearly the difficulties of dealing with certain key challenges to socialists in underdeveloped settings — stand as virtual archetypes of what not to do in Africa when seeking to build anything that might be thought of as socialism.[11] While the new government was prepared to be pragmatic in certain respects (for example, as regards its inherited linkages with South Africa), the various crises of the transition encouraged its ambitious leaders to embrace too many tasks at once. Moreover, with the limited room for manoeuvre available for progressives in power in the then-polarized world of the Cold War, the party's development agenda (as regards both political and economic choices) came to be distorted by the impact of assistance from the Eastern bloc, upon which it became overly, if almost inevitably, reliant.

In the event, the movement was drawn away from the peasant roots of its liberation struggle towards a model that, by fetishizing (with Eastern European encouragement) the twin themes of modern technology and "proletarianization," forced the pace and scale of change precipitously, both in terms of inappropriate industrial strategies and, in the rural areas, of highly mechanized state farms and (against the evidence of experience elsewhere in Africa) ambitious plans for the rapid villagization ("aldeias communais") of rural dwellers. The Mozambique case thus exemplified a situation in which the possibility of defining an economic strategy that effectively linked a more apposite program of industrialization to the expansion of peasant-based production was lost. Moreover, the failure to forge this link (and the severe reproduction crisis that the government's alternative policies produced for the peasantry) was to be a key material factor in jeopardizing Frelimo's parallel hopes of mobilizing popular energies and transforming consciousness.

For, in the political realm, there were already negative tendencies at work. The authoritarianism of prevailing "socialist" practice elsewhere reinforced the pull of the movement's own experience of military hierarchy and of the autocratic methods conventionally associated with African nationalism, leading to the "vanguard party" model of politics that was officially embraced at Frelimo's Third Congress in 1978. The simultaneous adoption of a particularly inflexible official version of Marxism-Leninism had a further deadening effect on the kind of creativity (both vis-à-vis the peasantry during the liberation struggle and as further exemplified in the transition period by the encouragement of grassroots "dynamizing groups" in urban areas) that the movement had previously evidenced. Such developments substantially contradicted any real drive towards popular empowerment, tending to turn the organizations of workers, women, and others into mere transmission belts for the Frelimo party. It is true that the kind of "left developmental dictatorship" now created by Frelimo witnessed successes in certain important spheres (health and education, for example); and advances in the principles (if not always the practice) of such projects as that of women's emancipation were impressive.

Moreover, the regime took seriously the challenges to its emancipatory vision posed by the structures of institutionalized religion, by "tradition" and patriarchy, and by ethnic and regional sentiment. But the high-handed manner (at once moralizing and "modernizing") in which it approached such matters often betrayed an arrogance and a weakness in methods of political work that would render it more vulnerable to destructive oppositional activity than need otherwise have been the case.

At the same time, I would repeat my judgment (to be further elaborated upon in chapter 4) that the central finding of William Minter's study of Mozambique (and Angola) stands: that without such external orchestration Mozambique's own internal contradictions would not have given rise to war.[12] Once launched, however, the war did serve to magnify Frelimo's errors and to narrow its chances of learning from them. Indeed, such was the war's destructive impact on Mozambique's social fabric that what began as an external imposition slowly but surely took on some of the characteristics of a civil war. Given the nature of its own violent and authoritarian practices, Renamo could not easily pose as a champion of democracy (except in some ultra-right circles in the West). Nonetheless, it had some success, over time, in fastening onto various grievances that sprang from the weaknesses in

Frelimo's own project — Renamo seeking to fan the resentments of disgruntled peasants, disaffected regionalists, and ambitious "traditionalists" (for example, displaced chiefs). Meanwhile, under pressure both from the war and from the international financial institutions that now circled around Mozambique like vultures, the Frelimo state itself buckled; its original sense of high purpose and undoubted integrity began to be lost. Thus, by the time open elections did finally occur in the 1990s as part of the peace process, Renamo had gained sufficient popular resonance to give Frelimo a close run, albeit on a terrain of political competition reduced to the lowest kind of opportunistic calculation of regional, ethnic, and sectional advantage and without any residue of socialist discourse and debate whatsoever. Indeed, by the 1990s such trends had witnessed a full-scale surrender by Frelimo and the Mozambican state to the globalizing logic of neo-liberalism.[13]

## South Africa

South Africa's claim to our attention is based less on what was attempted there by the forces of liberation from apartheid's quasi-colonial grip than by what the situation had seemed to promise. If there was ever a dog that did not bark in the night for latter-day Sherlocks to reflect upon, it is the absence of a socialist vocation on the part of both the South African liberation movement leadership and, perhaps more importantly, that country's apparently well-developed and assertive working class once apartheid had been defeated.

As with the Mozambican case, hot debate continues as to the reasons for this outcome. Some will see the ANC leadership's embrace of a starkly neo-liberal policy ("Just call me a Thatcherite," said Vice-President Thabo Mbeki in announcing the government's programmatic move to the right in 1996) as reflecting that, at the present time, "There is No Alternative" on a world stage set by the untrammelled hegemony of global capitalism. Others will be more inclined to see in the apparent apostasy of the ANC a confirmation of the petty-bourgeois ambitions that are said always to have characterized that movement's leadership. As for the working classes, broadly defined, in that country it may simply be too early to tell whether they have been definitively sidelined by the rightward turn of the chief spokespersons for the anti-apartheid/national liberation thrust that seemed to many to also house such strong anti-capitalist potential.

Whatever the best explanation of the outcome that has occurred in South Africa, many socialists on the continent had come to look for a vindication of their hopes in, precisely, that anti-apartheid struggle. But not only on the continent. In 1986, after all, observing the situation from the United States, Magdoff and Sweezy had waxed eloquently on the ripeness of South Africa for revolution and the "seemingly irreversible" nature of the revolutionary struggle there.[14] Given the ANC's links to a highly mobilized and radicalized network of mass organizations on the ground — including, by the end of the 1980s, the country's large and vibrant trade union movement — there seemed good reasons for such optimism. Here, in a setting far more "developed" than elsewhere in Africa, was promise both of an ongoing and cumulative democratization of the transition and of an emergent set of economic policies with transformative promise.

On the policy-economic front, many of the ANC's pre-liberation formulations emphasized the need to impose a strong measure of social control upon the workings of the market and over a capitalist economy that was very much more developed in South Africa than elsewhere on the continent. Much was heard of the prospects for nationalizations and, of special interest, of economic strategies designed to facilitate "growth through redistribution." Linked implicitly to a radical notion of "structural reform" that had as a goal the progressive closing in on the prerogatives of capital by movement and state, such strategies would have sought to press capital to slowly but surely gear an increasingly high proportion of its productive energies to meeting popular needs (rather than permitting capital to freely pursue the logic of its own global ambitions). Yet the difficulties of confronting the post-Cold War global economic power structure in these terms were soon apparent and, in combination with the increasingly self-interested ambitions of at least some amongst the ANC leadership, produced a markedly neo-liberal post-apartheid development project, one premised on "global competitiveness," the centrality of foreign investment, and the rule of the market.[15]

Moreover, the reluctance to place popular needs at the centre of economic strategy was, not surprisingly, linked to the narrowness of the ANC's agenda in the sphere of democratic empowerment. One should not distract attention from, or deny credit to, the ANC's considerable accomplishment in easing South Africa's shift away from apartheid authoritarianism. But the negotiations process that saw this result was also rendered more palatable to established power both by the extreme nature of the compromise with neo-liberal economics and by the limitations on mass democratic empowerment facilitated by the ANC. These latter limitations were defined by the demobilization attendant upon the establishment of liberal-democratic (as distinct from popular-democratic) norms and institutions and by the firming up of a dominant-party system (the comparison with the Institutional Revolutionary Party [PRI] in Mexico is sometimes mentioned) rather than anything more overtly authoritarian. Increasingly unions are merely bullied into line (despite ongoing resistance on their part) and the stirrings of progressive organizations in civil society are merely "managed" by the ANC, rather than being embraced as part of some shared struggle to constrain capital. It begins to appear that, in order to reactivate more transformative aspirations in that country, South Africans may eventually have to invent both a new politics and, beyond the primacy of the ANC and its alliance with the South African Communist Party (SACP) and Congress of South African Trade Unions (COSATU), a new movement grounded in the wide range of popular grievances and organizational initiatives present on the ground.[16]

# What Is to Be Learned?

## Framing defeat

Students of Marx will understand why Africa provides a particularly extreme case of the challenge that haunts all Third World socialisms. This challenge is defined by the absence of what are conventionally thought of as the "objective conditions" necessary for building socialism. Among the variables here is a lack of the prior development of the productive forces and of the advanced measure of accumulation that would, at least in theory, have made the appropriation and rational use of capital by the collective labourer a relatively smooth operation. The conditions of underdevelopment under which a necessary measure of planned accumulation must now be carried out by the new "socialist state" are generally defined, in a situation of "economic backwardness," by shortfalls of many of the societal skills, training, and education necessary to guide a state-centric process of development. Even more importantly, some fear that the "accumulation" that still needs to be accomplished must involve forms of surplus extraction from the populace by the state — forms of extraction that, while essential to such accumulation, are difficult to achieve democratically.

Moreover, this very difficulty reinforces a second crucial dimension of Marx's overall argument regarding the socialist project: his notion that a principle enabling condition for socialist possibility is the creation by capitalism of its own gravediggers in the persons of the industrial working class. Self-conscious and self-organized workers — and not some party substituting itself for them — would drive the revolution forward democratically. Whatever we may think of such a premise in light of how little has been realized of the revolutionary promise of working classes in the advanced capitalist countries, socialist revolutions have actually occurred in what at best have been semi-industrialized, and more often than not primarily rural, settings; and this tendency has raised questions about the social base for sustaining the democratic thrust necessary to keeping popular needs and egalitarian principles on the agenda.

For Gavin Kitching, himself a student of Africa in his formative years, democracy is indeed the central issue. In his *Rethinking Socialism* he makes the negative case regarding Third World socialisms quite starkly:

> I believe that a necessary but not sufficient condition of the creation of socialism is a materially prosperous society. And I believe that socialism is impossible to construct in materially poor and deprived societies. Or rather, I believe that [and here he quotes Paul Baran] "socialism in backward and underdeveloped countries has a powerful tendency to become a backward and underdeveloped socialism."

Kitching acknowledges that certain countries can lay a certain minimal claim to the label "socialist" because they have "abolished private property in the means of production, distribution and exchange." But, since they cannot be democratic, their "socialism" will inevitably be a "poor and stunted thing." Cannot be democratic? Here's Kitching again:

> I hold these countries are not socialist democracies because (a) many of them are poor and poverty has certain social and cultural consequences which mean that there is little or no effective popular support for democratic forms, and (b) they build socialist economic institutions primarily in order to commence or speed up the process of industrialization and economic growth. Such a process is, I believe, incompatible with meaningful democracy, because it is so unpleasant for the majority of the population in the societies affected by it that if such people had any genuine control over political and economic power they would use it to prevent such a process occurring. Since certain elites in these countries have an interest in this process succeeding and believe that its success is in the interests of the long-term welfare of their people, they will not allow this popular will open or effective expression.[17]

Strong stuff, this. Moreover, for Kitching, the only left alternative (under conditions of underdevelopment) to this kind of bastard socialism is a version of peasant-centric populism (and he places Nyerere's efforts firmly under this category), albeit one he suggests to be equally doomed to failure.[18]

But are the conditions of underdevelopment really so hostile to mounting a socialist project? There is, some have argued, a certain promise to be found in the "weakest link" theory of capitalism's global reach, a theory that suggests the system's peculiar vulnerability to challenge precisely under the conditions that exist on its periphery and semi-periphery. Moreover, this is an argument reinforced by the obvious occurrence of "socialist revolutions" in such settings. Ken Post and Phil Wright (in their valuable *Socialism and Underdevelopment*) set out a related perspective:

> The working out of capitalism in parts of the periphery prepares not only the minority working class but peasants and other working people, women, youth and minorities for a socialist solution, even though the political manifestation of this may not initially take the form of a socialist movement. In the case of those who are not wage labourers (the classical class associated with that new order) capitalism has still so permeated the social relations which determine their existences, even though it may not have followed the Western European pattern of "freeing" their labour power, that to be liberated from it is their only salvation. . . . The objective need for socialism of these elements can be no less than that of the worker imprisoned in the factory and disciplined by the whip of unemployment. These prices are paid in even the most "successful" of

the underdeveloped countries, and others additionally experience mass destitution. Finding another path has thus become a desperate necessity if the alternative of continuing, if not increasing, barbarism is to be escaped.[19]

Not that such "disparate forces" (as Post and Wright term them) can be expected to spontaneously produce revolutionary outcomes. A measure of leadership to "combine" (their term) and guide such forces — by contributing in the spheres of organizational innovation and ideological probity — seems necessary. And yet, as Post and Wright also note, the kind of leadership that has been offered, especially by Marxist-Leninist intellectuals, under such circumstances, has too often led to "an authoritarian dead end" in countries "marked by 'intermediate integration' into the world economy" (read: underdeveloped countries).

Post and Wright give their argument a rather grating edge when they turn to Africa, stating:

International capital is now reproducing a new sub-category of country . . . places, above all in Africa, so poor that they have almost fallen off the edge of the US State Department's map of the world, places where the physical well-being of the people has been reduced below the level at which the mobilizing force of ideas can be expected to have much impact.[20]

But it is also the case, more generally, that as Post and Wright move beyond discussing the Third World's potential for facilitating the "combination of disparate forces" in potentially anti-capitalist movements and turn to a consideration of the practice of socialists once in power, they begin to sound more like Kitching. For they underscore, as "an innate economic tendency," the severe conflicts that must arise in arbitrating the distribution of scarce resources when planning for accumulation is done under conditions of underdevelopment. And they assert, for the political sphere under these same circumstances, "the innate political tendency to the assertion of state control, eradicating all autonomous elements in civil society." These are both challenges that we have seen in our case studies to be real enough, and we will return to them below when we seek to explore, in light of the African experience, the ways in which the apparently negative imperatives of both accumulation and authoritarianism might have been countered. What bears noting here, however, is the way in which these "imperatives," in both the economic and political spheres, are said to arise for socialists precisely because of the special circumstances of underdevelopment.

Finally, it is worth noting yet another question mark that hovers over the project of any Third World socialism; and this is a particularly challenging question for all those who would seek to conceive and forge socialist futures under the circumstances of African underdevelopment. Those who have queried the feasibility of such socialisms have always noted not merely the internal contradictions inherent in seeking to build them under forbidding objective conditions; they have also emphasized, quite correctly, the vulnerability of all such attempts to external pressure. Thus even so committed a socialist as Ralph Miliband could feel compelled, in a book (*Socialism for a Sceptical Age*) written just before his death in 1994, to suggest that "in the 'third world,' it is quite clear that where economic development occurs, it will be under capitalist auspices, with Western capital much involved in the process." Of course, Miliband also understands the weaknesses of capitalism as a globally transformative agent and, in consequence, he is not sanguine about the prospects for much "economic development" occurring under such capitalist auspices in many parts of the world. And yet, for him, virtually all "governments in the 'third world' have accepted the hegemonic role of the West and adapted their economic and social policies to it. *The price for not doing so is beyond their capacity and their will.*"[21]

For Miliband, then, this vulnerability is principally defined by the pressure of global capitalism and Western states, quick to intervene in order to disrupt, even when possible to overthrow, socialist regimes in power. In Africa, in an age of intensified globalization, direct pressures (the physical assault of Mozambique by a Reagan-backed apartheid South Africa, for example) have been complemented by the intrusive role of the international financial institutions; the IFIs have used the lever of Africa's debt crisis to impose "structural adjustment" packages of one kind or another on most countries on the continent. It was these pressures, complementing physical assault, that helped produce a recolonization of aspirant-socialist Mozambique,[22] and it was the apparent prison of an overbearing global capitalist economy that provided the ANC, once in power in South Africa, with the (semiplausible) excuse that "There Is No Alternative" to its own dramatic capitulation to neo-liberalism. It was also this situation that wrenched from a defeated Nyerere in Tanzania a particularly expressive cry of pain regarding the role of the IMF. That institution, Nyerere said:

> has an ideology of economic and social development which it is trying to impose on poor countries irrespective of their own clearly stated policies. And when we reject IMF conditions, we hear the threatening whisper: "Without accepting our condition, you will not get our money, and you will get no other money." Indeed, we have already heard hints from some quarters that money or credit will not be made available to us until we have reached an understanding with the IMF. When did the IMF become an International Ministry of Finance? When did nations agree to surrender to it their power of decision-making?[23]

Other kinds of costs have had to be borne in Africa for its external vulnerability, to be sure. The Cold War context in which many African socialisms have tried their wings meant the possibility of some succour from the so-called "socialist countries." In the case of the imperatives of armed struggle (a sometime seedbed of socialist awakening), assistance from the Eastern bloc was often essential, but the existence of that "Second World" also provided an alternative pole of reference and assistance when Africans, once in power, chanced radical alternatives to neo-colonialism. Such assistance often carried a heavy cost of its own: as seen in Mozambique, the apparent haloing of a mode of "socialist" discourse imported from the bad old days of official "Marxism-Leninism." This, in its high-tech, highly centralized definitions of the "correct" modalities of economic development and in its authoritarian/vanguardist political predilections, would have at least as much a negative as a positive impact on socialist undertakings in Africa. The removal of this model from the field is therefore a mixed blessing for African socialists. For whatever the long-term benefits of the passing of the Soviet bloc and the discrediting of its bankrupt legacy (both in theory and in practice) to the freeing up of space for the renewal of radicalism in Africa, it is equally true that the East's demise has left Africa more vulnerable than ever to the dictates of global capitalism.

The demise of "socialism." The ever rawer ascendance of "global capitalism": such developments focus the mind. There is, of course, a long tradition on the left of seeing revolutions in "the centre" as being necessary to facilitate any real advance on the periphery. But even if we decline to fall back too comfortably on such formulations and their potentially Eurocentric subtexts, the vulnerabilities of small, poor countries (small, in Africa, often in numbers, but, with the partial exception of South Africa, also small in terms of economic weight and substance, and they are all certainly poor) are legion. It is no accident that Kwame Nkrumah in his radical heyday stated categorically that "Africa must Unite," and socialists in Africa will, as time goes by, have to think more effectively in terms of region and continent as terrains for struggle and for economic action. Moreover, the present worldwide context — of neo-liberal market mania and monolithic capitalist globalization — is at least as hostile (if in novel ways) to progressive aspirations in Africa as was the old Cold War world. How much, one is led to ask, are African radicals dependent on dramatic changes at the global level to facilitate their own efforts? Indeed, Colin Leys has come close to arguing, along these lines and in his own recent contributions to the debate about "development theory," that there exist quite severe limitations upon what any African state might hope to achieve in the absence of radical changes being realized at the global level itself.[24] Not that African assertions cannot be part of some larger global struggle, but even those who consider that the national framework still offers some room for manoeuvre on the continent will have to think long and hard about the question of the scale (nation, region, continent, worldwide) at which their various radical assertions are to be pitched and the kind of alliances against global capitalism that it would be wise to enter into.

## Three Challenges

We must not, then, forget the complexities produced by the general framing conditions of "underdevelopment" for all efforts to mount socialist challenges under such conditions; but we must also seek, even if somewhat artificially, to keep such complexities at arm's length if we are to undertake a second task germane to this discussion: an assessment of the strengths and weaknesses of concrete socialist practices and programs that have been attempted in spite of/because of these very conditions. Following Post and Wright, we can identify three different arenas of relevant practice. The first arena concerns the "seizure of power," a phrase these authors use to reference the theory and practice of socialist movement-building as geared to the actual taking of power in the first instance. The other two areas are those germane to the practices of socialist-intentioned regimes: economic strategies (the issue of "state socialist accumulation" is the way Post and Wright signpost this theme) on the one hand, and political strategies ("the politics of state socialist societies") on the other. Of course, in any discussion of the causes of the failure of socialist aspirations in Africa, it is extremely difficult to distinguish those causes that spring from the forbidding circumstances that prevail (socialism as being historically impossible!) from those causes to be identified in the actual weaknesses of socialist practice on the continent. Still, socialists in Africa have attempted (been forced to attempt) socialisms under prevailing circumstances, however difficult, and there are indeed lessons to be learned, in and of themselves, from such attempts.

Let us take first the question of how socialist projects have been launched in Africa and how they might come to be launched again. It bears emphasizing that in most cases to date they have been produced as part of the apparent unfolding logic of specific nationalist and national liberation movements, borne to the fore by anti-colonial energies and then carried further by the nationalist leadership itself as it has turned to the left. That socialist aspirations have emerged in a very real sense from above (as in Tanzania and Mozambique) has created problems that, if not preordaining authoritarianism (however quasi-benevolent), at least have facilitated it. The importance of the issue of establishing a positive dialectic between leadership and mass action has been well illustrated in these cases; but it is also demonstrated, from a rather different angle, by the South African case, in which much more of the energy for socialist transformation seemed to spring from below, from the mobilized set of social/class actors that drove the anti-apartheid struggle on the ground. The ANC's ability to wrap itself in the mantle of anti-apartheid and national liberation rectitude in such a way as to pre-empt a deepening of the process of transformation in that country is therefore instructive.

For it is worth underscoring that, however much the socialist impulse in Africa heretofore has been cast within the framework of simultaneous, even pre-eminently, nationalist aspirations, the nationalist moment in African history is now drawing to a close. Efforts to build freshly radical, socialist movements geared to the seizure of power in contemporary Africa will increasingly have to stand firmly and self-consciously on their own two feet in this respect. This is quite likely to prove a considerable blessing. Note, for example, the terms in which Patrick Bond several years ago hailed the initial emergence of a new opposition politics in Zimbabwe, one rooted in the assertions of civil society (including those of a strong trade union movement), as heralding a new phase of progressive activity on the continent. "What is crucial," he wrote, "is that the opposition's political orientation is potentially both post-nationalist and post-neoliberal, perhaps for the first time in African history."[25]

Subsequent developments in Zimbabwe have not borne out the promise thus perceived by Bond. But his emphasis on both the novelty of the moment in Africa and the potential role of a range of new, more actively assertive actors in (urban) civil society to the next round of struggles in Africa is important — even if the urban tilt of his formulation may also suggest the need, simultaneously, to define more overtly, as writers as diverse as Amilcar Cabral and Mahmood Mamdani have urged, the kind of positive links that such a movement must seek to establish with rural actors similarly inclined.[26]

I have sought elsewhere (see, for example, the concluding chapter here) to contribute to a discussion of the kind of grouping of Africa's "disparate forces" of contemporary dissent that could yet drive forward a new phase of struggle for popular power and socialism there.[27] Suffice to summarize here that the situation is far from being static, with various promising instances of resistance, particularly at the local level, beginning to cut against the simultaneous pull towards further continental decay. Such instances help define (again using Monga's term) the "collective insubordination" of Africa,[28] as directed not only against parasitic governments but also IFI-induced austerity. This "renaissance" of "popular resistance from below" (in Fantu Cheru's phrase)[29] is wide-ranging: from IMF riots, through the more structured activities of an impressive array of actors — itemized by Stephen Riley and Trevor Parfitt as "lawyers, students, copper miners, organizations of rural women, urban workers and the unemployed, journalists, clergymen and others"[30] — that have shaken numerous African governments in recent years, to the local manifestations of "street-level democracy" in various "political settings at the margins of global power" that Jonathan Barker identifies in his recent writings.[31]

True, African experience has taught Cheru and others that there are no shortcuts, via nationalist organizations, liberation movements, or vanguard parties (the chimeras of an earlier moment of African struggles), towards building a bottom-up hegemonic project: "Instead of focusing on a unifying conception of society and transformation, we must look for a workable sense of cohesion to emerge out of seemingly irreconcilable modes of resistance waged from below."[32] Others still have placed greater emphasis on the urgency of bringing immediate organizational and ideological focus to such diverse resistances: emphasizing both the need to build, democratically, "nation-wide movements and/or parties capable of exercising state power, and making [such power] felt in supra-national institutions"[33] and the importance of developing potentially counter-hegemonic discourses — including the revival of a socialist imaginary — in doing so. The experience of the Movement for Democratic Change in Zimbabwe in attempting to do just this may demonstrate how difficult that task is likely to be. Nonetheless, Graham Harrison and others have highlighted related emanations of resistance across the continent — in Nigeria, for example — that may yet manifest greater potential along these lines.[34]

What will prove "historically possible" in this regard remains to be seen. Meanwhile, it also behooves us to look more directly at the lessons that any new movement successful in achieving power along such lines might expect to learn from prior continental experience when it, in turn, seeks to mount its own attempts at (socialist) transformation. Recall, then, our suggestion that the actions undertaken, once in power, by movements and leaders identified as being socialist can themselves be investigated on two principal fronts, the economic and the political. In doing this we are imagining that, for purposes of learning such lessons, we have positive answers to the range of questions raised earlier here: that is, we are imagining that Africa can still provide one plausible framing context for some kind of genuinely socialist endeavour and that a movement reflecting social forces that are increasingly self-conscious about the need to undertake such socialist endeavour can in fact emerge to centre stage. What, on this basis, are the lessons thrown up by previous socialist practice in Africa?

Although the challenges arising in the economic sphere are legion,[35] one may wonder whether either the imperatives of "accumulation" and "planning" or the dangers said to be inherent in these imperatives need be quite so implacable as observers such as Kitching, Post, and Wright argue them to be. Isn't this to accept, however regretfully and/or resignedly, the necessary logic of a roughly Stalinist model of "socialist" practice as being the most appropriate (and/or inevitable) under conditions of extreme scarcity? This model, put into practice in the Soviet Union of the 1930s, did indeed witness a developmental "solution" based on extreme centralization; an emphasis upon "primitive socialist accumulation" at the expense of the peasantry and in the one-sided interests of heavy industry; and the granting of priority to state farms in the rural sector.

But in fact there does exist a possible alternative to this model of "primitive socialist accumulation" — one that shifts the emphasis towards the facilitation of more equal urban-rural exchanges as a key to driving the economy forward. The accumulation process could then be advanced precisely by finding outlets for industrial production in meeting the growing requirements, the needs, of the mass of the population, including the rural population. The key to "expanded reproduction" — "expanded socialist reproduction," as I have termed this in writing where I have described the failure of socialists in Mozambique to realize just such a possibility[36] — would then lie in those more equal urban-rural exchanges, with food and raw materials moving to the cities and consumer goods and producer goods (including such modest items as scythes, ploughs, hoes, axes, and so on) moving to the countryside. As Clive Thomas, William Luttrell, and others have argued,[37] accumulation — collective saving geared to investment — could then be seen as being drawn essentially, if not exclusively, from an expanding economic pool, rather than merely being squeezed from the population. And wouldn't such a developmental ethos also be more open to acknowledging the claims of environmental sensitivity, human scale, and collective consumption than do many of the all too heroically modernist socialist schemata of the past?

Any such strategy would also be premised on taking the peasants seriously. This is something that Stalinoid Marxism has had grave difficulties in doing everywhere, and yet it is no less necessary to do so on a continent where even non-Marxist socialists in power (Nyerere) have tended to fall back on their own versions of forced collectivization as a plausible solution to their rural development problems. Taking the peasantry seriously might still involve reaffirming the virtues of the co-operativization of the peasantry, albeit a co-operativization won democratically rather than one forced upon rural dwellers in the name of "more proletarian" forms of production. It might also be one that found more room for allowing market mechanisms to structure some of the necessary exchanges between urban and rural, worker and peasant, thereby also protecting the state from being overwhelmed by the requirements of micro-management. Of course, in the process of socialist construction the precise role to be assigned to the market — with all its inherent dangers (for example, class formation) — on this and other fronts opens up an additional range of difficult questions. But we need not go as far as Alex Nove and others have gone in the direction of "market socialism" in order to recognize that the question must remain open — and open as well (even as the new socialist economy becomes more promisingly auto-centric) concerning just what kinds of "necessary" entanglements with the global marketplace are possible (and/or unavoidable) before their costs begin to outweigh the benefits.

As we have seen in the cases of Tanzania and Mozambique and also in the debate, cut short by the ANC leadership, about alternative economic strategies in South Africa (where the late, lamented "growth through distribution" model might have produced a promising variant on the theme of "expanded socialist reproduction"), the track record of African socialist practice underscores just how crucial it is that new economic thinking begins to occur along some such lines. This rethinking is essential to strengthen the economic prospects of any novel socialist effort (national, regional, or continental) that seeks to counter the malignant grip of capitalism upon Africa. But it is also the case that any such rethinking has potentially positive political ramifications. For (recalling Kitching's dour formulations) just how much more likely would be a democratization of the "socialist" development process if it were twinned to an economic strategy that placed the real needs of the people at the centre of policy-making? But of course the democratic deficit — the denial by socialist leadership once in office of mass democratic empowerment that has stalked twentieth-century socialist practice, not least in Africa — has not merely been an offshoot of presumed economic imperatives; it has had other roots as well.

We know that, on this second front of socialist practice, a veritable witch's brew of negative ingredients has gone into producing such outcomes in "socialist Africa": the intellectual arrogance of newly ascendant elites; the cumulative precedents of nationalist movement practices elsewhere on the continent (even when these precedents were established by leaderships in pursuit of much less benign ends than the socialists themselves); the inherited hierarchies deemed necessary to movements and liberation forces previously engaged in intense struggles, sometimes armed, against colonial masters; and the "progressive" vanguardist discourses learned from overseas parties in the "successful" Marxist-Leninist tradition.

Indeed, in the cases of Tanzania, Mozambique, and South Africa, the pattern of smothering (however often "with the best of intentions") the kinds of mass political activism that could have helped sustain the democratic and socialist charge was repeated over and over again. Was this inevitable? Not necessarily. There were, after all, in each of the countries under consideration, real expressions of popular energies that had actively to be disabled in order for self-appointed vanguards to consolidate themselves. True, the alternative of advocating mere spontaneism is not a sufficient answer here. A complicated dialectic between leadership and mass action is required to sustain socialist endeavour. Nonetheless, a sensibility that takes seriously the need to sustain this dialectic in a manner that is cumulatively democratic is something that can be learned. Fortunately, such a democratic outcome is one that will most likely be insisted upon if new movements for transformation are to emerge, as they must, primarily from below rather than from above.

Do such aspirations sound merely utopian? Their achievement in practice will certainly be something new for socialists, although the recent experience of the Workers' Party in Brazil seemed at first to give some earnest of what such a future might look like. Moreover, experience does suggest that creating the political space necessary to ensure the kind of self-organization from below that can alone drive popular democracy and meaningful socialist struggle requires as a necessary (although decidedly not sufficient) condition institutionalized guarantees of open debate, freedom of political and social organization (including independent trade unions, women's organizations, peasant associations, and opposition political parties) and unfettered ventilation by the media of any and all issues. Socialists have conventionally been suspicious of such apparently "liberal" preoccupations. But don't calls for such institutional guarantees actually reflect a much clearer acknowledgement of just what is necessary — in Africa and elsewhere — to give democratic forms the potential to be real and meaningful (that is, to release revolutionary energies and to advance class and other popular struggles) for those who need them most?

What then are we to make of the record of socialism in Africa? And where does consideration of that record bring us? There can be little doubt that, given the global and continental defeat/failure of regimes and movements that presented themselves as socialist, and faced with the hegemony of neo-liberal orthodoxy worldwide, the language of socialism had, by century's end, lost a great deal of its credibility on the continent. Indeed, writing some years earlier of socialism in Africa, Colin Leys could only conclude, somewhat elegiacally:

> The accomplishments of African socialism are not, on the whole, to be measured in terms of growth rates. They are primarily social and political, above all in having posed the question of the form in which development is to occur, in having made it comprehensible to ordinary people that they do have collective historical choices which they may try to exercise if they will. The achievement of the Tanzanians and the Ghanaians [and, we may add, the Mozambicans] in this respect is epochal. One can also say that the accomplishments of actually existing African socialism lie partly in its failures; to paraphrase Marx, what succumbed in these failures was not African socialism but the "persons, illusions, conceptions, projects, from which the idea of socialism in Africa was not free, from which it could be freed only by a series of defeats.[38]

At the same time there are those in Africa and outside (Leys among them) who argue that any such setback need prove only temporary. Given that global capitalism shows no more sign of producing socio-economic transformation in Africa than it has heretofore, and that the costs of the ongoing socio-economic crisis for the continent are mounting, the claims of the social over the workings of the unalloyed marketplace, and of the "left developmental state" over those of capital, may yet reassert themselves as crucial dimensions of emerging popular-democratic demands. If so, the analytical categories and political practices linked to socialist critique and practice — albeit free of the authoritarian propensities and of the narrow economic thinking that often characterized such initiatives in the past — will ultimately have to be revived in Africa.

CHAPTER 3

# LIBERAL DEMOCRACY VS. POPULAR DEMOCRACY IN SUB-SAHARAN AFRICA

Although the necessary revival of a socialist imaginary still represents a crucial challenge in Africa, the language of "democracy" is one much more widely heard, honoured in the breach if not often enough in substance across a broad spectrum of African — and Africanist — opinion. Nonetheless, as Tanzanian scholar Issa Shivji (who is amongst those who have been writing most eloquently on the question of democracy in Africa) argues, the distinction that must continue to be made between "liberal democracy" and "popular democracy" has tended to become blurred in the process.[1]

Indeed, Shivji himself has experienced difficulties in defending this distinction in intra-African debates. He speaks, for example, of an important continental conference in Harare at which "the liberal perspective seemed to be dominant." In his keynote address, he says, he "attempted to address the key issue of constitutionalism within the larger question of democracy and situate it in a popular democratic perspective." This approach, he says, was "understandably . . . not particularly well received. Former radicals trying to find a niche in the rising tide of liberalism felt a bit embarrassed; liberals were irritated and the statists saw in it their traditional *bête noire*." In short, as he complains, liberalism held firm sway. And yet, for him, it was clear that "in the current debate on democracy, the divide between the liberal . . . and the popular perspective — thoroughly anti-imperialist — from the standpoint of popular classes" ought to define the opposing, perhaps too implicit, positions. "If not, we are likely to get a celebration of the liberal triumph; jump indiscriminately on compradorial (for that is what liberalism degenerates into in most of our imperialist-dominated countries) bandwagons and confuse the long human struggle for democracy (equality) with its particular historical form — western liberalism (individualism)."[2] And yet, as Shivji further states, much that "would clearly distinguish the popular perspective — [its] position on imperialism, state and class, class struggle, etc. — remains unsaid by its intellectual proponents for fear of being condemned as old-fashioned or demagogic."[3]

The main reasons for the prevalence of such an intellectual atmosphere are not hard to find. In part, as Shivji suggests, this atmosphere is defined by the difficulties that even radicals have in defining what the alternative model — "popular democracy" — might actually be expected to look like, concretely, under African conditions; this is, self-evidently, a point to which we will have to return. But another element in the present milieu is even more central. Thus, in the kind of circles Shivji describes, the discussion of democratization has tended to be elided with, even subordinated to, a parallel discussion of the related process of economic liberalization that has swept the continent so dramatically in recent years. Too often these processes — political democratization and economic liberalization — are seen to be merely two sides of the same coin. Moreover, this approach tends, in turn, to proceed as if the debate regarding the wisdom (and/or inevitability) of "neo-liberalism" as the essential framing premise for both economic policy and democratic possibility were pretty much settled — and settled, overwhelmingly, in neo-liberalism's favour.

True, one of the best of recent books on the impact of neo-liberalism/structural adjustment on Africa counsels some measure of caution with regard to such premises. "There may be more tension," its editors write, "between fostering individual freedoms and good governance on the one hand and creating rapidly growing marketing economies on the other than many people might like to admit."[4] But even these authors seem hostage to a liberal perspective on "market economies" that, in its own way, blunts the possibility of having the kind of root and branch discussion of African alternatives counselled by Shivji.

In short, the ubiquity of the liberal/"neo-liberal" perspective tends, crucially, to frame the scientific discussion of democratization in Africa. One other distinction might help us to think through the impact of such a narrowing of the terms of the discussion of democracy. For, within this intellectual milieu, such discussion has come to focus all too exclusively on what might be termed the "political science of democratization" — with any simultaneous consideration of the "political economy of democratization" assumed to be foreclosed (as being "old-fashioned" perhaps). I will elaborate on this distinction — between the "political science" and the "political economy" of democratization — later. However, in order to offset the temptation to operate at too high a level of abstraction in doing so, I will also draw briefly on the experience of the two "transitions to democracy" that I had the opportunity in the 1990s to study at first hand, those that centred on the national elections of 1994 held in South Africa and in Mozambique.

## The Political Economy of Democratization

Much of the literature on Third World democratization has come to turn on a very narrow reading indeed of democratic possibility, one rooted in the political elitism of Joseph Schumpeter and the u.s. theorists of "polyarchy." The most baldly stated variation on the theme is probably the best known, that advanced by the ubiquitous Larry Diamond in his various writings. As he puts the point: "Perhaps the basic tension in democracy is between conflict and consensus. Democracy implies dissent and division, but on the basis of consent and cohesion. It requires that the citizens assert themselves, but also that they accept the government's authority. It *demands that citizens care about politics, but not too much.*"⁵ As he further warns:

> If reform is to be adopted without provoking a crisis that might destroy democracy, the costs to privileged economic interests of overturning democracy must be kept greater than the costs of the reforms themselves. This requires realism and incrementalism on the part of those groups pressing for reform. It also requires sufficient overall effectiveness, stability and guarantees for capital on the part of the democratic regime so that privileged economic actors will have a lot to lose.⁶

Moreover, this concern for the sensibilities of capital, phrased here, commonsensically enough, in tactical terms, is merely one dimension of a much more fundamental conceptual slide — expressed in its most unabashed form in Diamond's influential work, but present in the bulk of the transition literature — from "democracy" through "liberal democracy" to (Diamond's own phrase) "liberal capitalist democracy." It is fortunate, he writes, that:

> the past four decades of Third World economic development have furnished invaluable lessons for distinguishing the policies that work from those that do not. Broadly speaking, market-oriented economies develop while state-socialist economies fall behind. Internationally open and competitive economies work; closed (or at least rigidly and persistently closed) economies do not. Economies grow when they foster savings, investment and innovation and when they reward individual effort and initiative. Economies stagnate and regress when bloated, mercantilist, hyperinterventionist states build a structure of inflexible favoritisms for different groups, curtailing change, experimentation, competition, innovation and social mobility."⁷

This, then, is the loaded way in which Diamond and his colleagues lay the foundations of the case for their brand of democracy.

Small wonder that for Diamond the effort to create "a balanced [democratic] political culture — in which people care about politics but not too much" — requires, "in Eastern Europe and much of the developing world, restraining the partisan battle [by] deflating the state and invigorating the private economy."⁸ And beyond that — at the conclusion of his text we have the customary invocation of polyarchy and of "democratic elitism" — there lies, precisely, the crucial role of "political elites" and of the pacts they create amongst themselves:

Elite actions, choices and postures can have a formative impact in shaping the way their followers approach political discourse and conflict. Opposing party leaders must take a lead in crafting understandings and working relationships that bridge historic differences, restrain expectations and establish longer, more realistic time horizons for their agendas. . . . Competing party elites must set an accommodating and civil tone for political life.[9]

The thrust of much recent literature is, then, to define the terms of any transition to democracy ever more narrowly and cautiously.[10] Another example comes in the much-cited work of Giuseppe di Palma, in which he emphasizes the importance of accepting certain stern limitations in the "crafting" of democracies — a process he defines as the "setting up [of] government [under conditions of marked] diversity as a way of defusing conflict."[11] As he argues, "One factor that reconciles to democracy reluctant political actors tied to the previous regime is that in the inaugural phase coexistence usually takes precedence over any radical social and economic programs." He continues:

Such precedence stems from understanding the limits of democratic (and other politics) as natural harbingers of material progress. It stems as well from a fuller appreciation that willfully using democracy as a Jacobin tool of progress not only is ingenuous but may also raise intolerable political risks; namely, authoritarian backlashes and, in anticipation, escalation into a virtuous "guided" democracy. Past democracies — the most instructive example from the 1930s being the second Spanish republic — have foundered on such Jacobin instincts. By giving reform precedence over coexistence and making support for reform the test of legitimacy, they have unintentionally fulfilled a prophecy: the losers would be unwilling to reconcile themselves to a nascent democracy. The example looms large among political practitioners in Europe and Latin America. Indeed, the importance of coexistence has not gone unnoticed, despite its significant policy sacrifices, by those who still sympathize ideally with a more Jacobin democracy.

There is bluff "good sense" in this, of course. A preoccupation with how a would-be democratic society develops norms of tolerance and due process is not irrelevant. Yet how easily such an approach can emphasize this issue at the expense of any real concern about socio-economic outcomes; how easily it can underwrite, conservatively, a tendency to "blame the (wilfully unrealistic) victims" rather than their oppressors for any failed transitions. Thus di Palma is quick to identify "mobilizational models for the Third World" based on *dependencia* paradigms and undue popular suspicion regarding the role played by the "advanced industrial democracies" in the "global economic order" as representing a particularly clear danger to "democratic crafting." Not surprising, then, is his comfortable conclusion that "democracy's *disengagement from the idea of social progress*" is "a silver lining because it has actually given democracy more realistic, more sturdily conscious grounds for claiming superiority in the eyes of public opinion and political practitioners."[12]

Is it any wonder that Perry Anderson can write of such tendencies that "what is missing [in contemporary political thought] is any conception of the state as a structure of collective self expression deeper than the electoral systems of today. Democracy is indeed more widespread than ever before. But it is also thinner, as if the more universally available, the less active meaning it retains."[13]

Indeed, Barry Gills, Joel Rocamora, and Richard Wilson present the new orthodoxy as converging around a practice of "low intensity democracy" — this being a practice designed both to help legitimate the present global status quo and to limit/contain possible challenges to it.[14] Identifying the tacit (and not-so-tacit) premises that lie behind such a narrowing of the democratic optic is not difficult. What is at stake is, quite simply, not only a dramatic abandonment of the politics of public purpose but also a fetishization of the market — the latter being part of a broader and now quite omnipresent world view recently characterized by Colin Leys:

> Our leaders are currently directing a process of self-destruction of our societies in the name of a utopia no less irrational than the beliefs of the Solar Temple. . . . This utopia is the idea of a world-wide market in which the people of the world relate to each other directly as individuals, and only as individuals: and "globalization" [linked in turn to acceptance of the unchecked "freedom of capital to move across national boundaries"] is the process of trying to realize this idea.[15]

And what about "democracy" under such conditions? Manfred Bienefeld continues the argument:

> Unfortunately genuine democracy is hard to reconcile with neoliberalism's mystical belief in the magic of disembodied markets, its fierce hostility to the notion of state and society as organic entities capable of defining and pursuing a common interest, and its insistence on pervasive deregulation. Under such conditions, the state loses the capacity to manage economies in accordance with democratically determined social, ethical or political priorities. Only the shallowest and most meaningless democracy will survive in a "cowboy capitalism" where property rights become virtually absolute because states and electorates are disempowered by the mobility of capital.[16]

In Africa, Leys suggests, the result of such globalization — with its attendant processes of structural adjustment and the like — "has not been a market-based social and economic recovery based on individuals and their initiatives in the marketplace. It has been, instead, an ethnic-based regression, as people have been pushed back into reliance on precolonial social bonds for survival; and in some cases it has resulted in economic and social catastrophe."[17]

In short, if the realities of Africa's present-day political economy so temper the democratic prospects on the continent, they also create conditions that undermine the prospects for any smooth consolidation of domestic peace and "state-building." Even Larry Diamond is sufficiently nervous about this possibility to qualify his celebration of "low intensity democracy," stating that "democracy cannot endure if massive inequality and exclusion go unchallenged" and that "getting reform on the agenda requires that the disadvantaged and excluded economic groups organize and mobilize politically."[18] But such qualifications remain, by and large, to the side of his ideological exertions in defence of "liberal capitalist democracy."[19]

Not every observer is as sanguine as Diamond regarding the capacity of neoliberalism to be both the universal solvent of the development problem and the guarantor of democracy in the Third World (including Africa). But even for those who have more doubts, the difficulties of mounting a more promising alternative can also seem daunting. In such a context, some critics seem prepared merely to choose a posture of resignation. In this respect, the words of Adam Przeworski, one of the more astute students of the global "transition to democracy," might be taken to exemplify most starkly the tone of a defeated left, when he talks about how capitalism is "irrational" and socialism "unfeasible," and "in the real world people starve" — all of which leads to discouraging conclusions.[20] In such a context, Przeworski asserts, transitions from authoritarian to more democratic politics will tend to find their transformative content constrained by the continuing strength of the holders of socio-economic power: "A stable democracy requires that governments be strong enough to govern effectively but weak enough not to be able to govern against important interests. . . . Democratic institutions must remain within narrow limits to be successful."[21]

Under such circumstances, Przeworski concludes, the best-case scenario for a "successful" transition is one in which "reformers" within the erstwhile power structure distance themselves from their own "hardliners" and agree to negotiate a form of democratic outcome with "moderates" within the democratic camp — those who, in turn, are prepared to distance themselves from the "radicals" who occupy a position further over on the ideological spectrum. True, this probably implies acceptance by such moderates (Przeworski terms theirs to be "the traditional dilemma of the Left") "that even a procedurally perfect democracy may remain an oligarchy: the rule of the rich over the poor. As historical experience demonstrates, democracy is compatible with misery and inequality in the social realm and with oppression in factories, schools, prisons, and families".[22]

Self-evidently, the tone here is very different from anything that the Diamonds and di Palmas might adopt. Yet, in the end, there is little more that Przeworski can offer us, given his premises ("socialism is unfeasible"): a left bending over backwards to avoid "chaos"; a left propitiating the powers that be; a left that is nothing if not "prudent." Such is the shrunken vision of the transition to democracy that the "realism" of the epoch would seek to fashion for us.

Nor is Przeworski alone in his realism/pessimism. Thus even Ralph Miliband, as we have seen (chapter 2), feared that in the Third World economic development could only occur under capitalist auspices, and particularly the auspices of Western capital.[23] But what if this were to mean, in turn, that the vast majority of people in the Third World are merely doomed, by the present illogic of imperialism, to underdevelopment and to ever more severe versions of social distemper — unless dramatic structural changes, both global and national, begin to occur? There is certainly one stream of authors on Africa who attest as much, focusing on the "stranglehold" presently exerted on Africa by international forces (and their local agents) and, in particular, on the policies of the international financial institutions in further promoting such a situation. Thus John Loxley and David Seddon, in introducing a valuable issue of the *Review of African Political Economy* on the subject, comment:

> Where the IFIs identify failure they blame the domestic policies of African governments, but many observers . . . would insist that Africa's problems today are predominantly "external" in origin and that the IFIs in particular have played a significant role in reducing Africa's capacity and prospects for development. We share this view and suggest that the strategy adopted and the lending policies and conditions imposed by the IFIs are heavily to blame for the dismal performance of most African economies over the last decade or more — although there are also "internal" factors which should not be discounted and "external" factors which precede the interventions of the IFIs.[24]

Adopt such a premise for a moment — that, as argued in the first chapter of this book, capitalism really is irrational and destructive in its workings in Africa — and the otherwise cosy and "reasonable" world of the new democratic theorists turns very sour, very quickly. Take di Palma's image of "Jacobins" wilfully wielding democratic claims in order to realize "progress," for example. In practical terms, isn't he actually evoking the "danger" that the vast mass of the Third World will begin to demand a different, more rational world order than the present process of globalization can be expected readily to provide? Others, even some professing to approach these matters from the left, attempt to shuffle such difficulties aside in other ways: by implying that global capitalism (now in its "post-imperialist" phase, according to David Becker and Richard Sklar[25]) is, in the end, profoundly developmental — although, to be sure, in need of somewhat greater (if rather unspecified) pressure from below in order to operate more equitably. In such a context, Becker and Sklar argue, "Capitalism versus socialism is no longer the prime issue of class analysis; it yields pride of place to the question of liberty versus dictatorship."[26] But what if global capitalism is, cumulatively, making the situation of African countries worse: how sanguine can one really be about proclamations as to the probable "unfeasibility" of the socialist alternative?

There is, to be sure, one other alternative, one exemplifying, in the recent lit-erature on Africa, a kind of "postmodern turn." This approach also suggests an abandonment of the "grand narratives" of "socialism" and "capitalism," of the developmental/predatory state and of the world market, and proposes instead an embrace of the village and the locality. "Africa's potential for democracy," Becker and Sklar state, "is more convincingly revealed by the creation of small collectives established and controlled by rural or urban groups (such as local associations) than by parliaments and parties, instruments of the state, of accumulation and of alien-ation."[27] But this is only partly helpful. True, Africans must strengthen their capac-ities to act from the bottom up. But the negative impulses that spring from an irra-tional (global) capitalism and/or the typically predatory state will not merely leave them alone to do so. The sources of these impulses must be transformed as well; we simply must not make things easier for ourselves by pretending that this is not the case, however difficult/impossible the task of transforming them may seem. As Leys suggests:

> I would say that the African state, for all its record of abuse, remains a potential line of defense for Africans against the depredations of the world economic and political system: part of the solution, if there is one, and not necessarily part of the problem, as the drive of the IMF and the World Bank to weaken the African state in the name of market efficiency implic-itly acknowledges.[28]

Yet how is any such state to come to act consistently in this way if not in response to pressures from below? Clearly analysts who see capitalism as part of the prob-lem and not part of the solution, and who insist on taking "imperialism" serious-ly, have pressing reasons of their own for valuing democracy — would it not be a "popular democracy"? — highly.[29]

## The Political Science of Democratization

"Popular democracy"? We will return to a consideration of this concept. However, what will be apparent is that, precisely because it does not take the question of imperialism seriously, much of the current literature on democratization in Africa finds itself limiting the conception of democracy with which it works — the bet-ter, as noted, both to legitimate the neo-liberal project and to insulate it against any unmediated claims by popular classes from below. This implies a firm step away from any consideration of an alternative economic project, prompting the suspicion that, from such a perspective, "democracy" is valued more as a plausible narcotic than as the route to any kind of genuine popular empowerment. With "political economy" (concerns about imperialism, class struggle, and the like) now bracketed off, the democratization debate can proceed on other fronts without bad conscience.

The result: whether it is because they feel the left/socialist alternative to be irrelevant (Diamond), dangerous (di Palma), or impossible (Przeworski), these and other theorists are prepared to shift quite sharply the centre of gravity of the debate about democracy towards what I have called, for want of a better term, "the political science of democratization."

We must avoid caricature, however. The emphasis upon "the political" within democratization theory can take different forms, and those forms are worth distinguishing. Only at its most crass — as in much of the literature on "governance," for example — does the narrowing of the democratic optic take an overtly manipulative turn, with "democracy" viewed as being as much problem as opportunity, its claims hedged in accordingly. As Susan George and Fabrizio Sabelli document, the World Bank has been a particularly important reference point for generating this discourse: its earlier efforts to downgrade the claims of the state to a developmental role are now qualified by a clearer recognition that some kind of viable state-like structure must be in place to maintain a minimum both of order and of legitimacy.[30] In order to put "governments . . . on notice to get their acts together" and to specify "this process and this requirement," the Bank "has chosen the rather archaic word governance." ("'Government,'" George and Sabelli add, "would have been a bit too blatant since the Bank, according to its Articles, is not allowed to intervene in politics at all.") They then document the cautious dance that World Bank authors, in their texts on governance, weave around the notions of "transparency," "public choice," "responsiveness," and "accountability." In fact, George and Sabelli's conclusions do not differ from Gerald Schmitz's summary of much the same literature: "In contrast to self-empowerment and grass-roots democratic action, it is 'we professionals,' with access to our reams of paper, who know best how others should do participatory development. Extending the paradox, more 'participation' ends up reinforcing the Bank's role, even though more real democracy in developing countries would quite likely reduce it!"[31]

The result: academic advocates of the Bank's approach find themselves saddled with the unenviable task of theorizing, in Joan Nelson's formulation, a working balance between the "contradictory pressures of political opening and economic management" in situations of "simultaneous dual transitions" (that is, situations witnessing both economic liberalization and some form of political democratization). Not surprisingly, they are forced to twist themselves almost out of shape in their efforts to do so. Thus Nelson notes, "Recent research on the politics of economic reform suggests a need to insulate key economic management functions from direct political pressures and at the same time to improve the channels for ongoing consultation between the government and concerned interest groups on other aspects of economic policy and reform." As an example, she argues that the question of "how to contain yet also integrate organized labour merits particular attention." She adds:

The process of economic liberalization inevitably hits labor hard. . . . Most Third World successes with sustained economic liberalization in the past two decades have entailed periodic or consistent repression of unions: among the obvious examples are Korea, Bolivia, Chile, Mexico, and Turkey. Some theorists have suggested that labor restraint is crucial not only for sustained economic development but also for consolidation of democratic openings, in order to encourage confidence and loyalty from business. Yet failure to integrate labor into democratic processes can also threaten democratic consolidation.[32]

I find it difficult to know just where to add the emphases in such quotations, the tensions within them being so close to the surface. Small wonder that various "hired guns" from the academy have been working overtime to smooth down the rough edges of the "governance" approach. In African studies a key figure in attempting to do so has been Goran Hyden, whose essay on "Governance and the Study of Politics" is widely cited. His work is also all too typical of this genre: seeking to give us an "objective" model of governance — one that, in its abstraction, only obliquely evokes the socio-economic policy content that such a model is designed to ensure — he nonetheless produces something readily available for use by neo-liberals. For, within this model, "democracy" is, once again, a safely contingent and manipulable variable, not a defining requirement. Hyden argues:

In its assumption that what matters now, and in the future, is whether politics is good or bad, the governance approach is cast in a postmaterialist and postpositivist vein. . . . This is where it departs from the literature trying to measure democracy or freedom. While that literature is important in its own right and obviously overlaps to some extent with the concerns of this approach, the study of governance is performance-oriented. It examines how well a polity is capable of mobilizing and managing social capital — both fixed and movable — so as to strengthen the civic public realm. In this respect it comes closer to the literature on business management. In the same way as business management theory treats the organization as crucial to business success, the governance approach treats regime — the organization of political relations — as essential for social and economic progress.[33]

Meanwhile, in sharp contrast to the calculated blandness of such a way of presenting things, Schmitz feels able to conclude from his counter-efforts to demystify the governance approach and to evoke "a more truly democratic . . . praxis" that "manufacturing 'democratic consent' is (fortunately, I believe) proving to be more difficult at the mass than the elite level."[34] Time alone will tell.

But if "governance" encapsulates one fashionable, and highly suspect, "political science" approach to democratization, still other, much better reasons exist for a preoccupation with the political interactions that mark an attempted transition to democracy. In taking seriously such approaches, we will see that the main charge against them is not that they are wrong-headed but rather that, in their tendency to ignore or downplay the political economy of democratization, they are one-sided. Two emphases in particular are worth noting in this respect. First, practising democrats in Africa, as well as those who theorize their activities, stress the importance of establishing democratic institutions in order both to discipline entrenched autocrats and to help pre-empt the authoritarian tendencies that have become so much a part of African political life. Second, both practitioners and theorists also stress the possible importance of democratic institutions to the reconciling of "differences" — especially those that are "communally defined": by *ethnie*, by religion, and by race — and the facilitating of "order" and "nation-building."

Take the first point first: the demand to democratize the "predatory state" in Africa. This demand is quite understandable in light of recent African history and indeed has a rich history of its own. As the editors of a special issue (on "Surviving Democracy?") of the *Review of African Political Economy* remind us, "The present struggles form part of the long African struggle for democratic politics and systems, visible in the radical nationalist movements of the post-war decade in South and West Africa, in the populist revolts of the early 1980s in Ghana and Burkina Faso (and the related victory of the NRM in Uganda), and in the continued record of opposition, dissent and resistance to authoritarian and repressive regimes of the last 20 years."[35] Of course, it is this upsurge that Shivji found so often to be presented in exclusively "liberal-democratic" terms (as he saw at the Harare conference): some African writers have been so preoccupied — for very good reasons — with breaking the elision long central to continental political discourse between "democracy" and "the single-party system" that they have tended, themselves, to embrace alternative notions of "pluralistic democracy" (and its "most manifest criterion . . . a multi-party system") quite uncritically.[36] True, such authors have thrown up a variety of relevant considerations about the constitutional means by which the promise of a more open society might be more permanently and effectively realized in Africa.[37] At the same time they tend to be not nearly so alert to the kind of nagging questions that the *Review* editors — from a more "political economy"-driven perspective — ask as they conclude their editorial:

> Multi-partyism and the rule of law, indeed even the codification of basic human rights, do not of themselves imply participation, representativeness, accountability or transparency. They may be essential to the possibility of reducing inequalities and of removing oppression, but do not accomplish this of their own accord. Much more commonly democracy serves as a system through which class dominance and various forms of systematic inequalities are perpetuated and legitimated. The challenge of those African nations undergoing a process of democratization is to use the space it opens to press for greater justice for the mass of the population.[38]

Some African commentators do recognize the danger that the democratization process in Africa may merely halt "at the level of periodic decorative elections." Sidgi Kaballo provides a case in point, arguing forcefully the need to establish, alongside electoral mechanisms, a much deeper culture (and attendant institutionalization) of "universal human rights" than has heretofore existed in post-colonial Africa. Kaballo even notes in passing the possible class determinants of such a culture, in his case lamenting the very weakness of the class on whom he might otherwise pin his hopes, the African bourgeoisie.[39] Even more suggestively, Peter Anyang'Nyongo, an influential Kenyan advocate of democratic processes and human rights, notes the existence of diverse cases of democratization in Africa. In some cases he finds that "profligate bureaucrats and politicians came under severe attack for corruption and mismanagement" from the "vocal middle classes" (who found their "standard of living . . . threatened by a tight economic atmosphere"). In others (he highlights the case of Zaire, mentioning the writings of Nzongola-Ntalaja) he finds democratization to be driven by the yearnings of "the popular masses" for a "second independence."[40] These points are suggestive, yet in the end, Shivji might argue, too little is made of the possible implications of such distinctive social bases for the substance of diverse democratization processes. Of course, some, like Claude Ake, are prepared to expand Nzongola's point evocatively to the rest of the continent:

The ordinary people of Africa are supporting democracy as "a second independence." This time they want independence not from the colonial masters, but from indigenous leaders. They want independence from leaders whose misrule has intensified their poverty and exploitation to the point of being life threatening. And they are convinced that they cannot now get material improvement without securing political empowerment and being better placed to bring public policy closer to social needs.

[Nonetheless] democracy is being interpreted and supported in ways that defeat these aspirations and manifest no sensitivity to the social conditions of the ordinary people of Africa. Generally the political elites who support democratization are those with no access to power, and they invariably have no feeling for democratic values. They support democratization largely as a strategy of power. . . . The people can [only] choose between oppressors and by the appearance of choice legitimise what is really their disempowerment[41]

By and large, however, the class analysis of Africa's democratization boom remains to be done.

As for Kaballo, he also acknowledges that "the prevailing economic crisis and the harsh austerity measures required by the international financial institutions and donors decrease [the bourgeoisie's] chances of reaching compromises on the demands for better living conditions of the masses" (quite possibly creating conditions within which "the way to authoritarian politics opens up again") His conclusion: "It is not enough to include the respect of human rights and the establishment of multi-party democracy as a new political conditionality in international and bilateral relations: the democratization process . . . needs [international] backing by relaxing the austerity measures and the provision of more economic assistance."[42] Interestingly he quotes, in support of this conclusion, Larry Diamond. But Kaballo gives no more reason than does Diamond to anticipate the kind of global turnaround that guaranteeing such a benign context for democratization would require. He is, in short, as unsuccessful in carrying the contradictions of the global economy as he is in carrying the contradictions of Africa's domestic class structure into the centre of his analysis.

What, secondly, of the question of order? In a world, and a continent, scarred by the extreme tearing of the social fabric that has occurred in such settings as (the former) Yugoslavia, Rwanda, and Somalia, it would be unwise to trivialize the preoccupation of political scientists with this issue. This is, in fact, the other side of the coin of Przeworski's pessimism regarding the (unlikely) radical/socialist dimension of any transition from authoritarian rule. For Przeworski also argues passionately for the possibility that, under certain circumstances, protagonists to such transitions will agree (if it proves possible for them to agree at all) "to terminate conflicts over institutions because they fear that a continuation of conflict may lead to [or perpetuate] a civil war that will be both collectively and individually threatening. The pressure to stabilize the situation is tremendous, since governance must somehow continue. *Chaos is the worst alternative for all.*"[43] In a parallel manner, James Dunkerley — in examining the "resolution of civil wars in Nicaragua (1981-90) and El Salvador (1980-91) where laborious and intricate negotiations terminated conflicts of great brutality and bitterness" — writes of the "collapse of communism and the outbreak of other civil wars, the terrifying images of which should serve to remind us of the merits of what Cromwell called 'settling and healing,' even if this is achieved in unheroic manner, at the cost of dreams, and through the concession of often vital interests."[44]

As it happens, Przeworski and Dunkerley both cast their concerns primarily in terms of the compromises amongst classes and contending power blocs that might be necessary to facilitate a transition. In the African literature, with its own distinctive tilt towards the political science of transition, far greater attention has been paid to another possible route towards "chaos," that threatened by the uncontrolled escalation of "identity politics" — particularly as driven by an extreme expression of the politicization of ethnicity (although regionalism, race, and religion have also been mentioned as other possible modalities of such hyper-politicized identity). From this angle, too, "settling and healing" have seemed important goals, with "democracy" then assessed primarily in terms of its projected contribution to the underwriting of an effective level of societal order (di Palma's "setting up [of] government in diversity as a way of defusing conflict").

LIBERAL DEMOCRACY VS. POPULAR DEMOCRACY

In the two case studies — of South Africa and Mozambique — that follow in this chapter we will see the way in which the introduction of electoral, and other, related, constitutional solutions to outstanding situations of deep-seated social conflict have helped to produce far more stable societies and polities than had previously existed. Of course, as scholars have also warned, the implications of "democracy" for the securing of order in fragile societies may sometimes be far more negative; the competitive aspects of democratic processes may serve to exacerbate the claims and counter-claims of different communal interests rather than to assuage and domesticate them. Still, we would be unwise to ignore the contribution that the exercise of political imagination, of "statecraft," can and must make — both during the period of constitution-making and the run-up to the initial elections, and after them — to the ongoing reconciling of such claims and the creation of some greater sense of enlarged community and shared citizenship.

There is one major limitation to this way of formulating things, however. It is a limitation anticipated earlier when we noted the roots in Africa's contemporary political economy of the intensity of many such "claims and counter-claims." The fact remains that any sense of "enlarged community and shared citizenship" or of national institutional consolidation that is won, momentarily, by statecraft may already be in the process of being lost, once again, to the fragmenting logic of "underdevelopment" and of peripheral capitalism. True, the specific tensions that mark the various fragile societies we study are the product of quite specific histories and circumstances. But their weaknesses are exacerbated — make no mistake — by the global capitalist disorder (and by such corollaries as the undermining of any sense of a possible developmental role for the presently existing nation-state). Sapped of confidence in socialist and other related projects ("modern," collective, and humane), people turn for social meaning to more immediate identities, often to grasp them with fundamentalist fervour (as Leys suggests).

Here is Ralph Miliband's "extremely fertile terrain" for the kind of "pathological deformations" — predatory authoritarianisms and those "demagogues and charlatans peddling their poisonous wares . . . of ethnic and religious exclusion and hatred" — that now scar the landscape in Africa and elsewhere.[45] For, as Nancy Fraser effectively argues, it seems extremely unlikely that tensions rooted in struggles for "recognition" can be resolved, in the long-term, in any very effective and healing manner unless tensions rooted in struggles for "redistribution" (broadly defined) are also being addressed.[46] We are drawn back, in other words, to a consideration of the necessary simultaneity of the moments of "political economy" and of "political science" in the discussion of Africa's transition to democracy and of the links of that process to "nation-building." The brief case studies that follow are designed to put further flesh on the bones of this approach.

# South Africa: A Liberal Democracy ?

The South African election of 1994 was a crucial event, so overwhelmingly significant as a "liberation election" from white minority rule that it is, indeed, rather
difficult to view it in any other terms: the drive for democratic rights in that country by and for the vast majority of its population is a well-known story that has
captured the imagination of the world. At the same time, South Africa also has
seemed to provide an almost classic case of the kind of transition that Przeworski
has in mind when he writes of the "extrication" of democracy from authoritarian
regimes in which "political forces that control the apparatus of repression, most
often the armed forces" remain strongly positioned. Joe Slovo, South African
Communist Party (SACP) leader and one of the major protagonists of the South
African transition, writing in the midst of the negotiations stage in that country,
characterized the South African situation in much the same terms:

> We are negotiating because towards the end of the 80s we concluded that, as
> a result of its escalating crisis, the apartheid power bloc was no longer able to
> continue ruling in the old way and was genuinely seeking some break with the
> past. At the same time, we were clearly not dealing with a defeated enemy and
> an early revolutionary seizure of power by the liberation movement could not
> be realistically posed. This conjuncture of the balance of forces (which contin-
> ues to reflect current reality) provided a classic scenario which placed the pos-
> sibility of negotiations on the agenda. And we correctly initiated the whole
> process in which the ANC was accepted as the major negotiating adversary.[47]

Moreover, this military stalemate was itself seen as merely the tip of the ice-
berg of other conflicts within the society, conflicts driven by the realities of "difference" (as defined by racial, cultural, and political party/movement identifications) that have been so visible and so close to the surface and dangerous in South
Africa.[48] For example, one informed observer, assessing the racial dimensions of the
situation, suggested, "The balance of power and the potentially catastrophic effects
of a descent into civil war dictate that negotiated transition rather than revolutionary transformation is the order of the day — and that a settlement . . . requires
significant compromises to allay the concerns of the white elite."[49] As the negotiations unfolded, the ANC was prepared to make a number of such compromises to
meet white concerns, and also prepared, on occasion, to make them towards Gatsha
Buthelezi and his Inkatha Freedom Party (despite this party's sustained posture of
intransigence and provocation).

Under the circumstances of a divided South Africa, the realization in April
1994 of a nation-wide election that witnessed the transfer of power from a racial
oligarchy to a new, pan-racial majority was a dramatic achievement.[50] Small wonder that the negotiations that served to realize such democratic possibilities and to

hold in check such dangerous contradictions have been a magnet for the attention of students of the "political science" of transition. Here was a case, if ever there was one, of the "setting up [of] government in diversity as a way of defusing conflict": accordingly, the temptation has been irresistible for political practitioners and political observers alike to draw the ebb and flow of political in-fighting, of intra-elite tradeoffs, and of constitutional compromise to the centre of their analyses. Thus a book by Alaister Sparks usefully documents the manner in which the relevant negotiations had actually begun well before the release of Nelson Mandela from prison in 1990 and traces their continuation right up to the 1994 election.[51] Even more impressive in this regard have been the two important volumes on the South African transition prepared by Steven Friedman and his colleagues: The Long Journey: South Africa's Quest for a Negotiated Settlement and The Small Miracle: South Africa's Negotiated Settlement.[52] These books contain painstaking analyses of the intense interactions that took place, over the four-year period 1990-94, amongst political elites regarding transitional political and bureaucratic arrangements, long-term constitutional dispensations, and the proposed workings of the electoral system that would eventually come into play in 1994.

There is even some discussion in such works of the moments at which political actors outside the formal negotiating framework broke into the process: the mass-action campaign spearheaded by the trade unions in August 1992 and the more chaotic events at Bisho that same month are examples. Of course, on the left, there was concern that such mass action had come to be treated merely as a "tap," to be turned on and off at the ANC leadership's whim as short-term calculation of advantage at the bargaining table might dictate: "We must not confine or inhibit mass struggle. . . . Instead we need to encourage, facilitate and indeed build the kind of fighting grass-roots organizations that can lead and sustain a thousand and one local struggles against the numerous injustices our people suffer."[53] But what most academic analysts seemed to accept both as inevitable and as benign was that, on balance, the negotiation process had tended to sideline many of the bearers of popular resistance who had done so much to place negotiations on the table in the first place. "Elite coalescence has been the hallmark of South Africa's transition," wrote Timothy Sisk approvingly, adding, "Elite-concluded accords do not work unless elites are able to demobilize their own constituencies."[54] The election itself was hailed, in effect, as locking the results of such "coalescence" — and such judicious "demobilization" — into place.

Some of the celebration by political scientists of the South African negotiations process that culminated in the 1994 election has been more qualified. The actual electoral process was often chaotic, for example. Given the heroic scope of the overall undertaking, most observers were inclined to be tolerant of many of the flaws in the process, but some flaws did seem to demand special attention. Most controversial was the manner in which the outcome of the election was itself a "negotiated" one, notably in KwaZulu/Natal, where, in the context of considerable fraud and malfeasance and in the interest of safeguarding a peaceful outcome, the ANC and Inkatha leaderships merely agreed on the outcome in secret.[55] There could be no guarantee that so sanctioning Inkatha's victory in its "home province" would actually discipline its rogue tendencies; the electoral process seemed likely to be merely one more avenue along which it would choose to advance its disruptive project. (Indeed, some observers argued at the time that additional constitutional concessions — an even more decentralized form of federalism, for example — were necessary so as to meet, in the interests of further guaranteeing order, Buthelezi's apparently insatiable demands.[56]

A handful of other authors queried the actual scope of the democratic outcome in South Africa in quite other terms. Notably, Herman Giliomee expressed fears that the elections may merely have produced "a one-party-dominant system" ("along Mexican and Taiwanese lines").[57] And there are precedents in the region that might feed such concerns, notably that of Zimbabwe, where according to Richard Saunders the continuing electoral successes of the ZANU-Patriotic Front (ZANU-PF) can be traced, paradoxically, to "the grim model of multi-party democracy which Zimbabwe's ruling party has moulded and refined since coming to power in 1980." Saunders points out: "It is a model which has mixed western-style liberal democratic political constructs with ZANU-PF's increasing partisan domination of state and civil society, to produce a pro forma democracy that evokes little popular enthusiasm and diminishes active participation from ordinary Zimbabweans."[58]

But if "the gradual depopularization of the formal political process" is also a risk in South Africa it might be mistaken to seek its roots primarily in any authoritarian proclivities that the ANC may have.[59] Pace Giliomee, some left observers have seen a more serious risk of such an outcome to lie in the ANC's comfortable commitment to the liberal nature of the democratization process in South Africa, rather than in not having committed itself to it enough.[60] Giliomee seems to have only two points to his political compass: authoritarianism vs. liberalism — with no space for "popular democracy." However, we cannot make sense of South Africa in these terms: to understand why this is so it becomes necessary for us to expand the scope of our inquiry beyond the confines of the currently fashionable discussion of the South African transition.

For the weakness of such discussion springs, once again, from that severing of "political economy" from "political science," with all the dangers that holds. Here one dramatic citation may suffice, although a more sustained canvassing of the literature would bear additional witness to much the same point. This citation takes us back to the two Friedman books singled out earlier for praise for their handling of the intricacies of the political horse-trading that characterized the negotiations process. The special significance of this citation bears emphasizing. Note that it is the only moment in all the 543 pages of these books when any of the collected authors acknowledges that there existed, in effect, a second level of "negotiations" in South Africa, albeit one clearly visible only within the optic of the political economy approach. Thus, on pages 290-91 of the second of these volumes, Chris Landsberg — writing a chapter entitled "Directing from the Stalls? The International Community and the South African Negotiation Forum" — notes:

> But the SAG [South African government] was not the only target for persistent pressure from abroad. The ANC also came in for its share of the pressure. Since 1990, when the democratization process began, some foreign governments, notably the US and some of its allies — Britain, Germany, Italy and Japan — successfully induced the ANC to move away from its socialist economic policies, including that of nationalization. Instead, they succeeded in persuading the movement to embrace Western-style free market principles which the ANC increasingly, albeit reluctantly, adopted. It is interesting to note, for example, that Mandela's evolving position on fiscal responsibility was a direct response to pressures from foreign investors and governments.[61]

This dimension, involving the moderation of the ANC's aspirations for socio-economic transformation and the movement's consequent increasing acceptability to powerful vested interests, worldwide and local, was at least as crucial as any constitutional compromise to guaranteeing the smoothness of the transition to "democracy" in South Africa. Yet even in the context of Landsberg's own chapter it is noted only in passing, and certainly never presented — as it should have been — in such a way as to be integrated into these books' overall interpretative framework.

Permit me one other citation, in order to cap the point: it is drawn from another book that painstakingly traces the South African negotiations process, Timothy Sisk's *Democratization in South Africa: The Elusive Social Contract.* Sisk's priorities are established on his very first page and in no uncertain terms: "Determining how conflicts driven by identity politics are reoriented from the battlefield to the conflict-regulating institutions of an inclusive democratic state is the critical challenge of our era."[62] In fact, Sisk does acknowledge at various points later in his book that critical questions of "redistribution" have also been at stake in a deeply inegalitarian South Africa.[63] He even suggests that such questions must now be dealt with or the consequences might be disastrous. But his discussion of such issues is prisoner of his starting point: his framework does not allow him to see that the very nature of the negotiations process that centred on "identity politics" also shaped, in crucial ways, the terrain for any ongoing struggle over redistributional politics. As the ANC became more "liberal" — adapting itself to the seeming imperatives of the global capitalist economy and, through "elite-pacting," to the prioritizing electoral models of political contestation (which, some feel, has encouraged a further demobilization of its constituency) — did it also become less able to effectively champion the struggle for "redistribution"?[64]

There is certainly evidence that the ANC has adopted a broadly "neo-liberal" economic agenda (see chapter 2 and the chapters in Part III).[65] We can, however, speculate further as to what will happen if the movement's gamble on free-market capitalism — expected to provide both a sustainable solution to South Africa's economic problems and also sufficient surpluses to permit at least some redistribution of resources — does not work. The growing indifference of the black population, its transformation into mere spectators at the political-cum-electoral game, was earlier suggested to be one possible outcome. That there were already some indications of this by early 1995 was apparent in the initial run-up to the local elections to be held later in the year. According to one report, in April:

> Anxiety is starting to mount in provincial governments at the slow pace of voter registration, three weeks from the deadline. But registration has been slow in all parts of the country, and in some of the previously most politically active areas it has been slowest. . . . The 90-day voter registration exercise has met with a lukewarm response despite high-profile media campaigns. Last Saturday an ANC local government election rally at the Union Buildings in Pretoria attracted fewer than a hundred supporters. Rally organizers had been expecting up to 20,000. The lack of enthusiasm is being put down to disappointment about the failure yet to see material improvements after the last voting exercise, in April last year. An expectant black community has yet to see the houses, improved education and health facilities the ANC promised in its election campaign.[66]

By September the situation had not much improved. One high-profile study from the Centre for Policy Studies warned, "Large-scale apathy on election day could lead to local government based on a thin slice of popular support, which is not representative." As Paul Graham of the Institute for Democracy in South Africa added, "In terms of internationally accepted criteria for free and fair elections, the forthcoming elections are getting to the point where it is sadly failing."[67]

Moreover — to build on the analysis developed in the previous section of this chapter — popular indifference may not be the worst thing that can occur under such circumstances. Might not any "demobilizing" of popular constituencies for purposes of consolidating "inter-elite accords" (à la Timothy Sisk) merely make such constituencies available for other forms of mobilization than developmental ones? Winnie Mandela's tendency to translate socio-economic contradictions into starkly racial terms offers few solutions to South Africa's structural problems, but it has proven to be attractive in some of the popular circles in which she moves; and this kind of cultural nationalist politics could prove to be even more attractive in future. In addition, if South African blacks are not effectively mobilized in terms of class interests and for purposes of national developmental goals and socio-economic transformation, they may well fall back on more exclusively ethnic loyalties to ground their search for moorings in the unstable social universe that is the new

South Africa. And if these things were to occur, might not the "chaos" that nego-tiations are said to have pre-empted merely be found to be bubbling up again, within the electoral arena[68] and elsewhere, in new and even more dangerous forms? This may be too bleak a picture, however. South Africa is also marked by other, much more progressive, efforts to keep alive the popular term in the polit-ical equation, and to strengthen initiatives that might qualify global capitalism's hold over policy-making. Within the ANC coalition itself there are cross-cutting ten-dencies, for example, leading some close observers to predict that "the 'broad church' of the ANC will eventually split into its component elements," and largely along class lines, leading to new party-political alignments.[69] Others have argued that different class projects will continue, for the foreseeable future, to play them-selves out within the ANC itself, suggesting such contradictions to be already visible within the movement's Reconstruction and Development Programme/RDP[70] — a key document developed, through a process of internal debate and public con-sultation, to serve as both election manifesto and policy guide for the ANC once in power. Thus the RDP largely accepted the existing capitalist framework for purpos-es of macro-economic policy-making. Yet its dramatic first section locked into place a clear statement about the centrality of meeting "basic needs" as the chief per-formance standard against which to measure the success of the new South Africa, one to which all sectors, including the business community, could be held account-able. This was a powerful point of reference for challenging any easy slide into acceptance of a Brazilian-style "fifty per cent solution" (or worse) as "good enough" for South Africa. Even more importantly, later sections of the document affirmed in dramatic terms the necessity that an ongoing process of popular empowerment from below would keep the process of transformation alive. One is reminded, in this connection, of one of Nelson Mandela's more intriguing state-ments of those early years: thus, speaking to the COSATU annual congress in 1993, he warned the assembled workers' representatives to be "vigilant." "How many times," he asked, "has a labour movement supported a liberation movement, only to find itself betrayed on the day of liberation? There are many examples of this in Africa. If the ANC does not deliver the goods you must do to it what you did to the apartheid regime."[71]

As it happens, this was not always the message that Mandela delivered after assuming power. It is, however, the kind of language that continues to drive much of the left in South Africa, as they have looked to the assertions of trade unions, civics, women's organizations, and the like — operating, from sites within "civil society," both inside and outside the ANC — to keep a progressive agenda alive. As ANC/SACP loyalist Jeremy Cronin told a Johannesburg conference in 1994:

> The challenge is to engage with the democratic transition process, with a per-spective and a movement that is more democratic, more far-reaching in its popular empowerment implications, a perspective that extends political

democracy beyond the critically important institutions of representative democracy to embrace direct and participatory forms as well. And we need to extend democracy beyond political institutions, into the social and economic realms.[72]

Opinions differ as to how effectively popular demands can make themselves felt by such means. Some observers are inclined to despair regarding the prospects for progressive endeavour in the near- to mid-future; others insist that "the powerful grass-roots forces behind liberation can regain momentum," the current situation "compelling the still formidable — as well as many brand new — organizations of the poor and working-class to demand that their representatives and leaders take an entirely different direction."[73] In any case, it is argued that it is only along some such path that the way could lie open to a deepening of democracy and the retaining of a radical momentum in South Africa. As Glenn Adler and Eddie Webster argue (in their critique of the rightward pull of much of the transition literature, especially that of Przeworski), "disciplined and sophisticated social movements" may yet be able to:

> inject more progressive content into the democratization process and wrest important concessions from reformers and moderates alike [recall Przeworski's use of these terms]. In other words a conservative outcome is in no way given in advance. . . . Rather than being a force to be restrained by the alliance between reformers and moderates, a mobilized civil society and powerful social movements — especially the labour movement — played a central and constructive role in creating the conditions for the transition, in shaping its character, and indeed in legitimizing the transition process itself. Whether the labour movement can continue to play this role is an open question. With the advent of parliamentary democracy and the creation of corporatist-type policy-making fora and institutions, as well as the emphasis on national reconciliation, pressures towards incorporation and demobilization have never been stronger. However, countervailing trends point towards the persistence of these movements and their democratic culture and toward a postapartheid politics of continued contestation within the new democratic institutions.[74]

## The Mozambican Case: What Kind of Transition?

We will return — in light, in particular, of more recent developments in South Africa — to an assessment of the likely strength of any such possible revival of radical endeavour there in later chapters. Note, however, that certain ostensible alternatives to the liberal-democratic framework have already been tried and, it is argued, found wanting in Africa. Mozambique is a case in point, much cited in South Africa as an example of what not to do. After all, didn't Mozambique attempt to mount a "socialist alternative" to the dictates of global capitalism — and that in the days when there at least existed an apparent global counter-hegemonic force (the Eastern bloc) to which a country could link its radical fortunes? And look what happened.

There are those who will argue that Frelimo's activities in Mozambique did not actually comprise a genuinely socialist project even in its earliest days. I cannot agree with this reading. Elsewhere I have argued the necessity of distinguishing "left developmental dictatorships" from "right developmental dictatorships" and suggested that Mozambique under Frelimo leadership once fell within the former category: concerned precisely with those issues — a "position on imperialism, state and class, class struggle, etc." — that we have seen Shivji identify with a "popular perspective."[75] Moreover, in its early days, Frelimo quite self-consciously presented itself as embodying a "radical democratic" thrust: it both highlighted within the terms of its overall project the needs and interests of ordinary Mozambicans and it sought to institutionalize in real ways the active participation of those people (through the formation of "dynamizing groups" and mass organizations of women, workers, and the like). But recall that Shivji also placed, alongside his models of liberal and popular democracy, a "statist" model, embracing regimes whose own distinctive "democratic" rhetoric (and authoritarian practice) he sardonically epitomizes in the phrase "what-use-is-free-speech-to-a-starving-peasant." Viewed in such terms, the initial Frelimo experiment was both "left developmentalist" ("socialist") and, ultimately, "statist" (authoritarian).

Interestingly, recent interviews I have had with the more committed of the first generation of Frelimo leaders find a number of them admitting ruefully that the undemocratic, "statist" nature of their undertaking contributed importantly to the failure of their initially progressive project — laying a dead hand over the very institutions of democratic activism that the movement was ostensibly willing into place. To be sure, Mozambique's inherited circumstances (the relative backwardness of Portuguese colonialism, the absence of trained cadres, the extreme vulnerability of the economy) were far from favourable to both radical endeavour and economic transformation. And the ruthlessness of South Africa's policy of destabilization — concretized in Mozambique in the practices of the Renamo movement but part of a much broader regional strategy of defending apartheid — must still be considered the single most important factor in undermining Frelimo's efforts.[76] Yet the fact remains that, domestically, grievous errors in the sphere of economic policymaking were twinned with high-handed political practices, practices that undermined precisely the popular empowerment that might have set Frelimo's own project on far firmer foundations.

Empowerment? In principle, one might imagine such a "left developmental dictatorship" deepening its project in democratic terms — in line with its initially very real commitments to the popular classes — and moving towards a more genuinely (rather than notionally) "popular democracy." But the anti-democratic impact of a tendency towards militarist hierarchy, an embrace of the presumed centralizing imperatives of "developmentalism," and a fixation with quasi-Stalinist notions of socialist practice combined to negate any such trajectory in Mozambique.[77] Very soon, in any case, the effects of war, and of the penetration of the country's faltering politico-economic structure by the IFIS and the aid community, meant that little remained of Frelimo's initial left vocation. What Mozambique was experiencing under Frelimo leadership was something very like a "recolonization" (in the pungent formula suggested by economist David Plank).[78] Now, if the party's authoritarian instinct did remain in place, it was increasingly the instinct of a dictatorship ("developmental" or otherwise) of the right.

There was to be no easy resting place for the Frelimo leadership at this point, however. The Frelimo state was in tatters, and the war ground on. Western interests, now ever more prominent (and unchallenged) actors in Mozambique, were increasingly insistent upon brokering a negotiated, "democratic" settlement to the country's "civil war." Moreover, Renamo, at first merely a vicious cat's-paw of external actors (Rhodesia, South Africa), had begun to root itself ever more indigenously in Mozambique's broken-backed society. Its sheer continuing presence in areas where it could not be driven out militarily increasingly allowed it to ground a certain "giveness" for itself within the emerging Mozambican political equation. And it had also managed to carve out some space for itself by (for example) linking up with quasi-traditional structures and fanning regional resentments. Thus, even though much of its external backing (from such former sponsors as apartheid South Africa and Banda's Malawi) was beginning to evaporate, its political claims could not merely be wished away.

It was also the case that, in ideological terms, much less now separated Frelimo from Renamo than had once seemed possible: both had little choice but to embrace the conventional nostrums of neo-liberalism (and, apparently, little desire not to do so). Add to this that, at a certain point, the government's own morale seemed to snap, with mounting corruption and the increasingly arbitrary use of power by both military and civilian authorities threatening to drag Frelimo's own project down to Renamo's level. Thus, by the time of the 1994 elections — with Renamo finally cajoled (by various international actors, most prominently) into taking up a more conventionally peaceful political role — a great deal of the distance separating the two movements-cum-parties had begun to disappear. As South African journalist Eddie Koch commented, that election seemed to be marked by a kind of "moral amnesia," with Frelimo's own high purposes at independence now but a distant memory and Renamo's history as, first, Rhodesia's and then South Africa's brutal cat's-paw also obscured by time and changing circumstance.

In consequence, to observe closely Mozambique's first multi-party election in October 1994 was a very different experience from that of observing the South African election earlier in the same year. For whatever the ambiguities that attached to the South African transition process, the overriding mood of most South Africans in April had been one of euphoria. Theirs was a "liberation election," one in which a large majority felt themselves to be voting, quite literally, for their freedom. Mozambique offered a far more sombre context for exercise of the franchise. Indeed, large numbers of Mozambicans seemed to be voting, first and foremost, for the very idea of voting itself. Their apparent hope was that the election would prove to be an arena within which political differences might, at last, be resolved peacefully and the violence that had scarred their lives for so long might end. Was this not, then, a virtually archetypal case study in the "political science of democratization"?[79]

Moreover, in these terms the election did "work," albeit as part of a much broader peace process, one that was orchestrated to a signal degree from outside the country by interested players within the international community.[80] (For more detail on this, see chapter 4.) Both the United Nations and a number of Western countries (as well as various arms of the Catholic Church) placed strong pressure on Frelimo to cede a more pluralistic political structure, while also going to considerable expense to encourage the Renamo leadership to transform itself from guerrilla movement into a more conventional political party. The result was, indeed, a smooth-running electoral process, financed in large part by substantial foreign subventions (notably from the United Nations), although cleanly organized and run by the Mozambicans themselves.[81]

Moreover, Renamo did surprisingly well in the election, even though Frelimo's Alberto Joaquim Chissano scored firmly over Renamo's Afonso Dhlakama in the presidential balloting and Frelimo also scraped out a rather narrower majority in the National Assembly. In the run-up to the election there had been much pressure on Frelimo to concede — the South African precedent was mentioned — Renamo participation in a post-electoral "Government of National Unity," which Frelimo refused to do. Moreover, despite the narrowness of its victory, the post-electoral Frelimo government seemed inclined to operate, rather high-handedly, on a "winner-takes-all" basis.[82] Might this not, at best, produce a Mozambican version of the de facto one-party state, and at worst be so provocative as merely to reactivate civil strife? In the event, Renamo was apparently reasonably reconciled to the new system.[83] It seemed, for the moment at least, that a democratic resolution had brought closure to one of the most horrific, chaos-producing wars in Africa: no small accomplishment.[84]

And yet the kind of politics that was facilitated by the electoral process, if measured against the aspirations of advocates of "popular democracy," was not particularly empowering of the Mozambican populace. We have seen that the scope for national decision-making had become quite narrowly defined by the global circumstances in which Mozambique found itself, with the state eviscerated and any immediate prospect of political contestation over alternative socio-economic visions sidelined. In the election, Frelimo, once the proponent of a clear (if controversial) socialist development alternative, ran a campaign centred on "show-*micios*" (a play on the Portuguese word "*comicio*") and rallies in which show business (including bands and parachutists), the trivialization of issues, and the glorification of the candidate took precedence over real substance. For its part, Renamo tended to fall back on the quite calculated manipulation of various regional, ethnic, religious, and (advanced in the name of "tradition") gender-oppressive particularisms and animosities in building its own electoral base, thereby setting a number of dangerous precedents for the texture of future political interactions in the country.[85] The upshot, ironically, was that the introduction of the institutions of pluralist democracy was, in some ways, disempowering for ordinary Mozambicans: rendering them less, not more, able to engage in meaningful debate about the nature of neo-colonial structures in their country and about possible alternatives to them.

As with South Africa, this way of interpreting the situation does need qualification. The liberalization/democratization of political space in Mozambique has had implications that stretch beyond both the opportunities and the mystifications of the electoral arena. As trade union and women's movement structures have been liberated from the deadening hand of monoparty control, for example, they have begun to assert themselves in new ways. Agricultural co-operatives, emerging in particular in the peri-urban green zones, are also believed to hold considerable promise in some areas, while the freeing up of space for a more creative brand of journalism has also had an often positive impact, albeit one felt primarily in the urban areas. If such varied initiatives can indeed root themselves firmly in Mozambique, the necessary socio-political underpinnings for pressing more powerful democratic demands upon governments, parties, and the electoral process itself may prove to be that much more firmly in place. Or take the recent observations regarding rural Mozambique by Ken Wilson, who finds — in trends towards decentralization, in the mounting of local elections, in the new sensitivity of various governmental bureaucracies to grassroots demands and initiatives, and in the waning of politicians' high-handed devaluation of existing cultural sensibilities — the necessary context for a new and much stronger voice from the peasantry to be heard.[86]

Wilson may be overstating the positive side of the "opening to the villages" that he emphasizes; other observers have tended to stress more strongly the possible dangers (for the transformation of gender relations, for example) of a negative compromise with "traditional" structures that such an opening might entail in practice.[87] Still, in reading his intervention, I was forcefully reminded of a conversation I had in 1994, during the run-up to the elections in Mozambique, with Graça Machel, former minister of education in the Mozambican government and widow of Frelimo leader (and the country's first prime minister) Samora Machel. Saying that she would not herself be standing for the Assembly this time round, she told me that she would, however, be voting for Frelimo. I was taken aback. This was an answer to a question that it would not have dawned on me to ask.

Yes, she went on, Frelimo still represents more of a national project — Frelimo's most crucial historical accomplishment, in her view — than any other alternative on offer. But in terms of deepening democracy and ensuring the

eventual revival of other more progressive strands of Frelimo's original undertakings for the country (including the building of ever more secure foundations for a
genuinely stable Mozambican national political system), she saw the chief hope as
lying in the strengthening, in her phrase, of "the institutions of civil society." And
this is the sphere towards which, for the foreseeable future, she said she intended
to direct her own considerable energies.

## The Missing Alternative: A Popular Democracy ?

Are the seeds of alternative democratic possibilities to be found here, as in South
Africa, in the building from the ground up of an invigorated "civil society"? This
is the kind of question to which we turn in conclusion. One thing is clear, however: it is the refrain of "liberal democracy" — drawing, as Shivji says, "its inspiration from western liberalism centred around notions of limited government, individual rights, parliamentary and party institutions, the centrality of the economic
and political entrepreneur of the market-place, etc."[88] — that is hegemonic in South
Africa, and even (however much more tentatively) in Mozambique. This hegemony,
the apparently "commonsensical" nature of liberal-democratic discourse, is one
reason why progressive political actors and analysts have difficulty mounting the
case for an alternative. But are such actors and analysts not also stymied by the difficulty of giving concrete form to their own ideal type, that of popular democracy?
Are they only able to contrast glibly that model's abstract claims to the perceived
imperfections of the real-life system of liberal democracy, while incapable of specifying what it might mean to put their own imagined alternative firmly on the
political agenda?

Of course, if liberal democracy is indeed likely to prove to be an oxymoron in
Southern Africa, that would be a point worth making whether or not any more
progressive alternatives to it, and to the neo-liberal economics with which it intersects, were readily forthcoming. Again, the "historically necessary" is not always
the "historically possible." Nor is someone like Shivji prepared to apologize for the
difficulty of evoking, for purposes of comparison, the experience of any "real-life"
popular democracies in Africa — since, in fact, the attempt to build them has only
just begun. As Shivji states:

> The popular [perspective on democracy] remains most undefined. It opposes
> both the statist and liberal in their typically top-down orientation by empha-
> sizing popular struggles and mass movements from below. It challenges the
> universality of liberal values and the authoritarianism of statist positions.[89]

> As an ideology of resistance and struggle . . . [its] exact contours and forms
> of existence can only be determined in actual social struggles in given, con-
> crete social conditions. Yet, at the minimum, it has to be an ideology which
> articulates anti-imperialism and anti-compradore-state positions.[90]

Must we leave the argument there, however? Have we not already begun to spec-ify the ways in which the "concrete social conditions," the contradictions, of peripheral capitalism in Southern Africa are even now throwing up "resistance and struggle" of the kind necessary to ground increasingly "popular" expressions of democracy? I will return to this point in the concluding chapter, but it is worth asking, first, in however preliminary a way, whether we can begin to identify exist-ing practices that exemplify the promise of just such resistance and struggle? To this question many observers would answer "yes," looking to a range of organiza-tions in "civil society" as exemplifying precisely the promise in question. Indeed, this is a key emphasis on the left both in South Africa and in Mozambique.

True, "civil society" has become something of buzzword in discussions about Africa. The term often masks as much as it reveals about the class content of strug-gles there (as elsewhere). As Ellen Wood forcefully reminds us in a number of her writings, it is a deeply ambiguous concept, tilted in its origins towards the inter-ests of emergent entrepreneurs, yet also used, more recently, to encapsulate the claims of broader publics and a wider range of interests.[91] It is noteworthy, in any case, just how central the notion has become to those who press the case for some-thing considered to be more empowering of ordinary people than mere liberal democracy. A case in point, perhaps, is Benjamin Barber, one of a handful of Western political thinkers who have defied the hegemony of the theorists of "poly-archy" and "democratic elitism."[92] Writing in 1984, Barber anticipated my argu-ment here by asserting, "We suffer, in the face of our era's manifold crises, not from too much but from too little democracy." He continued:

> From the time of de Toqueville, it has been said that an excess of democracy can undo liberal institutions. I will try to show that an excess of liberalism has undone liberal institutions: for what little democracy we have had . . . has been repeatedly compromised by the liberal institutions with which it has been under-girded and the liberal philosophy from which its theory and practice has been derived. . . . Liberal democracy is . . . a "thin" theory of democracy, one whose democratic values are [a] prudential . . . means to exclusively individualistic and private ends. From this precarious foundation, no firm theory of citizenship, par-ticipation, public goods, or civic virtue can be expected to arise.[93]

Barber's alternative? "Strong Democracy . . . defined by politics in the participatory mode," a politics through which "active citizens govern themselves directly, not necessarily at every level and in every instance, but frequently enough and in par-ticular when basic policies are being decided and when significant power is being deployed." Note that Barber, in arguing the case for "strong democracy," is care-ful to distinguish this from anything smacking of "unitary democracy," a quite different concept and one much closer to the kind of "statist" formulation of "authoritarian quasi-democracy" that Shivji critiques.[94] A strong democracy is one in which consensus, community, and a sense of the "public realm" are won through political interaction, not imposed from above.

In more recent writing Barber worries about the arena within which such politics might best be pursued, asking where, in effect, meaningful citizenship must come to be defined. For he is well aware that the surge of globalization (his "McWorld") has grouped many of the forces that most deeply affect people's lives at that global level. But whether in the community, national, or worldwide arena, the challenge is "to make government our own" through a recasting of "our civic attitudes"; this, in turn, "is possible only in a vibrant civil society where responsibilities and rights are joined together in a seamless web of community self-government."[95] Barber is by no means naive as to the prospects of so "making government our own," especially at the global level. Yet it is his very underscoring of the necessity to do so that marks him as a genuine democrat: "How civil society can be forged in an international environment is an extraordinary challenge. Recognizing that it needs to be forged is, however, the first step towards salvaging a place for strong democracy in the world of McWorld."[96]

It is here that Barber's concerns intersect with Southern African progressives: there is a shared sense that it is genuine popular empowerment that must be struggled for in the name of democracy. And there is something more: even those in South Africa who have already lived the intense history of popular activism that was so much a part of the anti-apartheid struggle realize that the bases of such empowerment can never be taken for granted: they must continue to be built painstakingly — conceived, renewed, struggled for, given institutional form — from the bottom up. There is no short cut to popular democracy, nor is there any elite pact or refined constitutional dispensation that can guarantee it, however important these accomplishments can sometimes be in opening up space for the pursuit of a more deep-cutting process of democratization.

Identifying the goal of "strong democracy" can therefore make an important contribution to our understanding of democratic practice and of truly effective institution-building. Measured against it, the insensitivity, even brutality, of the formulas of Diamond ("citizens [should] care about politics, but not too much") and Samuel Huntington (his fear of an "excess of democracy") are unmasked.[97] Here is the kind of "political science of democratization" that could really help us to get somewhere.

Still, even Barber can only take us so far. In the end his writings run the risk of valuing democratic activity for its own sake, and for the sake of producing a more meaningful "community," but without really spelling out the concrete policy ends that a more effectively empowered citizenry might be expected to produce. Thus, while the global system churns on, he can satisfy himself with the bromide "that neither capitalism nor socialism has much to do with the economic realities of the modern world."[98] This is not an emphasis that the South African "strong democrats" whose concerns we have linked with those of Barber would be comfortable with, however. For they are much more inclined to be political economists than Barber is; their "strong democracy" has far more in common with Shivji's "popular democracy" in underscoring the fundamental importance of bringing capital under social control: the importance, in short, of a preoccupation with "imperialism, state and class, class struggle" in the grounding of democratic assertion.

For an approach that is both realistic and long-term must be part and parcel of this aspect of the progressive agenda as well. In Africa, as hard experience (and our previous chapters) have shown, the building of a socialist alternative in socioeconomic terms can be no more of an overnight enterprise than can be the building of a popular democracy on the political front. Few radicals in South Africa, for example, advocate any kind of ultra-left adventurism as the necessary antidote to the vaguely reformist neo-liberalism that many within the ANC now seem tempted by. Elsewhere I have argued that the notion of "structural reform" — a measured yet revolutionary project of closing in on the prerogatives of capital and shifting[99] the balance of power over the production process slowly but surely in the direction of the popular classes — epitomizes what the best of South African progressives still believe to be both necessary and possible. Statements by such important once-socialist-minded South Africans as then prominent trade union leader Enoch Godongwana and leading ANC activist Pallo Jordan serve to document this point, even if these two have themselves now moved some distance away from such perspectives. Acknowledging that "if we want a socialist alternative in the absence of an insurrection, that poses a challenge for us," Godongwana suggests:

> We argue a socialist alternative, but within the constraints of saying we cannot simply storm and seize power tomorrow. Therefore we should be creative — how do we make sure that, in the process of struggling for socialism, we assert ourselves as a class with the objective of having a class rule. . . . We must begin, while we assert a leading role in various areas of society, to build certain alternatives within the capitalist framework that will tend to undermine the capitalist logic.

Or, from the same debate, consider Jordan's similar interest in a kind of strategy

> which doesn't necessarily imply grabbing hold of the state or nationalization of the commanding heights of the economy, but in a sense establishing a number of strategic bridgeheads which enable you to empower the working class and the oppressed, and from these bridgeheads you begin then to subordinate the capitalist classes to the interests of society in general.[100]

As it stands, much of this kind of argument remains at the level of mere metaphor, even in South Africa. Spelling out what it would have to look like in practice requires real imagination, with respect both to the concrete mechanisms of state activity to be employed (the use of tariffs, taxes, procurement policies, and the like) and to any complementary actions that might have to spring from civil society (via collective bargaining structures, for example, or through the full range of existing socio-economic forums). Nor is a reliance on mere populist spontaneity likely to produce the subtle tactics and deft timing that we can see as being necessary to realize such ongoing struggles: clearly, effective leadership must come to complement the kind of mass energy and action that is so essential to radical undertakings. Nonetheless, the language in which the challenge now confronting South Africans is framed does make a difference.

For seeking to discipline capital to service socially defined priorities cannot be done merely by wielding the rhetoric of shared national purpose. Instead real, countervailing power — social power, class power — must be brought to bear upon it. This will not be easy. Yet it is precisely here that the goals of popular democracy and socialist assertion — of the political science and the political economy of democratization — come together. It is also true that any such efforts will be that much more difficult to realize in other African settings (Mozambique, for example) in which global capital (the IMF, World Bank, aid industry, multinational corporations) has an even more unqualified run of the shop and local elites have become so corruptly compromised by the "opportunities" offered them by "free-market" capitalism, in which the instruments of possible popular empowerment within "civil society" are much less developed, and in which parties and states that might begin to express a new set of progressive demands are far more distant on the horizon than is the case in South Africa. Yet there, too, the struggle continues.

The question of whether the strength of popular forces-in-the-making can build up enough to stem the logic of recolonization and the further underdevelopment of Africa that is occurring in the name of an ascendant neo-liberalism remains a very open one. Should we not admit, in fact, that it is difficult to be sanguine regarding the prospects for democratic empowerment in Africa — in large part because it is difficult to be sanguine about the prospects for the social and economic transformation of Africa under the current regime of neo-liberalism and global-market hegemony?

This is a painful truth, but, unfortunately, it is one that is not as "old-fashioned" as it is sometimes made to appear. Nor should acceptance of this truth serve as an invitation to trivialize other concerns that drive the debate about democracy in Africa: the need to discipline abusive authority; the need to create fresh space for individual and collective self-expression; the need to institutionalize the possible means of reconciling communal (ethnic and racial) differences and of reviving and refocusing some more positive sense of national purpose. The "political science of democratization" must not be allowed to displace "the political economy of democratization," but it must never again be merely reduced to it either — as the left has too often been tempted to do in the past.

Yet the fact remains: institutional ingenuity in the name of democracy can only do so much to contain and humanize Africa's contradictions so long as the socio-economic "terrain" remains so "fertile" for "pathological deformations" (to allude to Miliband's formulation). Indeed, under such circumstances, the tendency for democracy in Africa to exacerbate, rather than resolve, the difficulties of "nation-building" may well be the predominant one. Must we not conclude, in short (and *pace* the likes of Becker and Sklar), that the twin issues of "capitalism versus socialism" and "liberty versus dictatorship" are inextricably linked in Africa? But if this is true, are we not also left with a mere counsel of despair (socialism being "unfeasible," after all)? Certainly, as Colin Leys has put the point so tellingly, ideas that might begin to effectively address the question of Africa's economic crisis "could come to seem rational only in a world that was in the process of rejecting the currently predominant ideology of the market. While this world must come, it is not yet in sight, and meantime the African tragedy will unfold."[101]

"While this world must come . . ."? Would that it were so. Still, Leys's sentiment parallels that of Miliband: "Such a situation cannot endure." As Miliband concludes his final book:

> Change in the political system and the advent of "democracy" do not change the social order; but the demand that it too should be radically changed is certain to come into focus. . . . The specific demands and forms of struggle which [are generated] will vary from country to country: there is no single "model" of progressive or revolutionary change. But everywhere, there are common goals and aspirations — for democratic forms where they are denied, and for more democratic forms where they are a screen for oligarchic rule; for the achievement of social order in which improvement in the condition of the most deprived — often a majority of the population — is the prime concern of governments; for the subordination of the economy to meeting social needs. In all countries, there are people, in numbers large or small, who are moved by the vision of a new social order in which democracy, egalitarianism and cooperation — the essential values of socialism — would be the prevailing principles of social organization. It is in the growth in their numbers and in the success of their struggle that lies the best hope for humankind.[102]

Not least in Africa.

PART II

# SOUTHERN AFRICA:
# A RANGE OF VARIATION

# PEACE AND RECONCILIATION, AUTHORITARIANISM,

# AND "AFRICAN SOCIALISM"

We turn, in Part II, to four more detailed case studies: two, of Mozambique and Tanzania, deepen our analysis of countries already discussed in previous chapters; and another two, of Namibia and Zimbabwe, break fresh ground. The case studies also explore, in turn, four themes important to the recent history of Southern Africa: the making of peace in a wartorn region and in a country, Mozambique, ravaged by the fallout of the Thirty Years War for Southern African liberation (and, in particular, by the destabilizing actions of the cancerous apartheid state); the meaning of reconciliation, not only between black and white (South Africa's Truth and Reconciliation Commission comes to mind in this regard) but also amongst blacks who were themselves differentially affected by the often hard politics of the liberation struggle (which is a prominent feature of the Namibian case); the fact of authoritarianism, too often — as in Zimbabwe — the bitter outcome of the great victory that liberation from white-minority rule had undoubtedly represented; and, finally, the further reflection on the challenges of socialist construction that a revisiting of the Tanzanian case makes possible.

Of course, the issue of effecting "peace" in countries ravaged by heightened violence, ethnic hostility, warlordism, and the like has a continental resonance that stretches far beyond Southern Africa. The case of Mozambique is no doubt less well known than it should be, and it was thus important to remind ourselves, in Part I, of just how much was accomplished there through the anti-colonial struggle in the 1960s and the 1970s.[1] Nonetheless, as chapter 4 specifies, Mozambique had become, by the 1990s, a country so blighted by domestic conflict and the transformation of an externally inflicted (by South Africa) conflict into a virtual civil war that the mere negotiation, in the political realm, of a peace settlement could come to be considered, with some good reason, as an accomplishment of heroic proportions. Nonetheless, chapter 4 emphasizes — as does chapter 3 — that it is profoundly misleading to consider these matters outside the framework of political economy. The preoccupations of political science must be complemented with insights derived from an understanding of, precisely, the political economy of capitalism in Africa in order to understand both the strengths and the limitations of the kind of democracy, the kind of peace, that have been established.

The focus of the following analysis of Mozambique is, then, on the peace process that brought a measure of stability in the 1990s to that wartorn country.[2] For me, both the war and the terms of the peace make grim reading in light of the high hopes that Frelimo cadres had for their country when I first knew them in

Dar es Salaam in the mid-1960s. Moreover, in 1972, after my Dar es Salaam sojourn, I had the opportunity to accompany Frelimo guerrillas in Tete Province, not just visiting the front lines of the movement's war against the Portuguese but also seeing the future being built in the already liberated areas. In 1975 I was an invited guest, chosen to represent Canada at Mozambique's independence celebrations. As it happens, my own government was seen, correctly, as having been much too supportive, through NATO, of Portugal's wars in Africa to warrant an invitation of its own. And I was to return numerous times over the next decade, including a stint in the early 1980s spent teaching at the Frelimo Party School and the University of Eduardo Mondlane in Maputo. I was thus able, in my numerous writings on the subject, to trace in considerable detail the rise and fall of Frelimo's struggle for humane outcomes in its country. The peace process brought to a close a distinctive chapter — the period of the Frelimo revolution — of Mozambican history, both for better (in light of, amongst other things, the sheer human costs of the continuing war) and for worse.

"For worse"? With elections becoming, yes, a peaceful but nonetheless largely nominal exercise in primarily passive political "involvement" for the populace as a whole. And with the newly stabilized and "peaceful" economy not only now producing statistically impressive growth rates but also, as is the norm for many such countries, deepening inequalities between regions and between the handful of wealthy elites and the broad mass of the population. Thus, in 2002 Mozambique's own governor of Sofala Province, Felicio Zacarias, criticized the one-sided reports of both the World Bank and the IMF, stating clearly that the poor were not benefiting from the widely acclaimed "growth" of the country's economy (Mozambique, in any case, remained the "fourth worst-off country in the world"): "When we talk about the seven percent growth, if you ask the people nobody will say they feel anything in their pocket, so something must change."[3]

Noted Mozambican economist Carlos Nunes Castel-Branco was similarly sceptical, stating that postwar Mozambican "success stories" were misleadingly based on "excessively aggregate data" that said little about either the extreme maldistribution of wealth or the level of poverty, which was "so huge and deep rooted that it will take significantly faster growth and improvement in wealth distribution, and for significantly longer periods of time," to reduce it "in a way that people can feel." Indeed, he continued, "Growth of the Mozambican economy has been, for quite a few years, determined by what happens to a very small handful of firms (12-15), all of which are large, foreign-owned, capital intensive and develop almost no linkages within the Mozambican economy."[4] Similarly, in 2003, such sceptical economists could view, against IMF claims to the contrary, the pattern of "immiserating growth" as producing a Mozambican economy that is increasingly narrow and, based ever more exclusively on aluminum, gas, and titanium megaprojects, carries increasingly dangerous political and economic implications. Castel-Branco concludes that the IMF "makes the claim about our economy being a success story because they desperately need a success story, even if they have to invent one."[5]

Moreover, the Frelimo government was beginning to sound a warning of its own. In a surprisingly frank official report it criticized its own anti-poverty program by noting that "real spending on poverty reduction is falling [the IMF having capped such spending severely], too little money goes to the poor north and officials lie in their reports" about the extent of achievements in fundamental areas.[6] Here, it seemed, in the early days of the twenty-first century, was the consolidation of a far deeper pattern of neo-colonial-style "economic dependency" than would ever have been anticipated by Frelimo cadres during the long march of their original liberation struggle.

The case study (chapter 5) of the politics of (non)reconciliation in Namibia during the first decade of rule under the South-West Africa People's Organization (Swapo) may call for something more here by way of an introduction.[7] The struggle to free South-West Africa from South African rule was crucially framed by the internationalization of the question of the territory's future. South-West Africa was originally ceded to South Africa as a League of Nations mandate, but in the 1940s the United Nations refused the territory's formal annexation by South Africa. Instead, after extensive negotiations, the General Assembly terminated the mandate (1966), declared South Africa's occupation illegal (a reading endorsed in 1971 by the International Court of Justice), and established a Council for Namibia to exercise formal trusteeship over the territory. In practice South Africa would successfully defy the UN by continuing its occupation until 1990.

Under such circumstances, it was perhaps inevitable that Namibians, as they themselves developed a remarkable range of initiatives to liberate their country, focused first and foremost on this international terrain. The Herero Chiefs Council played an important role in early Namibian initiatives at the UN, for example. Meanwhile, additional foci of opposition began to emerge in the late 1950s. A group of left-wing intellectuals crafted the South-West African National Union (SWANU) from previously existing student organizations. But it was Swapo that would now place itself at the very centre of the nationalist movement.

The roots of Swapo's precursor, the Ovamboland People's Organization (OPO), lay in the community of Ovambo migrant labourers working in South Africa and within South-West Africa itself, but from 1960 OPO adopted a more inclusive nationalist strategy signalled by its new name. Confirming OPO president Sam Nujoma as Swapo president, the organization relocated the centre of gravity of its operations, moving into exile in Tanzania. There, with the failure of unity efforts, Swapo moved skilfully to gain exclusive international status for itself as voice of the new Namibia-in-the-making. Swapo's courting of the Organization of African Unity and its Liberation Committee, combined with a promise to launch military activity within South-West Africa itself, led, in 1964, to OAU recognition of the organization as the "sole and authentic" representative of Namibia. Then, as pressure against South Africa's occupation of South-West Africa mounted at the UN, that body's General Assembly granted Swapo, in 1973, the status of "authentic representative of the Namibian people."

From the time of their first operation at Ongulumbashe in 1966, courageous guerrillas had penetrated the country sufficiently often to earn the attention of the South Africans. Nonetheless, Swapo was never able to mount a serious challenge to South Africa's military grip on Namibia. Efforts to consolidate international support for Namibia were therefore crucial. For South Africa was to try various schemes to legitimate its hold on Namibia, including the Odendaal Plan of the late 1960s for the "bantustanization" of Namibia and the 1975 launching of the Turnhalle process designed to give the appearance of a devolution of power to Namibians themselves. Moreover, even though these various "reforms" failed, they were complemented by savage repression that was far more successful. Although South Africa allowed a limited space for oppositional political activity in the southern and central "Police Zone" of the country, Swapo activists were harassed even there. Against the populace in the north the violence committed by the South African Defence Force and attendant locally based special forces (especially the notorious Koevoet) was even more extreme. This was particularly true of densely populated Ovamboland, which also provided the staging grounds for South Africa's many incursions into Angola against both the MPLA government and Swapo (a massacre at Swapo's Cassinga camp in 1978 produced as many as nine hundred casualties, for example).

Still, the Swapo leadership did continue from exile to firm up its centrality within the emergent Namibian polity, and its international status complemented its popular credibility internally in doing so. These efforts helped sustain common cause against the apartheid state's presence and various schemes in Namibia, albeit, some would argue, at the cost of permitting a damaging degree of control by the external Swapo over strategic initiatives inside the territory. These costs were perhaps most visible in the late 1980s, when organizations of workers, students, women, and church people who sought momentarily to broaden the terms of internal struggle and the autonomous empowerment of civil society along lines then being exemplified in South Africa were effectively discouraged from doing so by the exile leadership.

Even more certain, however, were the costs of the leadership's ruthlessness in crushing tensions within its own ranks in exile. Swapo members who questioned the organization's practices in exile were first imprisoned, with help from the Tanzanian authorities, in the 1960s; but the movement's internal crisis in Zambia (Swapo had shifted its base there in the 1970s) was much more serious. Inside Namibia the early 1970s had witnessed a vast popular upsurge, including a dramatic strike of migrant workers in 1971-72 and an impressive wave of youth-inspired resistance throughout the country. When this revolt was crushed by the South Africans, thousands of young Namibians flooded into exile to join the liberation movement. They soon discovered a Swapo that many of them considered to be militarily ineffectual, undemocratic, and corrupt. In 1975 they called for a congress, as promised at Swapo's previous 1969 Tanga congress, to discuss such matters. Nujoma instead persuaded the Zambian army to arrest some two thousand of these Swapo cadres, while also having the putative leaders of this "coup" jailed in Tanzania with the connivance of his fellow presidents, Kaunda and Nyerere.

The Swapo leadership largely whitewashed these events in a subsequent internal investigation while continuing with its pragmatic course of pursuing external backing. Swapo had long since cornered Soviet support, for example, and was prepared to make various left-sounding pronouncements to seal this relationship, even as it complemented these statements with more moderate assertions aimed at other potential constituencies overseas. More difficult to finesse was the further playing out of the movement's authoritarian tendencies, which erupted at its Lubango base in Angola (Swapo had shifted its centre of operations to that country in the 1980s) in a wave of often arbitrary incarcerations and torture (and even murder) involving hundreds of alleged "spies" from within the movement. Set in a context of military frustration and considerable paranoia, these developments evidenced a security apparatus now almost completely out of control. Its reign of terror manifested ethnic, intra-ethnic, and regional tensions as well as the targeting of the more educated amongst Swapo's cadres. As this deadly machine began to close in on even the most senior of the Swapo leadership in the late 1980s, the movement was very close to the point of self-destruction.

Meanwhile, Namibia's broader fate had become hostage in the 1980s to the Cold War machinations of the United States. After 1977 a Security Council-based "contact group" of five Western powers largely took over the Namibia issue at the UN, rejecting further sanctions against South Africa but promising to facilitate resolution of the issue with the apartheid regime. This group in turn soon yielded to U.S. pressure to "link" Namibia's fate to the ending of Cuban support for the Angolan government (itself under siege from South Africa, with U.S. backing) and thus helped stall international progress on Namibia. It was therefore fortunate that by the end of the 1980s the apartheid government, facing (after its failed siege of Cuito Cuanavale) a costly military stalemate in Angola, was also seeing a need to reconsider its intransigent strategies closer to home. It now became party to negotiations over Namibia that (in a context that also registered the Soviet Union's own waning interest in Southern Africa) finally realized the implementation of Security Council Resolution 385, which, ever since its passage in 1976, had called for UN supervision of free and fair elections in Namibia as a prelude to independence.

Significantly, Swapo was largely excluded from these negotiations. Nonetheless, the movement had managed to so consolidate its political credentials within Namibia, and especially in the northern, more populous, Ovambo-speaking part of the country, as to be a near-certain winner once the complicated process of clearing the ground for elections was finally realized. In the event, Swapo won forty-one of seventy-two seats in the UN-supervised elections of November 1989, permitting the new assembly to unanimously elect Sam Nujoma the first president of a liberated Namibia. Independence itself came on March 21, 1990.

Encouraged by new realities, both local and global, to abandon many of its more overtly authoritarian practices from exile as well as the socio-economic radicalism implied in some of its earlier rhetoric, Swapo now came to preside over a liberal-democratic constitutional system and a full-blown market economy. The darkest side of the movement's past practices seemed likely to re-emerge only if any lack of success of that economic strategy were to polarize social contradictions dangerously and/or if a political opposition were to emerge with enough credibility to jeopardize Swapo's electoral grip on power — that, amongst other things, would threaten Swapo's military, security, and political elites with a reopening of questions regarding the movement's abuses of power in exile. In the meantime a group of dedicated "ex-detainees" and their allies have sought, albeit with mixed success,[8] to keep the issue on the political agenda in their country (see chapter 5). In tracing their efforts we learn something more about the mixed legacy of the liberation struggle in Southern Africa and also about the complexities of postwar "reconciliation" as advocated and practised within the region.

The phrase "mixed legacy of the liberation struggle in Southern Africa" is, perhaps, one that describes the history of independent Zimbabwe even more accurately than it describes that of Namibia. For there the pull, during the Mugabe years to date, towards an authoritarian denouement was, if anything, even more powerful — a danger I wrote about in the early years[9] but return to here even more sombrely after twenty-five years of Zimbabwean independence and in the context of the country's present grim situation. I do so writing jointly with Richard Saunders, who had spent the past decade and more in Zimbabwe and writes authoritatively about this recent period. In light of the cruelly racist character of the white settler regime that preceded Mugabe's coming to power, it may have been too tempting to give Mugabe and ZANU the "benefit of the doubt" at independence and to momentarily stay criticisms of the new regime during and after Zimbabwe's heroic moment of freedom at the turn of the 1980s. Nonetheless, the fact of independence was, more or less, from the outset qualified by Mugabe's ambitions towards power and by ZANU's own drive towards ethnic and political party hegemony rather than by any real attempt to transform, in a genuinely egalitarian direction, the imbalanced socio-economic structures inherited from the past. Of course, the unhappy story of the country's passage to the present is not entirely straightforward. Rather, it provides a complex mix of external determinations and internal malfeasance that are teased out further in chapter 6.

Finally, as was the case for Mozambique, the materials presented here on Tanzania (chapter 7) need little introduction because the broad outline of that country's early experience with socialism has already been sketched (chapter 2). The writings grouped together in this chapter are, in any case, less detailed and systematic of argument than are those to be found in the other three chapters in this part of the book. During the first years of my work on Africa I wrote a great deal about Tanzania,[10] where I was living at the time, but I did not return to Tanzanian themes for several decades thereafter. Nonetheless, the death of Mwalimu Julius Nyerere, the country's first president and amongst the most highly regarded of African leaders, provided me with the opportunity, in several forums, to revisit some of my earlier writings and those of others on that period and to reflect further on key issues raised by Tanzania's long since aborted experiment of what Nyerere sometimes claimed to be a distinctively "African Socialism." As I suggest in chapter 2 — but the point is reinforced here — there are still lessons for the future, both positive and negative, to be learned from the early efforts to realize *ujamaa* in that country.

Is another "long march" in prospect, then? For, despite the successes of the original liberation struggle vis-à-vis the obscenity that was white minority rule, the evidence presented in this part of the book suggests that a "second liberation struggle" — for the freedom of the mass of the population from the impositions both of overbearing domestic elites and of a high-handed global capitalist system — is as much in order for Southern Africa (including, as we shall also see, in Part III, for South Africa) as it is for the rest of the continent. The next liberation struggle? We will see, once again, whether the "historically necessary" is, indeed, the "historically possible."

# CHAPTER 4

# ON WAR AND PEACE IN AFRICA:
# THE MOZAMBICAN CASE

Recently students of "internal wars" in Africa have reacted against an earlier tendency, both on the left and the right, to explain domestic conflicts there in terms of external determinations — in terms, say, of the machinations of the various global protagonists of the Cold War or, sometimes, those of a neighbouring "rogue state" that is understood to be meddling aggressively in the troubled nation's affairs. Any such analytical tendency was badly oversimplified, the critics argue, even in the heyday of the Cold War, and it has become all the more so in today's "unipolar" world. Moreover, as part of a general trend within African studies to give greater pride of place in our analyses to a sensitive understanding of the concrete circumstances and lived experiences of the African peoples themselves, turning inward seems to represent a valuable refocusing of emphasis. It was small wonder, perhaps, that the editors of the book in which this chapter originally appeared encouraged just such an emphasis.[1]

The Mozambican case — important in its own right — can serve as a useful point of reference in this kind of analytical discussion. Certainly an earlier orthodoxy saw Mozambique's "internal war" as having been imposed largely from outside, by (albeit in some complex manner) "Western imperialism" and by (more straightforwardly) apartheid South Africa's regional strategy of "destabilization." More recently, in a brisk debate that has occurred within and without Mozambique regarding this kind of interpretation, a number of observers have argued for a "new paradigm" that would place central responsibility for Mozambique's disastrous tumble into "civil war" on internal factors and internal actors. This chapter will seek, then, not only to deepen the allusions to Mozambique to be found in the earlier chapters of this book, but also to further illuminate the roots of the country's recent (post-liberation struggle) conflict by alluding specifically to this scholarly division over the relative importance of internal and external factors to that conflict's emergence.

I will argue that both internal and external factors were important, but I will also suggest, against those who would now "shift the paradigm" of explanation, that they now risk bending the stick of explanation much too far back in the direction of their own chosen emphasis upon internal explanations. After all, when an earlier version of this chapter was first published in a book edited by Taisier Ali and Robert Matthews, it bore the title "Inside from the Outside? The Roots and Resolution of Mozambique's Un/Civil War." Parallel concerns also ground this more abbreviated analysis of the eventual "resolution" of armed conflict in Mozambique in the early 1990s. Thus that more detailed version of this chapter traced the negotiations that, at their most formalized, saw Frelimo, the party in power, and Renamo, its counter-revolutionary antagonist, meeting in Rome between 1990 and 1992 to hammer out a peace accord. It also examined the on-the-ground transition between 1992 to 1994 that saw implementation of this accord, the winding down of the war, and nationwide, "democratic," multi-party elections in 1994. Indeed, at each stage of this "peace process" both internal and external actors played prominent parts — and yet, against the grain of much current commentary, I continue to insist that the crucial role of external forces be given its proper weight.

## Political Science/Political Economy

Inside? Outside? This argument would be difficult enough to make if there were not a further complication that tends to be overlooked in much of the recent literature on both peacemaking and the transition of democracy. This is the distinction between what I have designated (chapter 3) as the "political science" of such processes and their "political economy." Certainly, one could comprehend both the emergence and the resolution of conflict in Mozambique in ways that privilege, almost exclusively, political explanations. This happens in part because such explanations do have some value. Mozambique's liberation struggle was indeed politically defined, representing a contestation between the Portuguese colonial authority and the country's key liberation movement, Frelimo, for state power. Nor did the crystallization of Frelimo's anti-colonial project occur in isolation from broader political realities. Thus, it formed one front in what was, in effect, a region-wide struggle across Southern Africa against the anachronistic structures of white minority rule.[2] Frelimo chose to play an active role in that broader struggle both before and after achieving independence in its own country, notably vis-à-vis Rhodesia — by operationalizing international sanctions and by lending crucial logistical support to ZANU — and also (albeit in a far more modest way) vis-à-vis South Africa. And it was to pay a very high price for adopting, so high-mindedly, this set of regional policies.

Inevitably, too, Frelimo's struggle was framed by larger global geo-political realities, notably those defined by the Cold War. The Soviet Union and its allies, which had been a major source of material support to Frelimo in the war against the Portuguese, continued to be a key actor in Mozambique in the post-liberation phase. This in itself would have placed Mozambique on the enemy list of the Western powers, especially the United States. But it was on that list for another, albeit related, reason: because its own domestic project was some sort of socialist one, mounted in self-conscious defiance of the unquestioned hegemony of inter-national capitalism. Indeed, Frelimo's "progressive" commitment across a broad front was actually a key reason for its associating itself with the ongoing war for Southern Africa in the first place (compare its record in this regard to Malawi or Botswana, for example), and it was this commitment that led it to look upon the Eastern bloc as its "natural allies."

It was also this involvement that helped increase the already high stakes in Mozambique for various external actors. Specifically, with the coming to power of Ronald Reagan in the United States, Mozambique found itself more clearly than ever in the line of fire for rollback, not merely as a "Soviet puppet" but, even more importantly, as a regime with (in the phrase of U.S. Assistant Secretary of State for African Affairs Chester Crocker) "Afro-Marxist fantasies" about domestic economic and political priorities.[3] It was no accident that South Africa moved to escalate its "destabilization" of Mozambique — a development so crucial to the fate of Frelimo's initial post-liberation project — within hours of Reagan's moving into the White House. And it is also no accident that when Frelimo did finally seek, under enormous military pressure, to sue for peace, it chose to run its attempts to do so in no small part through Washington — and to make that peace, to a significant degree, directly with international capitalism.

Interpreting Frelimo's original project as being at least in part defined, in its strengths and its vulnerabilities, by its socialist character remains controversial. Nonetheless, it is the final point of the above paragraph that bears underscoring: Mozambique's making of "peace" with international capital itself. For my argument is, in essence, that the politics of peacemaking in Mozambique have been framed by socio-economic processes — comprehensible only in terms of a political econ-omy approach — that add up to a recolonization of the country. Of course, as regards the task of peacemaking, privileging political explanations that are in part independent of that recolonization process also makes some sense. By the late 1980s and early 1990s the country was in tatters,[4] and what had begun as a war largely imposed from outside had taken on many of the attributes of a civil war. Therefore the political processes that brought Frelimo and Renamo together to negotiate and implement a peaceful resolution to their differences have been of great importance in their own right, not least because they provided the vast mass of the population with, at minimum, some of the basic rudiments of personal secu-rity that full-scale war had denied them. But still these processes were, in the end, greatly facilitated by Frelimo's abandonment of virtually all vestiges of its progres-sive ideology, both domestically and internationally.

Why is it so easy to lose sight of this abandonment as crucial to our under-standing of peacemaking in Mozambique? In part it is because Mozambique's orig-inal socialist project was plagued with so many problems and contradictions that the project itself may have come to seem merely improbable — and therefore more or less of an irrelevance to the "real" history of the country. More importantly, however, it is now virtually impossible, more generally, to imagine an alternative to the conformity to a globalizing neo-liberalism that Mozambique's most recent socio-economic policies have come to exemplify. Indeed, most of the scholarly literature takes this "necessary" conformity as so commonsensical a premise that it scarcely bears commenting upon. As Colin Leys argues, new and effective ideas about how to deal with Africa's problems could "seem rational only in a world that was in the process of rejecting the currently predominant ideology of the market," and that "is not yet in sight."[5] In the meantime, in the climate that does prevail, the actual socio-economic content of such "peace" as is achieved in Mozambique — and such "democratic structures" as are established — tends to fall between the cracks of both observation and explanation. In a unipolar world the one-eyed man is king. What I argue here is that, in contrast, the processes of both peacemaking and recolonization have occurred, in Mozambique, very much in tandem.

## The Roots of War and Peace in Mozambique (1962-84)

In the case of Mozambique's recent history — which is undoubtedly a highly complex matter — one thing is clear: the internal war that has plagued the country had its roots in the original liberation struggle carried out by Frelimo cadres against Portugal's long and brutal colonial presence in their country. Founded in 1962, Frelimo launched its armed struggle in 1964 and, by the time of the Portuguese coup (1974) that paved the way to Mozambique's independence (1975), had established significant liberated areas in the northern provinces and a strong legitimacy in most other parts of the country. As well, as we've seen, the movement committed itself to playing a continuing role in the further struggle to liberate the subcontinent.

There is little argument that the other chief protagonist to internal war in Mozambique — the armed movement that was to become Renamo — was, in the first instance, the creature of outsiders, comprising a mix of Mozambican mercenaries and forced recruits mobilized and orchestrated by Rhodesia's security forces and, with the fall of the Smith regime, by the South African military. Nor can there be any doubt as to the ruthlessness of the militaristic agenda set by those sponsors of Renamo: destruction of the infrastructure of economy and state, the heightened insecurity of the mass of the population.[6]

Much of Frelimo's initial legitimacy within Mozambique was cast in terms of a fairly conventional anti-colonial nationalism. But the leadership of Frelimo had become much more radical than the anti-colonial norm by the very necessity of armed struggle, then setting an increasingly left-wing agenda for itself. Something like a socialist project emerged, which involved a certain defiance of imperial political and economic dictate and, at least in principle, the empowerment of the mass of peasants and workers in the society. As Jorge Rebelo, one of the early Frelimo leaders, phrased the point in an interview on the occasion of Mozambique's twentieth anniversary of independence:

We all agreed that we were going to gain independence, but this was not the ultimate object; that was in fact the creation of a progressive society which would bring an end to misery in our country. This was not merely a slogan. It was inside of us. . . . But we can't help but be shocked by the distance between that which was our objective and what is the reality today.[7]

Rebelo also recalled leaving a meeting at the Ponta Vermelha Palace just after independence and hearing President Samora Machel say, "Now we have the power and we can finish with misery in Mozambique in two years." When someone said, "No, two years is too short a time," Machel replied, "Okay, three years then."

"We have to say now," Rebelo continued, "that this was a bit of voluntarism [voluntarismo] on our part. We were imagining things that in reality were not possible. But that's what we wanted to do."

Of course, Rebelo is signalling both the leadership's sincerity of intention and the making of profound errors of judgment and mistakes in policy — errors and mistakes springing, not least, from this kind of "voluntarism" and leading Frelimo to try to do too much, too fast. The early years did witness heroic efforts to transform Mozambican society: programs in the spheres of health and education are the most widely cited in this regard. But there can be little doubt that, in seeking to "mobilize" Mozambique's "workers and peasants" for "progressive" purposes, the Frelimo leadership also proved itself far too insensitive to the cultural complexities of the situation in which they found themselves. The party was tempted to ride roughshod over the various regional, ethnic, racial, and quasi-traditional fault lines that cut across Mozambican society, rather than finding more deft methods of political work to advance their project. In fact, Frelimo's arrogance of purpose, meshing with a firmly vanguardist bent (inherited, perhaps, from the movement's military past but also, once in power, all too easy to rationalize in classical Marxist-Leninist terms), drew the leadership towards markedly authoritarian practices as well as a vision of socialism too exclusively cast in an Eastern European mould.

Could Frelimo have righted itself and, left to its own devices, discovered a socialist practice at once more realistic, more democratic, and more successful? This is too large and speculative a topic to be properly broached here.[8] Suffice to note, for present purposes, that it has now become fashionable to seek the principal roots of Mozambique's war in the weaknesses, even malignancy, of Frelimo's own project.[9] And there can be little doubt that the weaknesses in Frelimo's practice did render it vulnerable to destabilization by Renamo and its sponsors as they moved to prey upon regional sensibilities and "traditional" loyalties in grounding their activities a little more firmly within Mozambique. In the end, William Minter's finely balanced weighing of the evidence seems closest to the mark on this issue:

If one considers Angola and Mozambique at the time of the Portuguese coup in 1974 — imagining away both the regional Southern African and the Cold

War conflicts — what kind of wars, if any, might have resulted from internal factors alone, with the external environment similar to those of other African states? The most likely answer is: no war in Mozambique. . . . In Mozambique it is simply not plausible that a coherent military organization such as Renamo could have emerged without external initiative. . . . The war came from outside. Once it started a variety of internal factors fed into the conflict, but they did not become responsible for continuing the war. Ethnic and regional tensions, while they existed, did not divide Mozambicans so deeply as to have sustained a war on these grounds. Nor were the policies towards peasants, economic ideology or the one-party state what the war was about. These were real issues, of course, but it is a bizarre misreading to see Renamo as fighting for a better deal for peasants or as speaking for the emergent civil society.[10]

Renamo had very little positive ideology, certainly, except a vaguely pro-Western predisposition. True, the relatively closed nature of the political structures sponsored by Frelimo lent credibility to the democratic claims that Renamo came increasingly to employ to legitimate its war. But in view of its own brutal practices in the zones that it controlled, such claims, as made by Renamo itself, can only be seen as opportunistic. Nor (as we will emphasize below) were its "free-market" proclivities long to differentiate its position from those of Frelimo as the latter felt itself increasingly forced to share a neo-liberal agenda with its adversaries.

Indeed, what we find in Mozambique is a subtle slide from a war brought, primarily, from outside to a war much more internally sited — and also from a war cast in meaningful ideological terms (Frelimo's liberationist-cum-socialist project vs. its array of enemies) to a struggle between two domestic protagonists for the spoils of office. Ironically this outcome was much less the result of any success that Renamo may have had in rooting itself within the fabric of Mozambican society than it was a result of the slow but sure collapse of Frelimo's own project. Eventually the chief thing that would remain of Frelimo was its authoritarian propensities; these were now drained to a very considerable degree of the "good intentions" and higher purposes in whose name such propensities had sometimes been explained and excused. As the war wore on and the socio-political situation in the country deteriorated, Frelimo's tattered armed forces, reduced to living off the land, could seem to some parts of the population as almost as great a menace to their security as was Renamo. So, too, many Frelimo politicians and officials now seemed more preoccupied with looking to their own personal interests than ever they had in the past. If there was now increasingly less to distinguish Frelimo from Renamo in ideological terms, there was also much less to distinguish the two protagonists in terms of their domestic political practices. Instead, what was now most visible on both sides was a naked desire to hold — or gain — power at almost any cost. Hence, in Minter's trenchant summary, came "the popular perception in Mozambique — the more widespread the longer the war continued — of a war between two armies, with neither of them representing the people despite the over-whelmingly more abusive behavior of one side [Renamo]."[11]

Here, in short, was a war that cried out, in the name of simple humanity, to be ended. Moreover, Mozambicans had become war-weary to a very considerable degree. Yet humanitarianism and war-weariness are not always sufficient reasons for conflict to cease. Nor was it sufficient that the main protagonists to the war would increasingly feel themselves to be stalemated — and therefore increasingly willing to think in terms of seeking to realize their interests by other means than continuing military confrontation. In the Mozambican case, other powerful actors had to shift their ground for a process of peacemaking to take hold. By the end of the 1980s, as the peacemaking process accelerated in Mozambique, the South Africa government — whose aggressive regional strategy of defence of apartheid had done so much to sow the seeds of war in Mozambique — was itself (with the passing of P.W. Botha from the scene and then with the release of Nelson Mandela) retiring to the sidelines of the regional war. The same was true, for other but equally obvious reasons, of the Soviet Union and its Eastern bloc allies. Even more important, however, was the long-term shift in Western, principally U.S., evaluation of the nature of the Frelimo regime itself, a crucial point to which we will return.

The key to this shift was, however, the recolonization of Mozambique. Whatever balance sheet one strikes on this history of Frelimo's retreat and Renamo's advance (an advance eventually signalled by that movement's relative success in the 1994 multi-party election in Mozambique), the process still left a Mozambique dependent in its poverty and its vulnerability on the behest of the World Bank, the IMF, and the external aid community. And it left a leadership that had certainly lost touch with the aspirations of ordinary people. As Graça Machel, now active in the NGO sector, put it forcefully to me during my visit in Mozambique in the early 1990s: "Workers and peasants don't count for anything in this country any more." True, in the 1980s the Mozambican leadership tried to find ways of dealing with the external financial institutions in a way that would protect achievements in social spheres like education and health, while keeping some kind of state involvement in the direction of the economy. Thus, the country's first economic recovery program sought to finesse the World Bank and others into allowing space within which the government could give a more humane face to the compulsory restructuring. But that didn't last long, and soon privatization had become the alpha and omega of policy.

Much recent writing on Mozambique — as, for example, Joseph Hanlon's eloquent Who Calls the Shots?[12] or work by David Plank — focuses on the extent to which policy is, in these and other ways, being dictated from outside. Indeed, it is Plank who introduces the concept of "recolonization" most self-consciously into the discussion as something more than a mere metaphor, demonstrating, in an important article and on the basis of his findings in Mozambique, that "the most likely successor to post-colonial sovereignty will be neo-colonial vassalage, in

which Western powers assume direct and open-ended control over the administration, security and economic policies of 'deteriorated' states under the banner of
the UN and various donors."[13]

What this process of recolonization had begun to look like from the U.S. angle
can best be grasped, perhaps, from a reading of Crocker's own smug account of
the taming of the Mozambican revolution. By 1982, writes Crocker, "the
Mozambicans sought U.S. understanding and diplomatic support in checking tough
South African military and economic pressures" as well as seeking "official encouragement of private investment . . . [and] humanitarian and development aid from
the Americans." As Crocker continues, "Our priorities in these early encounters
were to shift Mozambique away from its self-destructive confrontation with
Pretoria, to foster rethinking about its ruinous domestic policies, and to explore its
readiness to abandon its close Soviet and Cuban alignment."

> By early 1983, this dialogue was paying off. In the months to come, U.S. food
> aid began to flow, and talks were held on an aid program to support the pri-
> vate sector and agricultural policy liberalization. . . . Mozambique decided to
> freeze or curtail security ties to Communist states, to seek "associate" status
> with the European Community under the formula in place for other African
> states, and to apply to join the World Bank and International Monetary Fund.
> As a signal to the Western private sector, an oil exploration contract was signed
> with Exxon, and Lehman Brothers was signed on to provide advisory services
> on debt restructuring.

As for the regional front, "It was no longer difficult to persuade Machel, [Joaquin]
Chissano, [Fernando] Honwana and their colleagues that the primary victim of the
Front Line State strategy of confrontation with South Africa would be the Front Line
States themselves, and especially Mozambique." Indeed, writes Crocker, "we came
to view the Mozambicans as partners."[14]

What did this partnership look like on the receiving end? Compare Crocker's
account with the forlorn flavour of a remark I heard President Chissano make in a
1990 Maputo speech, on the very first months of embarking on the formal negotiations process with Renamo:

> The US said, "Open yourself to . . . the World Bank, and IMF." What happened?
> . . .We are told now: "Marxism! You are devils. Change this policy." OK.
> Marxism is gone. "Open market economy." OK, Frelimo is trying to create
> capitalism. We have the task of building socialism and capitalism here. We
> went to Reagan and I said, "I want money for the private sector to boost peo-
> ple who want to develop a bourgeoisie." Answer: $10 million, then $15 mil-
> lion more, then another $15 million. You tell me to do away with Marxism,
> the Soviet Union and the GDR and give me [only] $40 million. OK, we have
> changed. Now they say, "If you don't go to a multi-party system, don't expect
> help from us."[15]

What could more starkly reveal just how supine Mozambique had been forced to become vis-à-vis Western dictate? Crocker also cites Chissano as visiting Washington, as early as October 1987, to assure Reagan of "his readiness to work with us and other countries to find a 'political solution.'" Ironically, Crocker and his presidential patron soon found themselves defending the Mozambican government against other right-wingers, in Congress and beyond, who chose to back Frelimo's antagonist, Renamo, unilaterally and uncritically. "In Washington," writes Crocker, "partisan strife over Mozambique became one of our biggest headaches during most of the second Reagan term. . . . Amazing as it may seem the challenge we faced from within and beyond the administration was the demand that we abandon and cut off aid to the struggling Maputo regime and help Renamo as 'freedom fighters' under the Reagan Doctrine."[16] In response, in order to disarm their critics Crocker and his officials sponsored and widely distributed a well-researched report by Robert Gersony documenting Renamo's brutal politics, and they otherwise sought to press forward with their Mozambican agenda.[17]

Simply put, with the recolonization of Mozambique locked ever more firmly into place, the United States now emerged as a central protagonist of the unfolding peace process in that country — with internal war increasingly interpreted as undermining the stability of a new "partner" in the global enterprise of peace, capitalism, and democracy. Indeed, by the dawn of the 1990s the way was clear for various Western actors to follow the United States into the vacuum left both by the withdrawal of South Africa and the Soviet Union from the fray and by the taming of Frelimo's radicalism. In such a context, bringing together the two sides in Mozambique's "internal war," two sides increasingly indistinguishable in ideological terms, could now become the order of the day — and the "internationalizing" of the resolution of the Mozambican conflict that now occurred could also be valued as one further step towards ensnaring both of the country's chief partisan protagonists, Frelimo and Renamo, within "safe" and relatively predictable domestic structures, economic and political.

## Peace, Democracy, and Development ?

An earlier version of this chapter traced in some detail both the checkered negotiations (1984-92) that led to the war's "resolution" and the terms of that "resolution" itself, which, as a kind of complex end-game, produced, eventually, the election of 1994, marked by not only a Frelimo victory but also a strong showing, especially in provinces in the centre of the country, by Renamo itself. As then-UN head Boutros Boutros-Ghali concluded, "ONUMOZ [United Nations Operation in Mozambique] was one of the most effective peace-keeping operations in the history of the United Nations.[18] It brought peace to Mozambique and, equally important, it contributed directly to the profound political transformation that has enabled Mozambique to set a firm course towards greater peace, democracy and development."[19] There can be little doubt, of course, that the UN was anxious for a peacekeeping success after a dismal record of recent failures elsewhere in the world, and that it was prepared — with the backing of its principal funders, who had a stake of their own in producing a certain kind of peace in Mozambique — to throw a great deal of money at the country in order to produce that success. And (*pace* Hanlon), alongside a number of other factors, the UN operation did make a significant contribution to producing that "certain kind of peace."

In the years immediately after the 1994 elections the peace, in most of its particulars, did hold. Nonetheless, the precise resonance of Boutros-Ghali's final triad — "greater peace, democracy and development" — calls for some further reflection. Obviously, to begin, the coming of peace of any sort is not something that we should downplay glibly, not after what ordinary Mozambicans had experienced in the preceding years. True, the legacy of the war continued to make itself felt negatively across a wide range of related fronts: the markedly high level of criminality, for example, being as much a reflection of the wholesale availability of arms and of war-induced lack of moral scruple (on the part of many of the recently demobilized former combatants, amongst others) as it is of the desperate economic situation in which the country found itself. Land mines, widely and cavalierly planted across the country during the war, continued to take a deadly toll.[20]

Politically, certain patterns from the past were also carried over. A December 1995 issue of the *Mozambique Peace Process Bulletin* captured some of these contradictions.[21] Certainly, one of its lead articles, "Renamo Needs Money," carried a bit too much of a feeling of *déjà vu* (sabre-rattling and economic blackmail):

> "The international community is just playing with us," complained Renamo leader Afonso Dhlakama, and is trying to starve Renamo until it disappears. In an interview in the Sunday newspaper *Domingo* (10 September) he suggested that although he was committed to peace, there were people in the party who might return to war if Renamo did not get more money from the international community.

Moreover, the *Bulletin* noted, Renamo continued to control some of its old areas and refused to yield them up to any process of integrated administration. Not that Renamo, at this late date, had the capacity (or, very likely, the inclination) — it was very different in this respect from its Angolan counterpart, UNITA — to remount a full-scale war. Douglas Patrick Mason seemed to capture the mood correctly when he suggested that in the wake of

> Mozambique's multi-party elections that capped the negotiated settlement to the civil war, the erstwhile combatants, the governing Frelimo and opposition Renamo parties, have settled into an uneasy relationship in the fledgling democracy. Despite intemperate exchanges, a stand-off over control of the rural areas, and the existence of a not so secret Renamo armed force, both parties have largely accepted the framework of democratic contest.[22]

Peace, then, but what about "democracy"? Some may think it enough to say that the establishment of a certain kind of democratic framework did help seal closure to one of the most horrific, chaos-producing wars in Africa: no small accomplishment. Yet we have also presented reasons for scepticism regarding the brand of democracy whose emergence was witnessed in Mozambique. Closest to the surface, in this regard, was the post-electoral Frelimo government's inclination, despite the narrowness of its victory, to operate on a "winner-take-all" basis; and the possibility remained that Renamo might yet try to play, within limits, a wrecker's role. In short, Mozambique was very far from having consolidated a democratic culture, and there were certainly those, on both sides, who might wish themselves back to the salad days of their more authoritarian pasts.

Still, there were many others who would accept that there were real benefits to be found in consolidating even the most formal of democratic structures. Thus one erstwhile senior Frelimo politician, himself an architect of some of the most undemocratic features of Frelimo's original national project, admitted to me self-critically that if the present kind of democratic structures had existed in the old days (including the far greater freedom of the press that now prevailed) obvious abuses of authority like the disastrous "Operation Production" of 1983 would not have been possible. And there was also the possibility that even the limited, liberal form of democratization that now existed in Mozambique would create terrain — beyond the opportunities/mystifications of the electoral arena — in which popular empowerment of a far more meaningful kind might yet be consolidated: empowerment that could spring from the assertions of actors in civil society, such as trade union and women's movement structures (now liberated from the deadening hand of monoparty control), and from the claims advanced by more self-confident peasant activists and agricultural *cooperativistas*.[23]

And yet the sense persists that the kind of liberal democracy achieved in the 1994 elections might also, by its own logic, cut precisely against just such a process of empowerment. Thus, for me, there was a particularly sad irony in the observation of a Mozambican friend, a journalist and a firm supporter of freedom, not least of the press, in his country. He wished for no return to the bad old days of government dictation of the "party-line" to his newspaper. Yet, he confessed, he couldn't escape the feeling that the workers and peasants in Mozambique had actually had more power under the "old" Frelimo regime. Then, he said, the leadership took their interests more seriously (even if it never found ways of institutionalizing a genuinely popular democracy in any very effective way), and their voices were actually heard more clearly than they were now, under liberal democracy: in the present system their votes were merely canvassed in a competitive manner that had little to do with advancing their life chances or helping them to clarify their socio-economic options.

Recall, too, the international framework of recolonization within which the 1994 Mozambican election occurred; and note, by way of updating and reinforcing this point, the sad description by one new member of parliament of the state of democratic Mozambique in the wake of that election: "The biggest moment of Mozambican politics this year [1995] was when the government went to Paris to meet with the donors. That was where parliament really was held in Mozambique this year, the donor meeting in Paris." Or, as another MP explained: unlike other countries and parliaments, "we accept that our budget is really set by donors at the annual Paris conference. We accept that our priority is to develop a donor accept-able budget." The claim that he then advanced for elected politicians was corre-spondingly modest: "But the assembly must be part of that process, that is what democracy means in Mozambique."

What, finally, of the promise of shared and even "development" under such circumstances? Is there any very good reason for assuming that a process of recol-onization — however much it may be consolidated on more peaceful ground and within a rather more stable social order — could actually deliver a level of eco-nomic progress that would transform in meaningful ways the lives of the vast majority of Mozambicans? Only his willingness to give a positive answer to this question could possibly ground Boutros-Ghali's confidence that development would flow from the peace in Mozambique. A far more sceptical response is certainly at least equally plausible. As Leys writes, "For all countries of the world, recapturing control over their own destinies requires the reestablishment of social control over capital and the resubordination of markets to social purposes [and] for the weaker regions of the world, such as sub-Saharan Africa, this is literally a matter of life and death." Recall, too, Leys's formulation to the effect that ideas that might premise such policies would appear to be rational only in a world that had come to jetti-son the prevailing fetishization of "the market," but until that necessary transfor-mation occurred, "the African tragedy" would continue to unfold.[24]

Could failure in this sphere mean, in turn, renewed tragedy for Mozambique? Of course, it would be naive at this late date to argue that the era of the old "Frelimo state" — a "left developmental dictatorship" with deeply compromised economic, social, and political policies — did not have its grievous flaws. Nonetheless, someone reflecting, in 1995, on the first twenty years of Mozambican independence, years most recently marked by destabilization, civil war, and peace-making, might still conclude by observing that what had been lost, most visibly, from the earliest period of post-independence Mozambican history was something terribly important. It was, precisely, that strong sense of purpose, social and pub-lic, whose loss Leys also decries, a purpose premised on the envisaging of society-wide transformations that could actually change the lives of the vast majority of Mozambicans in positive ways.

That such commitment to the collective weal has been lost will bring no tears to the eyes of a Chester Crocker, of a World Bank, or even, perhaps, of a Boutros-Ghali. But nevertheless its loss has been the price both of the kind of war inflicted on Mozambique and of the kind of peace achieved there. If development in any meaningful sense is ever to occur in their country, Mozambicans will eventually have to rediscover just such a sense of purpose. Without that — and here political economy and political science really do come together in an inextricable manner — something worse even than mere political somnolence and elitist rule might befall the country. For the Mozambican society, the Mozambican polity, may merely begin to fragment all over again.

CHAPTER 5

## LUBANGO AND AFTER: "FORGOTTEN HISTORY" AS POLITICS IN CONTEMPORARY NAMIBIA
(with Colin Leys)

Throughout the 1990s a good number of Namibians (notably members of the Breaking the Wall of Silence committee) have made considerable efforts to keep alive the issue of the Swapo leadership's alleged abuses of power when in exile. These activists' key focus has been the torture and killing of many innocent cadres (labelled "spies") of Swapo in the movement's detention centre at Lubango, Angola, in the 1980s. Such critics have had their difficulties — within both the formal political arena and civil society (including the churches, so important a sphere of Namibian life) — in setting the record straight about such events and/or in obtaining any kind of redress of grievances. The chief roadblock has been the unwillingness of the Swapo leadership to allow its own record in exile to be opened up to public scrutiny and, indeed, its active role in discouraging any such outcome. The leadership's advocacy of the wisdom of silence on these matters has tended to be cast in terms of the presumed imperatives of "reconciliation," but, we suggest here, this policy may have at least as much to do with the leadership's seeking to hide the blood of the past that it has on its own hands. We also raise a further question, which is whether models such as South Africa's process of "Truth and Reconciliation" might be applied to resolving such issues in Namibia; and we note the considerable challenge of realizing any such outcome in the country's immediate future.

## A Ticking Time Bomb?

In its issue of May 26, 2000, South Africa's *Mail and Guardian* featured prominently an article from Namibia entitled "Who Killed Swapo's 700 Missing Detainees?" There it was in black and white: history that refused to remain "forgotten." The immediate trigger: a claim by Swapo that testimony in the trial of South Africa's "Doctor Death," Dr. Wouter Basson, to the effect that amongst other "dirty tricks" he ordered the poisoning of more than two hundred Swapo fighters, "explains the whereabouts of missing Namibians Swapo has been asked to account for."

According to the article, the self-proclaimed champions of human rights "should in fact now go and demand from those who are making these disclosures to explain the whereabouts of the missing Namibians they have been calling on Swapo to account for since independence." The reply from other Namibians was immediate. Pauline Dempers was herself detained and tortured by Swapo in one of its notorious detention camps in Lubango, southern Angola, in the late 1980s, accused of being a South African spy, a charge she vehemently denies. Speaking now as chair of Namibia's Breaking the Wall of Silence (BWS), an advocacy group that includes a large number of former Swapo detainees, she issued a list of some seven hundred Namibians said to have disappeared while in the hands of Swapo during the liberation war. She went on to argue:

Does [Swapo's claim] mean that [it] handed over those people arrested [as being apartheid spies] to Basson? As far as we are concerned Basson's trial has got no connection to what we are asking Swapo to account for. We are asking Swapo to account for the people they arrested or killed. The case is not closed at all. We will take Swapo to task until they account for the missing Namibians.

At the same time, according to the *Mail and Guardian* report, "The Windhoek-based National Society for Human Rights (NSHR) challenged the Namibian government to set up a South African-style truth and reconciliation commission 'if Swapo leaders have nothing to hide.'"

Historians of Namibia yet unborn will long study the history of the Namibian liberation struggle; and they may well examine questions as to the character of Swapo as a liberation movement, the goals and actions of South Africa's intelligence establishment during the 1970s and 1980s, and how many people were incarcerated in Lubango, and why, and what happened to them, with the same relative dispassion that we can now bring to such issues as "The Establishment of the Ukwangali Kingdom" and the role played by the Damara in the 1904-08 war.[1] That time is not yet, however: as the *Mail and Guardian* news report underscores, in Namibia a slippage seems almost unavoidable between seeking to provide a plausible account of recent history on the one hand, and acting politically on the other. Nor is this particular episode the first time during the post-liberation decade that the history of Swapo's liberation struggle has become real politics in Namibia. Indeed, we may even suspect that this history could have had — and might yet have — even more serious political repercussions. Thus some Namibian observers argue that the issue of Lubango remains a ticking time bomb, one that might yet blow Namibia's "democratic miracle" out of the water. This could happen, they maintain, if it ever looked as though a political party with an agenda that included reopening the historical record on the detainees question was on the verge of

defeating Swapo at the polls. As one of our own most trusted Namibian interlocutors suggested to us, some members of the present military and security establish-
ments speak openly amongst themselves of the possible necessity of their then
launching a coup in order to pre-empt any investigation of their behaviour in
Angola and elsewhere during the pre-independence period.[2]

Whether or not this is an accurate account of their intentions, such people, and
others in the political elite, would appear to have, at the very least, a case to answer.
For there is no room for doubt as to the seriousness of the indictment levelled
against the Swapo leadership regarding its human rights abuses in exile. There is a
wide range of recorded testimony (some of it cited in our book *Namibia's Liberation
Struggle*), including, for example, the evidence given at successive press conferences
by the Swapo detainees who returned to Namibia in July 1989 (and reproduced in
related publications of the time); the interviews contained in Richard Pakleppa's
powerful film *I Have Seen*; the stories recounted by Siegfried Groth in his book
*Namibia: The Wall of Silence*; and the accounts by other ex-detainees in our
possession.[3]

Our purpose here, however, is not to rehearse all these charges yet again. It is
instead to examine how the demand for an investigation of the facts has been consistently resisted in Namibia, and the reasons for this resistance. Our focus is on
what is, in effect, the history of this history as it played itself out in Namibia during the decade of the 1990s, and on the public debate that has occurred over how
much of such history should remain forgotten, how much exposed, and, if it is to
be exposed, by what means. For the Swapo leadership has been determined to keep
this history forgotten, and to do so it has used a variety of means, ranging from
mere inaction to, apparently, measures of intimidation. It has also deployed a number of substantive arguments, some more plausible than others, against making the
historical record any more public than it already is. Meanwhile, in sharp contrast,
certain bold souls in Namibian society have sought instead to keep alive the
Lubango story — to actively remember it, as it were. As we will see below, these
activists have worked to find innovative means for bringing their history of events
in Angola to more widespread and sympathetic public attention, thus holding up
their own end of a dialogue, muted and unequal and underexposed though it still
may be, about coping with recent history in contemporary Namibia.

## To Forget or Not to Forget

To forget or not to forget? The contrast between, on one side, the government's
thinking on the linked questions of Lubango, the so-called "spy crisis," and the
missing detainees, and, on the other, the thinking of its critics is a wide one. In its
public statements on the issue, the Swapo government argued for "reconciliation"
vis-à-vis its former enemies, offering a particular variant on this process and a particular rationale for doing so. Lauren Dobell, writing on related themes, has con-
trasted this approach not only with that advocated by Swapo's Namibian critics but

also with that adopted by the ANC, a liberation movement that actually did wrestle with the issue of reconciliation in the context of a negotiated resolution of a liberation struggle. As she observes:

> Swapo's policy of national reconciliation, the essential contours of which were determined before independence, differs significantly from the ANC's. In confronting similar legacies of suffering, of communities and families torn apart in the war against apartheid, the Namibian and South African governments came to opposite conclusions regarding the best way to put the past behind them.[4]

Succinctly summarizing the model of the ANC's Truth and Reconciliation Commission (TRC), Dobell notes that, in contrast, "Swapo adopted a more cautious approach to reconciliation. In the government's considered opinion, resurrecting the past would serve no constructive purpose. A successful transition, it was argued, required cooperation among former enemies. Delving into past injustices would only incite a desire for vengeance and distract a still fragile nation from the paramount tasks of reconstruction and development." As Namibian Prime Minister Hage Geingob argued in 1992:

> When Swapo decided to promote reconciliation, its primary objective was to lay the ground work for peace and harmony in a country that was ravaged by long years of war. It was an attempt to heal the wounds created by hatred between blacks and whites, between father and son, and between families. Many of you will recall that it is not unusual for one person from a family to be a member of Koevoet [the police counter-insurgency unit] and the other a fighter with the liberation movement. Only an attempt at reconciliation could restore peace and harmony at various levels of our society. We saw no alternative.[5]

Up to a point Swapo's argument for this kind of reconciliation through studied silence is plausible, even convincing, especially in its appropriateness to Namibia's specific circumstances (including that it was perhaps easier for Swapo leaders to take this line because the regime overthrown had been, to a significant extent, one of illegal occupation, now departed). Much careful reflection is in order, in any case, on the relative merits of diverse approaches to (in Dobell's phrase) "knitting shattered societies together in the wake of dismantled authoritarian regimes" before making a judgment as to the wisdom of choices made in this sphere in any given country. But, we might ask, is Dobell actually correct to explain the choice made in Namibia by arguing that "in the government's considered opinion, resurrecting the past would serve no constructive purpose"? "Considered opinion?" "No constructive purpose?" Swapo's critics would find this far too polite a gloss to place on the leadership's approach to these matters. Moreover, Dobell herself is too astute an observer not to qualify the position. As she further writes:

An unspoken but critical sub-text for what detractors derided as a policy of national amnesia [in Namibia] was the Swapo leadership's uncomfortable awareness of the skeletons in its own closet. . . . In contrast to the ANC, whose Skweyiya Inquiry and Motsuenyane Commission acknowledged violations of human rights in the ANC camps, Swapo never officially admitted to any wrong-doing.

Indeed, it is difficult not to believe, in the Swapo case, that this particular consideration is the primary one, trumping many of the other arguments that might, in principle, be posed as to the merits of various differing strategies of national reconciliation. The Swapo leadership appears to have had too much to hide to put itself on an equal footing with the torturers, murderers, and informants on the other side, at least for purposes of open, quasi-judicial, TRC-style proceedings.[6]

This is not straightforward terrain, of course. No one would argue for some simple-minded equivalence between, on the one hand, the apartheid state and its functionaries (whether operating in South Africa or in Namibia) and, on the other, those who struggled, against enormous odds and often under the most desperate of conditions, to challenge it. Nonetheless the ANC has, up to a point, been prepared to put itself in the dock, this being a key factor allowing the TRC to make as much progress on a broad range of other fronts as it did in South Africa.[7] And this approach on the part of the ANC was not something new. As Dobell notes, the ANC had already facilitated, in the early 1990s and therefore well in advance of the TRC, the public scrutiny of its record by both the Skweyiya Commission and, when that was not deemed adequate, the more independent Motsuenyane Commission — and before that there had been the Stuart Commission Report of 1984, now also in the public domain, inquiring "into recent developments in the People's Republic of Angola."

One may criticize the adequacy of these prior reports and of the ANC's own response to them, whether in terms of disciplining perceived perpetrators of injustice, making just compensation to victims of any excesses, or self-critically examining the political premises (beyond the imperatives of war) that could have produced such problems. Nonetheless, they remain of real significance. Moreover, both the ANC's initial statement to the TRC itself and its second, more detailed one deal with questions of abuses of power by the movement in exile in something more than a purely defensive manner; and the TRC's own final report has some particularly strong sections on these events.[8] This is, in fact, so much more than has been accomplished in Namibia along similar lines that it is small wonder that some Namibians have looked to the TRC, with all its limitations, as a possible model for their own country.

For Swapo's domestic critics have continued to make it clear that in their view it is not differing philosophies and strategies of reconciliation but rather Swapo's desire to cover its own tracks that does indeed provide the most convincing explanation of the path of silence that the movement has chosen. In arguing for a more public processing of the issues, such critics have come to present the link between truth and reconciliation in a very different way than that advocated by Swapo. As Bience Gawanas, Namibia's ombudsman and herself an ex-detainee, argued:

> We are called upon to become a single nation in the process of reconciliation. If this means forgetting the past, then it will be very difficult for many of us. We can forgive but we cannot forget. We cannot dissociate ourselves from our history and our past, because if reconciliation is to be genuine and sincere, we must learn from the past and avoid old mistakes. We must know and we have a right to decide with whom we want to be reconciled and why. If we have made mistakes, we must be able to say, "I am sorry," even when it is the most difficult thing to say. Those who have been wronged must be able to accept the hand of reconciliation and say, "I forgive you!" When we remember the past, we do not dig up old ditches or open up old wounds. We merely avoid the curse of repeating the same mistakes.[9]

It is also true that beneath these general arguments there have been more personal agendas, sometimes with a sharper edge, even if, generally, the intention is equally honourable. Thus some of the victims seek not merely truth but also "justice" — the exposure, even punishment, of people, some of them now in high office, who they say are torturers and murderers. Others seek to have their own names cleared of the allegation of treason that was the official reason for their detention and torture, or they seek simply to find out what happened to detainees who never returned. Still others, relatives of detainees, want death certificates issued for those who must be presumed dead, so that they can get on with their lives. But not everyone who advocates a more open approach has so direct an involvement. Some supporters merely want to see a searing moment in Namibian history dealt with openly and honestly. They may also find it difficult to accept that Namibia is truly "new" so long as the commander of the armed forces is the alleged "butcher of Lubango" and interrogators from the Lubango detention centres have been reincarnated as members of the Security Service or the president's Special Field Force, which has been involved in numerous reported instances of illegal intimidation and harassment in recent years.[10] In short, the feeling that the secret political culture of the Lubango detention centres has been dangerously carried forward, unexamined and unchecked, into independent Namibia, is not confined to the Lubango detainees and their families.

# The History of the History

Some Namibians did challenge the writing of official history even as that history was being made. As early as 1977, for example, the Reverend Salatiel Ailonga wrote from exile to alert Bishop Auala of the Lutheran Church of the North to the Swapo leadership's abuse of its power in Zambia.[11] The Parents' Committee, formed in 1986 by the families of Swapo members detained in Lubango, likewise struggled to win the ear of the Namibian people, and especially the Namibian churches, for a critical accounting of what Swapo was doing to its detainees in Angola during the 1980s. The churches proved reluctant to embrace the issue, however, in part because of a fear of giving aid and comfort to the apartheid enemy. Indeed, the churches only began to feel forced to do somewhat more as the regional and global conjuncture worked to accelerate Namibia's march to independence after 1989. In particular, it became difficult to ignore the testimony of detainees released from Swapo dungeons when the first 153 of them returned to Namibia, under UN auspices, after their release in Angola in mid-1989.[12]

The Parents' Committee linked up quickly with the returned detainees, who also set up a Political Consultative Committee to try to get the full story of their Angolan experiences into the public arena. In 1989 the Committee produced a widely circulated document, "A Report to the Namibian People: Historical Account of the SWAPO Spy Drama." Moreover, the story obtained additional resonance, albeit of a rather contradictory kind, when it was taken up as part of the election-linked "disinformation" efforts by the sympathizers and/or functionaries of the apartheid regime. Ironically, much of this "disinformation" was actually true, despite the malignant purpose of the South Africans in distributing it: the volume *Call Them Spies: A Documentary Account of the Namibian Spy Drama* provided an important case in point here (at once both informative and, paradoxically, somewhat suspect in its provenance).[13]

Given the nature of Namibian society, a strong stand by the churches, taken not to block Swapo's rise to power but to help it relieve itself of the damaging burden of its past, might have given such criticism the kind of resonance it needed. In the event, the churches were reluctant (as they had been before and would be in future) to push the case vigorously. For, in the opinion of Cristo Lombard, a University of Namibia professor of theology, an unhealthy symbiosis, established quite early between Swapo and the churches, helped to damp down controversy over the political organization's abuses of power in exile. Thus, he cites as an early example of this pattern the uncritical acceptance by Dr. Shejavali, the general secretary of the Council of Churches of Namibia (CCN), of the misleading announcement by senior Swapo leaders Theo-Ben Gurirab and Hidipo Hamutenya in London in 1986 that Swapo had discovered a "spy ring" of at least one hundred of its own members. This acceptance helped the CCN to dismiss the concerns of the Parents' Committee.[14] Lombard's assessment of the churches' record during the transition process itself is even more critical. Now operating under close international and local scrutiny, "Swapo came closest to accepting full responsibility for any abuses committed before independence during the run-up period to the elections, in 1989-90." In this context, Lombard suggests, "It is easy to see how proper pressure from the churches in Namibia could have redefined the whole process of reconciliation." And yet "Swapo was let off the hook, and allowed to continue its authoritarian and uncompromising culture, and take over the governing responsibility without having accounted for its own human rights abuses."[15]

But was Swapo actually vulnerable to more pressure at that point? It had, after all, released at least some of its prisoners from Lubango in April-July 1989. This it did under a certain measure of international scrutiny and in line with the terms of a long-standing UN Security Council Resolution, number 385 of 1976, that had called for both South Africa and Swapo to release all political detainees prior to any independence election. But the move was also in line with the adoption by the Swapo Central Committee in February 1989 of a national reconciliation policy that, in view of the prospect of a settlement, promised to pardon those "misguided elements who infiltrated the rank and file of Swapo with the aim of serving the war aims of the enemy," and a further decision, announced in May 1989, "to release them all." But how significant was this? After all, debate would continue as to how many such prisoners Swapo had actually had in the first place and what had happened to those not accounted for. When ordered in a November 1989 court case to produce five named detainees, for example, Swapo simply denied having these prisoners and, in any case, failed to produce them. Even more revealingly, in its electoral campaigning the party rejected across the board the various allegations made by the Parents' Committee and other critics, thus falling back on (in Lombard's phrase) its "culture of silence and denial" and its shrivelled notion of reconciliation, "in which the injustices of the past could simply be swept under the rug, and the wounds of war left to heal themselves."[16]

There is some evidence that not all senior Swapo leaders found this stance an easy one to adopt. Lombard, for example, quotes a speech made before the pre-independence elections by Theo-Ben Gurirab, who was to become Namibia's foreign minister. The issue of the former detainees was a painful subject affecting virtually every family in Namibia, Gurirab said; it would not go away by being ignored; the time for dialogue on this painful issue had arrived.

> At the end of the day we will have to sit around the fire and take inventories: who is alive, who is dead, how did it all happen? As a Swapo leader I will never defend the humiliation and suffering of torture. If the allegations are true, I apologize to the victims and to their parents and pledge to you now that the Swapo leadership will take the necessary steps to bring those involved to book.[17]

Less than a year later (in May 1990), however, Gurirab "dissociated himself" from, as he put it, "the quotations made in my name."[18] By then any lingering disposition there may have been on the part of some members of the Swapo leadership to deal with the detainee issue openly and honestly seemed to have been extinguished.

Nonetheless, the parliament that met immediately after independence had inherited from Martti Ahtissaari, the United Nations Special Representative in charge of the transition to independence, a UN report, made in October 1989, on an investigation into the fate of 1,077 people who were alleged to have been in Swapo's detention camps earlier that year but had not returned. The report said that 71 of the people on the list had not been detained, but confirmed that 639 of those on the list had been detained and had either died (155) or been repatriated (484). There was insufficient information to identify 52; a further 315 remained unaccounted for.[19] Ahtissaari said that the problem "was now in the hands of the Namibians" and the new parliament contained a number of opposition MPs willing to pursue the issue.

As for Swapo, it also had to tread carefully. It still lacked a two-thirds majority, and so could not override the civil liberties entrenched in the constitution; and in any case it was anxious to reassure overseas investors. Nonetheless, any investigation of those missing would have had to look into the whole Lubango story and hear testimony from those who had survived. So, from the first, the new government resisted all attempts to have the detainee issue investigated, even when this took the form of a call for an all-party committee chaired by the parliamentary Speaker. Moses Garoeb, Swapo's secretary-general, said the party had taken on the duty of drawing up "a full and comprehensive list of all those Namibians who have died and disappeared in the war while they were under Swapo's care and responsibility," but that "many are simply unaccounted for." He categorically denied that Swapo was still holding "any Namibians anywhere as detainees." Hidipo Hamutenya, the Swapo minister of information (who, with Moses Garoeb, had visited the detention centres and was involved in showing the videos of the alleged confessions abroad), also stated that Swapo was compiling a list of "those who have died and disappeared under its care." He acknowledged that dying in detention was "one of the circumstances" in which people died, "but not the only one."[20] The debate was heated. Eventually Prime Minister Hage Geingob got all sides to agree to suspend the discussion while he tried to find a "diplomatic" solution in the form of a "small" all-party committee, albeit one with very vague terms of reference. What finally emerged in November was an agreement to ask the International Committee of the Red Cross (ICRC) "to trace the missing people."

The ICRC said it could only respond to requests from governments, and the prime minister therefore made the request. The ICRC submitted a series of reports, which were tabled in parliament, the last of them in June 1993. It reported that it had found no missing Namibians in the forty-eight Angolan prisons it visited in

1991-92, or heard any reports of such persons in Angola, Zambia, Zimbabwe, or Botswana.[21] For whatever reason, the ICRC reports were not debated in parliament, and the central issues — the fate of those missing, and the facts of what had happened at Lubango generally — remained unresolved.

One more attempt was made to use parliament to deal with them. On August 23, 1994, with a new general election pending in December, Eric Biwa MP, the sole Patriotic Unity Movement (PUM — an ex-Swapo detainees party) candidate elected to the first parliament, called the house's attention to its failure to debate the ICRC's final report. According to him, the report made it clear that the ICRC had in frustration abandoned the effort to trace missing people, having failed to secure the co-operation of "parties of critical importance." He moved that there should now be "an inquest in a competent Namibia court of law," not to prosecute those allegedly responsible for the death or disappearance of anyone, but to "determine the fate of the missing persons, so that where such persons have died, death certificates be issued."[22] A few brief quotations from this debate suffice to illustrate the positions taken — and what was implicitly at stake for the Swapo leadership.

First, Justus Garoeb of the United Democratic Front (UDF), an ally of the PUM, said that in addition to the many Namibians killed in the fighting, or who died from illness or accidents or suicide and other causes,

> We are also mature enough to know and to accept that given the war situation that prevailed those days and the human nature, for the good or for the worst, a great number of our children died at the hands of our own Swapo security people charged with various crimes they might have committed. Some died in detention under unhealthy conditions and shortage of nutritious food and/or unbecoming foodstuffs. Young girls were alleged to have been raped and died for lack of professional medical treatment. Others are alleged to have been literally beaten to death and some were reported not to have returned to detention after allegedly being taken away by the security people for interrogation. They just vanished into thin air.[23]

Even so, Justus Garoeb stressed, the UDF did not want to "pave the way for charges against the culprits," but just to "close this very sad chapter and make a new beginning."[24]

Swapo secretary-general Moses Garoeb merely reiterated that the party was compiling a list of all those who had died or disappeared, and that this required more time. Nahas Angula, minister of education and culture, took the official Swapo line — that any investigation of the Swapo detainees alone would be unfair, and would prevent reconciliation — to its logical conclusion:

> When Swapo entered into a cease-fire agreement with South Africa [Swapo's abortive ceasefire offer of 1981], I remember Swapo having a meeting, saying, "look, we are facing the problem of a nation which [has] fought against

itself. Brother fighting brother and son fighting father." It did happen. Then we said, "how do we face this situation?" We were very conscious of what has happened in other situations like this. Many of us lived in Angola for a long time. We knew that on the departure of the Portuguese there was no political programme in place to bring people together and to start the foundations of nation-making. That is why the war in Angola continues. We said we should try something else. That is why Swapo came up with the policy of national reconciliation. We knew the tragedies we have gone through and we said if we are going to look back and try to investigate or try to find out who did what and when, we are quite sure we are not going to be a nation at peace with itself. We will continue to be a nation in conflict with itself. We knew about that [and that] we should try to look to the future rather than return to the past. If you want to return to the past, fine. . . . But we must know about the consequences of that. You will never stop anywhere. You will have to go all the way from the crimes committed from the Berlin Conference up to the 21st March 1990. That you have to do if you are to be honest and do justice.[25]

Prime Minister Geingob summed up for Swapo:

Yes, some people were detained by Swapo and some went missing. Some of those detained were genuine spies of the enemy, some were probably innocent and some were probably wrongly detained as a result of which their reputations were tarnished. Such things happen in guerrilla wars because of the nature of such wars and the absence of a normal due process of law. . . . As the Government of Namibia we will continue our efforts to find out what happened to the missing persons, but it does not mean that the issue should be politicized before every election.[26]

Eric Biwa summed up for the detainees:

In a nutshell, the strategy is simply to deny, conceal, trivialize, disregard and rule at all cost. . . . While I do agree that the issue is emotionally charged, I am not convinced that Mr. [Moses] Garoeb is interested in a solution or has the moral and political courage to do something about it, and if he has the political courage, I would like to challenge him that he tells us today what happened to the detainees who disappeared after and shortly before his visit to the dungeons in January 1989. That was long after Resolution 435 had been agreed upon and the war had stopped. Therefore, the excuse that missing Namibians died in war cannot apply [to them]. . . . Let me assure the Prime Minister that the issue of the missing persons shall be raised as long as it remains unresolved. I personally undertake to raise it, be it from the floor of this House or from the streets. I joined Swapo 23 years ago, an act I have no regrets for, because I was absolutely convinced it was the right thing to do and was prepared to die for that cause. I was detained by Swapo in an underground dungeon for five years, but remained a member because I was convinced throughout that the mistake would be rectified in due course. Soon it became clear to me that Swapo irreversibly degenerated into an enemy of human rights and democracy. At this point I left Swapo to struggle for human rights and democracy under new conditions. Thus only death will silence me.[27]

Biwa's motion was defeated, and Swapo would later that year win the general elections with more than a two-thirds majority. From then on the history of the history took place largely outside parliament.

Siegfried Groth's book next broke the silence in Namibia, with words thus becoming formidable weapons in the struggle to challenge the active forgetting of Namibian history. Groth, a German cleric with pastoral experience in Namibia, subsequently had a notable history of servicing the spiritual needs of those Namibians, living in Zambia, who had fallen out of favour with the Swapo establishment. Dobell notes that Groth's account of events in Angola and of the questionable silence of church persons, then and since, regarding those events, revealed little that had not been written before.[28] But, coming from a source within the Lutheran family of churches and hitting, in any case, so uncomfortably close to the target, Groth's book evoked dramatic responses: embarrassment on the part of certain church persons and anger from the Swapo hierarchy. Importantly, too, it reactivated the network of those who still wished to force Swapo to finally come clean on this issue. As Dobell writes:

> A Breaking the Wall of Silence (BWS) Committee was formed, comprising former detainees and their supporters, together with a number of CCN (Council of Churches of Namibia) employees, to launch the book under its own auspices, and undertook to translate it from English into the more widely spoken Afrikaans and Oshivambo, the latter directly addressing Swapo's traditional support base.[29]

Equally significant was the nature of Swapo's response. Thus Swapo MP Nathaniel Maxuilili led calls for the banning and burning of the book, while the notoriously intemperate Moses Garoeb issued dark threats of war against the "evil forces" that dared to challenge Swapo: "There could be a lot of bloodshed in this country. We are always reminded of the past and of being insulted and provoked and we have now reached a point where we can say 'enough is enough' and can fight back."[30] Even more threatening was the step taken by President Sam Nujoma. Availing himself of the national television network on March 6, 1996, he launched a vituperative attack on both Siegfried Groth and Christo Lombard, who was associ-

ated with the launch, characterizing Lombard as "an apostle of apartheid." Nujoma
evoked "our policy of national reconciliation, unity of purpose, tolerance and mutual
accommodation" while also calling "upon all Namibian patriots to remain vigilant"
against "divisive forces" and "all types of irresponsible reporting."[31]

The president added, "The Swapo Government under my leadership will not
allow Namibia to become another Rwanda or Burundi, Pastor Groth's agenda will
only lead to bloodshed in our country. That is something we cannot tolerate in
Namibia." Significantly, the abrasive tone of the statement, the rhetorical overkill
(blood to be shed: by whom, and whose would it be?) and the highly personal-
ized outbursts were characteristic of Swapo's use of character assassination and
intimidation in exile, providing further evidence of some of the negative attributes of the political culture that has pervaded the movement from quite early on
in its history.

Meanwhile, Swapo functionaries had been busying themselves in finally
preparing their own oft-announced accounting of the varied fates of Namibians in
exile, publishing, on August 25, 1996, *Their Blood Waters Our Freedom* (also referred
to as "The Book of the Dead").[32] This publication did provoke one last gasp of parliamentary activity on the issue, with Prime Minister Geingob seeking to use the
availability of its account to now shift the burden of truth-telling back to the old
occupying power and its allies within Namibia, even tabling a motion to that
effect.[33] However, Eric Biwa, himself once more rising to the debate (and now a
UDF MP) was having none of this, slamming the "Book of the Dead" as "a classi-
fied set of lies" that, in the newspaper paraphrase of his intervention, merely "further deepened the mystery of the missing and the dead." In fact, he noted, there
was now "more to explain than ever before."[34] Such was also the conclusion of the
National Society for Human Rights, which, in a sustained response entitled *Critical
Analysis: Swapo's "Book of the Dead,"* was able to document a wide range of what it
termed "discrepancies, contradictions and distortions or falsifications" in the Swapo
account.[35]

The NSHR claimed to have names of 772 Swapo detainees who had not returned
to Namibia and were still "missing."[36] Of these, 140 were now listed in "The Book
of the Dead" as having died; 99 of those were said to have died in Lubango (which
did not constitute a statement by Swapo that they had been detainees, because
Lubango was the site of the organization's main military camp as well as the detention camps or pit-prisons). Thus 632 of the people on the NSHR list remained unaccounted for. Although Swapo said "The Book of the Dead" was incomplete, and
promised more research, it seemed unlikely that if such research took place it
would reveal much about these 632 people.

As for Swapo, it merely maintained that the NSHR's allegations were unfound-
ed. But its own credibility was seriously damaged by some of the discrepancies and
contradictions that the NSHR pointed out. In particular, some well-known Swapo
figures in exile who had previously been publicly denounced as spies, such as

Tauno Hatuikilipi (who President Nujoma stated in 1984 had committed suicide after being detected as a spy, but who was widely believed to have been killed by Swapo security forces), were listed in the "Book" as dead heroes and heroines (Hatuikilipi himself was now said to have died of bronchitis).[37] While there might be innocent explanations of the fate of many, perhaps most, of those people still unaccounted for, Swapo's protestations that it had nothing to hide were discredited by the evidence that there were indeed things it had tried to hide.[38]

Clearly much more remained to be done to ascertain the details of Swapo's record in exile, adding a fresh reason for the party's critics to press for some kind of process of public fact-finding and accountability. For the moment, the chief hope of the Breaking the Wall of Silence members and others was that the churches would at long last take up the issue of Lubango in a satisfactory manner. And there were those who worked, both within the churches and without, to have that happen. Even at the time this must have seemed a somewhat fond hope, of course. We have already seen (and Groth's book also demonstrated) just how reluctant the churches had been all along to raise questions concerning Swapo's practices in exile.[39] Perhaps it was believed that after five years of independence the churches might no longer feel themselves in danger of giving aid and comfort to an apartheid enemy by interrogating Swapo's record, and would therefore be more willing to open up such important moral questions. In fact, as early as 1994 and even before the publication of Groth's book, some people working within church circles (and especially within the Council of Churches of Namibia) had been approached by ex-detainees and others to seek church support for a more open-ended reconciliation process than the government was willing to countenance. Most notably engaged in such efforts were CCN general secretary Ngeno Nakamhela and CCN staffer Samson Ndeikwila.[40] And when, in late 1995, both the executive of the CCN and its annual general meeting voted "to address the detainee issue" it looked as if progress, from the ex-detainees point of view, might finally be made.[41]

However, a clear signal that there would be a strict limit to church engagement with this issue came with the early 1996 decision by both the CCN itself and a number of key churches not to accept an invitation to participate in the launching of Groth's book.[42] True, some concrete plans were still ongoing at this point within the CCN to mount a public program of "reconciliation and healing" — including, most significantly, a series of planned conferences "on issues related to the ex-detainees during the struggle for independence." The first of these was to be held, the CCN's Executive Committee instructed (according to its press release of February 19, 1996), between May and July 1996. In the words of Reverend Nakamhela:

CCN sees the conference as one step in establishing the truth about human rights abuses during the years of struggle for independence as far as humanly possible. CCN's conviction, willingness and sensitivity call it to continue to be

involved in finding a permanent resolution to the ex-detainee issue and to promote true reconciliation as an ongoing process in our nation.[43]

Yet all was not clear sailing on this front either. Indeed, as debate resumed concerning the best ways of proceeding with this process and its correct timing, a
number of church leaders began to backtrack, especially after a group of them were
invited to a March 1996 meeting with the president at which he warned the
churchmen to be careful not to run the risk of "disturbing the peace."[44]
Nonetheless, the initiative only really ground to a halt when an angry president
held a further, more formal meeting with church leaders on August 13, 1996, and
warned them even more aggressively than before not to rock the boat.[45] Although
the full story of the churches' role (or lack thereof) during this period remains to
be written, most observers suggest that church leaders fearfully distanced themselves even further from the detainees question after this meeting.[46] About this time
a whispering campaign also began against Reverend Nakamhela, and Swapo members were warned publicly by the party not to take part in any church-related reconciliation processes of the kind promised in the "Year of God's Grace" proposed
for 1997. In short, history was to be forgotten — or else.

The church-centred initiative did limp along, the oft-delayed process finally
producing a rather anti-climactic series of workshops.[47] But the central fact
remained that the project had not been allowed to be taken seriously by the churches. As for the BWS, it nonetheless chose not to abandon the cause after 1996 and
was to find the means to ventilate the issue from time to time in coming years —
despite the deafness to its concerns of the bulk of the Namibian elite and also the
apparent difficulties, logistical and otherwise, of capturing the interest and attention of many ordinary Namibians.[48] It was, for example, the BWS that seized on the
TRC process that was by now underway in South Africa as providing both a possible lever for keeping the Lubango issue alive and a possible model for future
Namibian practice. Thus the organization's 1997 annual report is full of favourable
references to the TRC; indeed, in that year the BWS invited a member of the TRC, Dr.
Mapule Ramashala, to address its annual general meeting on "the relevance of the
TRC exercise to the Southern African Region." Dr. Ramashala quite specifically
argued that "the ANC's painstaking work of careful investigating and documenting
the dead and those who have disappeared should inspire Namibians to find a way
to do likewise" and concluded by seeking to speak directly to President Nujoma
himself (albeit in absentia):

President Nujoma, Sir, may I not be presumptuous, but may I suggest that
there is a way out of this, that you and your people can address this issue. You
were a victim also. You need to identify with the pain and suffering that is
going through your land. You need to provide incentives for full disclosure,
not just for you, for your Cabinet and for all other perpetrators in your country.

Listen to BWS. I don't think there is any malice in this group. I believe that they are determined to move their country forward. This is an appeal to you, Sir, that you open communication and find ways with your people to heal not only those who have suffered violations, to heal your land, but most of all to heal yourself.[49]

There was no sign, however, that President Nujoma took Dr. Ramashala's advice regarding how best to deal with "forgotten history" the least bit seriously.

To be sure, there were other ongoing efforts to keep the issue alive. Here the initiative taken in the late 1990s by ex-detainee Emma Kambangula to launch, with others, the Project for the Study of Violence and Reconciliation Trust is particularly noteworthy — as, unfortunately, is the fate that befell her. In the 1998 account of one of the members of this project's board of trustees, Christo Lombard:

> The aim of the Project was (and is) to help all victims of the Namibian war to get the help they need and deserve: to get proper counselling for the extreme trauma suffered, to tell their stories and have these published, to clear their names and to take legal action when needed. In the absence of something like a Truth and Reconciliation Commission in Namibia, the Project seems to be the only current initiative in Namibia that tries to address the complicated issues of truth and reconciliation on both sides of the conflict zone. In this effort the Project has solicited wide international support and is in the process of setting up counselling structures with the help of professional centers that have dealt with post-traumatic stress successfully in other parts of the world.[50]

Kambangula, the originator and manager of this initiative, was in that same year harassed with death threats (threats purporting to be issued, by those who conveyed them, in order "to protect the president of Swapo and the president of our country") and eventually was compelled to leave the country to safeguard her own life and that of her small daughter.[51] In addition, in the wake of such threats, the project itself came to be considerably watered down and deflected away from the most challenging of its reconciliatory purposes — although some of those originally connected with it are proceeding with the task of recording additional accounts from Lubango survivors.[52]

And there were other initiatives to keep the history of Lubango alive during these years. There was, for example, the production by Richard Pakleppa of his powerful and deeply moving film I Have Seen, on the Lubango occurrences and their implications for contemporary Namibia. This was both an artistic triumph and, in the interview material it contains (both from numerous ex-detainees and from the likes of senior Swapo ministers Hage Geingob and Nahas Angula), a vital source of pertinent documentation.[53] Indeed, Angula is even moved to say on camera:

When we start retracing our own steps we should be able to discover where we [Swapo] went wrong, and where we were right, separate myth from truth, truth from myth. Perhaps when we start doing that, reflecting back, it is only then we can start to recognize the kind of mistakes we might have done and the kind of pain we might have inflicted on other people who might have been caught because of the mistakes we have done. But that will take time, I must say. . . . Not only that, it needs some form of leadership, a leadership that should recognize the fact that as a leader you cannot be right all the time, sometimes he makes an error, and we have to accept that as a fact of life.[54]

Unfortunately, with respect to this kind of frankness, Angula has remained an all too lonely voice within Swapo circles; others from those circles did step forward in quite a different manner, for example to denounce the film itself, especially at the first of several lively and well-attended public screenings in Windhoek in October 1999. These screenings were significant political events, however, and received good press coverage, even though the government-controlled Namibian Broadcasting Corporation refused to show the film. Moreover, in the often moving and dramatic discussions that occurred after the viewings the minority who simply attacked the film were more than counterbalanced by a majority who wanted a full and frank dialogue on the issues raised. For example, according to one report Ombudsman Bience Gawanas asserted that "the silence of some victims had been bought with positions and comforts." The report continued:

She said that after nine years she felt she must publicly break her silence on this issue. She shared her horror and shock at seeing recent photographs of tortured Namibians in the Caprivi and how she was reminded of what had happened ten years ago and the scars on her back. She spoke of those who had recently died without having been rehabilitated.[55]

But numerous other interventions were at least equally revealing. The public performances (and CD) of the band "Minus Four" — so named because (as the band's leader Banana Shikupe explains) out of the original nine members of their band (Ndilimani) in exile four had died in the dungeons — also had some impact, not least at a 2000 session at the Warehouse Theatre in Windhoek held to mark the United Nations' International Day of Torture.[56] Although representatives of Swapo and its government declined to attend, a number of prominent church persons did participate actively (including the general secretary of the CCN, Reverend Nagula Kathindi). Moreover, in addition to the performance of Minus Four, a choir composed of women from the dungeons came together to sing the songs they had sung in detention — and they were even joined in doing so by (once again) Ombudsman Gawanas. Activists around these issues took some strength from such "successes," although it could perhaps be argued that the impact of events like this concert and the screening of the Pakleppa film was primarily confined to Windhoek and to relatively restricted and self-selected audiences.

In 1999, however, the issue did surface in an even more public way — with the Swapo response being, once again, all too predictable. Not coincidentally, the situation was again potentially dangerous for the party. In 1995-96 it was not merely Groth's book but even more the threat that the churches might take up the issue of the movement's "forgotten history" that had caused a stir. In 1999 the broader context within which the issue was revived may also have seemed threatening to Swapo. For in that year there was emerging, in the shape of the fledgling Congress of Democrats (COD), the first potentially serious political challenge faced by the movement since independence. Momentarily, it looked as though issues such as governmental corruption, complacency, and high-handedness on the one hand and the questionably constitutional manner in which Nujoma had been allowed to run for a third presidential term on the other might give Swapo defector Ben Ulenga and his COD a fighting electoral chance. This was to prove illusory (not least because of the familiar tactics of character assassination directed by Swapo against Ulenga during the election campaign). But the heightened political tension of the moment meant that Swapo was in no mood to politely field the raising of the detainees' issue in mid-1999 when the BWS sought, once again, to place it on the political agenda.

The flashpoint for Swapo was the BWS committee's decision to mark, on July 4th, the tenth anniversary of the return to Namibia of the first 153 ex-detainees in 1989. For it was when the BWS announced publicly its "Ex-Detainees Reunion Day,"[57] and also spoke of the eventual publication of further personal narratives by those Lubango detainees who had survived, that the Office of the Swapo Secretary General sprang into action. It chose to see these recent initiatives as part of a "chain of attacks on Swapo" and suggested that, of these, "the most vituperative is the demand that Swapo should engage in a process of public confession and apologize to those who were detained during the struggle."[58] In sum, this statement, entitled "It Is Either Reconciliation or the Opening of Old Wounds," reiterated the party's general policy in such matters:

> As part of its programme of nation-building and the healing of the wounds of the past, the leadership of Swapo formulated and adopted a policy of national reconciliation in 1989. The policy was intended to guard against the fact that, if the Namibian people allow themselves to engage in witch-hunting and retribution, the consequences of such an exercise will not be in the best interest of peace and stability.

And yet, just as one might have wanted to ask who was actually threatening "bloodshed" when President Nujoma evoked that danger at the time of his presidential attack on Pastor Groth, one could equally well ask now just who was threatening "peace and stability"? The Swapo statement may itself have given the game away, however, when it added that, if the BWS or the National Society of Human Rights "prefer that old wounds be opened up and that the policy of national reconciliation be buried, *Swapo will be adequately prepared to join the battle*" (emphasis added).

Pauline Dempers, responding to Swapo's outburst on behalf of the BWS, suggested that this once again demonstrated that the party's claim to have "always been measured when responding to the so-called unwarranted allegations" was a "decorated cake with a bomb inside it." The former detainees, she continued, had "experienced Swapo's brutality at first hand [and] no amount of decorated threats will scare us. Ruthlessness is Swapo's way of solving problems." More generally, she continued, for Swapo "reconciliation means stone-cold silence should prevail in a zombie-like manner. In the minds of Swapo chieftains, reconciliation means that we have not seen anything, we have not heard anything and we must not say anything." And yet, while "the Swapo leadership may wish to die without addressing the issue, as some did, the issue will remain with your children and the future generations. . . . The issue will be there until the whole Namibian population becomes extinct and no human beings remain in Namibia any more."[59]

Needless to say, this is quite a striking statement for historians to consider. However, in the event, no real "battle" took place in 1999. True, a faked list of donors to the BWS was circulated (reported in *The Namibian* under the headline "War of Lies Heats Up: Apartheid-type Tactics Make Comeback")[60] designed to discredit the movement. For its part, the BWS suspected Swapo of being behind this offensive, although the charge was quickly denied. And what of the "forgotten history" of Lubango in all of this? It was left to one of the key BWS members, Rosa Namises, to make the comment that historians may best remember from this exchange. "We will not go away," she said. The issue "will stay until it is resolved."[61]

## Insult to Injury

And so we come back to the year 2000 and the strange story of Swapo's reaction to the trial of Dr. Wouter Basson in South Africa. In fact, this episode in the continuing saga of the Lubango detentions is particularly revealing. As we have seen, some Swapo leaders, and notably Prime Minister Geingob, had not denied that there were abuses, but they had always resisted any proposal to talk about them in public; while others had tended to speak as if there was nothing to talk about.

In this case, however, it was Swapo that spoke out: "Self-proclaimed champions of human rights should in fact now go and demand from [the South Africans] to explain the whereabouts of the missing Namibians they have been calling on Swapo to account for."[62] What is interesting about this is that nothing in the immediate political situation required Swapo to say anything about the testimony in the Basson trial. The 1999 election in Namibia was over, and in its election campaign the COD, despite its links with members or supporters of the BWS, had not emphasized the issue; and in any case it had been soundly beaten. And in June

2000 the BWS had nothing new to say. It does not take the psychological penetration of an Inspector Maigret to detect a bad conscience behind Swapo's incautious outburst. So there were missing Namibians, then? As many as two hundred, anyway? Curious that Swapo had not previously acknowledged so much.

Most future historians will surely be forced to say that this just won't do. Nor, we might predict, will many of these historians view sympathetically Swapo's broader arguments for a policy of reconciliation by way of amnesia. True, a TRC conceived on the South African model may not provide the ideal point of reference for dealing with the Lubango issue in Namibia. While some who perpetrated war crimes on behalf of the South African army of occupation are still in Namibia, many more have gone back to their own country, South Africa, or, indeed, elsewhere. The reciprocity of responsibility for crimes against humanity that underlay the South African TRC (however unequally that responsibility was actually distributed between the racist regime on the one hand and those who resisted it on the other) would therefore be much more difficult to establish in Namibia.

After all, even in South Africa the ANC did not like having the very small proportion of its own undertakings that were deemed unacceptable by the TRC evaluated against the same standards that were being used across the board to judge the apartheid state and its operatives. There, in the end, Thabo Mbeki's ANC even went so far as to crassly condemn the published TRC report itself on just these grounds, thus undermining some of the positive impact that the report might otherwise have had. It is hardly more likely that Swapo would appreciate being held accountable for its crimes with its murderous counterparts on the other side largely in absentia.

But the TRC model is not, after all, the only one available for seeking to recuperate for positive purposes a politically charged history. A variety of possible formats for commissions of inquiry is conceivable, at least in principle, and these are all the more conceivable if linked to an amnesty provision (the one lesson of the TRC that might be most relevant to the Namibian case). Such was the clear intention of Biwa's 1994 call for an inquest, and even perhaps also of the all-party committee proposed by Moses Katjiuonga in 1990, a proposal effectively neutralized by Geingob's approach to the ICRC. Nor is the fact, appealed to by Nahas Angula in the 1994 debate, that so many Namibians were enlisted on the colonialists' side a real obstacle. For those pressing for a resolution of the missing detainees issue are evidently willing to accept the risk of being implicated on the South African side — because, it would seem, they believe themselves to be innocent of all such charges.

The problem is, in fact, not the impossibility of devising appropriate mechanisms for an investigation; it is that those in power have consistently believed it to be either in the country's broader interest or in their own much more narrow self-interest — and, as we have seen, it depends on your perspective which description of their motivation you favour — not to allow one. This official stance has thus far proven to be a very effective roadblock to any open processing by Namibians of the Lubango question. Contemporary historians must worry as to how much more we can hope to learn in this generation, until, that is, certain key actors with too much to hide have passed away. But, of course, such actors will then also have taken their stories with them.

Historians may have additional reasons to rededicate themselves to setting the record straight in any case, such as the challenge to their craft and their integrity that is presented by accounts like the one contained in President Nujoma's autobiography, *Where Others Wavered*, published in 2001.[63] This book is a true measure of the moral obtuseness that has become part and parcel of the Swapo project — an ironic index of the extent to which, over long years of struggle, the cruelty and callousness of the apartheid masters also entered into the souls of those who spent much of their lives fighting it. For the book can fairly be said to have raised the practice of "forgetting history" in Namibia to a new level. Thus, the seeds of an evasive narrative that ultimately seeks to obscure the full import of Lubango are first sown in Nujoma's account of Swapo's internal tensions in Tanzania in the 1960s, which are more or less reduced to a discussion of the case of Leonard Philemon Shuuya ("Castro"). This figure, whose bona fides were indeed rather suspect, was, says Nujoma, "handed . . . over to the Tanzanian authorities who kept him away while the struggle continued" — until his release, along with "others who had been held," in Nujoma's signally euphemistic phrase, some years later (that is, the Tanzanians locked him up without trial for eighteen years). Nothing is said by Nujoma about the treatment of the eight "Chinamen" — Namibians returning from military training in China — who, after an attempt to raise questions concerning the Swapo leadership's conduct of the struggle, were similarly "kept away" by the "Tanzanian authorities" on behalf of the Swapo leaders. Nujoma evidently still imagines that it is sufficient for him to dub all critics "informers and traitors" and, later, "spies," for Swapo's treatment of them to be accepted.[64]

This is also a trick that he returns to in a subsequent chapter when dealing (albeit in less than a page of his 466-page book) with the even more dramatic developments that occurred in Zambia in the 1970s.[65] Nujoma's account of the events in Zambia is almost entirely spurious, recycling the long-discredited tale of Andreas Shipanga's centrality to these happenings[66] and grossly distorting the role of the Youth Leaguers entering exile and who thought to hold the Swapo leadership already in Zambia to account for what they saw as their corruption and ineffectiveness — by calling, principally, for the holding of the long-delayed democratic congress of the movement. Nujoma conspicuously avoids even mentioning such demands while falsely implying that the exile movement had a working constitution. These critics too are then written off, predictably, as "elements sent by the South Africans to spy on Swapo" (a key phrase, just waiting to be used again)[67] — while he makes no mention of how he himself and his group had to call on the Zambian army to arrest the bulk of the two thousand Swapo soldiers on Zambian soil (during and after which action a significant number were killed), and then intrigue with the Tanzanian government to airlift the dissident leaders from Zambia to jails in Tanzania (where, unlike in Zambia, habeas corpus did not apply).

Where is this kind of account leading? To Nujoma's treatment of the Lubango events, of course, a dismissive couple of pages that nonetheless manage to ring the changes on the by now time-tested formula: there were spies, war is hell, reconciliation is good.[68] Once again critics of the time are presented as merely having been "used by the South African intelligence apparatus." Indeed, in the end, only one phrase is of interest for our present purposes. "If we are accused of ill-treating detainees, this is *very little* compared to the killing, cruel torture and brutal treatment the apartheid South African regime inflicted on our people over so many years," Nujoma writes. While it is not entirely clear from his words (purposely vague?) as to whether he is referring here to the accusation of "ill-treatment" or to the ill-treatment itself, the question stands as to what, precisely, he means to specify by the phrase "very little."

As for "those in the opposition who bring up this matter": they "think that they will gain some sympathy, but they forget that the people are not easily misled by their deceitful tactics and statements." He reveals nothing as to the nature or substance of such "statements," nor does he make any substantive effort to refute them.[69] What we have instead in these latest and most official of words on Lubango is an epitome of the ethical indifference that has come to characterize Swapo's response to the events in Angola.

And yet these are not, we suspect, the latest words on Lubango — not so long as there are those with the courage of a Pauline Dempers or a Samson Ndeikwila to keep the issue alive. Indeed, in the flurry of excitement over the Basson trial the BWS made good on its standing promise not to "go away." In late 2000 it published a series of newspaper advertisements that not only listed still-missing detainees but also accused a group of named individuals, including senior ministers and serving police and military commanders (with Chief of the Army Jesus Hawala at the top of the list), of being responsible for gross human rights abuses with respect to the events that had occurred both in Zambia and in Angola. In effect, Breaking the Wall of Silence, having despaired of the Swapo leadership ever dealing openly with the issue, was daring those named to sue, and when one of them (a former general and now Namibian ambassador to Angola, Ndaxu "Ho Chi Minh" Namoloh) threatened to do so, Pauline Dempers merely stated that the BWS "will not apologize as he is requesting but would encourage him to proceed with his claim of innocence regarding the ex-detainee issue," suggesting that there would be plenty of witnesses to be called in the cases if Namoloh and others were directly involved.[70]

It remains to be seen what will happen to these and other efforts to pry open the lid of forgotten history in Namibia. Here one can only express the hope that future historians will be equally energetic and at least as imaginative in pursuing the truth.

CHAPTER 6

# MUGABE, GRAMSCI, AND ZIMBABWE AT TWENTY-FIVE
(with Richard Saunders)

Many years ago, one right-wing commentator found it "difficult to escape the con-clusion that Robert Mugabe will soon be taking far-reaching and meaningful steps to turn his country into a socialist state on the Gramscian model." And, indeed, twenty-five years later there are still some, of left and right, who see the current, apparent "re-radicalization" of ZANU-PF's political project as a last, leftist, quasi-Gramscian gambit to recapture lost popular legitimacy. Many more, however, see it instead as reflecting the final throes of an increasingly compromised, corrupt, militarized, and anti-popular regime. In this chapter we will emphasize the extent to which present policies do indeed reflect the material-political consequences (and contradictions) of the historic class compromises that Mugabe and ZANU have made in Zimbabwe and the deep-seated confrontation between elite interests and those of the mass of the population that Mugabe now seeks to obfuscate with mere rhet-oric and opportunist policies.

For those who were active in the international support network for Southern Africa liberation in the 1960s and 1970s, the prospective coming to power of a majority-rule government in Rhodesia (henceforward Zimbabwe) in the late 1970s brought considerable joy, even though it produced a rejoicing that was somewhat qualified. Celebration was tempered not because of the nature of the incumbent regime to be dismissed with the coming of change, of course. This was, after all, the hated, and eminently racist, Unilateral Declaration of Independence (UDI) minority-rule regime of Ian Smith that was about to be dispatched to the trash can of history, and the end of that regime's time in power was long past due.

Moreover, behind Smith stood one of his own ostensible enemies, the histor-ical (and historically compromised) colonial power of Great Britain, which had, in fact, shown no willingness to confront the defiant Smith regime by force, and its proposed solution — sanctions — had been quickly revealed as the empty gesture it was. Various flimsy reformist gestures by the United Kingdom had been equally revealing of the British government's half-hearted resistance to Rhodesia's UDI. It was very soon apparent to all that only the militarized action of the territory's African population could hope to bring significant redress to Zimbabwe/Rhodesia's troubled present.

No, it was the nature of the resistance itself that gave observers pause. This was certainly not because the nationalist movement was beginning, slowly but surely, to make military headway against the Smith regime. Rather it was because it was equally clear, unfortunately, that the movement was itself completely divided. Not that this was necessarily a bad thing in the abstract (from the point of view of long-term democratic prospects in a free Zimbabwe, for example). Yet it certainly seemed so in the immediate case of Zimbabwe — given the empty juxtaposition of personal ambitions that polarized ZAPU and ZANU and inflamed hostilities between the two movements, and also the backward-looking and unproductive ethnic ambitions (Ndebele and Shona, to go no further) that hovered just beneath the surface of liberation movement rivalry. Thus, in the 1970s, it could be plausibly argued that the internal rivalries that racked the Zimbabwean nationalist camp "smacked more of the same old wasting kind of petty-bourgeois political infighting — centred upon personalities, intrigues, and the mobilization of constituencies around ethnic identifications, all long-time features of a Zimbabwean exile politics untransformed by effective struggle."[1]

Some observers hoped that a kind of "logic of protracted struggle" might yet produce the emergence of new popularly grounded political practices and a new kind of leadership that would be promising not just for the success of the struggle against white minority rule but also for realizing the kind of radical changes that might eventually be launched by a new, post-liberation, largely black government. However, a degree of scepticism soon crystallized as to the quality of the existing liberation leadership (including the scepticism towards it of the newly formed Frelimo government, which had witnessed the evolution of the Zimbabwe liberation struggle at close hand yet was nonetheless an active supporter of it). In fact, some, including Frelimo leaders, saw, however briefly and probably overly optimistically, a certain promise in the emergence of the Zimbabwe People's Army (ZIPA) — a new military and political initiative that began to surface as the more unified expression of less opportunist, more militant (and younger) cadres from both ZANU and ZAPU, possibly displacing the dominance at the top of "the old guard, Nkomo and Mugabe in particular."[2]

## Nationalism as Presumptive Hegemony

It was testimony to the resilience and strategic guile of the old guard that the ZIPA project met with a quick demise (with even Frelimo, as host government in Mozambique, coming, against its original instinct, to play a particularly heavy-handed role in facilitating the new formation's fall), and that the established militarized wings of the nationalist movement re-emerged to play a crucial part in the transition to majority rule. In the pre-independence election of March 1980 ZANU-PF (no longer joined with ZAPU in the "Patriotic Front" as it had briefly been at the time of the election, but willing to share a few cabinet posts afterwards) handily won and stood ready to take power with the coming of independence in April. Faced with such evidence of "success," however, some on the left who had been sceptical as to ZANU's claims were tempted to begin to rethink the movement's radical credentials. In doing so, they were encouraged by far more conservative commentators who now also cast Mugabe as a deft man of the left, one prepared to use short-term compromises to tempt the existing (largely white) bourgeoisie into acquiescing to change — while all along harbouring long-term goals of genuinely radical transformation. Indeed, one such commentator, David Willers, even evoked the figure of Italian Marxist Antonio Gramsci to capture the subtlety of Mugabe's ultra-left manoeuvring. For, in Willers's view, Mugabe was "no wishy-washy African socialist." Like Gramsci, who avoided premature confrontation and counselled "tactically winning influence and control over the trade unions, cultural agencies, media, education, religion and the main production centres," Mugabe, Willers said, "appears to be following the Gramsci line in every respect and [has] thus far averted a rebellion by the bourgeoisie."

> Tactically, Mugabe has been without fault: a primary objective, namely to persuade the Rhodesian bourgeoisie that ZANU-PF is a national, credit-worthy part of reconciliation, free of obedience either to the Russians or the Chinese, has largely been achieved. The emphasis, aimed at wooing the middle classes, has been on moderation. Lulled into a sense of security by a projection of ZANU-PF as a party of economic sanity, the bourgeoisie have not complained. . . . One hopes that Rowan Cronje will be proved wrong when he feared that the whites would be kept on in Zimbabwe merely for economic expediency or as neutral factors of production. However, it is difficult to escape the conclusion that Robert Mugabe will soon be taking far-reaching and meaningful steps to turn his country into a socialist state on the Gramscian model.[3]

Much of this was mere cant, of course. Gramsci, for all his care to distinguish deftly between the necessary imperatives of wars of "position" on the one hand and of "manoeuvre" on the other, was a committed Marxist and a genuinely socialist revolutionary: as his position has been summarized, "an integral opposition" or, indeed, a revolutionary government in power "could only come about by the proper political work of organizing and mobilizing the masses, not in terms of corporate interest, but in terms of the hegemonic leadership of the working class organized in a revolutionary party with an active mass basis."[4]

It would soon become apparent that Mugabe and his ZANU-PF government colleagues were not similarly inclined, their strategic goals being in fact far removed from those anticipated by some on the left — and by the majority of Zimbabweans — in the early 1980s. There were, to be sure, important popular gains, notably on the health, education, and Africanization fronts, to be made in the early days — gains that reflected ZANU-PF's skilful negotiation of powerful political-economic undercurrents thrown up by local, regional, and international forces. These gains did lend some credence to the view that a new popular-democratic hegemony was being built in Zimbabwe. Indeed, perhaps the categories of a Gramscian mode of class analysis (as distinct from Gramscian guidelines for consolidating revolutionary power) of the holding and entrenching of bourgeois power can be applied to our understanding of the role claimed by many a victorious nationalist movement, like ZANU, presenting itself — and, in ZANU's case, doing so still — as the sole legitimate voice of "nation-building" and "national purpose." Then, the use of a battery of cultural (if, ultimately, much cruder and more forceful) methods to register ZANU-PF's claim to unchallenged power in this regard can be interpreted, in Gramsci's terms, as being part of the attempt to have "the supremacy of a social group [ZANU] manifest itself in two ways," as both "'domination' and as 'intellectual and moral leadership.'"[5]

Yet although very real and widely celebrated gains, sustained if not comprehensive, continued to be made by the popular sector up to the mid-1980s, the political centre of gravity of the ruling party leadership had begun slowly but surely to shift to the right. Thus Mugabe would eventually reveal himself to be merely an authoritarian "nationalist" who proved quite adept at playing the role accurately predicted for him and for ZANU by author Ibbo Mandaza at the time of the transition: that of chief spokesman of "the gradual embourgeoisement of the African petit bourgeoisie as they found their class aspirations fulfilled."[6] There was also Mugabe's temptation — one open to many apparent-militants in Southern Africa, but not to more principled leaders in the region such as Nelson Mandela or Samora Machel — to see the class contradictions of an unequal society in merely racial terms: ZANU's radical rhetoric thus intermittently disguising racist resentment (and ethnic chauvinism) rather than guiding a more profound transformation of colonial society in the interests of ordinary Zimbabweans.

In short, the national-popular political program of ZANU-PF soon withered to become nationalism of a very weary and worn kind. Significantly, the popular elements of Zimbabwean society would themselves begin to move in the other direction, broadly leftwards, to create new political spaces in a burgeoning, reborn movement of civic organizations outside the aegis of party and state. In consequence, a profound crisis of hegemony would eventually emerge and deepen sharply in the 1990s, resulting in the first substantial challenge to ZANU-PF's political rule since that of ZAPU in the early years of independence — even if the terms of that crisis has been occluded somewhat by Mugabe's recent vocal return to the popular radical-cum-racial language of the past, and to a key theme of the liberation struggle: land.

How then to understand the current "re-radicalization" of ZANU-PF's political project: is it a last, leftist, quasi-Gramscian gambit to recapture lost popular legitimacy — or the final throes of an increasingly compromised, corrupt, militarized, and anti-popular regime? In answering this question, contemporary observers have the data of two decades of shifting class politics and a remodelled — if not, in the end, transformed — state to consider. In examining this record and its troubling outcome one senses two phenomena. First is the recrudescence of attempts by Mugabe and ZANU to reground popular power in Zimbabwe in populist-cum-racial terms. But there is also the profound and wide-ranging negative consequences of the long-term abandonment by the leadership of a genuinely democratic politics grounded in any residual national popular legitimacy of the dominant state form.

For Robert Mugabe, arch-strategist and Machiavellian power-broker though he may be, has now been forced to confront the material-political consequences of the historic class compromises that he has made. The implications of the developing set of tensions and contradictions fostered during Mugabe's twenty-five years in power — driven in no small part by a deep-seated confrontation between elite interests and those of the mass of the population that Mugabe now seeks to obfuscate by mere rhetoric, brute coercion, and opportunist policies — are in fact our main focus here. For we will assess just what has been produced during that quarter-century in terms of both the opportunities for, and the obstacles to, the resumed transformation of struggle claimed by Mugabe to be ZANU's goal.

## The 1980s: ZANU, and Mugabe, Consolidate Their Power

With the taking of power in 1980, Mugabe and the ZANU leadership saw two principal challenges facing them: the consolidation of state power (and, not unimportantly, ZANU's own presumptive hegemony within both that state and the overall society) and the articulation of a "development" strategy for the country. It seems clear that consolidation of a ZANU-centred one-party state was a key initial instrumental, strategic goal, although the complexity of the constitutional bargain struck with the Rhodesians and the British on the one hand and the diversity of Zimbabwean society on the other meant that this goal was never actually achieved. Nonetheless, as the politics of consolidating power went forward apace on other fronts it was plainly evident that what was presented as the "logic" of nation-building most often had a highly partisan intent.

There was, for example, an intensifying clampdown on ZAPU and other forms of organized political opposition. This was consolidated by the further firming up of a securocratic vision of state politics under emergency powers and, for some time in the 1980s, the repeated playing of the "ethnic," ostensibly Shona, card against ZAPU and its popular base in Matabeleland and western Zimbabwe. As Mugabe put it in 1984, "ZAPU is irretrievably bent on its criminal path . . . time has now come for us to show this evil party our teeth. We can bite, and we shall certainly bite."

Such rhetoric served to rationalize the brutal activities of the army's Fifth Brigade (and other state-linked bodies such as the Central Intelligence Organization and ZANU Youth Brigades). These operations were much more fully exposed, in their deserved notoriety, later rather than at the time; thus, a report by churches and legal foundations documented in great, horrifying detail extensive official abuses in terms of killing, detentions, torture, deprivation, and "disappearances."[7] Under such circumstances the eventual subsumption of ZAPU through a ZANU-dominated (labelled ZANU-PF) merger of the two parties in 1987-88 enabled a series of legal changes that aimed to circumvent constitutionally enshrined provisions for rights protection. These also allowed coercive intimidation of the political opposition to be extended to the realm of legal regulatory control and confinement.[8]

At the same time as the assaults on ZAPU, the government also made moves to flood the space available to "civil society." This meant building out from the party and state and into society itself: thus the ZCTU (trade unions), co-op movement, most student and intellectual groups, residents' associations, and women's organizations were either created under ZANU-PF's patronage, or soon came to function as refractions of the party's broad political policies.[9] Meanwhile, in the important realm of the national media, the nationalization of what became the public print media, combined with intimidation of the remaining private-sector press, placed critical limits on the space open for national debate and independent provision of information and reportage.[10] Inevitably, too, this context also weighed on electoral processes, where ZANU-PF manipulated unscrupulously both nationalist trappings and the regulatory regimes to sanction and deepen its control of all levels of the state.

Hegemony? After all, as Carol Boggs points out:

By hegemony, Gramsci meant the permeation throughout civil society — including a whole range of structures and activities like trade unions, schools, the churches, and the family — of an entire system of values, attitude, beliefs morality, etc. that is in one way or another supportive of the established order and the class interests that dominate it.[11]

Perhaps, momentarily, this might have seemed an apt description of the ZANU-PF leadership's own petty-bourgeois nationalist project. Yet it was soon apparent that this ZANU-PF vision of a new Zimbabwe could not so readily become the hegemonic "common sense" of a now stable situation. The exclusion of the people from the material and formal political advantages of freedom was, over time, too dramatic, the rewards to the ruling elites too gross, for domination to work so seamlessly. Already by 1990, John Makumbe's article on the 1990 elections as being "not free, not fair" had noted this — a carefully considered opinion that Makumbe would, with co-author Daniel Compagnon, extend in a book-length scrutiny of the 1995 elections, terming these later flawed elections as representing further steps "toward an entrenched authoritarianism," not the ongoing consolidation of "hegemony."[12]

Not that there was, at first, any marked attempt by ZANU to deny the popular demands that had underlain the original independence struggle. The initial constitutional bargain did allow some land reform, subsidized by the British (approximately seventy thousand families were resettled), but, by the mid-1980s, a reluctance to act further on the existing deeply racist maldistribution of land was rationalized in terms of the same constitution's restrictions, the honouring of which had been made necessary, it was argued, as part of the smoothing of the way to independence.[13] As well some real substance was given to populist themes on various social service fronts in the first years. Yet, even here, where these began to encroach on the growing privileges of the rising black state-dependent elite, there was a strict ceiling on how far such rightful demands could be expected to reach. Similarly, there was a limit on the rhetorical sweep of officially sanctioned "Marxism-Leninism." Ibbo Mandaza is not wrong to assert:

> As the African petty bourgeoisie began gradually to find access to the same economic and social status as their white counterparts so, too, did it become increasingly unable to respond to the aspirations of the workers and peasants. . . . It became imperative as an act of survival for the new state to put a rein on its mass base. . . . Political principles and ideological commitment appeared mortgaged on the alter of private property.[14]

Or, in the words of the economists Carolyn Jenkins and John Knight, "The rapid convergence of interests of old white and new black elites . . . reduced the will to redistribute and increased politicians' desire to accumulate."[15] Moreover, the alacrity with which the residue of any such "populist" commitments was cast aside with the coming of "structural adjustment" in the 1990s is further testimony to the new elite's ambiguous commitment to its original ostensibly socialist project. But note: the existence of (legitimate) mass expectations of entitlement also explains the widespread backlash against the government that would become so much a part of the Zimbabwe political scene in the 1990s, especially in the urban areas.

In fact, it was not long before ZANU-PF, having abandoned any pretence of socialist aspiration, edged Zimbabwe towards settling down to its fate as neo-colony — while the elite settled down to enjoy its comforts. As Lee Cokorinos could already write in 1990, "By now there is ample evidence that ZANU-PF, while containing within its ranks dedicated and honest representatives and members of [the popular] strata, is dominated by what Tsvangirai has called 'the old nationalist leadership' seeking to 'close off challenges to their long-term benefits.'"[16] Morgan Tsvangirai, a Zimbabwe Congress of Trade Unions leader, was soon to become more involved in the struggles to which such antagonisms were leading, but in the early 1990s their political form was merely an uneasy truce: between unkept promises and economic stagnation on the one hand and elite privilege and presumption on the other. Indeed this was already clear by the end of the 1980s, as both within the party and without there was a gradually emerging challenge to both the degeneration of party core principles (participation, democracy, social equity, land reform) and the quite evident emergence of increased corruption (epitomized, most notoriously, in the Willowgate scandal of 1988).[17]

In future, many civil society organizations (in Zimbabwean parlance, "civics") would begin to slip the leash of party control, while confrontations between the state and some of the better organized civics — the ZCTU, human rights organizations, students, independent-minded journalists and the independent media, and the like — would become ever more important. In short, slowly but surely the exposure of all concerned parties to the bracing reality of public debate began to have a positive impact. Here, ironically, the same process that helped consolidate ZANU-PF's legal-juridical power — the merger of ZAPU into ZANU in 1987, and the effective disappearance of political party opposition in parliament — also led to the temporary easing of restrictions on public debate. In fact, the likelihood that public criticisms would be labelled "acts of treason" or "dissident" activity as a matter of course, as they had been for much of the post-independence life of ZAPU, was now diminished.[18] With other rapidly changing conditions in the national and regional political-economic environment, this temporary breathing space, and the effective marginalization of state politics as a terrain of meaningful, contested popular debate, would nurture profound challenges to ZANU-PF's emerging new "consensus."

## The Dawn of the 1990s: ZANU Further Exemplifies Both Its Class Belonging and Its Global Subordination

The downward spiral in the country's "development" has been dramatic during its first twenty-five years: defining the palpable "economic decline of Zimbabwe," as Jenkins and Knight entitle their book on the subject. As they write:

> In April 1980 Zimbabwe was formed with lofty aspirations for national unity and pervasive prosperity based on economic growth and greater equity. By April 2000, real income per capita was lower than before Independence, the rates of both unemployment and inflation exceeded 50 per cent, there was unprecedented violence in the towns and the countryside, and the same government that has swept to power in 1980 could maintain its grip on power only by intimidation.[19]

The economic and related political decline began not in 1980 — there were significant if not consistent popular advances for much of the 1980s, in the face of sometimes hostile circumstances — but with the creeping movement towards neo-liberalization beginning in the late 1980s and formalized in the early 1990s with the introduction of ESAP (Economic Structural Adjustment Program).

The initial evidence of this shift was seen on Independence Day 1989, which

marked the first time that Mugabe did not explicitly invoke Marxist-Leninist principles in his annual address to the nation — and the first time mention was made
of "trade liberalization" policies for the sake of resuscitating employment
prospects.[20] But this slide became much more precipitate with its degeneration into
a firm embrace of the ESAP, as proposed and implemented from 1991. The broad
and costly implications of this formalization of the presumed core nature of mar-
ket-centric, capitalist principles have been much discussed (with reference both to
Zimbabwe and to the rest of the continent). Yet it seems clear that this was not, at
least in the Zimbabwe case, exclusively a policy imposed on an unwilling local elite
by the IFIS and the "global bourgeoisie." "Did they [ZANU] jump or were they
pushed?" asked Lionel Cliffe a number of years ago.[21] One possible answer rested
in "domestic dynamics," which for Hevina Dashwood appear to have been much
more important than international factors "in explaining the shift in Zimbabwe's
development strategy," notably "the domestic support for ESAP" by "the dominant
class, the ruling and economic elites." As Dashwood states:

> The embourgeoisement of the ruling elite has been significant in a number of
> respects. . . . Also members of the ruling elite enriched themselves, they lost
> touch with their traditional basis of support, the peasantry and the working
> class. Instead, they came to identify their interests increasingly with those of
> the economic elites. This was a consequence of the ruling elite's own increas-
> ing stake in the economy and their coming to embrace a capitalist ideology.[22]

This assessment assumes that the bulk of the ZANU leadership had ever been "in
touch" with its ostensible "traditional base" in the first place or, indeed, now
embraced "capitalist ideology" in some extremely sophisticated sense. To be sure,
much of the leadership evidenced opportunism on this front, and they also, in the
main, comfortably pursued class-strategic ends. But not all were easy with the "sell-
ing" of this new package, and real differences as regards both ideas and interests
remained within the ZANU leadership.[23]

Moreover, the costs exacted from the mass of the population by following the
ESAP option — in terms, for instance, of social service cutbacks and lost employment opportunities — were extremely high and well documented, and they were
later admitted to even by the ruling party as it sought to legitimate its poor development performance and to shift blame to the IFIS and donors. The political fallout
from ESAP was great. As Finance Minister Bernard Chidzero said, the government
found itself in a "Catch-22, caught between the politically unpopular demands of
the IFIS and the dynamics of society which cannot easily be controlled."[24] For much
of the 1990s, Zimbabwean politics was shaped by popular responses to ESAP — and
ZANU-PF's increasingly brutal attempts to come to terms with them.

At the start of that decade a second factor emerged that for a time affected,
indeed momentarily narrowed, ZANU's political options. This was the rapidly shifting

regional/international geopolitical arena. Thus, with the fall of regimes in Eastern Europe (1989), it became less easy to rationalize authoritarianism under the cover of supposed progressive claims made on behalf of "the one-party state." In addition, changes in South Africa from 1990 removed from Zimbabwe the excuse of alleged "security imperatives" said to spring from apartheid destabilization. ZANU-PF was caught completely off guard by these developments.[25] Indeed, just what mix of legitimating ideology, regulatory manipulation, and brute force would be tried by the ZANU-PF leadership to contain the regime's emerging and growing legitimacy crisis would take a few years to work out.

Perhaps, at first, there seemed little reason to hurry. Truth to tell, the political arena and any kind of real formal political participation had been long abandoned, and this was a pattern that stretched up to the late 1990s. For a large number of organizations and interests, the most appropriate way of interacting with the state for much of the 1990s was to lobby government, engage formally with what was acknowledged as ZANU-PF's privatized parliament, and play supportive "development" roles. Yet as ESAP wore on and ZANU-PF's commitment to liberalization appeared entrenched, many non-governmental organizations became less open to playing this kind of role. As for more active critics, the immediate response by ZANU-PF was typically more aggressive, using both legal and extra-legal means of attack. Thus they made changes that hurt students and academics (the University of Zimbabwe Act was altered to allow greater government meddling in university affairs); trade unions (amendments to the Labour Relations Act sought to undermine trade union unity and the national labour centre, and, not coincidentally, to also satisfy local capital); and the independent media (reduction of their very independence by a clampdown on independent journalists within the state media, for example, and by sealing off entry to aspiring new players in the key area of broadcasting).[26]

While the existing power structure continued to give ZANU privileged opportunity to mobilize (and to undermine the organizational platforms of perceived opponents), the broader contradictions of the party's project were also increasingly clear. These tensions were reflected in rising activism, particularly in urban areas that were both deeply bruised by the effects of ESAP and also more amenable to organization because of a greater density of established membership associations and better access to information and public debate. Among the building blocks of new potentially hegemonic coalitions were constituencies ranged against the political status quo, as well as others whose numbers were swollen by economic decline — including impoverished "war veterans" and marginalized unemployed youth — but whose political affiliation was more open to contestation. The stage was set for the unfolding of a new round of contestation over the direction of the state, and a struggle for survival by the increasingly beleaguered liberation movement nationalists.

## The 1990s: Increased Resistance and Intensified Repression

The growth of resistance in the 1990s is primarily a story of deepening hostility towards the status quo and of the widespread reorganization of popular constituencies around core issues of economic and political disenfranchisement.[27] In this process key organizations, notably from the national labour movement, would emerge with the deepening crisis in economic production to challenge the state and ruling party.

The combined impact of ESAP and the 1981-92 drought created an economic crisis for ZANU-PF that the government attempted to manage, initially, by calling for national-patriotic belt-tightening. But when it became clear to much of the populace that the state and dominant political grouping was being fundamentally and negatively restructured and that earlier commitments to providing equitable access to health, education, food security, land, and other resources would be reneged upon, the foundations of new popular movements outside the party were relatively quickly consolidated. A critical development here was the growing hostility of the state towards engagement with the civic sector, including with comparatively benign long-standing organizations whose main functions were to provide economic survival skills to members.

By the mid-1990s the government made it quite clear that it would tolerate only limited engagement from below, and on its own terms, and that it was willing to intervene inside "autonomous" civil society organizations in order to shape "dialogue" from both sides. This negative situation was compounded by the failure of the 1995 elections to produce any significant political party opposition — a development that would actually serve to boost the legitimacy and energy of the civics as they sought alternative means of engaging the state. A period of widespread and intensifying state-civic conflict emerged.

In the mid-1990s the state's earlier legal and coercive attacks on the student movement and ZCTU were extended, at first without comprehensive success. Amendments to the Private Voluntary Organizations Act in 1995 permitted the state to seize the assets of any specific voluntary organization, remove its executive and replace it with one of the state's choosing (even setting the salary levels for the new executive), and otherwise constrain the activities of such groups. The first point of attack was the Association of Women's Clubs (AWC), an organization noted more for its deep network of roots in rural society and its established infrastructural assets than for its political outspokenness. In the event, the AWC successfully challenged the constitutionality of the PVO amendments in the Supreme Court — and the civic became profoundly politicized, to ZANU-PF's disadvantage, in the process.[28]

More broadly, the PVO debacle offered concrete evidence that ZANU-PF's reconsolidation of authority required the restructuring of the role of popular groups into a distinctly subordinate position with regard to party and state. Thus it was at this time that leading civic organizations began raising the question of the state as an obstacle to democratic participation. They strategized about how to "discipline" the state by means of constitutional renewal aiming at entrenching fundamental rights, enforcing due process in what was perceived as an increasingly arbitrary, executive-dominated legislative process, and resolving outstanding issues of mandated participation by ordinary citizens and popular organizations in decision-making processes. The primary institutional reflection of this development was the emergence in 1998 of the National Constitutional Assembly (NCA), a strongly bound coalition of dozens of civic organizations, including leading labour, women's, faith-based, student and youth, professional, and human rights organizations.[29]

In all of the alliance-building, the ZCTU and national labour movement played a particularly important role, for several reasons. Firstly, apart from faith-based organizations, constrained as they were by their own internal politics and limited degrees of grassroots accountability, the labour movement was effectively the only national civic organization outside of the ruling party. Secondly, the movement had some degree of professional/technical presence: that is, it had a cadre of professionals and organizers (including a group of full-time national office-bearers), a capacity to undertake policy critique, a monthly newspaper (and other information networks), and several popular and widely known leaders, including ZCTU secretary-general Morgan Tsvangirai. Thirdly, and importantly, the ZCTU was the only organization of any weight that had spent considerable energy publicly addressing the failures of structural adjustment and the need for another model of national development.[30] Moreover, despite some sceptical views regarding the precise implications of ZCTU's "Beyond ESAP" program, the union had a strong education and information campaign focusing precisely on the detrimental impact of ESAP and international capital, and on the need to rein those elements in and subordinate them to national needs. All of this resonated strongly with workers, and, indeed, with other social constituencies — particularly at a time when Zimbabwe's economy was being rocked by a series of additional shocks, including revelations of massive public-sector corruption, the "buying-in" of "war veterans" with very large unbudgeted cash payouts, and Zimbabwe's costly involvement in the conflict in the Democratic Republic of the Congo.

While the labour movement's organizational strengths were key in the building of a new cross-constituency, as economic conflict grew its members' roots in the shattered economy and society helped to catalyze and focus civic struggles. Moreover, they signalled that the class compromises of ESAP had been identified and needed to be confronted. The wildcat — and later organized — "political" strikes of 1995-97 played a catalytic role. The strikes of 1996 (the public sector walked out), 1997 (unprecedented waves of mostly wildcat strikes) and especially 1998 (protests over cost of living and the emergence of "War Vet" politics within the state) were important landmarks, attracting much popular sympathy as well as fierce counterattacks from government.[31] The December 1997 and March 1998 general strikes — which shut the country down completely on unambiguously "political" issues — set the stage for a more formal challenge to the ruling party: the formation of a political counter-party to ZANU-PF resulted from the government's unwillingness to take its own offers of tripartism and inclusion seriously.[32] Thus, one year after the nationwide general strike of 1998, the Movement for Democratic Change (MDC) emerged, following a period of negotiation and alliance-building among a range of civic organizations, and with leading figures from the labour movement and NCA at its core.[33]

Faced with the appearance of a popular-sector-led political party and social movement, ZANU-PF responded by remilitarizing the state in form and content, thus raising the stakes for the democratic challengers confronting it. The first steps in this direction involved the militarization of the ruling party itself. Firstly, through the 1997 buying-in of a critical, until then unallied, group, the "war veterans" were incorporated by means of a bank-breaking and unbudgeted payoff. Secondly, the involvement in the DRC war in 1998 shifted significant political, human, and economic resources into the hands of the military and gave the military unbridled access to loot and power. The "war vets" were particularly important. They constituted a flexible category of those who both maintained unmet grievances from the past, seeking payouts from the government, and could become available as potential shock troops for ZANU's partisan purposes, once their loyalties were won. Yet as the scale of their use in coercion grew, their numbers (and in many instances, loyalty) proved insufficient. They were then supplemented by a less ambiguous and more easily manageable cadreship for delivering brute force: the "youth brigades," the first of whom were trained in state-run centres in 2001, thus became the third component of the state's militarization.[34]

The ruling party was directly transformed by this process of militarization, as Mugabe and his allies in the leadership used the newly empowered security elements against the regional structures of ZANU-PF to discipline and re-establish lines of authority within the party. This militarization soon extended to the state, with several security personnel strategically slotted into senior bureaucratic and political posts. The middle and lower levels of the bureaucracy and public service were "cleansed" too: from above (notably in the educational and health sectors) and from below (through the intimidation and "raiding" of structures by war veterans and others).[35]

Moreover, the long semi-dormant land issue also fed into this volatile politics of aggressive regime. In it, there were themes of both legitimate grievance and racist resentment that Mugabe would soon show no reluctance to manipulate. Indeed, "land" would become a flashpoint for his emerging practice. The stage was thus set for the dramatic developments of the late 1990s and beyond.

# From 2000: Land, the War Veterans, and Unvarnished Authoritarianism

The continuing political-economic crisis of 2000 and after is the direct consequence of the construction by the opposition of the real beginnings of a counter-hegemonic, popular-democratic program. The defeat of ZANU-PF in the February 2000 constitutional referendum; the defeat, in actuality, of ZANU-PF in the 2000 parliamentaries; and the widely recognized rigging of the 2002 presidential election: all reflect the deeply unpopular and failed — non-hegemonic — "national" project that ZANU-PF reconstructed in the 1990s. Not surprisingly, ZANU-PF's response was to rely increasingly on straightforward domination by intensifying the militarization of the state and key institutions within it and by closing down democratic spaces within the courts, parliament, civil service, health and educational professionals, and the media. Simultaneously ZANU-PF sought to revive its old nationalist rhetoric of populist anti-colonialism, in order to provide an ideological and moral basis, in the name of national rights and "justice," for its eradication of individual and community rights. (This line, arguably, has been more evocative for a wider audience outside of Zimbabwe than it has been inside the country, where individual rights have been so negatively and clearly prejudiced by their effective loss.)[36]

The "fast track" land reform program was at the core of all of these developments, and of the attempt, more generally, to sustain ZANU-PF's otherwise unpopular position. This is because it aimed to accommodate several functions at once: ideological (by exemplifying the supposed fulfilment of the original nationalist struggle); redistributive (albeit not to the landless, generally, but to the party/skilled elite and to the security apparatus, melding these new proto-bourgeois elements into a new alliance with common claims to valuable assets guaranteed legally by the state);[37] and political. On the political front, a key goal of the first phase of the land invasions in 2000-1 was the disorganization and marginalization of commercial farmworker communities, the constituency that played an important role in defeating ZANU-PF in the February 2000 referendum by voting in numbers against the party.

For ZANU-PF it was essential, then, to disrupt substantially the opposition's access to this constituency — and also to the electoral process itself — in advance of the June 2000 parliamentaries. This strategic and tactical imperative was underlined in the subsequent process of land redistribution, which witnessed the widescale corralling and marginalization of large sections of the former commercial farmworker community and the effective stripping of "opposition" links to the rural areas, which included not only structures of the MDC but also many civic organizations and media sources (including the independent newspaper *Daily News*, which was finally shut down by the government in 2003 under new repressive media and information legislation). Since the 2002 presidential elections, and with the much criticized parliamentaries of 2005, the stark militarization of the countryside took on various forms and visited a quiet reign of terror on many rural communities. The use of food rations is merely the latest tool in this regard.

An unprecedented degree of militarization of the state and politics was the result, along with a political economy characterized by its subordination to the survival of the ruling party. It is an extremely dangerous period, not least because militarization solves none of the underlying problems to which the democratic movement was reacting in the late 1990s. Indeed, those problems — of popular marginalization, a shrunken state sector, concentration of wealth, declining employment, and growing national debt — have been made worse by the crisis. National accounts are in a shambles; investment is nil; skilled professionals have flooded out and will not easily return; the professionalism of the state has been fundamentally and profoundly diminished; and, due to its fiscal crisis, the very reach of the state into the areas of social services has been truncated.

The "securocratic scenario" might enable ZANU-PF to hold on to power, but not to legitimacy. Yet, ironically, the party can now only hope to both stay in power and seek to rebuild the country through a further move in the direction of neoliberalization of the economy. Reserve Bank Governor Gideon Gono's desperate attempt in 2004 to get the foreign exchange rate into a semblance of normality, and the IMF's resumed visits to the country turning on discussions of how Zimbabwe could re-enter the fold are indications of this tendency. More worrying still is that this further shift to the right would be quite easily accommodated by those brought into the restructured party leadership — those whose base in security functions has bought them political influence in ZANU-PF and access to state-mediated accumulation, and who have no real connections to any popular political economic program of the kind seen in the 1980s. For their interests lie in defending the new status quo of asset redistribution, which has benefited and continues to directly benefit them, and ensuring that the whole question of redistribution and reallocation is not opened up for reconsideration now, or in any post-Mugabe dispensation.[38]

## The Future

It is tempting to see much of this negative trajectory towards authoritarianism and irrationality in Zimbabwe since 1980 in terms of Robert Mugabe's own motivations and personality. Irascible and vindictive, Mugabe also suffers from the "occupational disease" of too many successful liberation leaders: the tendency to elide the ascendancy (and the vagaries) of his own person, movement, or party with the expression of the singular "national will" of his compatriots. This trait overlaps with a tendency to present inequality (when convenient) as being primarily structured by race, not class. Yet as Linda Freeman notes:

> The membership of the coalition opposing Mugabe is primarily black as is the independent press and judiciary. . . . The reality is that it is opposition to the

regime, not the purported racist prejudice of a tiny white minority (some say now as few as 30,000 out of 11 million) and their external supporters that the government finds unacceptable.[39]

However, Mugabe's narrow racial formulations, taken together with such other crude prejudices as, to take merely one example, the bizarre homophobia that he has demonstrated on so many occasions,[40] provide a potent recipe for the current crisis.

But, what next? It is important to emphasize that much more than Mugabe, and the eventual succession to his person, are implicated in divining the possible future of Zimbabwe. For example, it is difficult to escape the conclusion that the security elements of the state and paramilitaries have been so cleverly and deeply integrated into the ZANU-PF leadership's project that it will be very difficult to disentangle and discipline them by normal, legal-juridical democratic means. Thus, Freeman contends, for the time being and regrettably, perhaps "the old forces of liberation have triumphed over the new."[41] Note, too, that it will now be more difficult, even should "new forces" eventually win, to recover the assets — land being only one — that have been looted by well-placed Zimbabweans. Yet unless this is done there can never be the kind of land reform with the genuine redistribution that is needed and that is the only way of beginning to redress rural poverty and underdevelopment.

How, then, can even the most minimal conditions of a popular-led transition to some kind of genuine "social democracy" and/or "socialism" be ensured, in the face of the array of vested interests (those of senior officials in the military, the state, and the dominant party, in particular) that feed off the status quo? For even if those conditions (not least the context, in the broadest sense, for free and fair elections) are set in place, there are no guarantees, since the MDC and other elements of opposition remain, after such a battering as they have taken, far more a diverse collection of voices and interests than an entirely coherent alternative in the wings. The process of rebuilding Zimbabwe under a post-ZANU regime would first involve constructing a consensus position on the way forward, followed by the dismantling and reconstruction of the security-fixated state. Then and only then could a more full-fledged program of redevelopment be undertaken.

Imagine, however, for the moment, the likelihood of ongoing success in the rebuilding of Zimbabwe by popular interests. What of the inhospitable global environment that exists for realizing any such effort? And closer to home, in Zimbabwe itself: what of the degeneration of the state that any progressive opposition would inherit? How does one reconstruct the state? In what guise? And with which personnel? Who could be expected to ever trust the self-declared "national-popular" state and its policies again? In short, the challenge will be daunting. Yet the means and manner by which the popular legitimacy of the developmentalist state can be re-established will have to be found.

Not that such a task should be viewed only negatively, of course. For in the wake of the obfuscations of conventional anti-colonial nationalism (now a good twenty-five years past its sell-by date) a transition period would be the time to use popular power to build in and entrench the social obligations of the state which, previously, were only adopted as a matter of transitory policy. It would be the time, too, to erect institutional and constitutional safeguards that could prevent a renewed system's easy overturning in the future. Moreover, it is also true that, while the opposition may be thinking about the return to more genuinely and humanely left policies, they have yet to take proper stock of how the progressive social services state of days gone by no longer exists in Zimbabwe. This means that, at a bare minimum, the tools of service delivery will need to be reconstructed before any more expansive set of policies can reasonably be implemented.

Yet, as Freeman concludes, "The broad coalition of opposition forces in Zimbabwe, battered and bruised though it may be by government repression, held and may still hold within it the promise of a different phase in the political life of the country and the region."[42] However, if such opposition forces were ever to be successful in both winning power and relaunching a process of genuine liberation, we would then be talking about the return to Zimbabwe of a very different Gramscianism than that envisaged earlier by Willers, or exemplified, if only in Willers's imagination, by Mugabe. For in Gramsci's own words (from his justly celebrated *Prison Notebooks*):

> With the extension of mass parties and their organic coalescence with the intimate (economic-productive) life of the masses themselves, the process whereby popular feeling is standardized ceases to be mechanical and causal (that is, produced by the condition of environmental factors and the like) and becomes conscious and critical.[43]

We have alluded to the power of materially limiting conditions in constraining any successful counter-hegemonic project (one of Gramsci's key concepts) that would seek to go beyond mere rhetoric while also transcending the present cold realities of militarization, institutionalized violence, and the sacrifice of people on the alter of the marketplace. Negative conditions are to be found not only, in the short run, within Zimbabwe itself but also, of course, more globally. Nonetheless, it is only in the recognition of the importance of subordinating the state to popular forces, of exemplifying in practice those popular forces' tangible interests and demands, and of maintaining their organizational power, grouped and focused politically certainly yet also outside of the claustrophobic apparatuses of both high-handed state and quasi-official party, that real promise can be found.[44] For the future of this kind of hegemonic project, in Zimbabwe as elsewhere, the struggle continues.

CHAPTER 7

# JULIUS NYERERE'S SOCIALISM: LEARNING FROM TANZANIA

## The Theory and Practice of (Un)Democratic Socialism

The career of Julius Nyerere as public actor can, I would argue, best be evaluated on three fronts: as a nationalist, a socialist, and a democrat — although, as we will see, these three strands of his theory and practice cannot be readily disentangled.

I will say least about Nyerere as nationalist, although it is perhaps too easy to forget that dimension of his undertakings: so much has since happened to the original project of anti-colonial and anti-racist nationalism. But Nyerere was a key player in that first generation of successful African nationalist leaders who in the postwar period refused to accept the refusal of the likes of Winston Churchill, that quintessential Colonel Blimp, to "preside over the dissolution of the British Empire." Nyerere also took the "unfinished business" of Southern Africa very seriously, placing Tanzania squarely in the middle of the Thirty Years War for Southern African liberation, as essential rear-base and as the most active of protagonists of such essential pan-African initiatives for liberation as PAFMECSA (Pan-African Freedom Movement of Eastern, Central, and Southern Africa) and, subsequently, the OAU Liberation Committee.

The nationalist moment in post-colonial Africa tends now to be consigned to the back pages of the history books. No doubt this is in part because its denouement, as prophetically foreseen by Frantz Fanon, was to prove so lacking in purpose and promise for the vast mass of Africans ostensibly liberated under its banner, and this has proven to be as true for Southern Africa, including, most notably and most dispiritingly, South Africa, as it has been for Africa north of the Zambezi. Where Nyerere went further than most, however, was in how he complemented his nationalism with his own version of a socialist analysis and a socialist vision.

In saying this I tend, up to a point, to discount Nyerere's own professions that he was not so much realizing socialism in Africa as he was realizing "African Socialism" — this despite his famous statement about socialism being "an attitude of mind" that was "rooted" in Africa's "own past — in the traditional society which produced us." When writing in this way, Nyerere might almost seem to be speaking to a postmodern audience, honouring the integrity of indigenous culture against the pull of more Eurocentric leftist formulations. And yet this whole African Socialism discourse, so often associated with Nyerere (and others, such as Senegal's Senghor), seems flaccid and, in any case, for Nyerere, to have been rather less central to his thought, in the long run, than was the (relatively) hard-nosed analysis that actually came to provide the underpinnings for his own socialist practice. For Nyerere's overall project was, in the end, nothing if not modernist and developmental (not swear words in my vocabulary, but words that nonetheless flag ambiguities to which I will return).[1] In the end, too, his analysis of actually existing Africa was at least as much Fanonist as Senghoriste, if not more so.

Take, for example, Nyerere's observations as to the nature of the new class already all too visible across the continent in its rush to power and its naked self-interest. For example, in a speech I heard him give to a vast crowd in Dar es Salaam in September 1967, he warned the people against the very real possibility that their leaders were "purchasable" ("African leaders have a price these days," he once wrote) and all too likely to become a new class of indigenous "exploiters."[2] Or take his statement in *Education for Self-Reliance* as to the likely impact of an untransformed education system on such processes of class formation:

> The educational system introduced into Tanzania by the colonialists was modelled on the British system, but with an even heavier emphasis on subservient attitudes and on white-collar skills. Inevitably, too, it was based on the assumptions of a colonialist and capitalist society. It emphasized and encouraged the individualistic instincts of mankind, instead of his cooperative instincts. It led to the possession of individual material wealth being the major criterion of social merit and worth. This meant that colonial education induced attitudes of human inequality, and in practice underpinned the domination of the weak by the strong, especially in the economic field.[3]

Other punchy and provocative statements about the potential costs of class formation (in the rural areas, for example) to the long-term future of most Tanzanians are to be found in abundance in his book *Socialism and Rural Development*.

There is, however, a second dimension of his move to complement nationalism with socialism that is of at least equal importance, and it is one that marks the interpenetration of these two projects even more overtly. Here a particularly important formulation is found in his essay "Economic Nationalism," which concludes, "The only way in which national control of the economy can be achieved is through the economic institution of socialism." Moreover, as he added, the policies that flowed from such an understanding "were not taken out of blind adherence to dogma." Rather, they "are intended to serve the society."[4]

"To serve the society." A moral imperative, then, but also a necessary development strategy, and one that is all the more relevant now, almost forty years later, in light of what we have seen as the necessity of a "renewed socialist thrust" in Africa (see chapter 2). But what, then, can be learned of such matters from the (relatively unsuccessful) record of the Tanzanian case itself in this respect? Debate will continue as to whether, on the one hand, lack of clarity in its self-definition and lack of subtlety in its practice were most responsible for undermining its prospects or whether, on the other hand, such a project had little chance of success in any case under the conditions that global capitalism offered Africa at the time. Some erstwhile supporters of Nyerere's policies have since become rather more sceptical about his approach. Thus Cranford Pratt was eventually to argue, in an obituary for Nyerere, and speaking of the Tanzanian's socialist policy measures, "Few would now claim that many of these were appropriate instruments for the development of a poor country, especially one whose public service was already overextended."[5] This judgment as to the appropriateness of Nyerere's policies is, as we shall see, very much open to debate. Here it is important to underscore the correctness of the basic premise from which Nyerere's policies flowed: the global capitalist system did not then, does not now, serve Africa well.

This is, in fact, a theme to which Nyerere would return over and over again, both while he was still president of Tanzania and equally vigorously after he had stepped down from that position and continued to play the role of international gadfly on development issues — as, for example, when he once sought to strike back at the strictures of structural adjustment with the charge that the IMF, with its "ideology of economic and social development," had become a self-appointed "International Ministry of Finance" that was forcing nations "to surrender to it their power of decision-making."[6]

Here, in Nyerere's words, is the "spirit of Seattle," well avant la lettre surely, a spirit of proto-socialist critique that, interestingly enough, also continues to inspire at least one of his daughters. Only a month after her father's death, Rose Nyerere was to be found speaking at a Jubilee 2000 workshop in Johannesburg and invoking, as part of a continuing struggle against the African debt, her father's attack of the early 1980s upon what he then called the "international debt cartel." It is the emphases and actions she invoked that, I would argue, make Nyerere's writings so important a resource for a new generation of Africans (like his daughter) as they reactivate their struggle for social, political, and economic transformation along, dare I predict it, socialist lines.

As for the question of Nyerere as democrat, much has been written of his political and constitutional innovations. Indeed, Pratt, in his obituary, was prepared to grant Nyerere far higher marks on this front than for his socialist socioeconomic endeavours. Yet in my judgment it is, in the long run, in the political realm that the most dramatic flaws in Nyerere's progressive practice were to be found.

There is a problem here, of course. I have used the phrase "Nyerere's socialism" — and we speak of "Nyerere's political initiatives" — as if these were relatively unproblematic formulations. But such undertakings were refracted through the real world of Tanzania's nationalist politics. Even Nyerere could not make policy just as he wished, as some will correctly emphasize while seeing in this fact an explanation or excuse for some of Nyerere's apparent failings, especially in the sphere of democratic practice. After all, the world of African nationalism in the 1950s and 1960s, like so many other political worlds, was a hard world, filled, albeit not exclusively, with hard and ruthless men (and I use the word "ruthless" advisedly). Nyerere, it could be argued, was a good man surrounded by many who did not quite share his vision or his high sense of moral purpose. There is something in this. I recall, for example, the struggle in the late 1960s over the succession to Mondlane with Frelimo, which was then still primarily domiciled on Tanzanian soil. The outcome, which saw the far more worthy Samora Machel defeat the Simango faction, was won in considerable part because Nyerere had the political will and craft to back down the "cultural nationalist" triumvirate, so strong within the Tanzania African National Union at the time, of Munanka, Sijaona, and Maswanya, a group that sought, initially, to have the Tanzanian state guarantee Uria Simango's ascendancy.

But this example of Nyerere's primacy also demonstrates the kind of power that Nyerere could exercise when he cared to do so. Indeed, if he is to be granted much of the credit for Tanzania's accomplishments he must also take his fair share of the blame for its more unsavoury by-products. But what blame? It has been argued, by Pratt most eloquently perhaps, that Nyerere's political project was a judicious initiative that found, at least momentarily, in the so-called "democratic one-party state" a way of staving off the divisive tendencies — ethnic, regional, religious — that elsewhere have torn African polities apart.[7] I even recall the theoretical acrobatics that Jonathan Barker and I performed in trying to make a related point about the judicious balance between the simultaneous imperatives of leadership and mass action that defined the 1970 Tanzanian election.[8] In retrospect we probably tried a little too hard to make that argument — although it also behooves me to now acknowledge the importance of the manner of Nyerere's eventual departure from politics: his charms, like Prospero's, all o'erthrown, he retired gracefully to the sidelines, opening the way to his successor while also sanctioning the transition to an electoral process far more open, at least in formal terms, than the one that he had himself fostered.

And yet there is something missing from an account so structured, if one allows for the moment the cold wind of reality to blow through it. I have personal memories, after all, of the invasion of the campus at the University of Dar es Salaam by the Field Force Unit in 1970 — the time when my student Akivaga, the Kenyan leader of the University Student Council, was dragged at gunpoint from the central administrative building, then tossed like a sack of old clothes into an army vehicle and sped away to expulsion both from the university and from the country. Nor can I forget other first-hand accounts — but by then I wasn't there, having, with many others, not had my contract renewed at the university — when protesting students were savagely beaten by security forces as they marched down the Morogoro road to town in 1978. Or take the case of my colleague Arnold Temu, a Tanzanian historian who held a Ph.D. from the University of Calgary, one of the very first Africans to earn the degree in Canada. Temu was first humiliated, even though an MP, for being one of a mere handful of Tanzanians who spoke out at the time of Akivaga's expulsion. Then, having rehabilitated himself sufficiently to become Dean of Arts at the time of the 1978 protest, he was summarily dismissed, sent into effective exile as an itinerant historian moving from Nigeria, to Swaziland, to the University of Western Cape in South Africa. Is it a kind of paternalism, or perhaps a certain brand of residual Stalinism, that made it so difficult for many of us on the left to take full account of the import of such actions?

Or perhaps something else was behind this undemocratic tick, at least in the case of Nyerere himself. Years ago I introduced a review of a book of Nyerere's writings by citing Lenin's statement about George Bernard Shaw: "a good man fallen among Fabians." I meant to refer to the studied blandness of some of Nyerere's least convincing statements about "socialism as an attitude of mind" and the like. But there may be another way of thinking about the *bon mots* of Lenin with reference to Nyerere, as I was reminded by an e-mail from a friend, himself once a Dar es Salaam academic, who reflected on what he chose to term "Nyerere's authoritarianism."[9] How to explain it? He refers to the missionary influence and suggests, too, that "the notion of 'Mwalimu' of the nation has always seemed to have a particularly missionary resonance: the shepherd and his flock, etc., perhaps combining with certain aspects of patriarchal authority in indigenous culture (more commonly remarked upon)." As he continues: "My feelings about this aspect of Nyerere also draw on observation of his style on certain occasions at UDSM when I was there: the way he handled 'critical' questions from the left, etc. — very much in the manner of the tolerant but potent teacher/leader, adjudicating what could be said and how."

Interestingly, in looking back over some of my own early writings, I found that I had made almost precisely the same point thirty years ago about the style of Nyerere in his visits to "the Hill" (the slang reference to the site of the university). But what of my "fallen among Fabians" reference? "Are you familiar with the Cowen and Shenton thesis on "Fabian colonialism?" my friend asked in his e-mail.[10]

> It gives a new and interesting twist to colonial paternalism/benevolent author-
> itarianism — the need to deliver to Africans the benefits of bourgeois civiliza-
> tion while "protecting" them from its costs (above all, divisive class forma-
> tion), not least, of course, by 'adapting' African custom to the new circum-
> stances and other modes of state intervention in and regulation of the condi-
> tions of social (and "moral") existence. I suspect that these factors/forces of
> liberal colonialism/missionary endeavour have been overlooked in the forma-
> tion of both Nyerere's ideas and practices.

These ingredients and others, then, helped to produce an unattractively undemocratic edge to Nyerere's politics. Nor can I ignore other evidence of Nyerere's fist beneath the velvet glove well beyond the Hill in Dar es Salaam. For example, in studying the evolution of the hard, authoritarian practices that characterized the politics of Swapo in exile and that culminated in the nightmarish torture and killings in that organization's camps in Angola in the 1980s, I find it difficult to lose sight of Nyerere's fingerprints all over the history that produced this outcome: in the Tanzanian state's incarceration of Swapo cadres who dared to ask embarrassing questions of their leadership at Kongwa in the mid-1960s, for example. Even more dramatic was the transfer from Zambia to Tanzania of the eleven most prominent spokespersons of the democratic movement that had sprung up in Zambia to, once again, question a corrupt and unresponsive Swapo leadership. Rounded up by the Zambian army, they were eventually spirited away, at Swapo's request, to Dar es Salaam, where they were unceremoniously left to rot in jail: precisely because Tanzania did not have the nuisance factor of Zambia's habeus corpus provisions. Here was Nyerere presiding, not very benignly, over what Colin Leys and I came to term the "Club of Presidents," a club that linked national leaders and liberation movement leaders around a common desire to stifle, often in the most brutal possible way, the seeds of any dissent that could grow outside a very limited circumference of acceptable discussion.

I'm also struck, more anecdotally, by the story that I once heard the late, estimable Zanzibari/Tanzanian politician Mohamed Babu tell at a public forum during his years of effective exile from his home country. It was a story about his own arbitrary detention during the 1970s and his own languishing, without benefit of hearing or trial, in a Dodoma prison for a number of years. One night (in his account), as the radio played on loudspeakers through the darkened prison, he heard a BBC interview with Nyerere, an interview in which, answering a direct question, the president stated that there were no political prisoners in Tanzania. Instantly, through the darkness, the voice of a fellow detainee, an ex-army officer, Ali Mafoudh, rang through the prison to the delight of the others: "*Nani sisi? Mbuzi?*" ("Who are we? Goats?") Amusing at one level, of course, but it is also the kind of textural specificity to the reality of "one-party democracy" that is too often missing from our discussions.

Even more important is how this discussion can and must be brought back to further illuminate our evaluation of Nyerere's socialist project. Of course, the manner in which the students were dealt with was emblematic enough: they were, after all and on both occasions when force was used against them, asking that the leadership act more effectively to implement the democratic injunctions and anti-corruption rules that were ostensibly in place within the national polity. And, as another example, the workers at the Mount Carmel Rubber Factory in 1973, without effective unions in the first place and then crushed — arrested, shipped off to the rural areas — were also making, in the spirit of Mwongozo, the TANU Guidelines, much the same democratic demands. But Mount Carmel was, in any case, merely the most extreme example of the tight stranglehold that TANU held over the organization of workers, women, and others on Nyerere's watch.

There is, finally, an even more emblematic moment: the shutting down of the Ruvuma Development Association (RDA) in 1969. This is not a moment that finds much resonance in most writing about Tanzania, although fortunately Andrew Coulson in his book on Tanzania does include an extended and extremely insightful appendix that gives the RDA and its demise its due weight. I say that I find the moment emblematic, although, to be honest, I'm not quite certain whether it marked a turning point in and of itself or instead merely epitomized clearly the limits of the vision — Nyerere's? TANU's? — that underpinned the *ujamaa* project in the first case. In any case, the incident does warrant a great deal of thinking.

In Ruvuma was to be found grassroots empowerment of a real and tangible kind — in the rural development sphere, in the education sphere, even in the sphere of local-level industrialization — a perfect example of the kind of "street-level democracy" whose importance Jonathan Barker highlights in his powerful book of that title — although in this case the "streets" were a few dusty roads in one of the most economically backward parts of the country.[11] The RDA also embodied a process that Nyerere himself, for a time, seemed to take strength from as he developed his overall socialist project and, centrally, his specific vocation for rural socialism in the late 1960s. Let me, to make a long and crucially important story short, merely quote the conclusion of Andrew Coulson's account:

> Given this support, the decision to disband the Association [RDA] could only be taken at the national level. In 1969 the Central Committee of TANU was reformed, to include a majority of members elected by regional party branches. Thus professional politicians from the regions suddenly achieved power at the centre of the Party. In July 1969 the new Committee met in Handeni to discuss ujamaa for a whole month, and decided that its members would spend five weeks living in some of the most advanced villages in the country, including four of the RDA villages. These visits confirmed their worst fears: the RDA was an autonomous organization receiving funds and personnel from abroad, and promoting a form of socialism which did not depend on a strong central party. If RDA organizations became the norm nationally, the professional politicians would be in a far weaker position. Moreover, by 1969 another model was available, much more attractive to them: good reports were coming in from the Rufiji valley, the first large-scale movement of all the people of an area into planned villages. This was organized by party officials (rather than by any grass-roots organization of the peasants) and gave the officials an obvious sense of achievement. It was soon to become the policy nationally, and it was entirely incompatible with the existence of groups of independent, politicized peasants, such as those of the RDA villages, which would be small, voluntary

and might well oppose central direction. On 24 September 1969 the Central Committee met in Dar es Salaam, under President Nyerere's chairmanship, and 21 out of its 24 members voted in favour of disbanding the RDA.

There was little or no planning as to how this decision would be implemented. On 25 September the Minister for Rural Development and Regional Administration flew by government plane to Songea, with members of the Central Committee, to announce the decision to the people. The assets of the Association were confiscated — the grain mill, the sawmill, the mechanical workshop, vehicles and equipment. The police were sent to take away any Association property in the villages. The expatriate staff left quietly within a few days. The villagers got on with their work as best they could. Within a week the teaching staff in the school was transferred to posts throughout the country — to Mara, Kigoma, Mbeya, Dodoma, and Singida regions. The model for *Freedom and Development* and *Education for Self-Reliance* had been destroyed.[12]

Grif Cunningham, a friend from Tanzanian days and later a colleague for over twenty-five years at York University's Atkinson College, reminds me that, just as the events described by Coulson were building up, he (Cunningham) had himself been freshly appointed, from his post as principal of Kivukoni College, to be special presidential advisor to the president on *ujamaa* villages. A first-hand student of Tanzanian rural development for many years, and not least of the whole Ruvuma experience, Cunningham was on a brief leave in Canada when the decision to close the RDA was taken. He arrived back in Tanzania to find that, with the decision to close down grassroots democracy as an essential building block of rural transformation, his job was now pretty much null and void. He spent the two years of his contract more or less in limbo as the disastrous policy of forced villagization gathered steam, tolling, as we can now see, the death knell of any democratic socialist aspiration in the country.

For me the lesson is clear, albeit, speaking personally, it has been a painful and difficult one to learn over the years. Indeed, I learned it perhaps even more as a fellow traveller of Frelimo's post-liberation left-developmental socialist project than I did in Tanzania. A socialist aspiration of some kind — a challenge to the illogic of actually existing capitalism, both globally and as it works its malign purposes on the African continent itself — must be at the core of any meaningful response that Africa is eventually to make to the crisis in which it finds itself. We learn that positive lesson from, amongst others but not least, Julius Nyerere. But, as that aspiration re-emerges politically, it must be a far more democratic project than anything Africa has witnessed in the name of socialism heretofore. In the end, and with all necessary qualifications, we learn that negative lesson, too, from, amongst others but not least, Julius Nyerere.

# Poverty Alleviation and the Revolutionary-Socialist Imperative

The abject failure of neo-liberal "reforms" since the 1980s, the malignant nature of global capitalism's continuing grip upon Africa, and the deepening conditions of poverty that face most Africans suggest that the search for genuine alternatives — revolutionary, socialist — must, with ever renewed force, find its way back onto the continental agenda. In such a context Africans will be encouraged (amongst other necessary tasks) to reflect critically upon earlier projections of heterodox futures for the continent, including the one exemplified by Nyerere's Tanzania during the 1960s and 1970s. Through a re-evaluation of the Tanzanian experience in particular we hope to draw creative stimulus as well as lessons, both positive and negative, and in doing so we focus analytically upon two principal themes worthy of attention in this regard. Moreover, even though each of those themes is central to Nyerere's own theory and practice, they also have important resonance beyond Nyerere's moment and remain pertinent, even crucial, for any ongoing discussion of the challenges that confront present-day, dependent, and poverty-stricken Africa. Thus, at the core of both Nyerere's political philosophy and his life work in the public sphere were his own imaginative takes on the theory and practice of "democracy" (think: "the democratic one-party state") on the one hand and of "*ujamaa na kujitegemea*" ("socialism and self-reliance") on the other. We explore these two themes here through further consideration both of Nyerere's own undertakings and of the Tanzanian setting within which those undertakings came to be grounded.[13]

## Democracy

"Democracy," its theory and its practice, is a contentious topic in Africa. Moreover, I am conscious that it was with reference to this issue that Cranford Pratt and I locked horns in an all-too-acrimonious debate several decades ago.[14] In this exchange Pratt professed to find in my criticisms of Tanzania's politics a preference for an approach, Marxist and/or Leninist, that was far more dangerously and self-righteously authoritarian than anything that Nyerere himself was inclined towards. Indeed, for Pratt, Nyerere's political practice was essentially democratic, albeit one that sought to shape and guide from above the consolidation of democracy in Tanzania in such a way that the country could weather the very real threats to this consolidation that characterized the immediate post-independence years. For my part, while rejecting Pratt's charge that I favoured an overtly dictatorial approach, I argued that Pratt himself actually underestimated both the authoritarian nature of Nyerere's own "democratic" practice and the very high costs that the Tanzanian president's chosen approach (and that of TANU, the party he led) inflicted on the movement for progressive change in Tanzania. Accepting, with Pratt, the prevailing framework of the one-party state, I argued that Nyerere's polity could only hope to provide a framework for nurturing democracy if popular forces —

workers, peasants, students, women — were empowered within it to act quite dramatically from below in order to ensure the safeguarding of their own interests and the maintenance of a socialist direction for the country.

What of this debate today? It remains of interest, I think, but only if, with the benefit of hindsight, we note that both Pratt and I were mistaken, in important if rather different ways, in our arguments about the nature and potential of Nyerere's one-party democracy.

Take Pratt's argument first. As suggested, he saw as being largely benign the kind of controlled democracy that Nyerere willed into place with his one-party democratic system. Thus, even in his more recent writing on Africa, in an article co-written with Hevina Dashwood, for example, he continues to suggest that it was benign at least for the early and formative years of the Tanzanian political system:

> Nyerere in the years 1964-5 devised and vigorously implemented an original set of political institutions, making up a democratic, one-party state. These institutions were intended to be sufficiently participatory and democratic as to limit the risk of the regime's becoming sufficiently authoritarian and corrupt but not so open as to threaten Tanzania's still fragile unity or weaken prematurely the integrating and energizing capabilities of the nationalist movement. The whole exercise in constitution-building was a brilliant and successful demonstration of democratic leadership.[15]

And, indeed, there is something to be said for the view that this system (especially when we assess the one-party structure in tandem with other initiatives of the time, such as the Leadership Code) successfully overrode a certain amount of intra-elite political opportunism and the negative mobilization of ethnic politics that has often accompanied it elsewhere in Africa. But it is also easy to underestimate the formidable costs that accompanied the kind of "guided-democracy by philosopher king" (or perhaps better put: by "philosopher Mwalimu"), costs to be measured in terms of the authoritarian manner in which progressive popular mobilization outside the boundaries of TANU's agreed policies was smashed.

The humbling of the workers at the Mount Carmel Rubber Factory and elsewhere in the early 1970s is an example of this problem (this being, in any case, merely the most recent stage in the enforced establishment, from quite early on, of a bloodless, state-dominated union movement in the country). Likewise the crushing of the peasants of the Ruvuma Development Association and the subsequent collapse of the project of *ujamaa* villages into a forced march towards collectivization were much the most revealing political moments of the Nyerere years.[16] Other cases come to mind: that of my own student, Akivaga, being forcefully expelled from the university, carried off by the Tanzanian Field Force Unit, because he had dared to question university administrative practices; and that of Arnold Temu, thrown out of Parliament for questioning the regime's handling of university matters, and, when later sacked from the university itself, sent effectively into exile as an itinerant academic.

As it happens, Temu's case also produced one of the most poignant moments in a research trip to Dar es Salaam in the summer of 2001. Sitting at the bar in the New Africa Hotel, I glanced to my right and eventually recognized, under the shared disguise of age, Arnold Temu himself. As it turned out, he had just returned to Dar to take up a job at the new Open University there. Further discussion brought, unsolicited, a startling statement from him: he had sworn not to return to live in Tanzania as long as Nyerere was alive. He thus offered a perspective on "Mwalimu" and his "democratic" sensibility that is, at the very least, worth recording.

These developments were at least as exemplary of the true meaning of "one-party democracy" for many ordinary Tanzanians as were the "democratic one-party elections" that those people were being encouraged to participate in — and the events actually gave the lie to certain of Nyerere's more general democratic pronouncements as well as to some of his claims to be empowering ordinary people in their struggle against nascent class formation in the country. Here I would reaffirm my judgment that Pratt was mistaken not to have taken these moments, and the underlying contradictions within Nyerere's own project that they revealed, much more seriously than he did at the time. Here, too, I would offer the hypothesis that Pratt was willing to temporarily shelve his liberal-democratic misgivings and give Nyerere's project of guided democracy too much the benefit of the doubt not only because of his own great confidence in, and respect for, Nyerere the man, but also because he took the potential challenges of "nation-building" much more seriously than he ever took the imperatives of class struggle and socialist construction in Tanzania.[17]

But what, then, of my own analysis? I still think that I saw the negative significance of these dimensions (Mount Carmel, the RDA, the university) of Tanzanian reality on Nyerere's watch more clearly than did Pratt and that I was correct to state as much. That said, my own view was that the one-party state could be genuinely democratized from within, albeit not so much by means of the intra-party competitive elections that Pratt emphasized as by the empowerment of workers, peasants, women, and students through their own self-organization within the one-party system and within the polity as a whole — and that hopeful view was no less mistaken in its way than was Pratt's.

Of course, developments at Mount Carmel, at the university, at the RDA (quickly twinned with a more generalized pattern of enforced villagization in the rural sphere) all suggested, soon enough, that a democratic transformation from below of the one-party state was not going to be allowed to happen in Tanzania. Still, slow to learn, I was to make a similar mistake with reference to the emerging situation in Mozambique, this time embracing (with, if anything, even more enthusiasm) the claim to "democratic substitutionism" made by the Frelimo leadership there — even while awaiting, once again in vain, for the empowerment from below that I hoped would provide the necessary popular complement to drive and sustain the initial revolutionary gestures and quasi-socialist breakthroughs being made from above by that leadership. In consequence of these mistakes in judgment, I have since come to think that self-organization for popular democracy requires as a necessary (although decidedly not sufficient) condition institutionalized guarantees of open debate, freedom of political and social organization (including independent trade unions, women's organizations, peasant associations, and opposition political parties) and unfettered ventilation by the media of any and all issues. This alone can provide the terrain upon which popular forces may hope to group and sustain the fight for their rights and the satisfaction of their needs. Is this a call for a greater degree of "liberalism" in Africa? It can be put that way if you like. I myself see it as reflecting a clear acknowledgement of just what is necessary, in Africa and elsewhere, in the way of democratic guarantees in order to give democratic forms the potential to be real and meaningful (that is, to release revolutionary energies and to advance class and other popular struggles) for those who need them most.

True, as Karim Hirji suggests in his recent article,[18] under some circumstances the introduction of a multi-party system can carry a society even further away from a practice of the empowerment of ordinary citizens than was the case under its prior one-party system. Perhaps this has even been the case, thus far, in Tanzania, where many citizens may have had their interests more effectively represented within Nyerere's so-called one-party democracy than through the later multi-party system. Indeed, as political scientist Paul Kaiser eloquently argues, the move towards a multi-party system facilitated in Tanzania a deepening pattern of elite corruption and opportunism and of wasting inter-ethnic and religious rivalry of precisely the sort that Nyerere might have feared.[19] Certainly, a litany of comments about such negative developments was the chief stuff of dinner-table conversation with Tanzanian comrades on my visit there in 2001.

Yet even this denouement does not strengthen the claim that one-party states empower ordinary people and advance their interests, even in the short run. While we should not on the one hand understate the importance of leadership to realizing processes of political change, or on the other romanticize the spontaneous militancy of "the masses," perhaps we have learned enough from the African experience (including that of Nyerere's Tanzania) to realize that the real, not notional, democratic accountability of leaders to their presumptive popular constituency must be a crucial part of the African development agenda.

## Socialism

The second dimension of my reflections has to do with "socialism and self-reliance" and the relevance of that strand of both Nyerere's thinking and Tanzania's practice to the present circumstances of Africa. Perhaps on this front Cranford Pratt and I were once in greater agreement than we are now, although our politics —

Pratt is more of a social democrat and I more of a revolutionary socialist in these matters — may well have given our support for Nyerere's own "socialism and self-reliance" rather different spins even in "the good old days." Still, I was surprised to find Pratt stating, in his powerful obituary for Nyerere — after sketching a list of the various socio-economic measures that Nyerere's government introduced:

> Few would now claim that many of these were appropriate instruments for the development of a very poor country. . . . These socialist measures cannot alone be blamed for the dramatic economic decline that Tanzania experienced, for these were also the years of soaring oil prices, the collapse of world commodity prices and the severe and extensive drought, which together reversed the development accomplishments of a great many African states, whatever their ideological orientation. However, they did make their own not inconsiderable contribution to Tanzania's economic decline.[20]

Too much socialism? Forgive me, but I continue to think that Nyerere's socialism, warts and all, was far closer to the heart of the matter as regards the socio-economic imperatives of a new Africa than have been the policies of almost all his successor-leaders in Africa. As Manfred Bienefeld has long argued, Nyerere's Tanzania, in terms of the principles underlying its economic policy, remains far more "model" than "anti-model." As Bienefeld argues, the Arusha Declaration, with its national-ization of the commanding heights of industry and finance, granting of greater priority to agriculture, leadership code, and restriction of TANU membership to those who supported its new strategy did not automatically increase the country's resources or its people's incomes:

> It did not even reduce the contribution which foreign capital and technology could objectively make to development, nor the need for hard work, nor the need to make wages and incomes commensurate with production and effort. What it did do was to give the Tanzanian state greater control over the investible surplus being produced in the country. It also further reduced private capital's direct influence within the Party and its indirect influence through its command over resources. As a result, it achieved greater freedom for determining a wide range of economic, social and political policies, including the country's foreign policy. . . . The primary objective of the new strategy was to permit a less uncertain, a more domestic needs-oriented and a more socially responsive utilization of investible resources. It was thought that it could elicit greater effort and commitment from those engaged in production, and that it could eventually capture dynamic external economies, through a greater freedom to direct investment towards nationally defined, long-term objectives.[21]

Of course, one can quarrel, from the left, with various aspects of Nyerere's actual "socialist" practice within the frame of these exemplary objectives (for example, Bienefeld himself emphasizes, amongst other things, the high costs of Tanzania's attempted quasi-socialist transformation of Nyerere's undemocratic propensities, not least in the rural sector). But even after Nyerere removed himself from power[22] he continued to reiterate his basic premise that the global capitalist system did not, and does not, serve Africa well. Indeed, his last book of published speeches, which primarily served to pull together many of his utterances during the 1990s, provides a running commentary on the continued subordination of Africa to global capitalism, and texts studded with references to the existence of "neo-colonialism" and the ongoing need for "economic liberation."[23] This general thrust of his later work culminates in the observation that:

Globalization has particular — and particularly adverse — ramifications for the countries of the South, with the poorest being the most badly affected. Further, I am suggesting that the capacity of developing countries separately to mitigate its effects is almost non-existent. . . . Thus, for example, the agreement signed at the end of the Uruguay Round is now part of International Law; almost all of its provisions in one way or another restrict the right of a government to protect its industries, control its development path, or discriminate by law in favour of domestic investment.[24]

This outcome is the precise opposite to that projected by and hoped for in the Arusha Declaration-related initiatives of thirty years earlier. But this critical note regarding the evolution of globalization and its negative implications for Africa was not a new one for Nyerere to strike. As early as 1980 he had given voice to similar misgivings, with one particularly dramatic (and often quoted) statement striking back at the strictures of structural adjustment as dictated by the IMF.[25] Here, as elsewhere, is the "spirit of Seattle," and of a continuing "proto-socialist critique." True, Nyerere himself seldom returned to the concept of socialism in his later writings, and when he did so it was with a rather defeated air: "Throw away all our ideas about socialism. Throw them away, give them to the Americans, give them to the Japanese, give them . . . so that they can, I don't know, they can do whatever they like with them. Embrace capitalism, fine!" And yet, since global capitalism had so little that was positive to offer Africa, he added immediately, "You have to be self-reliant."

Africa South of the Sahara is isolated. Therefore, to develop, it will have to depend upon its own resources basically. Internal resources, nationally, and Africa will have to depend upon Africa. The leadership of the future will have to devise, try to carry out policies of maximum national self-reliance and maximum collective self-reliance. They have no other choice. Hamna![26]

But isn't it difficult to see how such "self-reliance" could be realized except along socialist lines — the very point that Nyerere himself had made so forcefully some thirty years earlier in his famous intervention on "Economic Nationalism"?[27] That Nyerere could not bring himself to make that same point in the 1990s, even as he struggled with the contradictions of his own position, suggests how much ground socialists in Africa have now to make up in order to regain their credibility as plausible critics of the contemporary status quo. In the meantime, the spirit (if not always the substance) of Nyerere's own refusal, right up to the moment of his death, to abandon his efforts to parse critically the challenges that face Africa should be an inspiration in and of itself. Note, in this respect, the impact of his pronouncements on his own daughter. Note, too, the contribution of such younger African thinkers as the distinguished Guinean political scientist Siba Grovogui, who himself has come to argue eloquently, "Africa must return to the original ideal of self-reliance if it is to escape from its current crisis."[28]

I also take guidance here from the many students and activists whom I worked with during a term I spent teaching in South Africa in 2000. These were people for whom "socialism" remains a living point of reference. For I suspect that as a new generation of Africans seeks to reactivate the continental struggle for social, political, and economic transformation they will have — more than Nyerere himself seemed inclined to do in his latter years — to build upon a revitalized and overtly socialist foundation to advance their revolutionary efforts. Indeed, against Pratt's apparent assumption that "socialism" was more part of the problem than part of the solution for Nyerere and his compatriots, I would suggest that the need in Tanzania, then as now, was and is not less but more socialism. For a basic premise of African revival, as I argue (together with my co-author, Colin Leys) in chapter 1, must be that there is absolutely no prospect for sustained development for Africans within the terms dictated by the continent's subordination to actually existing global capitalism.[29]

This is, of course, the ground upon which Leys and I also rest our further case regarding the imperative of renewed socialist struggle in Africa. But one need not look only to our own writing for academic support for this premise. We can also look, albeit by means of a subversive and symptomatic reading, to the book *Closing the Circle: Democratization and Development in Africa*, by Richard Sandbrook, who begins his book with a provocative statement: "Mass poverty, economic stagnation, and ecological degradation are obviously cause as well as effect of political disorder. Nevertheless politics is primary: 'getting the politics right' is a precondition of rising prosperity as well as of the liberty, security, and services for which all people yearn."[30] This statement serves to frame his argument for the rest of the book as he explores the nature, the importance, and the prospects of (a certain kind of) democratization for Africa — until, that is, his final chapter. For there he acknowledges, in a no less startling, if seemingly contradictory, statement:

Democratic development, in Africa as elsewhere in the world, would be greatly bolstered by the reforming of economic globalization — towards what I call "social-democratic" globalization. . . . Although democratic development requires massive reforms of domestic institutions and policies in Africa, it depends also on certain facilitative changes at the global level. Chief among the latter are debt cancellation, social restrictions on global markets, and mechanisms for redistribution of income on a North-South basis.[31]

Oh, is that all? one is tempted to exclaim. Whither the primacy of the political under such a circumstance? One must, of course, give marks to Sandbrook for acknowledging that, if he is to sustain his argument as to the progressive nature of a liberal democracy in Africa (one that stops well short of popular democracy and social revolution), he cannot merely fall back on the nostrums of neo-liberalism. He sees (as many of his fellow North American political scientists do not) that it is necessary to make a case for the possible reform of a global economy that so constrains Africa economically and politically. And yet his proof, offered in this last chapter, that some kind of "social-democratization" of the global order is possible is singularly unconvincing. In any case, Leys had already, in his writing, come to this point and produced a far more accurate conclusion:

The rest of the world needs to start thinking about Africa in terms that correspond to what is really happening there. For example the "debt problem" needs to be dealt with honestly, and most of the debt written off. External support should be denied to kleptocrats and thugs in office, and given instead to popular movements for cooperation and reform. Special arrangements for African exports should be made, to sustain African export earning. Adjustment lending programmes . . . could be replaced by collaborative, but no less frank and intensive, involvement in policy-making and implementation in connection with very different kinds of long-term aid and trade packages. And so on. The problem with such ideas is that they have no attraction for those who currently own Africa's debt, buy Africa's exports or arrange official capital-assistance flows. Such ideas could come to seem rational only in a world that was in the process of rejecting the currently predominant ideology of the market. While this world must come, it is not yet in sight, and meantime the African tragedy will unfold.[32]

In fact, the choice in Africa must be between this kind of bleak admission of defeat and a much more revolutionary project of substantive democratization and real socio-economic transformation (this being the only meaningful hope for substantial alleviation of poverty on the continent) rather than on the basis of anything Sandbrook is prepared to theorize for us. For, extrapolating from Leys, I would suggest that it is much more naive to hold out hopes for the benign reform of the system of global capitalism than it is to suggest that Africans must find ways both of better insulating the continent from the main abuses of that system and of joining with others to advance the long-term revolutionary struggle to overthrow it. In short, we return once again to the notion that the alternative to the African tragedy can be, must be, neither capitalism nor social-democracy but, rather, socialism.[33]

## Popular democracy

Do we know with any precision what such a "socialism" might mean in concrete policy terms? Do we, in fact, need to know? Minimally, we can at least assert — and here we rejoin the discussion of "democracy" begun in the first part of this chapter — that the answers will spring (as emphasized in chapter 3) from the practice of "popular," not "liberal," democracy.[34] True, critics such as Sandbrook suggest that those of us who make claims for "popular democracy" are hopelessly vague in our formulations.[35] And yet how vague is it really to state, as Issa Shivji does in specifying his own advocacy of the practice of popular democracy, that it must be rooted in "positions on imperialism, state and class, class struggle."[36] Of course, such a revolutionary practice must be more open than have been left initiatives of the past to the challenge of creating institutional guarantees for free and open political interactions; to the complexities of defining a possible place for market mechanisms even while reasserting social control over the economy; to confronting the realities of gender and racially based oppressions, the legitimate claims of ethnic and religious diversity, and the imperatives of environmental sensitivity. Yet at the core, so Shivji asserts, will be resistance to capitalism and imperialism and the commitment to a reverberantly class-based politics. How difficult is it to grasp, one wishes to ask Sandbrook, that this is a universe of discourse — the political terrain of anti-imperialist endeavour, of class struggle — far removed from that of the liberal democrat?

It is tempting to leave the matter there, avoiding any pretence of having some ready blueprint for the programmatic innovations in the economic, social, and cultural spheres that a socialist movement freshly emergent as the bearer of a popular democratic impulse in Africa will eventually come to define. After all, as my York University colleague Robert Cox has put the point:

> A historical movement gets underway, it is shaped by the material possibilities of the society in which it arises and by resistance to its course as much as by the . . . goals of its supporters. [And this is why] critical awareness of the potentiality for change . . . concentrates on the possibilities of launching a social movement rather than on what the movement might achieve. . . . In the minds of those who opt for change, the solution will most likely be seen as lying not in the enactment of a specific policy program as in the building of new means of collective action informed by a new understanding of society and polity.[37]

And yet one hesitates to stop so short. For there are complexities to the long-term challenge of building revolutionary socialism in Africa that Africans, if their case is to seem plausible, must already begin to consider even as they seek to create from below the kinds of movements that can bring popular democracy and its future programs to centre stage. In this regard the positive themes that Bienefeld draws from Nyerere's original project in Tanzania are relevant. So, too, is the critique in South Africa of the ascendant ANC policies of unbridled neo-liberalism: critics in that country hark back to the earlier projection ("growth through redistribution") within South African progressive circles of an economy more centred on servicing basic needs, prioritizing internal linkages and advancing, against capital, a potentially transformative project of "structural reform" than on accepting mere subordination to the global marketplace.[38]

Moreover, in addition to conceptualizing a possible economics of "expanded socialist reproduction,"[39] the critics will also have to raise very large questions as to the relative salience of (and interaction between) local, national, continental, and global struggles for advancing novel initiatives in the policy sphere, as well as in the sphere of politics itself (movement-building; the institutional consolidation of both administrative capacity and genuine democracy).

It may well be, as Nyerere seemed to be arguing in the speeches of his later years, that for Africa the hour is growing late. But, as his own writings and his unflagging commitment to posing radical questions during that period also serve to suggest, there is still much to discuss, maybe even much that can be done.

PART III

# SOUTH AFRICA:
# DEBATING THE TRANSITION

# SOUTH AFRICA IN TRANSITION

The third part of this book subjects the transition in South Africa to even closer scrutiny, in the form, in the first instance, of three cross-sectional analyses of that process taken at different moments in time. The first (chapter 8) is from 1994, developed at the time of my presence in South Africa as a witness to the democratic elections that capped the negotiations process there. It sought to draw out, in a preliminary way, just how interested observers might begin to analyze the changes underway in South Africa and to consider what the future might hold.

Written at the very moment of the electorally sanctioned shift from a government dominated by the National Party (and led by President F.W. de Klerk) to one dominated by the ascendant ANC (and led by the new president, Nelson Mandela), chapter 8 — and the crucial analytical questions that it seeks to raise — provides a kind of benchmark for chapter 9, which seeks, in much more detail, to strike a balance sheet on the "new South Africa" created by the transition. This second cross-section was taken in the year 2000, at the end of an extended teaching assignment that I took up at Johannesburg's University of the Witwatersrand in the first half of that year. But it was also written in the wake of six years of post-apartheid freedom and of the second national election that, in 1999, marked the shift from Nelson Mandela to Thabo Mbeki as president. It paints a sobering picture of just what that transition had produced: the overthrow of racial tyranny certainly, which was no small accomplishment; but also the choice of the narrowest of neo-liberal strategies (with a mildly racially assertive overlay) by the new ANC government, a choice that seems to offer little promise of alleviating the deeply impoverished circumstances of the vast mass of South Africans. Finally, a third cross-section (chapter 11), coinciding with the ANC electoral victory of 2004, confirms this analysis.

The whimper that the "South African revolution" has become constitutes a particularly grievous setback in continental terms — almost certainly the most grievous of all, given the promise that a South Africa more economically developed and more substantially proletarianized than anywhere else on the continent once seemed to offer — to the cause of socialism. Although there are those, in the South African trade union and popular movements, for example, who continue to think and speak in terms of such a possible, even necessary, alternative, in many circles any such projection is deemed irrelevant indeed: even some of those who are sceptical about the promise of neo-liberalism are prepared to argue that, in any case, there is no real alternative.

As I said (gallows humour) in addressing various gatherings in Johannesburg, the most striking thing I discovered upon my return to South Africa in the year 2000 was just how easy it had now become to be considered an ultra-leftist! Still, as my chapter 9 also indicates, there are some clear signs to be found of disillusion with the leadership of the ANC and its questionable practices. An African population that acted so bravely to overthrow its racist masters may not sit still for long before querying more deeply its now somewhat more multi-hued ruling class.

It was in the context of both my academic pursuits and my long-time political involvements and activities that I first went to apartheid South Africa, and was able to witness at first-hand some of the horrors of the social, political and economic system of racial capitalism that tormented that country.[1] Tracing those negative impressions in an article in *This Magazine*, I was also alert to the changing atmosphere of post-Soweto South Africa. Indeed, I found inspiration, as I wrote at the time, in a moving visit to the battlefield of Isandhlwana:

> Isandhlwana was, on January 22, 1879, the scene of the last great military victory of the [then] Zulu nation against the on-rushing Afrikaner and British hordes, the latter [both] bent on seizing the Africans' land and, ultimately, yoking them to the country's industrial machine. . . . True, the military might of the imperial centre was ultimately to crush all such warriors, in Natal and elsewhere in Southern Africa, who were armed only "with lances and spears." Nonetheless, Africans had shown themselves quite capable of taking up successfully the gage of the conquerors and would be prepared to do so again.[2]

Indeed, as I wrote then, it was "hard not to hear," in the recent "anger of the Soweto students and the ANC's military actions at Rustenburg, Zeerust and Thabazimbi," the "echo from Isandhlwana, the spirit of resistance to seizure and oppression still alive in the land of *apartheid*." In fact, the example of Soweto seemed clear enough at the time to seek to rally Canadians to solidarity with the freshly escalating struggle, emphasizing that it should not be "difficult to be thankful for the fact that Africans, as they continue their fight, now 'know something of drill' and are armed, economically and militarily, with other, more effective, weapons than the spear."

No longer able to get a visa for South Africa after that first visit, I was only able in the following years to explore South African realities at a distance. Working in particular with Stephen Gelb, I wrote (in our book *The Crisis in South Africa*)[3] of the acceleration of resistances, from Durban to Soweto and beyond, that were "clear signs that the tide has at last begun to turn against South Africa's apartheid system." Indeed, invoking the work (on Europe), some decades earlier, of the eminent Italian Marxist Antonio Gramsci, we could, by 1981, already identify the existence of a veritable "organic crisis" in South Africa and document its terms at book length. Our book, banned in South Africa, was to lead something of an underground existence and for years afterwards I was to hear stories from political actors of the time of frayed photostated copies that they had read in clandestine circumstances during that period. Moreover, follow-up writing succeeded in identifying even then the continuing deep "crisis of racial capitalism," and the possibility of that crisis not only as increasingly deepening but also as being "resolved," eventually, "in favour of the popular classes" and "in socialist terms."[4]

But this was still analysis at a distance. As the 1980s wore on — a decade of marked escalation of the popular struggle in South Africa but also of increasing repression by the apartheid state — I began to feel that I needed to witness for myself the unfolding events (largely taking place inside the country as an urban uprising rather than as the guerrilla struggles familiar elsewhere in the region), whatever the necessary means of my doing so. By 1988, as I later wrote:

> I had not been to South Africa for almost a decade, unable to obtain a visa from the apartheid government. In July of that year I decided I should go anyway. It wasn't the first time I've crossed a frontier without proper papers. But in 1972 when I visited the liberated areas of Mozambique during the war against the Portuguese, I was accompanied by a column of Frelimo guerillas. This time I was on my own.[5]

So, that year, I entered the country once more, this time illegally, and spent a month there, a month characterized, as I wrote at the time, by a "few moments of tension" though even these moments seemed "pretty small potatoes . . . compared to the dangers South African activists must confront daily as they seek new ways to beat back the brutal repression of South Africa's current officially-declared 'Emergency.'" And although there did seem to be some momentary lag in the popular struggle in the wake of the regime's emergency restrictions, I saw enough, nonetheless, to understand that:

> I had stolen a month from Pretoria and I had passed close enough to the cutting edge of revolution in that country — to the people, the organizations (COSATU, the ANC, in particular), and the powerful yet undefinable ambience of resistance — to have sufficient reason to accentuate the positive. I had come away with the knowledge that, whatever the odds, the struggle to realize "transformation" is in good hands.

Nonetheless, the end of the struggle against the apartheid state was much nearer than I imagined; indeed, it is now clear in retrospect that the white regime was already seeking ways of significantly altering its tactics of survival — and that the mass of the (black) population was quite simply too much "on the move" towards freedom to be easily shunted aside. As a result, throughout the 1990s I was to return to South Africa on numerous occasions (now quite legally) to conduct research and to witness dramatic developments there.

First I was to track the "transition to a new South Africa" (with both the positive and not so positive connotations of that phrase) through the difficult years of "negotiations" between 1990 and the election that brought the ANC and Nelson Mandela to power in 1994. In chapter 8 I seek to draw together an analysis of this period that captures the complexities and contradictions of the process. For there was certainly a story to tell. Thus, during these first years it seemed increasingly clear that the ANC would emerge as the most successful voice for democratic change in South Africa, as indeed proved to be the case. But as the picture of the kind of ANC that would come to assume power also became clearer, it was increasingly apparent that the result of its ascendancy would not prove to be so great a triumph for ordinary South Africans as had originally been hoped.

This reality too I sought to illuminate, and fortunately I was granted the opportunity not merely to pay numerous short visits to South Africa but also, at the turn of the century, to spend a longer period there, teaching in Johannesburg. Chapter 9 represents the kind of balance sheet that I was then able to strike. For I was at once disheartened by the performance of the ANC and buoyed up by resistances to the exaggerated recycling of far too much of the previous reality of inequality and poverty that quickly came to characterize so much of post-apartheid policy-making. My written interventions, although crafted in part through close discussions with critical comrades in South Africa during my teaching sojourn there and well received by a number of them, nonetheless faced a very critical reception from other South Africans, also with strong records of struggle and with high repute there (notably Jeremy Cronin and Raymond Suttner). Fortunately their critical reflections did provide me with the opportunity, in the pages of *Monthly Review*, not only to reflect upon but also to further clarify, in my responses to them, my original points. These responses can be found in chapter 10.

I found in their criticisms no strong reasons to alter the rather negative picture I had come to when considering the outcomes, in socio-economic terms, that the ANC's success had overseen in South Africa and the great cost, in terms of widespread popular passivity and cynicism on the one hand and growing scepticism and some renewed resistance on the other, that the ANC's new hegemony (as reconfirmed in the 2004 elections, for example) in South Africa has produced. True, the ANC swept the polls in 2004, but the general passivity with which the bulk of the population absorbed the electoral event was much remarked upon; thus, veteran Robben Island prisoner (but ANC critic) Neville Alexander was moved to note the extent to which "South Africa has become a normal bourgeois democratic country in which the wealthy rule and the poor are marginalized."[6] In other words, for many this had become — already! — just another "ordinary" election, marking a further pacification and marginalization of the electorate rather than a deepening of its liberation.

What a contrast with 1994.[7] For there now existed merely "a disillusioned democracy" — or so Dale McKinley thought to characterize South Africa in the wake of its third national elections (April 14, 2004), noting, as others have done, that "only 56 percent (15,806,380) of all eligible voters (27,438,897) cast their ballots" — with roughly seven million people eligible to vote "who did not even bother to register." As he continued: "The national voting turnout has gradually decreased since South Africa's first, one-person one-vote elections. In 1994, 19.5 million people voted; in 1999 just over 16 million voted; and in 2004, under 16 million (remembering that the country's population has grown substantially over the last decade)."[8] Thus, argued McKinley, "South Africa has already entered into the terrain of low intensity and commodified democracy" characterized by "the increasingly devastating effects, on already poor South Africans, of massive job losses, privatized service delivery, market-led land policies, and the pursuit of [ruthless] cost-recovery mechanisms."[9]

Not surprisingly, I therefore felt confident, finally, to echo in my third cross-section in 2004 (chapter 11) the largely negative reading I had been forming of much of the ANC's post-independence project over the movement's first decade in power (at first led by Mandela and, subsequently, by Mbeki). I here view post-apartheid South Africa in comparative perspective and, sceptically, in the context of the experience of the Third World as a whole; but I also continue to take some comfort in noting that new oppositional voices are beginning to be heard inside the country — voices that point, in the long run, towards a continuing and ever deepening liberation struggle there as elsewhere on the rest of the continent. Still, as noted by Trevor Ngwane (one of South Africa's most impressive militants outside the ANC orbit, from which he was several years ago expelled), one must be careful not to take false hope from the figures of electoral abstentions or engage in "wishful thinking": for, in light of the ANC's 2004 electoral landslide (from the electorate who did bother to vote, that is), it is still far too early for such a process of disillusion to be said to have found full fruition.[10]

True, Ngwane emphasizes convincingly, "The rich are getting richer and the poor poorer in South Africa, all the major social and economic indicators [showing] that the majority of South Africans have not benefited economically or socially from the democratic order." It is indeed "clear that the ANC is pushing a neo-liberal capitalist agenda . . . in South Africa and, unfortunately, in Africa," managing only, in Alexander's words, to exacerbate the problems of the poor while "co-opting individual black wannabes into the charmed circle of the ruling elites."[11] Similarly, South African high court judge Dennis Davis notes that while, after ten years of democracy, ANC economic policy has enabled "some black South Africans to profit immeasurably," it "has not shown any prospect of changing the economic structure which disempowers the majority of the population." Davis finds this result to be wholly unsurprising given that "the ANC's dominant faction was a black middle class whose political aspirations stretched only so far as the attainment of the first stage of revolution — the national democratic revolution," and not socialism.[12]

Yet Ngwane also admits that, however important the low poll may have been, at the polls themselves no party really challenged the ANC, especially from the left or from amongst the black population, despite the manifest failure of the ANC "to fight poverty or reduce unemployment during its 10 year rule." There is no doubt, he sadly suggests, that "there are millions of workers who still believe in the ANC as both their liberator and guarantor of a better life now and in the future." Either that, or they are so exhausted by the battle against apartheid so recently won, that a new struggle, against elites of "their own," does not yet seem timely for many.

It is also true, as Ngwane states, that the ANC has cynically "used to the fullest its access to state power," while dominating the media, to ensure victory. But, on behalf of the opposition, he is self-critical as well. For "we," the new social movements, although apparently often quite significant on the ground, were remiss, he says, in calling for (at best) merely a "no vote" while failing, in this and other ways, to develop "a coherent and unified position." In consequence, he says, we merely "left an empty space exactly when [we were] supposed to deal with the issue of political power." Above all, we came to "celebrate the local struggle" in an "autonomist" manner and, in consequence, failed to develop either a larger vision of socialism or a strategic coherence in terms both of our program of action and the requisite "form of organization adequate to the task of implementing such a programme."[13]

Strong words: a reminder to South Africans that they will have to work even harder in future if they are to develop a truly hegemonic alternative to the situation that history has meted out to them. Nonetheless, Africans cannot afford, either in South Africa or elsewhere on the continent, to let time stand still. Indeed, this is a point that I make explicitly, for the continent as a whole, in a final chapter that follows this part of the book.

CHAPTER 8

# THE TRANSITION

Let us begin with a time capsule, one that, without undue anachronism, seeks to examine the terms that first defined South Africa's dramatic transition in 1994. For even at that early date it was difficult to avoid framing the discussion in terms of the ideology of the new globalism: the prioritizing of a certain definition of "democracy" and of the necessary centrality of the imperatives of "the market." As the country prepared for its first non-racial election in April, these twin terms — and the presumed link between them — had come to frame much of the dominant political discourse in South Africa. Obviously it was entirely appropriate to hail the resonance of a "democratic moment" that marked the removal of the last vestiges of the most resolutely institutionalized racist system in the world and the entry into office of Nelson Mandela and the African National Congress. But there already seemed something rather too anti-climactic about what was emerging from the "transition to democracy" in train in South Africa.

For, on the left (both inside the country and abroad), rather more had been expected from the dramatic mobilization of popular energies that, during the 1970s and 1980s, had come to stalemate the activities of the apartheid state and pave the way for "negotiations." Magdoff and Sweezy had, after all, offered their celebrated formulation to the effect that South Africa was "'objectively' ripe for revolution" and had "entered a stage of overt and seemingly irreversible revolutionary struggle."[1] Equally apposite, however, was a parallel observation, of somewhat earlier vintage, by so astute an observer as well-known sociologist Michael Burowoy, who argued, "By virtue of its history of struggles, its powerful state, its developed forces of production, the immiseration of its proletariat, the increasing insecurity of its white intermediate class, and the merging of race and class, South Africa has become the arena of the prototypical Marxist revolution."[2] Plausible though such expectations may have seemed at the time, how romantic they would soon sound.

As a less radical denouement began to emerge in South Africa, there were those who were quick to say "I told you so," in particular some leftists of various persuasions who had all along been suspicious of the ANC's own particular brew of petty-bourgeois African nationalism and quasi-Stalinist leftism. But more often than not such critics' points have been scored from abstract and rhetorical positions so far removed from the likelihood of being exposed to any "reality check" of their own as to be almost entirely unenlightening. Not that sharp criticism of the ANC was necessarily out of order. But if the lessons of the transition in South Africa are to be learned, such criticism cannot merely be extrapolated, with doubtful relevance, from some pristine set of revolutionary first principles. They must, instead, be grounded with reference to the real complexities of the situation that challenged the popular movement there — complexities dictated by the apparent imperatives of both global capitalism and the country's internal structure of power.[3] More generally, the difficulties that the ANC was already having, even as early as 1994, in sustaining an ongoing transformation of South Africa evoked dangers and dilemmas that confront the left the world over in the epoch of ascendant capitalist globalization. What distinguished South Africa, perhaps, was that certain of these "dangers and dilemmas" were being etched there all the more vividly against the backdrop of the high hopes that until so recently had prevailed.

We have discussed briefly, in chapter 3, the history of negotiations and the election-centred transition that, both before and after Nelson Mandela's release from prison in February 1990, prepared the ground for the 1994 election and its immediate aftermath. Here we will seek to set the limits of that transition in a somewhat broader analytical frame, while also seeking further to ground the analysis of the ANC's capitulation to neo-liberalism. The broader issues in particular are those evoked by the coupling of the terms "democracy" and "the market." Just what "democracy" could possibly mean in the emergent South African context calls for attention, as does the significance of the centrality of "the market," worldwide and local, in ANC thinking about the economy. How much space could be granted to the free play of "market forces" before the new government (or, more broadly, the popular movement itself) would forfeit any real prospect of dealing with South Africa's vast social inequalities and pervasive discrepancies of economic power in a productive and progressive manner? And — a closely related query — what meaning, if any, could one hope to see attached to the idea of "socialism" in an emergent, post-apartheid South Africa?

These difficult questions — which will be considered more fully in chapter 9, when we attempt to answer them from the vantage-point of the year 2000 and the new millennium — were already prominent as of 1994, when many South Africans had begun to ask them in reflecting on the profoundly contradictory nature of the transition that was unfolding in their country. Moreover, a second dimension to our discussion is of even more general relevance, one that concerns, precisely, the "ideology of the new globalism." In keeping alive a debate about transformation in their country, those South Africans who have continued to do so also find themselves forced to face down a particular "tyranny of concepts" — regarding "democracy," regarding "socialism" — quite specific to the global conjuncture of the last decade of the millennium. In reviewing their efforts we can also learn something about the challenges — conceptual, practical — that confront us all.

# Democracy, Pseudo and Substantive

While we must hail the transition to "democracy" in South Africa, how enthusiastically we do so will depend on just what, more generally, we take the notion of democracy to mean. For no word in the political lexicon is so ideologically charged; and to understand fully the import of the South African case it is necessary not only to unpack the concept but also to take note of the considerable struggle that now, in the post-Cold War world, centres on attempts to take ownership of it. At the same time, the very complexity of what was happening in South Africa during that country's transition provides us with a privileged opportunity to explore issues of crucial importance to the recasting of the left's project more globally.

By the early 1990s "democracy" had been placed on the agenda not primarily by theorists, but by peoples: in Eastern Europe, Latin America, the Far East, Africa. What is only slightly less remarkable, however, is the speed with which liberal and right-of-centre intellectuals (especially in the United States) seized upon this worldwide popular initiative, seeking not only to turn "democratization" into an academic growth industry but also to direct, even domesticate, the process — in part by taming and trimming the concept itself. What was occurring was, in fact, a recycling of "modernization theory," that earlier attempt to make the American political system — or, rather, an heroic abstraction of it — a model for the world. "In fact," stated Larry Diamond and Mark Plattner, "Liberal democracies today are widely regarded as 'the only truly and fully modern societies.'"⁴ How startling too was Diamond's further claim that democracy "demands that citizens care about politics but not too much."⁵

Much of the flavour of the democratization literature of the early 1990s is captured in Diamond's formulation. Central to his work and that of others was a reining in of the claims of democracy — a self-conscious narrowing of the definition of global democratic possibility that is consistent with emphases long current within mainstream (especially American) democratic theory. As Philip Green has argued extensively, such theory has come to collapse the notion of democracy into that of "liberal democracy," the specific type of "democracy" familiar in the West. This system is labelled, variously, by its theorists as "pluralism," "polyarchy," and "democratic elitism," but Green calls it "pseudodemocracy." He describes the system as "representative government, ultimately accountable to 'the people' but not really under their control, combined with a fundamentally capitalist economy." As he adds, this kind of democracy is "preferable to most of the immediately available ways of life of the contemporary nation-state. But it is not democracy; not really."⁶

I have cited Green here not only to reinforce my own argument but also to ground his juxtaposition of this very limited version of democracy to an alternative model: the "hidden" or "popular" face of democracy that he then espouses. From this latter perspective it is "the popular masses, not elites, who set the democratic agenda":

We would do better, at least initially, to understand this hidden face of democracy as a series of moments, moments of popular insurgency and direct action, of unmediated politics. . . . We would do better to conceive the real history of democracy as the history of popular struggle, in which the people learn, as Rosa Luxemburg put it, how to govern themselves. . . . To argue that only formal elections eventuate in representation is simply to argue by definition or to assume what has to be painstakingly proved. In this way the "democratic elitist" tends to make elections into virtually absolute trumps — the only legitimate method for ascertaining the will of the only definable cast of characters known as "the people." But when the "necessary condition" becomes the enemy of all attempts to eliminate injustices that are intrinsic to them, the good becomes the enemy of the better.[7]

"The great moments of the creative process," Green concludes, "are not parliamentary sittings or elections but strikes, demonstrations, marches, occupations, even funerals," and he proceeds to specify some of the ways in which the "direct expression" of "demands for equal rights" might burst through the constraints of polyarchy. It is in the same kind of spirit that (in chapter 3) we found the Tanzanian writer and activist Issa Shivji distinguishing "liberal democracy" (as "part of the ideology of domination") from "popular democracy" — the latter seen to be "an ideology of resistance and struggle of the large masses and popular classes of the people." As he further specified the point:

Democracy, for most of us [African intellectuals], whether we like it or not, is associated with the organization of the state and government structures (Parliament, courts, parties, accountability, elections) rather than a summation of the experience of struggles of the majority. Of course, these are not mutually exclusive: indeed we will all swear by our political science text-books that they are not. And yet in practice, and in our theoretical and political practices, we rarely let loose of the apron strings that bind us to imperialism or the African state or both, we rarely deviate from liberalism; and in our case therefore compradorialism.

For Shivji, this merely demonstrates "a total lack of faith in the masses of the African people."[8]

What writers such as Green and Shivji are grasping for is a definition of democracy geared to facilitating and/or expressing the widespread mobilization of the hitherto powerless against the structures of their political and socio-economic subordination. Identifying the programmatic substance of such a project (socialism?) in the face of the kind of difficult-to-discipline global capitalism that is now so dominant is, needless to say, no easy task. It is also the case that the practical day-to-day modalities of such a politics are much easier to conceptualize for an insurrectionary phase (South Africa, 1984-86, for example)[9] than they are for a situation of more "normalized" politics: finding the ways and means of consolidating the practice of "popular democracy" against the pull of routinization does dictate a more complicated search for entry points for struggle when that task must proceed within relatively stable institutions. Still, that the dominant voices seeking to frame the discourse of democracy in the current global conjuncture are not those of the Greens and Shivjis has helped to render the granting of any such expansive meanings to democracy that much more difficult to conceive of, let alone to consolidate in practice.

There is, in sum, a very conservative political charge to the bulk of the literature on the much-heralded "global resurgence" of democracy. Yet it is not only conservatives who have introduced the narrowest of premises into their discussions of what a transition to democracy must now mean. For instance, Adam Przeworski's model of a "necessary" compromise between "reformers" and "moderates" at the expense of "hardliners" and "radicals" in the "transition to democracy" does provide certain substantive insights into the transition that South Africa itself has been experiencing, but how sanguine can we be about Przeworski's conclusion that "democratic institutions must remain within narrow limits to be successful" because "chaos is the worst alternative of all"?[10] And if the very process of negotiations did indeed witness a kind of taming of the impulse towards genuine democratic empowerment in South Africa (with "moderates" within the popular movement having found it possible to rein in the "radicals" in the name of a "realistic" politics), should we not consider this to be a particularly sorry outcome — especially given the nature of the process of struggle that had brought South Africa to the brink of its "transition" in the first place?

## Elite-Pacting vs. Popular Mobilization

For this process that had led to this transition had been defined, over the previous two decades, by a remarkable series of those "great moments of the creative democratic process" that Green identifies as being so important: "strikes, demonstrations, marches, occupations, even funerals." Without doubt, mass action — first stirring in Durban and Soweto in the 1970s, then peaking in the near insurrection of 1984-86, and, ultimately, reviving in the late 1980s in the very teeth of the government's imposition of draconian emergency regulations — was the key factor forcing the apartheid government onto the path of "reform." Moreover, it remained an important ingredient of the negotiations round as well; massive popular demonstrations demanded more rapid advance towards a democratic outcome punctuating the negotiations at various key points during the 1990-94 period.

This political process had also meant the creation in South Africa of an infrastructure of popularly rooted groups and organizations quite beyond anything seen elsewhere in Africa. Perhaps the trade unions were closest to centre stage in this, but civic associations, youth groups, education-focused bodies, and women's organizations were all part of it. It is true that, especially beyond the union sphere, one could easily overstate the actual efficacy in organizational terms of many of these initiatives as well as the degree of internal democracy that, in practice, they manifested. Nonetheless, the mounting of such initiatives — which came to interface actively with the ANC — represented a major political accomplishment.

Moreover, this broad process of mobilization seemed to promise the possibility that a populace so organized would be able to continue to advance its claims in the post-apartheid period — even, if necessary, against the claims of its own ostensible political vanguard. There also developed, alongside this kind of practical politics, an important theoretical practice, a mode of discourse that served, simultaneously, both to encapsulate and to reinforce the most positive attributes of South Africa's emergent Mass Democratic Movement. Created as much by those directly engaged in the practical, day-to-day political struggles as by professional intellectuals, this discourse highlighted a quite radical notion of the importance of "civil society" (of "popular, progressive civil society," of "working-class civil society") to the ongoing struggle in South Africa, both before and after any elections that might occur.

At the same time, there was a strong counterweight within the process of negotiations against any such positive pressures as were coming from below. This counterweight lay in the threat posed by both the potential for "chaos" and the exercise of countervailing power by "important interests," and it came to loom large in the eyes of ANC negotiators. Thus the hard right, both white and black, undoubtedly demanded attention, as it threatened, by word and by increasingly evil deed, to undermine the viability of any possible transition to democracy. This continued to be true right through to 1994. Nor was de Klerk (the ANC's main interlocutor during the negotiations) an innocent bystander to all of this. Opinions still differ as to how to interpret the role he played. Still, it seems safe to say that, throughout the negotiations, he proved himself to be a "reformer" of a very particular type. Moved by circumstances beyond his control to a level of concession — the release of Mandela, the unbanning of the ANC, the entry into negotiations — to the democratic forces far beyond anything deemed acceptable by his predecessor P.W. Botha, he nonetheless continued, deep into the negotiations process, to try to have it both ways: appearing to offer a measure of reform sufficiently expansive to possibly co-opt ANC "moderates" into settling for a "liberal capitalist democracy" while also attempting, however incompatibly, to safeguard certain essential features of white minority rule. No mere prisoner of his police and military (although these indeed proved to be potentially crucial wild cards in the situation), De Klerk seemed himself to have sanctioned wide-ranging efforts to seriously weaken the ANC.

How are we to evaluate the compromises embraced by the ANC and produced by such varied emanations of right-wing intransigence? In 1994 it was still too early to say what the cost, if any, might prove to be for acceptance of a

"Government of National Unity" (GNU) principle that would lock the ANC — for five years (should it win the election) — into working through a cabinet compulsorily inclusive of its chief rivals. It was too early to say, as well, whether too many concessions were being made in the direction of regional decentralization; or in ensuring the continuity of the present civil service. Certainly the ANC was, in the context of such concessions, a very long way from "smashing the state."

True, Joe Slovo, in an overview of the process written at the time, could insist that these concessions be measured against how very much more both "reform" and "hardline" forces were actually demanding from the ANC going into the process.[11] Perhaps, he seemed to suggest, historians would come to grant the ANC considerable credit for having managed to produce, out of a set of rather unforgiving circumstances, the relatively favourable constitutional results that it did. And yet it was already apparent by 1994 that the main costs of the form that negotiations took lay elsewhere, in any case: in the crippling compromises in the sphere of long-term economic policy and, more immediately, in the political price exacted from the popular movement by the very nature of the process that produced the new constitutional guidelines set in place that year. In Slovo's opinion, this political price would not be high. Indeed, he presented negotiations as offering "the possibility of bringing about a radically transformed political framework . . . which will result in the liberation movement occupying significantly more favorable heights from which to advance" towards "real people's power."[12]

Nonetheless, others were far less confident that the kind of politics that came to characterize the negotiations process could actually provide so promising a stepping stone for the further mobilization of continuing popular democratic struggle. Such critics feared that there were already too many within the ANC leadership who appeared to be more comfortable with the kind of elite-pacting politics (polyarchy-in-the-making) that the negotiation process had encouraged than with any conception either of "real people's power" or of deep-cutting socio-economic transformation. In addition, the brand of horse-trading that the prospective GNU and other new structures seemed likely to encourage in the future promised to reinforce such tendencies. Wasn't there already prominent within the ANC a discursive practice that could lend itself quite easily to a narrowing of the political agenda, a conceptualization that, historically, had juxtaposed a "national-democratic" phase of struggle to any more transformative/socialist one, while also firmly prioritizing the former? How dangerous might that precedent become in the next round?[13]

The novel pressures upon the ANC to identify "upwards" that came from within the worldwide and local class systems were also known to be strong. That there should be those within the movement who would be inclined to so identify need not surprise us. After all, it was well known, even by 1994, that many within the ANC-in-exile had all along harboured aspirations that were petty-bourgeois nationalist rather than socialist in character. Moreover, these people, upon their return from exile, had been joined in the movement by others of a similar opportunist stripe; indeed, as the elections approached, an accelerating bandwagon effect drew even more of such elements to the ANC's colours. These are not actors who, if "democracy" were to prove to be the name of the game, would be terribly sorry to see the norms of liberal democracy pre-empt those of a more popular variant.[14] And, of course, the same was true of the various international forces — the IMF and World Bank, the corporate sector and international aid community — that now crowded in upon the ANC from all sides.

There was also the irony that even some of the more ostensibly progressive cadres within the leadership ranks of the ANC could find themselves lending untroubled support to tendencies hostile to a project of full-blown democratic empowerment. After all, like all Southern Africa liberation movements, the ANC had had its own internal political practices moulded, at least in part, by the hierarchical imperatives of organizing for military purposes and protecting security in a quite hostile environment. Moreover, this transpired within an exile milieu that surrounded the movement on all sides with few models besides the authoritarian practices of both conventional nationalist regimes in the host African countries on the one hand and the Stalinist regimes of their Eastern European backers on the other. Many cadres formed by this experience were, on their return from exile, at least as likely to be drawn (even if "for the very best of reasons") towards top-down, hierarchical models of change management in which the populace is directed, disciplined, "mobilized" as they were towards the rather messier business of helping facilitate more direct and unmediated expressions of popular energies and class demands. There were, in short, still lessons in democracy to be learned not merely by the ANC's opponents but, across a broad spectrum, by many within the ANC itself — in particular, as regards the modalities of "popular democracy."

It is the case that some critical discussion did continue, in tandem with the negotiations process, as to whether the ANC should not be pushing harder, not only seeking to realize a less compromised constitutional outcome but also consolidating a much more militantly democratic politics. Thus, within the ANC itself, some expressed the fear that concessions made by the party threatened to gut the capacity of a post-apartheid government to sustain any serious attack upon the severe socio-economic inequalities that continued to characterize South African society. Near the midway point of the negotiations, for example, senior ANC cadre Pallo Jordan responded to the movement's own "Strategic Perspective" document by suggesting that the ANC might have lost track of its broader goals of democratic transformation and begun to make the lowest common denominator of constitutional agreement an end in itself.[15] Of course, there was a plausible, if predictable, response to this: a claim that Jordan risked substituting mere rhetoric for political realism. Jeremy Cronin, South African Communist Party activist and one of the most prominent theorists in the camp of the democratic movement, wrote in criticism of Jordan: "To be sure, there are sometimes epic, all-or-nothing moments in politics. But when one is simply not in such a moment, then all-or-nothing tactics are liable to yield . . . nothing."[16]

And yet it was also Cronin who raised, during this same period, related questions regarding the dangers of a closely controlled mass action during the negotiations process.[17] As Cronin argued:

> It is critical that in the present we coordinate our principal weapon — mass support — so that we bring it to bear effectively upon the constitutional negotiations process. . . . Democracy is self-empowerment of the people. Unless the broad masses are actively and continually engaged in struggle, we will achieve only the empty shell of a limited democracy.[18]

For Cronin, as for others, it was the fact that powerful popular energies were continuing to bubble up from the base in South Africa that gave politics there its peculiarly vibrant potential. Hence the crucial question: would the emerging "democratic practice" of the ANC actually permit these energies to become focused in such a way as to drive forward a process of genuine social transformation? Time alone would tell, although it is sobering to note in this respect a comment at the time by another prominent SACP/ANC militant, Raymond Suttner. For Suttner, in reflecting on Slovo's celebration of the outcome of the negotiations process, could write: "JS [Joe Slovo] is absolutely right to underline the massive victory we have scored at the negotiations. He fails, however, to mention that the past three years have also seen the transformation of our organizations, particularly the ANC. This transformation could have a serious, long-term impact."[19]

Need the drive for genuine democratic empowerment in South Africa have found itself to be quite so compromised by the logic of negotiations and electoralism as this? And what, in any case, might such empowerment be brought to mean in practice — beyond these still relatively abstract invocations by Cronin and Suttner? Obviously, with respect to such questions, it would prove important to keep an eye on various concrete policy spheres in order to monitor whether the ANC was actually facilitating active assertions by the popular classes to redress their grievances and advance their long-term interests in structural change. For example, an analysis of the time of developments in the agrarian sphere served both to give some sense of what a substantive politics of empowerment might begin to look like, while also serving to identify some quite unsettling straws in the wind.[20]

Thus Henry Bernstein, after a careful analysis of the need for dramatic changes in the allocation of land and rural opportunity, suggested the parallel need for grassroots mobilization to make this possible:

> It is the political dynamic itself that provides a radical and potentially transformational content to any process of land and agrarian reform, rather than the scale of the immediate gains. The latter — how much land is redistributed in the foreseeable future, the conditions of redistribution and of the development

of black farming — will be constrained by both the general balance of forces, and the time it takes for the rural masses to develop their political capacities and cohesiveness. However, the limits imposed by the balance of forces in any conjuncture of struggle are only known by pushing against those limits, and developing the capacity of popular social forces itself shifts the balance and extends the terrain of political possibility.

The perspective outlined here is not a fantasy of immediate and total ("revolutionary") transformation: it envisages individual (if not absolute) title to land and individual or household farming, not socialist property or production. It is rather an assessment of the politics of potential "structural reform" . . . as opposed to what is otherwise on offer: a limited "deracialization" of land and farming designed by experts, delivered by the state, and driven by the logic of the market. This path excludes the agency of those whose daily struggles for existence bear the deepest imprint of apartheid.

As Bernstein concluded his article (its themes dovetailing in many ways with those of mine here), the "energies, hopes and ideas" of these thus-far excluded people are "the most important political resource for 'structural reform' in the countryside." And yet, while Bernstein asserts that "it is not too late for the ANC to start to connect with" such energies, the overall thrust of his analysis found him less than confident that the ANC would actually do any such thing.

In 1994 it seemed wise, though, not to overstate the negative case. Would it really be so easy for those who had come of political age within an ANC culture to downplay the massive population of genuinely deprived people in South Africa? And didn't this population have other organizational and ideological resources for pressing its own claims in any case? A note of encouragement, for example, was the moment late in the negotiations process when COSATU demonstrated to ensure provisions favourable to labour (regarding lock-out clauses and other issues) in the draft constitution. In Slovo's words, "There cannot be the slightest doubt that the COSATU intervention, and the massive COSATU led demonstration outside the World Trade Centre, at the beginning of November [1993], has a positive outcome on the negotiating process." Moreover, as Slovo continued, "the capacity for this kind of pressure will remain critical in the coming weeks, months and years."[21]

Some would see another promising sign of popular empowerment in the burgeoning, as part of the ongoing emancipation process, of forums for sectoral struggles — for, in effect, sectoral democratization — that grew up alongside the more high-profile negotiations forums (the Convention for a Democratic South Africa [CODESA] and Kempton Park negotiations) that had constitutional democratization on their agendas. The role played by the trade union movement seemed to be particularly promising in this regard. The alliance between the ANC and the country's largest trade union, COSATU, had been crucial to underwriting the politics of transition in South Africa. And recent efforts to consolidate a "Reconstruction Accord" between unions and the ANC represented a front on which COSATU had sought to extend that alliance in order to consolidate a workers' agenda for a post-election government.[22] But a second front upon which the unions now attempted to flex their class muscle more independently was the tripartite (unions-business-government) venue of the National Economic Forum, a forum that was soon to become, in the post-election period, the National Economic Development and Labour Council (NEDLAC).

Although critics from quite early on saw participation in such forums as representing a possible slide by the unions in the direction of co-optation and corporatism, the unions themselves believed that the forums provided an important context within which they could assert themselves. They argued so despite the evidence that some ANC leaders seemed uneasy about the establishment of this kind of autonomous realm of economic decision-making — however important such activity might have been in the past as one front of popular challenge to the old system. Would not such ANC leaders prefer, once in power, to draw national level decision-making back more firmly into the hands of the ministries they were about to inherit? Certainly, activists in the education sector expressed parallel concerns. ANC cadres returning from exile tended to turn for advice more readily to educational technicians (from the South African Committee for Higher Education, for example) than to the National Education Conference (born in the fires of mass struggle in the early to mid-1980s): there was already a suspicion that the nascent Education Forum — designed to facilitate, precisely, a sectoral democratization of the education sphere — was losing pride of place amongst the ANC leadership to a more technocratic, government-centric definition of future education decision-making.

The fate of the forums seemed likely to be one significant index of the strength of impulses towards "popular democratization" in the new South Africa. So too did such signs of unease regarding the likely strength of the ANC's long-term transformative intentions as were already discernible. Here the floating at the National Union of Metalworkers' 1993 Congress of the idea of launching a workers' party in order to keep progressive positions more firmly on South Africa's agenda offered a suggestive case in point. Nonetheless, whether wisely or not, most trade union efforts were still, in 1994, very much directed towards struggles within the ANC-led Alliance itself (ANC, SACP, and COSATU) in order to safeguard progressive policy initiatives at the government level — with COSATU's decision to place a number of its most prominent leaders on the ANC's electoral list providing a clear example of this strategic direction.

Not that the unions were the only actors in this process. Indeed, there were even some on the left who feared that the better organized workers could take on some of the trappings of a "labour aristocracy" in the next round in South Africa — unless, that is, they were to become ever more integrally linked to other South Africans, in the rural areas, in the townships, in the shantytowns, as part of a much broader alliance of social forces.[23] Hence the importance of Bernstein's preoccupations with the politics of the agrarian question. Hence the concern as to what kind of mobilization for progressive and transformative purposes would prove possible in the townships (whether through the existing civic associations or their successors, whether within the fold of the ANC or outside it). And what of other assertions — on the gender front, for example[24] — that also bore democratic promise: the promise both of helping to confirm the continued existence of a popular, potentially hegemonic, political project and of contributing to the further deepening of it?

In short, there seemed to remain a strong popular pull — from the streets, the countryside, the shop floor — on the ANC. Would the party come to warmly embrace such pressures from below, even to further shape them towards progressive ends, as a means of beating off demands from the right and from the global capitalist community? Or would it merely act to demobilize such pressures and embrace instead a rightward trajectory? In 1994 it was still tempting to find promise in Mandela's warning to workers gathered at the 1993 COSATU annual congress to be "vigilant" — to make sure that the ANC "delivered the goods" after liberation, to watch out for signs of betrayal.[25] True, Mandela's words of warning could be interpreted as an invitation to trade unions merely to act as one more pressure group within a pluralistic model of democracy (even if the language seemed to promise something more fundamental). But they also suggested that it might be a little too early to despair of the possibility of a genuine struggle within the ANC over the brand of democratization that would be encouraged in the new South Africa.

If such a struggle could occur, many believed, it might yet produce a more promising outcome than one influential South African analyst, Steven Friedman (a writer who sought to view South Africa through the optic of the orthodox transition literature), envisioned at the time. In a symptomatic article, "South Africa's Reluctant Transition," Friedman drew centrally on a distinction that juxtaposed "two strains within African nationalism — the 'liberal democratic approach' which seeks pluralist democracy, and the 'national approach,' which seeks 'national self-determination,' defined as a state in which 'the citizens of the nation are ruled by kith and kin.'"[26] For Friedman a temptation to drift to the latter pole, one risking an authoritarian outcome, was very much a part of the ANC's political baggage. Nor was this an entirely mistaken preoccupation on Friedman's part: there were indeed lessons in democracy that the ANC itself needed to learn. Yet note the narrow terms in which Friedman then continued his argument: as anything resembling "popular democracy" aimed at the redress of socio-economic inequality is allowed to drop from the equation, the choice facing South Africans is narrowed by sleight of hand to one between liberal democracy on the one hand and nationalist authoritarianism on the other, full stop.

Moreover, since these are the only resting places on Friedman's spectrum, he frees himself to suggest that the very best that can possibly be achieved is that "leaders . . . strike a compromise that is finely balanced and sturdy enough to prevent destabilization from both left and right and then to maintain support for it through a series of severe trials." But what, one might ask, of the probable costs to vast numbers of South Africans of only going so far as to establish a conventional liberal democracy? Are the socio-economic inequalities that persist merely to be endured in the name of prudence and realism and never, under any circumstances, to be "destabilized" from the left? So Friedman, like too many other contemporary students of the South African transition, seems to imply — having, like them, defined right out of his analysis the possibility that there could exist an alternative, more egalitarian form of democratic empowerment.

## Stigmatizing Socialism: The Market as Common Sense

Why was this foreshortening of democratic expectation occurring, even in a country like South Africa where something much more liberating might have been expected? Self-evidently, it had something to do with the renewed strength of the political right in the post-Cold War epoch. But it also had something to do with the state of the left itself. Consider the question: towards what end would any alternative, more "popular," form of democracy need to be mobilized? The conventional answer would once have been unequivocal: towards socialism. Now few people seemed quite so sure.

True, it is difficult to avoid the power of Marx's argument regarding democracy in "On the Jewish Question" — an argument that underscores the possible discrepancy between the appearance of formal political equality on the one hand and the reality of class inequality on the other. For Marx, "Political emancipation certainly represents a great progress. . . . It is not, indeed, the final form of human emancipation, but it is the final form of human emancipation within the framework of the prevailing social order." Still, the freedom that political emancipation embodies serves to reduce "man" to "abstract citizen," to an entity "infused with an unreal universality." In contrast, Marx states:

> Human emancipation will only be complete when the real, individual man has absorbed himself into the abstract citizen; when as an individual man, in his everyday life, in his work, and in his relationships, he has become a species-being; and when he has recognized and organized his own powers as social powers so that he no longer separates this social power from himself as political power.

The main effect of political revolution in the modern (capitalist) world is therefore paradoxical, in Marx's view: it has merely helped to "abolish" (or, perhaps better put, to obscure) "the political character of civil society," thereby "emancipating [that] civil society from politics and from even a semblance of a general content" while "dissolving" the social relations that characterize it (notably class relationships) into apparent congeries of (abstract) "individuals." Marx came to see the overthrow of the particular system of class power that so deeply shaped civil society under capitalism as necessary to giving real, human substance to any more narrowly defined political emancipation.[27]

Of course, some on the left have come to resist forging the link between democracy and socialism that seems to follow from such an analysis. Take, for example, the polemics of John Keane, who sees the aspiration towards socialism as an impediment to realizing progressive outcomes. Thus, for him, the demand for socialism, in its desire to "destroy the division between civil society and the state," is "undemocratic," while "the demand for democracy is much more subversive because it calls into question all heteronomous forms of power."[28] In this way Keane also seeks to impress upon us — as do Ernesto Laclau and Chantal Mouffe in making related claims for the centrality of a non-foundationalist "radical democracy" — the danger of allowing any excessive emphasis on class struggle to silence consideration on the left of other liberatory assertions (premised on gender and racial claims, for example).

But surely they are overstating the danger. In this regard Andrew Gamble's riposte to these remarks by Keane (as well as to related arguments by Laclau and Mouffe) is more convincing. Gamble associates himself with critics who are "disturbed" about the "sweeping condemnation" of classical Marxism expressed by these theorists — "and how flimsy and rudderless is the radical democratic politics they are proposing." As Gamble asserts, "In order to give [their argument] some coherence, they still have to draw on the concept of socialism and the socialist tradition." And "a socialism . . . without a workers' movement, without class analysis and class politics would hardly be socialism at all." This tendency "would become just another variant of liberalism."[29] To think otherwise, he implies, would be to cede far too much ground to those practitioners of capitalism who do know just how much their own class interests drive their undertakings and would like nothing better than to see class struggle downgraded in importance. Then too, Marx's analysis of the logic of capitalism is more relevant than ever in explaining the dynamics and depredations of capital's global reach. As Perry Anderson argues, "Intellectually, the culture of the Left is far from being demobilized by the collapse of Soviet communism, or the impasse of Western social democracy." After all, he points out, "The central case against capitalism today is the combination of ecological crisis and social polarization it is breeding," especially on the global plane. "Market forces contain no solution to these."[30]

Still, things are not quite that simple either. After all, the real drag on the left's self-confidence regarding the claims of "socialism" is not primarily to be found in the kinds of considerations raised by Keane or Mouffe and Laclau, or indeed in the absence of a convincing critique of the workings of "actually existing global capitalism." It lies more fundamentally in a generally decreased confidence about the possibility of realizing, in practice, a socialist alternative to such a capitalist system. Thus Anderson qualifies his remarks with a sobering reflection:

The case against capitalism is strongest on the very plane where the reach of socialism is weakest — at the level of the world system as a whole. . . . The future belongs to a set of forces that are overtaking the nation-state. So far they have been captured or driven by capital — as, in the past fifty years, internationalism has changed sides. So long as the Left fails to win back the initiative here, the current system will be secure.[31]

Even more pertinently here, we can return to Przeworski's grimly "realistic" analysis regarding the necessary pull towards the centre/right in most, if not all, democratic transitions. Przeworski frames this conclusion in the belief that only a very limited room exists for socio-economic manoeuvre in "Southern" settings — that "capitalism is irrational" and "socialism is unfeasible."[32] If socialism has long been the dream of those on the left, many will see in Przeworski's stark formulation the very essence of their present-day nightmares. What, indeed, can the democracy of "popular struggle" possibly mean within the constricting circumstances dictated by an all too arbitrary but enormously powerful global capitalist system?

It is cold comfort to realize that liberal-democratic thinkers have themselves virtually no resources within their own chosen framework with which to theorize the implications for them of the power relations of the new global economy; their response, as we have seen in chapter 3, is simply to ignore the issue[33] and to proceed with the further thinning out of their definition of democracy. The left, of necessity, has had to take the question of global socio-economic structure much more seriously as a constraint on its own hopes for meaningful democratization — not least with reference to the South African transition. Must we then lapse into Pzreworskian pessimism in the regard? In the first instance, it has to be acknowledged that there is absolutely nothing straightforward about developing a progressive economic policy, in South Africa or anywhere else for that matter, under current global circumstances. No one but perhaps the more obtuse of ultra-leftists can any longer expect a revolutionary alternative to emerge full-blown or very quickly anywhere on the globe — even if South Africa, with its running start of mass mobilization and popular contestation, did seem momentarily to be better positioned than most to keep the revolutionary flame alive.

Moreover, by 1994 one could already sense that the momentum that might at least have sustained a more subtle and apposite struggle for transformation was in the process of being lost even in South Africa. What, for example, were we to make of a remark like that of senior ANC negotiator Thabo Mbeki when he stated that, on economic matters, the National Party's positions "are not very different really from the position the movement has been advancing"?[34] Or of the resonance of the following smug report in a 1993 issue of South Africa's *Business Day*:

We can look with some hope to the evolution in economic thinking in the ANC since the occasion nearly three years ago when Nelson Mandela stepped out of

prison and promptly reaffirmed his belief in the nationalization of the heights
of the economy. By contrast, after delivering his organization's anniversary
message last week, Mandela — supported by SACP chairman Joe Slovo — went
out of his way to assure a large group of foreign (and local) journalists that
the ANC was now as business-friendly as any potential foreign investor could
reasonably ask. He indicated further that ANC economic thinking was now
being influenced as much by Finance Minister Derek Keys and by organized
business as anyone else.[35]

A plethora of statements by ANC leaders then rubber-stamped this apparent acceptance of the centrality of capitalist impulses to ANC economic plans — from the
almost slavish solicitation of foreign and domestic investment and the easy
acknowledgement of a key role for the IMF and the World Bank to the sometime
temptation to reduce the concept of black empowerment to the question of creating a black business class.[36]

Make no mistake: this was what one brand of "realism" had come to mean in
South Africa by 1994. True, there were counter-tendencies — and ones that had
some real social weight behind them, notably within the circles of organized
labour. While recognizing as naive the notion of some immediate revolutionary
seizure of economic power and subsequent dictating of an entirely new logic to
the South African economy, the bearers of such counter-tendencies had begun to
manifest a conviction that class struggle over social-economic outcomes could and
must continue in South Africa. They sought to blend "realism" and militancy in a
way that might, cumulatively, begin to box in the prerogatives of capital and
slowly but surely tilt the balance of power away from capital in some recognizably
socialist direction. At its best, as I have argued elsewhere (drawing on the writings
of the early André Gorz and Boris Kagarlitsky), such activity began to exemplify a
revolutionary practice that could be characterized as "structural reform"[37] — a possible project that others in South Africa (albeit with differing emphases on the revolutionary content of such an approach) have labelled "radical reform" or "revolutionary reform."[38] For example, the public pronouncements of such South African
political practitioners as trade union leader Enoch Godongwana and ANC activist
Pallo Jordan captured this kind of sensibility; and in 1994 Mandela himself stated
that he did "not believe South African businessmen could be trusted to develop a
post-apartheid economy without state intervention." As he said:

> We are convinced that left to their own devices, the South African business
> community will not rise to the challenges facing us. . . . While the democratic
> state will maintain and develop the market, we envisage occasions when it will
> be necessary for it to intervene where growth and development require such
> intervention.[39]

Of course, just what meaning contending class forces could be expected to breathe into such formulations in the post-election round in South Africa remained an open question. By 1994 this was already a controversial matter on the left in South Africa; a number of economic planning exercises that were particularly worthy of attention in this regard were already underway within the democratic movement. One of the most controversial of these was the work of the Industrial Strategy Project (ISP), an offshoot of the COSATU-linked Economic Trends Group. The ISP had developed the model of an industrial strategy motored by a preoccupation with export markets, technological innovation, and the need to be competitive internationally — with significant income and wealth redistribution seen as then flowing from the success of this burgeoning manufacturing sector (and, in addition, from a relatively unspecified program of "urban reconstruction and rural reconstruction"). Class struggle? The problem, as ISP co-ordinator and leading theorist Dave Lewis presented it at the time, was that "key fractions of capital do not necessarily have an interest in successful industrialization or in high rates of economic growth." Just as the authoritarian military state disciplined capitalists in Korea, so too would workers in South Africa — acting through their unions and worker participation in boards of directors — now act "to subordinate the narrow interests of capitalists to the logic of capital."[40]

This model was immediately subjected to criticism. SACP cadre Cronin, for example, objected strenuously to the idea of workers mobilizing to subordinate the capitalist class to the logic of capital and looked instead to the possibility of their submitting "the capitalist class to the logic of social need, of social demand, to the logic of a working class political economy."[41] As he put it:

I would begin with the material needs of people. To start with "we've got to be competitive" is to fall into the trap which I think Dave [Lewis] is in very self-consciously. He says we must submit the capitalist class to the logic of capital. Why? . . . So Dave remains self-consciously within the logic of capital. [But] as socialists we are trying to challenge that logic.

The ISP's central emphasis on "competitiveness" and an outward-looking growth strategy was also queried in light of experience elsewhere — not least by Canadian trade unionist Sam Gindin in a suggestive series of interventions.[42] Meanwhile, a second model — one proposed soon after by the ANC's own Macro-Economic Research Group (MERG) — suggested an economic agenda slanted instead towards structuring a new internal dynamic for the economy around the servicing of "basic needs." This model foresaw a beefing up of the state's role, although it remained less clear on the question of just how directive an ANC state might have to be in pressing capital to play a more effective developmental role. But such an approach at least began to touch base with other writings emphasizing the possibilities of inward industrialization, of "growth through redistribution," and of much more active kinds of direction of investment.[43]

The Macro-Economic Research Group at least momentarily inspired a sense of hope. At the time, its projections seemed to represent the thin edge of the wedge for the eventual realization of the kind of ongoing and intensifying struggle on the socio-economic terrain envisaged by Godongwana and Jordan. Perhaps an even greater effort to close in on the prerogatives of capital along these lines could be expected to bear significant fruit — helping frame the choices of capitalists more firmly within a progressive, increasingly expansive definition of South Africa's possible socio-economic direction (and doing so in ways that could go well beyond Lewis's interpretation of possibilities, for example). A more transformative vision could also help tip the balance of projections towards additional kinds of economic activities — less state-centred, perhaps, but popularly and co-operatively driven. Might these initiatives not find South Africans being empowered to act to service their own immediate and pressing needs (for housing, for example) in creative, productive, collective ways that would help, precisely, to give socio-economic substance to a broad-gauged, hegemonic political project?

To both left and right there were activists and analysts of the South African economy who saw the possibility of making revolution by means of structural reform to be fanciful, of course. For some, the terms in which options were thus being cast were still too narrow and insufficiently "revolutionary." They suggested, instead, the need for a shift "from basic needs to uncompromising class struggle" in which working-class leadership now positioned itself to "give leadership to the spontaneous uprisings" that were sure to spring up in response to the anti-climactic nature of the post-apartheid dispensation for most South Africans.[44] Consider, as well, the related arguments of Lawrence Harris, the well-known Marxist economist who, though British, had been close to ANC decision-making circles off and on over the years. Only a few years previously papers by Harris had been instrumental in forging for the ANC a promisingly leftist definition of a "mixed economy." He offered a conceptualization of change not far removed from that of "structural reform" as providing the terrain upon which the struggle for the long-term transformation of the South Africa economy could then be sustained.[45]

By 1993, however, Harris's writings were dismissing any possibility that the ANC could hope to lay the groundwork for that kind of socialist transition.[46] His position was premised on a decision to caricature the claims of a structural reform strategy and to now dismiss it as offering no more than a singularly unpromising corporatist tailing of capital.[47] He also undertook an extended attack on Joe Slovo's apostasy in moving away from his far more straightforwardly militant positions of the 1970s. Harris was too good an economist not to offer compelling arguments in support of a pessimistic outlook on South Africa's future. Thus we can sympathize with his concerns when he quotes Slovo, circa 1976, against himself regarding the substance of the South African transition of the 1990s. "The national struggle," Slovo had written, "is stopped in its tracks and is satisfied with the cooption of a small black elite into the presently forbidden areas of economic and political power." In Harris's view, the early Slovo had been prophetic.

But what then of Harris's own proposed solution to the contradictions now visible in South Africa? Unfortunately, his approach had merely collapsed into an all too abstract and high-handed invocation of the good old days of the "Leninist tradition" (once also embraced but now abandoned by Slovo). Having thus spared himself the task of discussing what an effective revolutionary strategy for avoiding a counter-revolutionary denouement in present-day South Africa might actually be, Harris could make little real contribution to the development of the radical imagination in that country.

There were also right-wing denunciations of "structural reform" to set against Harris's "ultra-left" critique. For, at the other end of the spectrum, approaches to struggle that attempted to keep alive a sense of continuing and deepening confrontation with capital earned the withering scorn of more orthodox economists in South Africa. Harris might now see such approaches as being far too meek, but Nicoli Nattrass, in a (symptomatic) paper of the time, could find even the relatively mild proposals of the ISP and MERG to be notably adventurist. Thus, in raising a range of more detailed questions regarding the specific modalities of intervening to shape capital's choices, her chief preoccupation remained "the limits to pushing capital around." These limits, she suggested, were strict and, in her formulation, familiar:

> Capital simply leaves (or does not enter) if the policy environment is unfriendly. Given the weakening of labor world-wide (as a result of prolonged recession), the increase in capital mobility and the expansion in overseas investment opportunities . . . the bargaining power of labor, like that of state planners, has been significantly eroded.[48]

Her conclusion: "It simply suggests that capital has to be courted rather than coerced."

Unfortunately — she represents a kind of mirror image of Harris in this respect — Nattrass excused herself from the necessity of taking seriously the probable upshot of this kind of narrowing of alternatives. Was there any reason to think that capital — left free, in effect, to determine the terms of its own seduction — would produce any real economic transformation in South Africa? And if this did not occur, did she really think that the political situation was likely to produce a viable equilibrium? Of course, for Nattrass, politics is most likely in any case to be defined as a vector for irrational intrusions into the technocratic world of rational economic decision-making.[49] Meanwhile, back in the real world of class struggle — where capitalism can still be deemed to be "irrational" — we find ourselves compelled to hypothesize a more positive vision of politics, and to the insist upon the link, apparently necessary, between meaningful democracy and the kind of socio-economic transformation that the practices of a developing socialist project can alone keep on the agenda.

For "revolutionary reform" can only be driven from below, premised on the sustaining of a politics of popular empowerment. As we have seen, within the ANC even by 1994 there were clearly visible tendencies that served to narrow the movement's definition of democracy and undermine its ability to facilitate expression of such mass assertions as might be expected to press against the presumed limits of the status quo. Indeed, the ANC's reluctance to present itself as an organization focusing on a class project (in however nuanced a form) would soon prove profoundly demobilizing of popular energies, something that would become even more apparent as the years passed. Elsewhere left/social-democratic parties, once in power (as now "the government of all the people"), have tended to retreat from continuing to advocate their project in class terms and have instead wound up acting, in the name of "realism" and "pragmatism," as spokespersons for the very worst kinds of market-liberal/monetarist policy packages. Unfortunately, a similar fate awaited the ANC, with an intensification of differences over such issues even finding a post-apartheid ANC government turning against the left — "the moderates" against "the radicals," in effect — much as Przeworski might have predicted.[50]

But these are themes that we will explore in the following chapter. In 1994 itself it was still possible to harbour hope that the existence of class struggle within and around the ANC might yet draw from that organization a level of creativity and leadership appropriate to the challenge of advancing the popular cause in South Africa. Self-evidently, the realization of an alternative vision of societal transformation, one premised on the goal of socialism and the practice of structural reform, would be no easy task. It even seemed possible that, between them, Harris, Nattrass, and Przeworski were correct and that there was, indeed, no "middle road" between an all too vague, nostalgic, and ultimately irrelevant "revolutionism" on the one hand and mere subservience to global capital's dictate on the other. Small wonder that, under such circumstances, there should be those comfortably situated in the upper echelons of the ANC who could come, whether in 1994 or later, to think socialism an irrelevance. Still, there were others who, like Colin Bundy (see chapter 1), believed otherwise — believed that what was necessary was a "leap of faith" to the left, exactly because "a milder mannered capitalist order" would never succeed in securing "a decent future for the majority of South Africans" or that a "deracializing bourgeois rule" would never "meet the aspirations of exploited and oppressed people" — whereas to believe that South Africa could "somehow be absolved of its economic history" truly did require "a leap of faith."[51]

Then too, and ironically, just as some within the ANC seemed inclined to make such a "leap of faith" to the right, it was possible to perceive abroad the first indications of a waning self-confidence amongst the very Western intelligentsia who so recently had brought us the notion of a post-Cold War "end of history." In 1994 a widely read *Atlantic Monthly* article, "The Coming Anarchy," by Robert Kaplan, precisely sought to demonstrate "how scarcity, crime, overpopulation, tribalism, and disease are rapidly destroying the social fabric of our planet."[52] It is true that, as Kaplan slouched from one catastrophic Third World setting to another, the general tone of his piece remained far more sensationalist than analytical. And certainly he traced none of his litany of desperate conditions and escalating barbarism back to any possible contradictions in the global production system. Nonetheless, there were signs of an interesting failure of nerve to be found in this and certain other writings of the 1990s. After all, how many basket-case economies can capital afford to walk away from before the shrinking horizons for expanded reproduction offered by such a world become a problem for it? Are these the circumstances under which the pendulum of power might begin to swing back in the direction of the popular classes, including those drawn towards action, in the first instance, within national boundaries? Might the space for imposing counter-hegemonic, left-leaning projects on capital — in South Africa, and more globally — and for releasing from the base creative and collective socio-economic energies open up sooner than we think?

# Beggaring the Imagination: The High Costs of Liberal-Capitalist-Democratic Ideology

Unfortunately, for the moment (as Bundy himself acknowledged), "leaps of faith" to the left are much less the norm than mere "commonsensical" acceptance, for better or worse, of the "inevitability" of a pretty much unalloyed capitalism. In his response to Keane, Gamble wondered aloud as to "socialism's fate" in the contemporary world. At best, might this not amount to socialism merely "lingering on as a critique of the shortcomings of liberalism, and as an analysis of the destructive effects of capitalist economics on individuals and communities"?[53]

For Gamble, however, "another possibility" remained: "The waning of belief in the methods and politics of state socialism makes possible the intellectual and political rebirth of the socialist project by setting free once more hopes of emancipation." But what if the "waning of belief" is in the very feasibility and efficacy of "the socialist project" itself — and of the practice of a genuinely "popular democracy" that might accompany it? For in South Africa, as elsewhere, it is not merely the strength of structural determinations that encourages people to reach this conclusion. There is also an autonomous cultural charge to what is happening. The threatened foreclosure of any sense of socio-economic possibility beyond "liberal capitalist democracy" involves both a hollowing out of language and a beggaring of the historical imagination. In part, this culture of ascendant global capitalism crystallizes spontaneously, but it is also driven by active efforts at ideology-creation on the part of liberal and right-of-centre intellectuals. And the costs of the grim fecundity of such an ideology are likely to be very high indeed, not least in South Africa.

This is not the case simply because the operations of capitalism, unalloyed and "irrational," will, in all probability, have little if any positive impact on the material lot of the vast majority of South Africans ("in the real world people starve"). It is also true because, at the cultural level, imaginations do not stand still. Thus the sidelining of socialist democracy may prove, in a world of continuing scarcity and inequality, to be a pyrrhic victory for global capitalism in many settings. Frustrated, balked of a sense of alternative purpose at the level of socio-economic vision, feeling merely disempowered as potential class actors are therefore cast into a political vacuum, people will begin to look elsewhere for presumptive routes to their salvation.

Sometimes this frustration may be framed in quasi-leftist terms, including the kind of populist-cum-racist rhetoric that, even by 1994, had become the stock-in-trade of Winnie Mandela and others like her in their appeals to potentially disaffected youth.[54] In such a politics South Africa's democratic imperative could be seen merely to curdle and fester dangerously. But more often, perhaps, popular frustrations will find voice through the politicized expressions of competing fundamentalisms: various extremes of religious, of racial, of national, regional, and ethnic mobilization. "Chaos" can spring at least as much from such sources as from the threatened backlash of the powerful classes highlighted by Przeworski, and the unravelling of the social fabric that is occurring in various countries around the world offers grim testimony to that fact. How ironic if "barbarism" should break out not in spite of, but precisely because of, the limited nature of the transition to democracy that is now being granted global sanction in both theory and practice.

South Africa does run a great risk of unravelling along such lines, and, as we will see in our next chapter, this would become even more of a danger by the early years of the new millennium, after 2000, than it was in 1994; as is well known, virtually all of the various societal divisions are present and available for potential politicization. Fortunately, there are also many activists, without and even within the ANC, who continue their efforts to avoid such a tragic denouement to their liberation struggle and who want to attach a more expansive meaning to the transition in their country. Perhaps it is here that progressive theory also has a role to play: as guardian — against the pull of "the ideology of the new globalism" — of the political imagination.

Opinions may differ, to once again echo Roger Murray, as to whether a "historically necessary" outcome, socialist and popular democratic, is "historically possible" in South Africa.[55] But many radical activists in South Africa do at least have a clear sense of the costs to their country of its not, as yet, having become so. And they are indeed working to ensure that, through struggle, the historically necessary remains at least the historically thinkable.

CHAPTER 9

# THE POST-APARTHEID DENOUEMENT

A tragedy is being enacted in South Africa, a country that is as much a metaphor for our times as Rwanda and Yugoslavia and, even if not so immediately searing of the spirit, perhaps a more revealing one. For in the teeth of high expectations arising from the successful struggle against a malignant apartheid state, a very large percentage of the population — amongst them many of the most desperately poor in the world — are being sacrificed on the altar of the neo-liberal logic of global capitalism.

Moreover, as I had occasion to remark during a stint spent teaching in that country in the year 2000, the most striking thing about the new South Africa, as I personally discovered, is just how easy it has now become to find oneself considered to be an "ultra-leftist." Thus, to talk with "opinion-leaders" or to read their public statements was to be drowned in a sea of smug: this is the way the world works; competitiveness is good; get with the program; GET REAL. One does not know whether to laugh or cry at this kind of "realism" — "magical market realism," as I have termed it elsewhere.[1] For there is absolutely no reason to assume that the vast majority of people in South Africa will find their lives improved by the policies that are now being adopted in their name by the ANC government. Indeed, something quite the reverse is the far more likely outcome.

Why this sad denouement? Are we mourning here the state of the world of globalization, marking soberly the wisdom of Adam Przeworski's famously bleak aphorism about the irrationality of capitalism and the lack of feasibility of socialism and accepting (albeit with less glee than some of them do) the oft-stated premise of many members of the new South African elite: TINA ("There Is No Alternative")? Or are we marking, instead, the failure of South Africa's popular movement, or even, as some would have it, a "betrayal" on the part of the ANC itself? The answer may well be that both emphases contain some truth, although just how we weigh them will depend a great deal on what we believe regarding the art of the possible for nationally based political movements and parties under present worldwide (and continental) conditions generally — or in South Africa more specifically.

# The Dual Transition

We must, of course, be circumspect. In South Africa the 1990s witnessed the transition from a system of racially driven authoritarian rule towards an outcome far more peacefully defined and democratically realized than most observers would have predicted at the end of the previous decade. Given the difficulties of such a transition the relatively peaceful consolidation of a functioning liberal-democratic system must be deemed a considerable achievement. Nonetheless, we must also ask ourselves just what are the most appropriate criteria for evaluating this dramatic process of change. In the mid-1980s, for instance, when Magdoff and Sweezy remarked on the buoyant revolutionary prospect they saw in South Africa, they left open the possibility of other, less palatable outcomes, going so far as to warn that the "stabilization of capitalist relations in South Africa" could prove a "stunning defeat for the world revolution."[2] Unfortunately, defeat now seems to be an appropriate description of what has transpired during the past decade in South Africa. For "the stabilization of capitalist relations" is, by any measure, one clear attribute of the country's transition.

True, the cause of "world revolution" has taken a fearsome beating since Magdoff and Sweezy made their observations, and perhaps South Africa will not now seem the most serious of the defeats that the presumed revolutionary-cum-socialist alternative has suffered in the intervening years. Indeed, a more basic question might well be whether invocation of the "S" word itself can any longer provide us with a relevant reference point against which we can measure the direction and pace of change these days. After all, the world was a very different place in 1986, and not just as viewed through the eyes of a Magdoff or a Sweezy. While there was already plenty of scope for "pessimism of the intelligence" on the left, there still seemed then to be room for a certain "optimism of the will." Much of this optimism has since been lost; public pronouncement and academic writing alike reflect the notion that an ineluctable and transcendent process of globalization is crushing the very plausibility of pro-active states and meaningful national jurisdictions. And even when some quasi-left observers grant more room for manoeuvre to states and nations, that room can consist of disciplining globalization only just enough to advance the competitive interests of elements of national capital. To think to act, nationally or globally, in order to challenge the underlying logic of capital or to realize some more social and humane purpose is, at best, seen as merely naive. Thus Paul Hirst and Grahame Thompson write, without apparent irony, of what they seem to consider the height of contemporary progressive aspiration:

> Such institutional arrangements and strategies can assure some minimal level of international economic governance, at least to the benefit of the major advanced industrial nations. Such governance cannot alter the extreme inequalities between those nations and the rest, in terms of trade and investment,

income and wealth. Unfortunately, that is not really the problem raised by the concept of globalization. The issue is not whether the world's economy is governable towards ambitious goals like promoting social justice, equality between countries and greater democratic control for the bulk of the world's people, but whether it is governable at all.[3]

To paraphrase Margaret Thatcher: there is no society, only corporations and their intermediaries.

Are we then setting the bar too high in even thinking of evaluating South Africa's level of accomplishment against the criteria evoked by Magdoff and Sweezy? Not necessarily. After all, South Africa's dramatic transition to a democratic dispensation ("one person, one vote, in a united South Africa") has been twinned with a simultaneous transition towards an ever more sweeping neo-liberal socio-economic dispensation that has negated in practice a great deal of the country's democratic advance. Still, it is also important to emphasize once again just how much of an advance has actually been made. Indeed, at the beginning of the 1990s, with the South African transition in process, nothing seemed quite certain about moving beyond even the system of racial authoritarianism.[4] At that point it was apparent that the passage from an apartheid South Africa was fraught with danger, the country still a killing field. And yet through the 1994 election and its aftermath South Africa was able to realize and stabilize the shift to a constitutionally premised and safely institutionalized democratic order — "making peace" without suffering the potentially crippling backlash from the right wing, both black and white, that many had predicted and without suffering the collapse into chaos or dictatorship that some had seen to be threatened by the establishment of majority rule. Moreover, this political stability was sustained through the five years of Nelson Mandela's presidency, reconfirmed by the very mundaneness of the 1999 election, and carried unscathed into the Thabo Mbeki presidency: a cause for celebration, surely, on a continent where apparently lesser contradictions have proven far more difficult to resolve.

It is true that the door to the transition was opened by some actors situated behind the barricades of white power: by the late 1980s it was evident to both dominant business circles and sufficient numbers within the ruling political elite that a situation of relative stalemate had been reached and steps would have to be taken to incorporate the ANC into the circle of legitimate political players. However, the full significance of this development would only became fully apparent in retrospect. What seemed more immediately pressing at the time was that, despite the release from prison of Mandela in 1990 and the unbanning of the ANC, President F.W. de Klerk and his associates had still not reconciled themselves to the notion of the ultimate establishment of an ANC government. Well into the transition period (1990-94), they continued to harbour hopes of safeguarding various attributes of the existing racial order within any new constitutional/political dispensation that would eventually emerge from negotiations. Moreover, de Klerk almost certainly was knowledgeable of various ongoing attempts by the South African military and police both to strengthen the hand of Chief Gatsha Buthelezi and his conservative Inkatha Freedom Party (IFP) in the jockeying for political positioning but also to actively undermine, in this and other ways (both direct and indirect), the capacity of the ANC to emerge as a hegemonic force in a new South Africa.

A significant threat to a peaceful transition also came from further to the right within the white polity. Both the Conservative Party and more overtly fascist organizations such as the Afrikaner Weerstands Beweging (AWB) remained players to be reckoned with, committed as they were to rolling back the clock to the days of unqualified apartheid. As Jonathan Hyslop convincingly argued, however, by far the greatest danger from the white right was represented by General Constand Viljoen. He, not Ferdy Hartzenberg (of the Conservative Party) or Eugene Terreblanche (of the AWB), had lines into a security establishment not otherwise inclined towards putschist activity and also had a much better chance of linking up with potentially divisive forces in the African community (with Buthelezi, for example, and with the "independent Bantustan" governments of the Ciskei and Boputhatswana). This was because, as a realist, Viljoen had concluded that the Afrikaners' last best hope lay in separatism, not apartheid overlordship. The foiling of white intervention to shore up Lucas Mangope's regime in Boputhatswana narrowed Viljoen's options, however, and when the ANC skilfully allowed space in the negotiations for the separatist notion of a Volkstaat to remain a possibility, the general chose, late in the day but fatefully, to commit himself to the electoral process. Despite a spate of bombings on the eve of the elections, the white right was thus largely corralled into the fold of peaceful transition. And even though his own last-minute entry into the election did not create quite so peaceful a process in KwaZulu, Buthelezi's decision to participate must surely have been produced, at least in part, by Viljoen's decision to abandon his own resistance.[5]

The ANC was equally adept in dealing with Chief Gatsha Buthelezi and Inkatha. The IFP brought to the table a bloody record of harassment of the ANC, often carried out hand in glove with the apartheid state. But it had also developed a significant base amongst many (although by no means all) Zulu-speakers in the rural areas and squatter settlements of the KwaZulu bantustan and in workers' hostels especially on the East Rand. Small wonder that, despite Inkatha's eleventh-hour conversion to participation in the 1994 polls, fraud, violence, and considerable chaos marked the electoral process in Natal — with "no-go" areas for one or the other of the chief protagonists in the election, especially in Inkatha-dominated rural Natal, imposing a firm limitation on open campaigning, for example. In the end, no accurate count of the vote proved to be remotely possible in Natal: the result was, quite simply, diplomatically brokered and in the IFP's favour, this being a choice of tactic made by the national-level ANC to draw Buthelezi further into the tent of compromise. This result also meant that the IFP would form the government in the province of KwaZulu-Natal, one of nine such provincial units established within the new federal system affirmed in the constitutional guidelines produced by the inter-party negotiations that preceded the elections.

Here Buthelezi found himself beneficiary of a process — that of constitution-making — that he had himself chosen to boycott. It was primarily white politicians, denied any more direct guarantees of minority privilege, who successfully held out for a federal division of powers as one means of hamstringing an ANC government that, they feared, might with victory seek to actively use the central government for progressive purposes. Another line of defence of established socio-economic inequalities was an attempt to bind the ANC to a constitutionally prescribed protection of individual human rights, in particular of the right to property. In addition, the so-called "sunset clauses" safeguarded for a period the positions of whites in public employment; the agreement on a "Government of National Unity" meant positions for both National Party and IFP politicians (including de Klerk and Buthelezi) in the cabinet formed by the ANC after its electoral victory; and an amnesty offered protection to those who had committed various gross abuses of power in defence of apartheid (albeit an amnesty sufficiently qualified to prepare the ground for the subsequent establishment of the Truth and Reconciliation Commission [TRC]).

These "constitutional compromises" could also be interpreted in other ways. Take the tilt in the constitution towards a preoccupation with human rights. There were those within the camp of national liberation who themselves championed such an emphasis not in any counter-revolutionary spirit but rather to help safeguard against the danger of abuse of power by an ANC that was, given its own hierarchical, even Stalinist, past, far from immune to temptations towards high-handedness. There were also those who sought to balance any concession to the privileging of the right to property with the writing into the constitution of a much broader range of economic and social rights designed to give validation to the ongoing claims of the impoverished in South Africa. Just how such rights (carefully qualified as they were) might be rendered operational in a post-apartheid South Africa remained to be seen (not easily is the simple answer), but that they appeared in the text at all suggests something of the balancing act between defence of privilege and demands for redress of historically embedded wrongs that the constitutional moment embodied.[6]

Nor has the limited federalism of the constitution presented any real impediment to the ANC's undertakings. True, the provinces have provided space for the expression of a degree of diversity in South Africa, even if such diversity has not always been of the most enlightened kind (KwaZulu-Natal government, after all, became a formally recognized shelter for the IFP, and the Western Cape government became a similar outlet for the quasi-racist preoccupations of the white and Coloured constituencies of the National and Democratic parties). Most often, however, the provinces have tended to become mere instruments in the hands of those who determine national budget allocations (and of a depressing brand of intra-ANC infighting) rather than vibrant political sites in their own right. It is surely no accident that the ANC did not seem to push particularly hard in either the 1994 or 1999 elections to win the two-thirds majority necessary to unilaterally change the terms of the constitution in this or any other particular (although on both occasions it was close to gaining just such a margin). If long-term constraints on the ANC's freedom of action have existed, or costs have had to be borne for the kind of negotiated transition that the movement did achieve, they have lain elsewhere than in the constitutional realm.

One place where a more obvious price has been paid can be found, many would argue, in the ANC leadership's tacit support for the demobilization of those popular energies that had been so crucial to the weakening of the apartheid state in the first place. To be sure, these energies did find political expression from time to time during the negotiations. Thus, amongst other actions, the Congress of South African Trade Unions, the country's largest trade union central and a key ANC ally, effectively manifested its unease at late-apartheid government policy initiatives (and at its own absence from the formal negotiations process) with a dramatic two-day general strike against a proposed new value-added tax. And negotiators were further reminded of the mass presence beyond the conference halls when, at a crucial moment, a series of rolling mass demonstrations (climaxing in the Boipatong massacre and the shooting by Ciskei soldiers into a large group of protestors marching on Bisho) were employed by ANC together with COSATU to reactivate stalled talks.

But, as Jeremy Cronin put it at the time, there was a tendency to view the latter kind of "mass action" primarily as a "tap" to be turned on and off at will by the ANC rather than as a foretaste of continuing popular empowerment.[7] ANC activist Raymond Suttner had similar doubts regarding the direction in which things were going: "The negotiations have had a dissolving effect on mass organization, a tendency for our constituency to become spectators. If we conduct the coming election campaign in a narrow electoralist manner, the dissolution could be deepened. Whatever the victory, we should not underrate the strong sense of demoralization in our organizations."[8]

Indeed, as Suttner feared, elections have fully revealed what little has become of popular mobilization in South Africa — and so too has the virtual collapse of the ANC as a mass political organization (although not as an electoral machine). The 1994 election had the distinction of being a "freedom election": one could not have asked for much more than that such an election would ratify, through a massive African vote for the ANC, the coming into the political kingdom of a population that had been denied any such place for centuries. By 1999, however, it was difficult to miss the significance of the election as being a mere popularity contest, the ANC still floating to a considerable degree on its legitimacy amongst Africans as a successful liberation movement rather than on any record of delivery on popular expectations during its first term in office. Meanwhile, the vote in KwaZulu-Natal continued to fall along quasi-ethnic lines, producing, once again, a narrow victory for the IFP, and the vote in Western Cape along racial ones, producing a National Party (NP)/Democratic Party (DP) government (with the two parties since merged into a new "Democratic Alliance"). Nationally, the DP became the official opposition (albeit with only 11 per cent of the vote compared to the ANC's near two-thirds poll): it did so, significantly, on the basis of a campaign pitched, to whites, Coloureds, and Indians, in terms of issues of crime, corruption, and the dangers of abuse of power inherent in a one-party dominant (read, also, African-dominant) political system, issues that were given, tacitly, a racist spin.

Of course, this tendency may also have reflected that there was not so very much more to campaign about. The DP hewed to a particularly business-friendly, neo-liberal line in its approach to socio-economic policy during the election, but by 1999 this tendency did not much distinguish the party from the ANC itself in policy terms: on many potentially important strategic issues the space for democratic disagreement and contestation had by then been papered over by a crippling consensus amongst the main political contenders regarding the presumed imperatives of economic orthodoxy. Small wonder that some observers have found it difficult to avoid a relatively narrow and unenthusiastic reading of what, substantively, was actually being accomplished in South Africa in democratic terms. Thus, David Howarth distinguishes the "democratic transition" that South Africa has achieved from the "democratic transformation" that it has not really attempted — using the term "democratic transition" to refer "to the process by which negotiating elites manage to oversee the installation of formal liberal-democratic procedures," and democratic transformation to designate "the longer-term process of restructuring the underlying social relations of a given society."[9] Since, in South Africa, these "underlying social relations" encompass a measure of socio-economic inequality that is virtually unparalleled elsewhere in the world (only Brazil and Guatemala are ever mentioned as being in the same league on the Gini scale that economists use to measure such things), it is not difficult to see what Howarth is driving at.

Some have viewed the incorporation of Buthelezi into the national fold as one particularly graphic instance of the high price paid for the kind of transition that has occurred. Certainly, this is true if one takes seriously the preoccupations of Mahmood Mamdani, who, in recent writing, has suggested that a clear distinction needs to be made between "citizen" and "subject" within the theory and practice of democratic struggle in Africa. In particular, he criticizes much thinking about democracy for focusing far too exclusively on urban pressures (by self-conscious "citizens") for change and overlooking the importance, if genuine democratic transformation is to be realized, of simultaneously helping rural-dwellers — people who are often still trapped as "subjects" within quasi-traditional structures of authority — to liberate themselves.[10] Does reflection upon Mamdani's model not raise the fear that the ANC, in the name of peacemaking, has merely handed over the rural poor (and the poor who are resident in the many peri-urban shantytowns around Durban and Pietermaritzburg) of KwaZulu-Natal to the ministrations of the caste of abusive chiefs and warlords who cluster around Buthelezi and his Inkatha structures?

This is, in fact, the argument made by Gerry Maré, the most articulate academic critic of Chief Buthelezi and his Inkatha project. Maré bemoans the extent to which the unsavoury Buthelezi has apparently forced the ANC to accept him as political player more or less on his own terms — this even though Inkatha won a mere 10 per cent of the vote in 1994. Maré adds:

> in spite of being named in the TRC report as carrying responsibility for "gross violations of human rights," Buthelezi has escaped with scarcely a blemish and with apparent absolution from the ANC itself . . . his position as elder statesperson acknowledged through the number of times that he has served as Acting-State President in the frequent absence of both Mandela and [then Deputy President] Mbeki.

As for his cronies, people "closely associated with horrendous acts of violence," they have "simply defied or ignored the storm and survived — often as members of various provincial parliaments or the central parliament, such as warlords David Ntombela and Mandla Shabalala, and the notorious prince Gideon Zulu."[11] Some critics may argue that such an outcome merely epitomizes the success of a judicious strategy of incorporation, a legitimate tactical ceding of ground to a dangerous and decidedly ruthless opponent, a purchasing of peace in one important region of South Africa at some real but nonetheless acceptable cost to principle. And yet one might be more inclined to accept such an argument were this not merely an example of the more general pattern of ANC peacemaking efforts: an across the board following of the line of least resistance towards centres of established power, a continued broadening of the scope of mere elite-pacting to consolidate, on every front, a turning away from the interests of the poorest of the poor.

For Buthelezi has not been the only, or indeed the central, target of such appeasement tactics. Far more important in this respect have been the wielders of corporate power who have lived to tell the tale of the dual transition with increasingly self-satisfied smirks on their faces. There can be little doubt that, in the end, the relative ease of the political transition was principally guaranteed by the ANC's withdrawal from any form of genuine class struggle in the socio-economic realm and the abandonment of any economic strategy that might have been expected directly to service the immediate material requirements of the vast mass of desperately impoverished South Africans. This withdrawal occurred in a society where the gap between rich and poor remains among the widest in the world: a society in which, as one mid-1990s survey demonstrated, "the poorest 60% of households' share of total expenditure is a mere 14%, while the richest quintile's share is 69%"

and where, across the decade of the 1990s, a certain narrowing of the income gap between black and white (as a growing number of blacks have edged themselves into elite circles) was paralleled by an even greater widening of the gap between rich and poor.[12]

Granted, the "negotiations" in the sphere of economic/class relationships were far less public than were the formal meetings of the Convention for a Democratic South Africa and the Kempton Park negotiations. But they were, perhaps, even more important. As one close observer wrote in 1994:

Since 1990, when the democratization process began, some foreign governments, notably the US and some of its allies — Britain, Germany, Italy and
Japan — successfully induced the ANC to move away from its socialist economic policies, including that of nationalization. Instead, they succeeded in
persuading the movement to embrace Western-style free market principles
which the ANC increasingly, albeit reluctantly, adopted. It is interesting to note,
for example, that Mandela's evolving position on fiscal responsibility was a
direct response to pressures from foreign investors and governments.[13]

Moreover, this brand of compromise was merely part of a decade-long process of accommodation, one hailed in retrospect by no less a source than South Africa's corporate think-tank par excellence, the Centre for Development and Enterprise (CDE): "The evolution of the ANC's policy position was . . . influenced by foreign perceptions and pressures (from foreign investors, potential investors, the World Bank, IMF and others). Other important policy influences were the *Growth for All* document of the South African Foundation (representing the country's 50 largest corporations) published in February 1996." The result: "Throughout the 1990s the ANC's economic policies have shown a clear shift towards greater acceptance of the market." That shift was sealed "finally in the Growth, Employment and Redistribution (GEAR) proposals of June, 1996."[14] But if 1996 was the crucial year for putting the finishing touches on the ANC's capitulation to neo-liberal orthodoxy, the die had already been cast during the transition period itself. As Hein Marais observes, "By 1994 . . . the left had lost the macroeconomic battle."[15]

## Liberating Capitalism

This defeat was no accident. From the mid-1980s the cooler heads in the camp of capital had begun to develop a counter-revolutionary strategy designed to shape the socio-economic transition that would now parallel the political one. The trigger: the near-revolutionary mobilization of popular forces against the established system that marked the 1980s. Faced with so serious a political crisis, Anglo-American business executive Zac De Beer enunciated his classic warning that "years of apartheid had caused many blacks to reject the economic as well as the political system." His corollary: "We dare not allow the baby of free enterprise to be thrown out with the bathwater of apartheid."[16] Armed with this sensibility, capitalists, both worldwide and local, prepared themselves to sever the marriage between the structures that had proven to be so profitable to them in the past: capitalist exploitation on the one hand and racial oppression on the other. Indeed, increased interaction with Mandela in prison and Mbeki and others in exile merely helped to confirm the growing sense that the ANC might be a potential participant in (and even possibly the best guarantor of) a transition that safeguarded the essentials of the established economic system. That a powerful stratum of Afrikaner capitalists had by now joined the upper echelons of South Africa's business community was also important. This group increasingly became protagonists within the National Party for reformist strategies for a deracialization of capitalism that began to jettison the interests of those Afrikaners — less well off and most vulnerable to colour-blind competition for jobs and other privileges — who had once formed its chief political base. Although de Klerk held out until quite late in the day for more firm guarantees of continuing racially defined privilege, that stand proved to be much less important to the outcome of negotiations than the underlying pull of capital towards the granting of extensive concessions on the racial-cum-political front.[17]

Intriguingly, this pre-emptive strategy was twinned to the saliency of a related perspective on the crisis that the late-apartheid economy was deemed to be confronting, a perspective that served further to underscore the need for "reform." For South African capitalism was increasingly viewed not only as prisoner of an outmoded (and increasingly politically dangerous) racial ideology but of an outmoded economic strategy as well: in an ever more neo-liberal age, the racially motivated interventions of the South Africa state were merely one way in which that state was now deemed to be unduly intrusive into the sacrosanct domain of the market and therefore a drag on economic progress. Thus, in its last years, the NP government itself had moved a long way towards the embrace of neo-liberal orthodoxy, a trend most clearly manifested in the centrality of "privatization, trade liberalization, spending cuts and strict monetary discipline" to the Normative Economic Model (NEM) that it released in 1993.[18] But the most significant conversion to such orthodoxy was to take place, under intense pressure from the world of capital, within the ANC itself.

There were some counter-tendencies to this outcome. True, many within the ANC were caught flat-footed in the sphere of economic policy in 1990, with only some vague if progressive nostrums from the Freedom Charter to fall back upon ("The mineral wealth beneath the soil, the banks and monopoly industry shall be transferred to the ownership of the people as a whole"). Perhaps it was such sentiments that initially allowed Mandela to state militantly, immediately upon his February 1990 release from prison, that "the nationalization of the mines, banks and monopoly industry is the policy of the ANC and a change or modification of our views in this regard is inconceivable." However, Mandela himself would soon so distance himself from that position that by 1994 he could tell the U.S. Joint

Houses of Congress that the free market was a "magical elixir" that would produce freedom and equality for all.[19] But even if Mandela himself was not to be counted upon in this respect, there was also available a more considered expression within the ANC of a radical sensibility relevant to thinking about the macroeconomic sphere — one grounded, for example, in early position papers developed by the Research Department (with the assistance of such figures as British Marxist economist Lawrence Harris), amongst other sources. This sensibility produced chiefly a kind of dirigiste neo-Keynesianism perhaps, but it nonetheless contained the possible seeds of a deepening challenge to capital's prerogatives in favour of a prioritization of popular needs in the sphere of production. Its impact was best exemplified by the then saliency of the proposed guideline "growth through redistribution" in ANC circles.

This perspective also found early voice in the ANC's new Department of Economic Policy (DEP), in fact in its very first major policy document:

> The engine of growth in the economy of a developing, non-racial and non-sexist South Africa should be the growing satisfaction of the basic needs of the impoverished and deprived majority of our people. We thus call for a pro-gramme of Growth through Redistribution in which redistribution acts as a spur to growth and in which the fruits of growth are redistributed to satisfy basic needs.[20]

Such emphases were reinforced by the report of the Macro-Economic Research Group, a report crafted between 1991 and 1993 by ANC-aligned economists work-ing with progressive counterparts from overseas. And it found significant public expression in such claims as that made in 1992 by then-DEP economist (and later governor of the Reserve Bank) Tito Mboweni:

> The ANC believes that a strategy of "growth through redistribution" will be the appropriate new path for the South African economy. . . . In our growth path, accumulation depends on the prior redistribution of resources. Major changes will have to take place in existing power relations as a necessary condition for this new growth path.[21]

This logic appeared momentarily compelling. After all, on the one hand the vast majority of South Africans were (and still are) desperate in their poverty for a wide range of the simplest goods and services, and on the other a very large percentage of people (most often the same people) were (and still are) equally desperate for jobs. Why, the ANC seemed poised to ask, can't those two key pieces at the centre of the South African economic puzzle simply be put together? Why must they be joined so indirectly and inefficiently through the circuits of global capital and the process of generating surplus value (profits) for those few who have the power to dictate terms and guarantee their massive cut of the action? But any such questions were very soon lost from view as Mboweni and other young ANC high flyers increasingly looked elsewhere for economic cues — in a rightward shift that was also congruent with that being made, alongside Mandela himself, by older heavy-weights such as Joe Slovo and Mac Maharaj.

For the voices raised against anything like the "growth through redistribution" model were ferocious, with attack dogs for capital like the notorious business economist Terence Moll quickly labelling it "macro-economic populism" and "a dangerous fantasy."[22] Moreover, a wave of much more capital-friendly scenarios — the Mont Fleur proposals, for example, and the recommendations of both the Nedcor/Old Mutual "Professional Economists' Panel" (entitled *Prospects for a Successful Transition*) and insurance conglomerate Sanlam's own Platform for Investment[23] soon washed over the macroeconomic debate — even as other global players "arranged for key ANC economic advisers and politicians to receive training at business schools and international banks and investment houses in the west where they were fed a steady diet of neo-liberal economics."[24] As DEP economist Viv McMenamin put the point frankly at the time, ANC economic thinking now registered "a shift away from policies that may be morally and politically correct, but which will cause strong adverse reaction from powerful local and international interests."[25] Ironically, even the chief trade union central, COSATU, which would eventually prove a somewhat sharper critic of burgeoning neo-liberalism in South Africa, found itself wrong-footed in this early going. Thus, its own team of academic advisors (the Economic Trends Group, the Industrial Strategy Group) began by advocating various interventionist measures vis-à-vis capital but soon found itself so taken with models of "shaped" and "competitive" advantage and with supply-side and external-market driven preoccupations as to offer advice that fit quite comfortably within the rising tide of orthodoxy. In the end, ex-United Democratic Front activist Trevor Manuel, instrumental in pulling the DEP to the right in the early 1990s, and ex-trade union militant Alec Erwin, patron of the COSATU academics, would become, as ministers of finance and of trade and industry respectively, the principal protagonists of the global conformism that had come to characterize ANC economic policy at the turn of the century.[26]

One last throw of the dice by the left within the Mass Democratic Movement was a document that became, in effect, the electoral manifesto for the ANC in the 1994 election campaign. To a considerable degree driven from below by the trade unions and civic organizations and adopted only rather opportunistically by a core group of ANC senior leaders, the Reconstruction and Development Programme (RDP) emphasized the centrality to the planning process of both the meeting of the populace's basic needs and the active empowerment of that populace in driving its own development process. Nonetheless, the central chapters on macroeconomic policy were already markedly compromised in the direction of free-market premises. The document as a whole was at best (as I wrote at the time) "less what it is, than what it might become" in the context of further class struggles.[27]

Unfortunately, it was the rightward pull that proved predominant, reinforced (as Asghar Adelzadeh has carefully recorded) in a range of government documents, each more neo-liberal in tone and substance than the last, that ran from the RDP White Paper of September 1994 through the draft National Growth and Development Strategy of February 1996 to the "Growth, Employment and Redistribution [GEAR], a Macroeconomic Strategy" document of June 1996.[28] As Marais notes, "Rhetorically, attempts were made to align GEAR with the socially progressive objectives of the RDP. But the central pillars of the strategy were fashioned in accordance with standard neo-liberal principles — deficit reduction, keeping inflation in single digits, trade liberalization, privatization, tax cuts and holidays, phasing out of exchange controls, etc."[29] And in March of that same year the RDP Office, until then strategically located in the President's Office as cabinet-level overseer of what was left of a popularly driven development mandate, was closed, its activities folded, ostensibly, into the various line ministries.

For many of the government's most sympathetic critics it is the extreme, precipitate, and unqualified nature of the ANC government's move towards a neo-liberal strategy that is so surprising. As Adelzadeh suggests, what has transpired appears to be in significant part a self-inflicted wound, an "adoption of the essential tenets and policy recommendations of the neo-liberal framework advocated by the IMF in its structural adjustment programmes," which is

> all the more remarkable in view of the limited, even negative impact of such programmes, especially in southern Africa, the lack of any leverage that the international financial institutions such as the IMF and World Bank have over South African policymakers, the lack of any dramatic shifts in economic and political environment to warrant such major shifts in policy orientation, and the lack of a transparent and fully argued justification for the adoption of an entirely different policy framework.

What there is, Adelzadeh concludes, is merely "a lame succumbing to the policy dictates and ideological pressures of the international financial institutions."[30] Moreover, the pronouncements of these documents have been paralleled by a range of concrete policies that epitomize just such a "lame succumbing." Crucial in the constitutional negotiations per se — alongside the property rights clause — was the agreement to guarantee formally the "independence" of the Reserve Bank, a reassurance to capital that removed from government hands any real leverage (especially in facilitating expansionary policies) over crucial monetary decisions. Moreover, as a member of the caretaker South African government, the Transitional Executive Council, the ANC spent most of 1993 signing on as party to a range of decisions that firmly cast the die for future policies once it was in power: inking an extraordinarily market-friendly letter of intent to the IMF in order to guarantee a balance-of-payments loan, for example, and joining the General Agreement on Tariffs and Trade (GATT). Perhaps the most noteworthy aspect of this latter move was that it set the stage, after 1994, for the ANC government to remove tariffs in key areas much faster than even GATT required — with catastrophic effects on many local firms. Moreover, Patrick Bond argues that the same kind of "moral surrender" to the market was evident in an ongoing propensity to cut back corporate taxation and in such decisions as those "to repay in full apartheid's $20 billion-plus foreign commercial bank debt and to phase out exchange controls in the name of attracting new foreign finance."[31]

These, and a number of other choices made in the early going, were crucial ones, rendering cumulatively more difficult and more unlikely any opting for the plausible alternative policies that existed at the outset of the transition. Left critics would argue that many of the ANC's more recent claims to be powerless in the face of the marketplace have a disingenuous ring when measured against how the movement itself had, early in the game, thrown away so many of the instruments that might have been useful in crafting a more assertive strategy towards capital.[32] Instead, and ironically, the ANC has come, full circle, back to the late-apartheid government's Normative Economic Model. For the central premise of South Africa's economic policy now could scarcely be clearer. Ask not what capital can do for South Africa but what South Africa can do for capital: an overwhelming preoccupation with foreign investment, an (at best) trickle-down approach to development more broadly conceived, and an attendant encouragement of a culture of stock markets (with even many trade unions becoming substantial players in the game through their own investment companies) and, for more marginal players, of institutionalized lotteries and other games of chance. All of this has occurred in a context in which a sophisticated case can and has been made against the continued prioritizing of supply-side economics and for an approach ("growth through redistribution") that highlights the far more central brake on economic growth that exists on the "effective demand" side of the equation.[33]

In light of such circumstances it is difficult not to feel, with Adelzadeh, that the option for neo-liberalism was, first and foremost, an ideological one. For in strictly economic terms the underlying premises of this wholesale capitulation to the market have been desperately shaky. The first chapter in this book suggests the shaky prospect existing for capitalist development in Africa and quotes Manuel Castells's warning that, even if South Africa has somewhat more room for manoeuvre within global capitalism than is the case elsewhere on the continent, the strong possibility exists of South Africa falling, like "its ravaged neighbours," into "the abyss of social exclusion."[34]

That strong possibility has been reinforced by numbers that indicate not the dramatic increase in employment figures forecast by those who launched GEAR but a spiralling downward trend in that regard (an estimated loss of at least a half a million jobs between 1994 and 1999). These figures are paralleled by evidence in such spheres as GDP growth, investment, savings, exports, and interest rates that "virtually all GEAR's targets were missed" and missed by a very great deal.[35] Indeed it is difficult to escape the conclusion that, in the summary of one analyst, "GEAR has been associated with massive deindustrialization and job shedding through reduced tariffs on imports, capital flight as controls over investments are relaxed, attempts to downsize the costs and size of the public sector, and real cuts in education, health and social welfare spending."[36] Of course, to highlight such negatives, it is sometimes said in South Africa, is to indulge in "Afro-pessimism." But it can much more easily be argued that the real "Afro-pessimists" are those who state that South Africa has little choice but to tag along behind a global capitalism that offers it very little by way of development prospects. Once again we recall Colin Bundy's bold formulation regarding the unpromising "leap of faith" required to imagine a transformative capitalist future for South Africa.[37] Surely there are stronger grounds upon which to build an "Afro-optimism" than through such a feckless flight to the right.

## Meridional Thatcherism

Interestingly the sensibility evoked by Bundy parallels the thoughts of leading left political economists like Greg Albo who also, in their more general work on such themes, juxtapose self-consciously the claims of "utopian capitalism" against the promise of "realistic socialism." For Albo, the latter objective would focus (amongst other things) on "more inward-oriented economic strategies" and the devaluation of "scale of production as the central economic objective," goals that "can only be realized through re-embedding financial capital and production relations in democratically organized national and local economic spaces sustained through international solidarity and fora of democratic co-operation." Not that the precise nature of such an alternative can readily be sketched in blueprint form. It would have to be specified in practice by those social forces who might yet mobilize themselves to place a more progressive agenda on the table in South Africa. Perhaps, as I have suggested elsewhere, the "growth through redistribution" emphasis that floated momentarily through the movement could still provide the starting-point for a process of "structural reform" with longer-term transformative potential. But there would also have to be a greater willingness to accept that the existent market-dominated global order — driven by "a minority class that draws its wealth and power from a historically specific form of production" — is (in Albo's words) "contingent, imbalanced, exploitative and replaceable."[38]

Unfortunately, this is precisely the kind of sensibility that the ANC's leadership has continued to devalue. It is true that, for all their talk of TINA, this group most often does not present itself as the reluctant slave of the imperatives of the global marketplace but rather as its enthusiastic, born-again, protagonist. Still, many explanations of the neo-liberal turn that the ANC has taken are cast in terms of the structural determinations upon their actions that are defined by economic necessity. For

Ann Bernstein and her big-business backers at the Centre for Development and Enterprise there is no doubt, given the strength of capital and the (benign) workings of the global economy, that "at the turn of the century, there is not much choice for South Africa. . . . There is only one road to follow if we want to . . . put the country on a sustained high growth path." Evoking the example of Britain's Tony Blair, who "has led the Labour Party away from its socialist and union-dominated past" and "is ruthless in ensuring that key members of the cabinet and party 'toe the new line,'" the CDE suggests that, similarly in South Africa, "a certain degree of toughness is . . . required to impose the new vision on the party and follow through with the chosen policies." And despite concerns about too slow a pace to privatization and too little government action to meet the need for greater "labour flexibility," the CDE survey is nonetheless pleased to point out that "business leaders who have met Mbeki are positive" and affirm, with minimal qualification, that "South Africa is fortunate to have a person of Mbeki's quality to lead it into the next century." Or, as one banker stated even more frankly in the wake of the 1999 elections: "The ANC are not fools. They know where the balance of economic power lies."[39]

The more detailed specification of just how the differing demands of diverse fractions of capital have shaped the policy substance of the transition is more debatable. At the most general level, there is a commonsensical reading that what determines government thinking is the presumed imperatives of retaining in the country as much as possible of the investment funds of large-scale domestic capitalists and of attracting fresh investments from abroad. Some observers also emphasize a less South Africa-centric logic to the choices made, suggesting the drive of certain key sectors of domestic capital to free themselves of the shackles of their South African siting as sufficient impetus to impose neo-liberal policies on the government. Here the emphasis is on the crucial role of "the Mineral-Energy Complex" that Ben Fine and Zavareh Rustomjee have shown as being so central, both historically and contemporaneously, to the South African economy.[40] The increasingly diversified global role of the main components of this MEC (and, in particular, of the vast Anglo-American conglomerate) and the extent to which the substantial percentage of its assets are now held in potentially footloose financial form provide another strong reason for it to seek as open a horizon as possible for its movements. Did this factor give an added edge to the pressure on government to lift capital controls, for example, and to give its blessing to the decision of a significant number of key companies to relocate their corporate centres offshore?

For critics the search for explanations continues, especially given that the government's choice of strategy has been quite so unqualified, its capitulation to the world of market signals and market forces quite so complete. Not surprisingly critics have sought additional explanations for the precipitous rush to go much further and faster to the right than even the most informed emphasis on the pressing nature of global constraints might seem to warrant. Was the ANC leadership pushed or did it jump? Is another structural determination not that of the "imperatives" of class formation, the upper echelons of the ANC having bought quite comfortably into a common class project with the white bourgeoisie, both global and local? Here, it is suggested, the best point of reference for analyzing the South African transition might be Frantz Fanon's notion of a false decolonization: the rising African middle class, both entrepreneurial and political/bureaucratic in provenance, merely sliding comfortably into their political positions as, yes, "intermediaries" of global empire and, from these heights, fending off the claims of the poverty-stricken they have left behind.[41]

Such critics find evidence for this interpretation in certain statements made by Mandela, who, as early as 1992, was warning a journalistic interlocutor that "we are sitting on a time bomb. . . . Their enemy is now you and me, people who drive a car and have a house. It's order, anything that relates to order [that's the target], and it's a very grave situation."[42] And they will find further confirmation in The Economist, which in 1996 could write (albeit more in glee than in anger):

> For all the fears that resentful ANC socialists would confiscate wealth, the new breed shares the same capitalist aspirations as the old. Though black incomes are barely a sixth of white ones, a black elite is rising on the back of government jobs and the promotion of black business. It is moving into the leafy suburbs, such as Kelvin and Sandton, and adopting the outward symbols of prestige — the BMW, swimming pool, golf handicap and black maid — that so mesmerize status-conscious whites.[43]

Or to take another equally sobering account:

> On an April evening almost exactly three years to the day after South Africans voted Nelson Mandela into power, you could watch, at a black-tie dinner in Johannesburg, the dynamics of South African power relations change before your eyes. The dinner celebrated the deal in which Anglo-American — the vast mining house that rules the South African economy — sold a controlling share of Johnnic, a $2 billion company with blue-chip industrial holdings, to a group of black businesses and trade unions called the National Empowerment Consortium (NEC), led by Cyril Ramaphosa. "I think," said Anglo-American's Michael Spicer when introducing Johnnic's new head, "we can call you chairman Cyril rather than comrade Cyril." Replied the former trade unionist who led the mineworkers' charge against the company a decade ago: "It's wonderful to have Anglo as a minority shareholder!" Ramaphosa, the man most responsible for organizing the working masses into the collective action that brought apartheid to its knees, now leads another charge: an advance, by the mushrooming black middle class, on the commanding heights of the economy. The corporate sector is crowing. "Cyril Ramaphosa was the man who built

the unions in the eighties," one very senior Anglo-American executive tells me, "and he'll be the one to break them in the nineties."[44]

Nor, despite Ramaphosa's own subsequent difficulties in keeping his place as a would-be captain of industry, is this an isolated incident. One can almost never find examples of prominent ANC personnel who, when resigning or being removed from office, announce their return to the ranks of the popular movement: like prominent former ANC provincial governors Tokyo Sexwale and Mathews Phosa, they tend to wind up following such pursuits as the diamond business or casino development in Mozambique. Small wonder that the authors of one careful analysis of the transition could conjecture:

> On the one hand, the government seems, in a way very reminiscent of equivalent groupings such as Swapo in Namibia or ZANU-PF in Zimbabwe, to resemble a club of old party militants who are more concerned to reap the rewards of their own earlier sufferings than to effect major changes in society. On the other hand, with the disappearance of the revolutionary vision which undoubtedly spurred such militants on in the past, what is left is largely a class promotion project, the promotion of a new class of wealthy and powerful African movers and shakers.[45]

One could easily overstate the positive significance of this trend in broader developmental terms, whatever its more immediately obvious negative implications for class formation within the country's black population. Structurally, black capitalism has proven to be a weak force, especially since the Asian crisis of 1998 and subsequent falling stock prices and rising interest rates that confounded black capitalists' hopes of repaying the loans with which they initially purchased shares in various enterprises. Recently, too, "black empowerment enterprises" (often in any case fronts for white enterprises) have had a sharply declining share of JSE listed stocks (after an early high-water mark of 9 per cent in 1996), with certain enterprises earlier devolved to "black" ownership even reverting back to their original owners (like the Afrikaner economic giant, Sanlam). In this and other ways, contemporary South African capitalism offers little room for the emergence of a vibrant and transformative "national (and/or 'racial') bourgeoisie," however much ANC statements (and certain of its affirmative action policies) may seek to imply otherwise.

All the more startling, then, is the saliency of the discourse that has come to rationalize the role of this ostensibly rising class. In the most general terms, a key trope has been Thabo Mbeki's evocation of the "African Renaissance" to describe the moment, continental and national, that he and his ANC now embrace. His speeches on this theme (notably his "I Am an African" address to the South African Constitutional Assembly in 1996 and his "The African Renaissance, South Africa

THE POST-APARTHEID DENOUEMENT

and the World" speech to the United Nations University in Tokyo in 1998) can sometimes sound notes of dramatic resonance.[46] Equally often, however, such ideas have come to be attached precisely to the rather narrower definition of "black empowerment," a note struck most dramatically in a speech by Mbeki to a meeting of black managers in late 1999.[47] There the emphasis was on the need to "strive to create and strengthen a black capitalist class," a "black bourgeoisie." Since "ours is a capitalist society," Mbeki continued, the "objective of the deracialization of the ownership of productive property" is key to "the struggle against racism in our country."

There is a problem, however: "Because we come from the black oppressed, many of us feel embarrassed to state this goal as nakedly as we should." Indeed, Mbeki said, "Our lives are not made easier by those who, seeking to deny that poverty and wealth in our country continue to carry their racial hues, argue that wealth and income disparities among the black people themselves are as wide as the disparities between black and white. Simply put, the argument is that the rich are rich whether they are black or white. The poor are poor, whether they are black or white." All of which, Mbeki continued, "frightens and embarrasses those who are black and might be part of the new rich." In short, the new black capitalist class are victims — of class analysis. Of course, structures of racial inequality are a continuing problem in South Africa. But can the issue of class formation, and its long-term social and political implications, really be finessed away so easily in the new South Africa? Like them or not, the statistics suggest otherwise: as it happens, "the rich are rich whether they are black or white."[48] One fears that as the celebrated "African Renaissance" comes to be more and more about the "embourgeoisement" of the favoured few, it becomes a very tawdry thing indeed.

Some hard-boiled analysts of the ANC's history profess no surprise at such an outcome, having interpreted the ANC's entire history as a nationalist movement as the expression, first and foremost, of a narrowly petty bourgeois project.[49] And certainly the knot of assertive nationalism, middle-class opportunism, liberal-democratic aspiration, and all-too-Stalinoid socialist ideology that have come to define the ANC's politics over time remains to be further untangled. As early as 1984 Mbeki was forcefully asserting: "The ANC is not a socialist party. It has never pretended to be one, it has never said it was, and it is not trying to be. It will not become one by decree for the purpose of pleasing its 'left' critics." True, he saw fit to add that the ANC represented the "notion of both an all-class common front and the determined mobilization of the black proletariat and peasantry," with this working class to be viewed as "a conscious vanguard class, capable of advancing and defending its own democratic interests."[50]

Nonetheless, despite this utterance, Mbeki seems to have had little trouble in adapting comfortably to a bourgeois milieu. In 1999 a columnist in the *Washington Post* reassured his readers by quoting a remark made to him by a prominent London-based investment banker: "Mbeki holds things close to his chest and makes decisions in a secretive way. However, he is not a populist, and has been a 'Thatcherite' in his fiscal ideas. His experience in exile introduced him to the financial world — he is unlikely to abandon the close ties to business developed in those years abroad."[51] Although there is no evidence of personal corruption, the account of Mbeki's preferred social circle, frequented on numerous occasions by shady figures from the soccer world and by business hustlers, in a recent (otherwise largely hagiographical) biography — in a chapter entitled, significantly enough, "The Enigma" — also makes for sobering reading.[52] As does the moment, at the public launch of GEAR, when Mbeki took particular delight in guying the left by himself declaiming: "Just call me a Thatcherite."[53]

That particular moment, in its self-conscious crassness, in its smug ultra-hipness, seems especially revelatory — its very bravado eloquently capturing the prevailing undercurrent of the ANC-dominated transition. Not the undercurrent represented by Mandela's contribution to that transition, to be sure. As Andrew Nash imaginatively argues, Mandela evoked a more traditional ethos ("a tribal model of democracy," Nash terms it) in playing his own crucial role in the first five post-apartheid years, muffling societal contradictions (for both good and ill) within a mythos of consensus.[54] Beyond structural determinations (of economy, of class formation), here was one way in which variables defined in terms of politics and personality must also be made part of the explanation of outcomes in South Africa. But Mandela's was not a politics that the younger generation, epitomized by Mbeki, either could or would choose to play. Their sense of self-importance bore no quasi-traditional markings. It was auto-produced: having pulled off the impossible, the overthrow of apartheid, they were very pleased with themselves indeed. Too smart now to be mere ineffectual lefties, they expected to play the only game in town (capitalism) successfully. It is this kind of coolly self-satisfied, self-righteous, and profoundly ideological thrust on the part of the new ANC elite ("sellout" is much too crude a term for it) that is the single most depressing attribute of South Africa's transition.

Worth bearing in mind is that such cadres had seen some kinds of "socialism" in tatters — in Mozambique, in the Soviet Union — and sensed the dangers of the fierce discipline, economic and political, that global actors might inflict upon South Africa if it stepped too far out of line. They also saw some of the weaknesses of the institutions of the state that they had inherited — and the limits that these weaknesses might impose on any attempt to undertake too heroic a collective project. Such considerations (including as well the very pointed sense of just what risky work it would be for them personally and collectively to choose to swim against a worldwide tide) may also have helped to counter any misgivings about the nature of the global capitalist system to which they now pledged allegiance. For there have been signs of such misgivings. For example, at the 1999 Davos forum that brought together heads of state and of multinational corporations to discuss the question "Is global capitalism delivering the goods?" Mandela was prepared to ask some questions of his own. "Is globalization only to benefit the powerful and the specula-tors? Does it offer nothing to men, women and children who are ravaged by pover-ty?"[55] In 1998, at the twelfth heads of state meeting of the Non-Aligned Movement, Mbeki observed that "the 'free market' path of development . . . has failed to live up to the expectations of the people of the South."[56] In the same year Mbeki pro-nounced that South Africans "must be in the forefront in challenging the notion of 'the market' as a modern God, a supernatural phenomenon to whose dictates every-thing human must bow in a spirit of powerlessness."

That last assertion, for all its seeming radicalism, was immediately fleshed out, though, by a statement of praise for the IMF, World Bank, and WTO as examples of the kind of "human intervention" needed to anchor any such challenge.[57] The tenor of Mbeki's celebrated 2000 tour of world capitals offers another example of this tendency. Mbeki touched base with the Clintons, the Blairs, and the Schroeders and with the doyens of the international financial institutions, the WTO, and the global business community. At every stop his emphasis, invariably well received, was on poverty alleviation. Yet this is a seemingly progressive trope that does not make those at the top, looking down, at all uncomfortable. Who could deny the exis-tence of poverty in Africa (including South Africa) and who would not be, chari-tably, against it? But what if the problem were named differently: as a deepening polarization of social classes across the colour line and around the world that is reinforced by the very logic of capitalist-centred development strategies? Unsurprisingly, this is not a language that either Mandela or Mbeki have cared to employ, let alone to use as reference point for drawing any more assertive conclu-sions for domestic policy from their occasional (and apparently quite fleeting) expressed suspicions regarding the magic of the market. More often such murmurs of dissent about global contradictions seem designed to make it that much easier, in terms of local mass consumption, to shuffle off responsibility for any lack of economic progress in South Africa to rather more shadowy forces deemed to be beyond the ANC's control.[58]

Indeed, in the context of a particularly subtle analysis of "how the ANC has reproduced its power since 1994," Hein Marais has identified such displacement of responsibility for the slow pace of change as one — albeit only one — dimension of the hegemonic narrative that ANC leaders have skilfully woven together.[59] But there is also the legitimacy, slow to dissolve, that accrues to the ANC as the histor-ical agent of black liberation/African nationalism — as well as the legitimacy that springs from the movement's continuing evocation of a project of racial redress. Moreover, despite its ambiguities in class terms, the project of racial redress does have a resonance: after all, there continue to be cadres within party and state who have dedicated themselves to the betterment of conditions of their fellow South Africans and availed themselves of the fresh opportunities opened up by deracial-ization and democratization to work for positive improvements in the lives of their fellow citizens. Perhaps such militants have too often taken comfort in the notion that half a loaf is better than none, but Marais suggests that in a range of sectors they have nonetheless staffed programs that have had pertinent and positive effects. "The often-valid critiques of ANC delivery mounted by the left — especially its impact on levels of inequality and poverty — have tended to play down its many notable accomplishments," he writes, and then to back up his point cites a range of encouraging official figures for areas such as water, electricity, telephone, nutrition, housing availability, and some spreading of welfare benefits.

Yet Marais himself is also forced to admit, "Sadly, some of these claims lose their lustre once scrutinized." Certainly, the squeeze on expenditure arising from fiscal conservatism and the prioritization of deficit reduction has been linked to such realities as the often rapid breakdown of what have turned out to be merely jerry-built services, the rising backlog in the quantity of public goods actually delivered and the parallel decay of many public health and educational programs (in a context in which private facilities have begun to multiply geometrically for the well-to-do).[60] Moreover, many possible areas for innovative policies seem merely untouched: land reform, for example, where "fewer than 20 of the 23,000 land claims lodged with the statutory Land Commission have been settled" and "less than 1 per cent of South Africa's farmland has been redistributed to poor, African households." There is, of course, the obvious question: why has the backlash to such realities (and to other, even more central ones, like the desperately high rate of joblessness) been so muted? Here Marais introduces another variable, what he suggests to be a shared and tolerant understanding on the part of the populace as to just how long the road to redress of widespread penury must be in a situation such as that inherited by South Africans from apartheid. As he puts it, "The majority of South Africans know that the road to freedom and a better life will not take just five (or ten) years." He suggests that this recognition is not a matter of "fatalistic patience . . . but the residues of knowledge accumulated through countless personal and collective struggles."

The country did not actually feel like that to me during my stay there, I must confess. On the left there was the sense that the road, however long, was not running in a very promising direction. But more generally, and even more striking, was, yes, quite a lot of fatalism (and/or cynicism). And, equally marked, the weakness, not the strength, of any sense of shared purpose — together with clear signs that the ANC, reluctant to facilitate a substantial mobilization of people for any more transformative purpose than fairly passive vote delivery, is content to allow the profoundly individualizing logic of a market society to help actively to demobilize and neutralize the mass of the population. No doubt this outcome has been reached because South African society is so deeply (albeit unevenly) marked by capitalist development, because it is a society in which a profoundly (if frustrated) consumerist culture, especially in the sprawling urban areas, now seems far more resonant than any presumed residue of the much-discussed traditional and collective-oriented spirit of "Ubuntu." Yet the ANC's choice to go against mobilization and for neo-liberalism has also helped to deepen this culture, a culture that has become, in turn, a crucial ingredient of the ANC's hegemony: the "common sense" of a South Africa that is, at least for the moment, only narrowly politicized. Can there be any doubt that this outcome represents a sad denouement for South Africa's mass democratic movement, a movement that in its march to victory promised so much more in terms of sustaining positive social purpose and releasing social possibility? Here, surely, will lie one of the harshest of the verdicts ultimately rendered by historians regarding the ANC: that it chose to sacrifice so much of that promise on the altar of the marketplace and, in doing so, squandered an opportunity of world historic proportions.

## Starting from Scratch?

In focusing upon the terms of ANC hegemony we should nonetheless avoid any underestimation of the hard edge that Mbeki and his party also maintain in order to lock their project firmly into place — the iron fist beneath the velvet glove of their undoubted legitimacy, as it were. The truth is that many members of that leadership group are people of limited democratic sensibility who simply do not like to be crossed. Most importantly, Mbeki's own approach to the exercise of power is far less avuncular and "chiefly" than Mandela's. The style of top-down control and micro-management was already visible during Mandela's term, when Mbeki effectively orchestrated much of the hands-on functioning of the state apparatus. Mbeki's peevishness was also on display during that period. It was he, for example, who seemed principally responsible for the ANC's initial rejection of the Truth and Reconciliation Commission's final report, an approach, based on a demagogic and wilful misrepresentation of that report's mild critique of the ANC's own abuses of power in exile, that undermined much of the positive resonance that report might have been expected to have. As president Mbeki has further centralized things in his own hands. That virtually no leading ANC politician would publicly critique his stubborn attempt to contradict progressive consensus on the question of the link between HIV and AIDS may provide some indication of just how far the writ of his own authority runs. But his very stubbornness on this issue may also suggest exactly what one would be up against in daring to cross him: in consequence, an air of considerable trepidation scars official circles, with only the occasional bold soul (like Johannesburg councillor Trevor Ngwane, suspended from the ANC for choosing to defy the government's sweeping privatization schemes for the city) daring to risk career prospects in defence of principle.[61]

Moreover, this distaste for disagreement has proven to be even more pronounced with respect to the policy-making centrepiece of the Mandela/Mbeki presidencies, the commitment to meridional Thatcherism epitomized by the adoption of the GEAR strategy document. From the outset this document — although never publicly debated or even, it would seem, vetted by Mandela himself — was declared "non-negotiable." Both Mandela and Mbeki took great pains to defend it.

At the 1999 conference of the South African Communist Party, the ANC's ostensible partner (along with COSATU) in a formally institutionalized political "Alliance," both men produced paroxysms of rage against any who would have the effrontery to criticize the policy. The language used to whip its allies into line was harsh, variously described by Southscan as "markedly aggressive," a "scathing . . . barrage," and a "public onslaught." Mbeki accused SACP leaders of "fake revolutionary posturing," terming them "charlatans" and "confidence tricksters" who were attempting to build their organization "on the basis of scavenging on the carcass of a savaged ANC."[62] As for Mandela, he stated firmly: "GEAR, as I have said before, is the fundamental policy of the ANC. We will not change it because of your pressure." He hinted darkly of the consequences that might well follow from any continued criticism of the strategy.

Although the rhetorical fury unleashed by Mandela and Mbeki at that conference was particularly vitriolic, this kind of attack has been linked to an offensive also directed in recent years against criticisms from COSATU and its affiliates. A particularly startling example was Mbeki's 1998 address to the South African Democratic Teachers' Union (SADTU) congress, where he contemptuously characterized the membership as a "bunch of drunken and ill-disciplined teachers" and lashed out at their union's expressed scepticism about GEAR:

> The members of SADTU stand out as competent practitioners of the toyi-toyi. We [Mbeki sardonically used the associative "we" in making his points] come across as militant fighters for a better pay cheque at the end of the month. We are seen as excellent tacticians as to when to disrupt the school programme so that we can extract from the Government the greatest material benefit for ourselves. . . . We behave in a manner which seems to suggest we are alienated from the revolutionary challenge of the education of our youth and masses and greatly inspired by the value system which motivates the traitor and the criminal.[63]

Flash forward to 2000 and the ominous report that now-President Mbeki "has lost patience with COSATU's and the SA Communist Party's opposition to government's market-friendly policy," with the union's national strike (May 2000) "against spiralling unemployment and grinding poverty (being) the last straw for the President." According to the *Financial Mail*, "What irks Mbeki most is the COSATU/SACP contention that his free-market economic policy mix is to blame for rising unemployment and poverty."[64]

Not surprisingly, perhaps, this virus of contempt for dissenters has been catching amongst ANC ministers. In 1998 Derek Hannekom, the minister of land affairs, launched an attack on the National Land Commission when that non-governmental organization advocated the scrapping of the property rights clause in the constitution in order to facilitate land restitution. Hannekom accused the National Land

Commission of being "stubbornly frivolous" and "ultra-left," the latter being precisely the phrase used about the same time by constitutional affairs minister Valli
Moosa to dismiss a campaign by the South African Municipal Workers' Union
(SAMWU) against the privatization of water and municipal services.[65] And when, a
year later, public service minister (and SACP member) Geraldine Fraser-Moleketi —
for her pains dubbed "Thatcher-Moleketi" by a sympathetic conservative Sunday
newspaper — also used that phrase in coldly backing down the wage and anti-privatization demands of public-sector workers, she even proposed that they read
Lenin's "Left-wing" Communism: An Infantile Disorder! Meanwhile, at COSATU's 1999
conference, Terror Lekota, minister of defence and chairman of the ANC, delivered
a speech on behalf of Mbeki in which he warned the union darkly that "the recent
trend on the part of some highly-placed comrades of ascending platforms or by
other ways criticizing or agitating against policies and actions of the movement,
inside and outside government, smacks of a lack of revolutionary discipline." Lekota
suggested that "sharp and uncontrolled criticism merely confused the masses" while
also creating a climate "in which agents provocateurs can thrive and advance their
counter-revolutionary agendas."[66]

Here is the "one-party dominant system" so feared by many liberal observers
in South Africa showing its teeth, albeit teeth that are more often flashed at those
on the left than those on the right. Not, as we have seen, that the ANC has much
to fear from the political right. But then, at the moment, some would argue that
it really hasn't too much to fear from the left either. Thus, despite the raw treatment they often receive, the unions have clung to the Alliance, once again acting
uncritically at election time in 1999 as a key political tool in mobilizing votes for
the ANC. It is true that some labour-linked analysts have seen COSATU, with this strategy, as continuing to be a potent player in the transition; that COSATU is still armed
within the Alliance and within forums like the tripartite National Economic
Development and Labour Council to carve out space for forcing upon capital a class
compromise that is, at least in some of its particulars, to labour's advantage.[67] They
cite, for example, certain progressive aspects of post-apartheid labour legislation in
support of their further hopes in this regard and suggest that, in any case, the world
for COSATU outside the Alliance with the ANC would be even colder than the one
that seems to exist within. And it does seem likely that COSATU will accept this
premise for the foreseeable future — despite the pounding it has taken and despite
a certain amount of open debate within the labour movement as to the costs and
benefits of the Alliance.

Perhaps all the unions can realistically hope to gain in this way is a bit of time.
Thus, early in 2000, born-again neo-liberal columnist Howard Barrell wrote that
the new president would certainly sustain the party's conservative trajectory even if
doing so somewhat more surreptitiously than some (including Barrell) would like.
Why? In order "to avoid disturbing the ANC's left-wing Alliance partners," and this
is because, he continues:

An open declaration of the depth of its resolve to privatize, rationalize, down-size and liberalize may provoke an unhelpful response from trade unionists, communists and some in the African National Congress. So much better just to slip things past the awkward squad, if at all possible, with a few pat or ambiguous phrases and empty reassurances.[68]

Nonetheless, Barrell concludes, "Government economic measures are unlikely . . . to be any less decisive for the stealth with which they may be implemented." Small wonder, then, that a figure such as Saki Macozoma, identified as chief executive of Transnet, one of South Africa's biggest soon-to-be-privatized companies, and a for-mer senior ANC leader, could hail Mbeki's ascension to the presidency by suggest-ing that his "term will be an opportunity to revisit legislation of the past, like mak-ing labour regulations more business-friendly."[69] Certainly, legislation that favours greater "flexibility" in the labour market has continued well into the mid-point of the first decade of the century, with the threat this poses of eroding gains already made by workers in terms of minimum-wage guarantees and other related provi-sions, attended, as well, by the ever more widespread use of "casual," part-time (most often women) workers who are relatively unprotected by those laws that do exist. So too has there been a continuation of the wearing grind of policies of pri-vatization and retrenchment and of macroeconomic strategies fated to produce, at best, the jobless growth that has become so marked a dimension of the South African labour scene in the post-apartheid period.

Inevitably, some will judge that trade union leaders have remained unduly naive and/or unduly timorous vis-à-vis the ANC and the Alliance. Still, their approach has not dictated absolute passivity. In May 2000 in a protest against job-lessness, the trade unions (COSATU, together with its allies in other, smaller federa-tions) were able to organize a day-long stayaway that pulled over four million peo-ple away from work and produced demonstrations by hundreds of thousands of workers in major cities. Despite the ANC's threats COSATU vowed to continue with its critical role. According to one report, "Undeterred [COSATU general secretary Zwelinzima] Vavi says he has put in place a second programme of rolling mass action if government and business fail to respond positively to COSATU's demands to stem job losses, stop privatization and for the state to play a direct role in correct-ing market 'imbalances.'" Vavi is quoted as asking: "The economy is not working for us. GEAR is not working. How can we support this?"[70] True, the unions have been weakened by the post-apartheid drain of trained personnel to government and business, and they have paid a price for their defensiveness[71] and for their difficul-ties in defining a countervailing political economy for South Africa. But they con-tinue to criticize and even to keep alive a debate about macroeconomic alternatives, as in their 1995 report *Social Equity and Job Creation* and the exhaustive 1997 report of COSATU's own in-house September Commission. In particular, the September Commission sharply attacked GEAR as spawning economic policies that would be "likely to lead to the strengthening of vested economic interests which have their roots in the apartheid era" and would thus promise "to strengthen capital, and specifically its financial interests, and weaken labour," in the end offering "very little redistribution of wealth and economic power in our society." The report also evoked the possibility of a "new kind of struggle" and of more ambitiously progressive economic strategies that would "reclaim redistribution as the fundamental goal of economic policy and as an instrument for generating economic growth."[72] Moreover, trade unions have the numbers, revenues, and level of organization that will continue to make them the most important players on the left in South Africa.

But not the only players. Indeed, in terms of such potential as still exists on the left in South Africa, it may be that the most immediate question for COSATU is not what to do with reference to the (capital "A") Alliance (ANC/SACP/COSATU). At least equally important is the question of how to reach downwards and outwards to actors in others sectors who also feel the pinch of neo-liberalism: to dust off the language, so potent in the 1980s, of "progressive/working-class civil society" in order to rebuild, from below, a movement of resistance to the strategic direction that post-apartheid South Africa has taken. One should certainly not romanticize the possibilities of reconstructing such a base and forging, in effect, a new (small "a") alliance. The popular forces start at a low ebb, as an important article by Shamim Meer reminds us:

A striking feature of the post-election period has been the demobilization of civil society. As the anti-apartheid struggle has waned, the organizations that sustained it have lost ground and influence in public life. Trade unions, civic associations, youth and women's organizations — in which the struggle was grounded — are all weaker.[73]

How much is rebuilding an effective popular movement therefore a matter of starting all over again, from scratch?

Not quite. As Meer also points out, "The poverty and inequality associated with apartheid — and which fuelled the struggle — remain." And it is not only trade unionists who have begun to reanimate their efforts to question this outcome. Take the churches, for example. In 1998 Anglican Archbishop Njongonkulu Ndungane was himself slammed by Mandela for questioning the gospel according to GEAR. Nonetheless, the churches returned to the charge at the tri-annual conference of the South African Council of Churches later in the year. There that redoubtable campaigner against apartheid (and former secretary-general of the South African Council of Churches), Dr. Beyers Naudé, argued that "while GEAR is a 'party political issue,' when it affects the poor, the church has no option but to intervene." At the same meeting, Mzwandile Nuns, representing the worker ministry in KwaZulu-Natal, noted the government argument that they are "cutting social spending in favour of lower company taxation which will subsequently create an environment for more companies to invest." But, he continued, "What we see on the ground is different. The bulk of poor people remain where they were many years ago." The lesson? As another delegate to the conference, Professor Takatso Mofokeng, put the point, the churches "should go back to the trenches, because it seems that is the language the government understands." He added: "People should demand what they are entitled to and use the methodology that works. GEAR didn't come up for referendum. If people are not happy about it they must stand up against it."[74]

This kind of sensibility continues to percolate through church circles, providing, for example, some of the clout for the growing strength of a local Jubilee 2000 campaign that focused on the question of apartheid debt. While it is true that the formerly prominent South African National Civics Organization (SANCO) is amongst those organizations hit hardest by post-apartheid institutional decay, circles of township militants, focused on issues of schools, health facilities, and services, remain. New voices are beginning to be heard, asking tough questions, and they may give more dramatic life to broader township-based initiatives.[75] Some fledgling reactivation of grassroots women's organizations — significantly demobilized both by too sanguine assumptions about the extent of the victory for feminism achieved with liberation and by the movement of many militants into the state — has occurred around struggles over such issues as the state's child benefit grant. Peasant-linked NGOs such as the influential National Land Committee and the Rural Development Services Network have taken fresh energy from developments around the land issue in neighbouring Zimbabwe. Moreover, these two organizations are among those feeding into an assertive umbrella body, the South Africa National Non-Governmental Organizations Coalition (SANGOCO), which has taken a number of signal initiatives, including, in the past few years, a revealing set of nationwide public Poverty Hearings and the establishment of an Economics Commission of its own in order to seek to design a new framework for economic and social policies.

Can such initiatives begin to add up, giving real thrust and substance to an effective (small "a") alliance of organizations of the dispossessed? Fortunately, there are some signs that this is already beginning to happen. Thus, a news item in the *Financial Mail* (May 19, 2000) highlights how "organizations aligned to the ANC-led alliance have regrouped into a formidable lobby, which, judging by their frustration with government policy, could develop into SA's real political opposition," this underscoring the point that "the real opposition in SA is not to be found in parliament, but in extra-parliamentary politics — as was the case before the ANC's unbanning in 1990." COSATU, Jubilee 2000, and SANGOCO are among those identified as key actors in this initiative, with the spirit they exemplify captured in the words of SANGOCO executive director Albie Dithlake, a key figure in the group: "The debate on economic and social policy needs to be broadened. We need a reconfiguration of the nature of politics in SA. A realignment of politics will allow space for fresh input into the economic debate." As the *Financial Mail*'s report continues:

The new grouping argues that with the lack of a serious black-led opposition to the left of the ANC, an alternative group is one of the few means of pressuring the government. . . . The May 10 national strike against job losses and rising poverty, led by COSATU, should be seen as the grouping's first direct action. A steering committee comprising representatives of COSATU, SANGOCO and civic bodies has been formed to take the campaign further. It is demanding greater openness and inclusiveness in economic policy formation. Quiet but authoritative, Dithlake captures the mood of the new grouping. He quotes Reserve Bank statistics to show that the income of the poorest 40% has dropped by 21% in recent years. "Figures like this prove that the social responsibility of the state is eroding. We (SANGOCO) need a close link to COSATU to present a consolidated front on macro-economic policy," says Dithlake. "With the State's delivery infrastructure being put into private hands, or corporatized and expected to make a profit, it will be increasingly difficult to win the war on poverty," he says. "Unless urgent measures are implemented to improve the standard of living of the unemployed, the social cohesion of our society will be threatened."[76]

It is, of course, far too early to evaluate the prospects of any such attempt by various forces in South African civil society — including not only trade unions but also organizations of women, the church, the environmentally engaged, those focused on issues of land or education or community concerns, amongst others — to link up more self-consciously, within and across sectors, in a popular alliance from below. But if it proves possible to do so, they can be expected to take strength from each other and encouragement to think beyond the boundaries of their separate assertions — and also to take further steps to crystallize the institutions of a (heretofore often only implicitly) shared theory and practice of struggle. Perhaps in this project, one that is still fugitive and under construction but increasingly visible and marked with tangible potential, we can begin to see the seeds of the kind of "structured movement" that Canadian trade union activist Sam Gindin has recommended in his own country: "something transitional that is more than a coalition and less than a party," as he puts it. Indeed, Gindin argues forcefully that the much-debated "party question" (the left-liberal New Democratic Party? a new party?) be postponed for, say, five or six years in Canada, while the left movement/alliance — without abandoning its immediate concerns regarding self-defence and more appropriate policies — gives priority to the development of its "political capacities" (specified by Gindin in terms of "our understanding, our ability to win others over, the creation of new forums and structures for studying, working and fighting together").[77]

For South Africa as well this kind of analysis may suggest a downplaying, at least for the moment, of divisive and repetitive debates over the merits or demerits, from a progressive perspective, of working with and through the ANC itself and/or the Alliance. It bears noting, for example, that the Financial Mail described the new grouping of actors, in 2000, as being located "within [the] ANC family," and it seems almost inevitable that this should be so, at least for the foreseeable future. As for the longer run, it is quite simply premature to say where a revived popular movement of the sort anticipated here might eventually fit into the South African political equation. There have been those within COSATU (especially within the National Union of Metalworkers) who speak, from time to time, of the possibility of forming a new workers' and socialist party outside the Alliance and to the left of the ANC. This seems an unlikely, certainly precocious, demand for the time being. Yet the "official" ANC has by now been pulled so far to the right that, whatever the degree of (sometimes grudging) legitimacy it may retain among the mass of the population, it would be unwise to consider it automatically to be some kind of natural, necessary, or exclusive home for progressive assertion. The current party leadership has surely sacrificed that mantle, even if one believes that the ANC could once have laid claim to it. Thus, if not now then eventually, the question will have to be asked as to whether and to what extent the universe of the ANC and the Alliance provides a fruitful context within which to advance a rejuvenated popular movement and, in Gindin's sense, "an alternative politics."[78]

Within the Alliance, some continue to argue the case that a promisingly radical role can be played by the SACP — even though the party's self-definition as an (ostensible) political formation that is at once both mere cheerleader for and occasional left critic of the ANC seems a near-impossible one (and one that must also be a contributing factor to its sharply declining membership figures). The fact that many of the most right-wing figures in the ANC government are senior SACP leaders provides additional grounds for scepticism. True, the party can produce some radical-sounding pronouncements of its own; the recent calls of SACP general secretary Blade Nzimande for a deeper commitment to socialism and for more state action in the economy offer interesting cases in point.[79] It is also true that in the party — as in many other sectors — a cadre of younger activists, their number still small but growing, is emerging that is less wedded to time-honoured icons and homilies. Still, it is difficult, on past and present performance, to feel any great confidence in the SACP's vocation for driving a revolutionary revival.

How likely is it, alternatively, that any new stirrings of organized mass-based dissent will find effective expression within the ANC and even, possibly, begin to push that organization in a more leftward direction? This is not entirely implausible perhaps, and I have personally been occasionally jolted by a surprising development or two on that front. An example was the 1998 publication of an internal ANC discussion document, "The State, Property Relations and Social Transformation."[80] The document — whose precise provenance is not entirely clear, although it appears on the ANC's official web page — ridicules any tendency "within the NLM [the National Liberation Movement] . . . to propose solutions that would be way out of line with current realities, such as punitive taxes."[81] Yet it is just as uneasy about an equally "dangerous tendency . . . to be so awed by financial cap-ital that we throw the NLM prostrate in front of this sector as if in pagan prayer." More specifically, the document allows the notion of "the developmental state," so much maligned by recent critics of the early years of post-independence experi-mentation in Africa, to assume centrality in its formulations:

> In terms of the broad array of economic and social policy, information and even political integrity, the state has lost much of its national sovereignty. This applies more so to developing countries. While on the one hand they are called upon to starve and prettify themselves to compete on the "catwalk" of attract-ing the limited amounts of foreign direct investment (FDIs), they are on the other hand reduced to bulimia by the vagaries of an extremely impetuous and whimsical market suitor!
>
> Can a developmental state survive, let alone thrive, under such conditions? The answer is yes! The starting point should be that constructors of this con-cept should not live in a fool's paradise. They cannot pretend that they oper-ate in an environment entirely of their own making. . . . [However] what is of even greater significance is that many forces, both within and outside the government, both in the developed and developing world, do appreciate the disadvantages of the dictates of the multinationals and particularly the preda-tory nature of international financial capital. A significant sector of humanity is honestly searching for answers to these problems; and the ANC alliance is part of this global movement.

In consequence, the document suggests, not only should this developmental state "use the resources that it commands to ensure redistribution of wealth in the interest of the poor and disadvantaged" but "it should put in place regula-tory and other mechanisms that not only seek to obviate market failure, but also afford the state the capacity to intervene in a pro-active way to facilitate growth and redistribution."

The significance of such formulations should not be overstated. Overall, the message of this discussion document is much more cautious and "balanced"; it is circumspect in particular (albeit not altogether mistakenly) about the limits of insti-tutional capacity and shortfalls of effective leverage that must qualify the rebirth of a more transformative government strategy in South Africa. Does it reflect, nonethe-less, a South African version of that souring of the neo-liberal honeymoon that has become more of a worldwide phenomenon than might have been hoped even a few years ago, a tack that could begin to put not just the "developmental state" but even socialism back on the agenda? In the event, the press told us, any such signs of second thoughts within ANC official circles was "not roundly welcomed by eco-nomic hawks like Deputy President Thabo Mbeki and Minister of Finance Trevor Manuel."[82]

Still, by mid-2000, there was the curious case of Kgalema Motlanthe, the ANC's secretary-general, who contradicted the government's own condemnation of COSATU's May 10th national strike by calling on union members to "intensely hate capitalism and to struggle against it" and who affirmed that "the ANC is not a bourgeois organization. The country's leading socialist minds are in the ANC. Anyone who argues for socialism will find allies in the ANC." But it is equally true that Motlanthe's reported statements have often been quite contradictory (he is much given to dismissing out of hand those he calls "limbo socialists . . . who write revolution from armchairs"), and there seems an opportunist underside to his emphasis that "the unions should hold the capitalist system's transnational units accountable for job losses in the country — not the ANC or government."[83]

Can we take more seriously the even sharper comments of some party militants that "the ANC is itself a site of class struggle" — and that, given the party's continued popular legitimacy, it is actually a privileged site of such struggle, one not to be cavalierly abandoned by the left? Can we also take heart from rumoured rumblings that the star of the Mbekis, Manuels, Erwins, and Mbowenis may be on the wane within the ANC? Or from accounts of (for example) the emergence of a deepening left/right division cutting across the ANC in vitally important Gauteng province?[84] It remains wise for the left to approach the ANC, as organized and led, with great suspicion.

And yet one does sense that within the ANC there are indeed militants who have begun to grasp that the leadership's macroeconomic strategy does not and cannot work.[85] And they may also suspect that, in the absence of material advance and with the ruling out of court of a class-based politics, the situation is unlikely to stand still: it can quite easily get a very great deal worse, deepening already existing conditions of social distemper and producing further morbid symptoms of both the free fall into "the abyss of social exclusion" so feared by Castells and the threat to "the social cohesion of our society" invoked by Dithlake. There is, as a direct reflection of socio-economic polarization and communal decay, the precipitous rise in the crime rate (much of it crime of an extremely violent nature). There is the cruel decline of health standards, most marked, albeit not exhausted, by the escalating HIV/AIDS pandemic.

There is also, Marais suggests, the danger of much more dramatic expressions of loss of "social cohesion." One of these dangers is inherent in the ANC's own propensity to shore up its hegemony by pandering to local chiefs, in KwaZulu and beyond — the co-optation of Gatsha Buthelezi is an example — people whose power is rooted "in a blur of ethnicized tradition, coercion and clientelism." As Marais argues, "The constant disbursal of tangible benefits is one way of easing" the resultant tension. "Drawing the subjects and their leaders into the fold is another — hence, for example, the ANC's courting of the IFP, and the salary hikes for chiefs and kings decreed by the ANC government shortly before the recent election." The problem: "If this largesse cannot be sustained, the tension between the modern and the traditional will increase, allowing politicized ethnicity to regain its muscle."[86] Add to this that the venal Winnie Mandela can still find fertile ground for her racist populism in the gangrenous inequalities that lie untreated in an untransformed South Africa — even as, at the other extreme, some whites seek, in the more "privatized" racism of their guarded suburbs and schools, defence against the levelling so necessary in such a society — and one gets a further sense of just how potentially dangerous are the tensions that seethe beneath the surface.

All of this further underscores the need to generate an "alternative politics." But is the ANC itself (like the old Institutional Revolutionary Party in Mexico) not more likely to fall back on ever more authoritarian methods as its preferred means of seeking to contain (rather than resolve) the contradictions that now scar the South African social formation? Time alone will tell what the remaining Mbeki years will bring. Still, one senses that for all his cocky self-confidence Mbeki is not always quite certain himself as to just how best to ride the whirlwind he has helped create. Despite his apparently unqualified commitment to his chosen role of architect of South Africa's appeasement of capitalism as presumptive engine of South African economic transformation, he still appears to be bobbing and weaving rather uncomfortably — as he did in the run-up to the 1999 election, when he permitted himself some pretty radical-sounding formulations of his own. One such instance saw his revealing attack not only on wealthy whites (afflicted, he said, by "social amnesia") but also on a "black elite" that abuses "freedom in the name of entitlement."[87] This black elite, he charged, was seeking "to hijack the sacrifices which millions of ordinary people made to liberate our country for noble purposes, in order to satisfy a seemingly insatiable and morally unbound greed and personal thirst for wealth and comfort, regardless of the cost to our society." He concluded by warning of "the danger of a mounting rage to which we must respond seriously."

An intriguing statement with which to conclude this chapter, then, but perhaps as much for what it says about present-day South African society as for what it tells us about Thabo Mbeki himself. Does the slightly desperate tone of such pronouncements suggest, for example, an uneasy sense on the part of the leadership of just how impossible it will be to overcome the grim legacy of racial inequality on a capitalist basis? And perhaps, too, a certain subliminal suspicion that even when local elites do everything possible to conform to global market dictate, the dependent capitalism they seek to facilitate simply cannot be expected to lift off the ground as once it (sometimes) did. Moreover, even if Mbeki and his team can continue, by and large, to dodge these realities, there are others who have begun to recognize that it is precisely in the failure of the promise of neo-liberal deliverance that lie both the tragedy of South Africa itself and the broader global resonance of the South African case.

We have also posed a further question: if the leadership of the ANC cannot be expected to act upon any such understanding — cannot be expected to respond to the looming South African crisis by focusing "mounting rage" and potential political volatility into positive and transformative popular energy — who (if anyone) can? Whatever the answer to this question, the stakes are certainly high: for the phrase "socialism or barbarism" has rarely had more meaning than it now carries in contemporary South Africa.

CHAPTER 10

# STARTING FROM SCRATCH? A DEBATE

*My essay "Cry for the Beloved Country: The Post-Apartheid Denouement" (see chapter 9) sparked discussion in South Africa when it was first published in January 2001 and later reprinted, as did earlier briefer articles published in South Africa's Mail and Guardian newspaper.[1] The sharpest attack in the public realm came from long-time ANC and South Africa activist Jeremy Cronin, a distinguished poet jailed by the apartheid state in the 1970s for his political work. Cronin was serving as deputy secretary of the South African Communist Party and as an ANC Member of Parliament when he wrote his response. Following is my reply to Cronin.*

It is interesting that, on one of the two main fronts of inquiry opened up in my original essay, Jeremy Cronin professes — despite the wounded tone he adopts throughout and for all his talk about my "frozen penultimates," "sneers," and "derision" — to be in considerable agreement with me. This concerns my reading of the overall trajectory of socio-economic policy that the ANC government has adopted since 1994. As he puts the point, "Saul goes on to argue that the ANC liberation front has erred seriously on two critical fronts — the choice of economic policies, and the relative demobilization of our mass constituency (except during electoral campaigns). I agree with Saul on both counts." Indeed, he adds, "I agree substantially with the broad analysis of the last 12 years or so in South Africa that Saul makes in his pessimism of the intellect mode," including, it would appear, my criticisms of the "Government's macro-economic policy (the Growth Employment and Redistribution framework/GEAR), privatization policies, excessive liberalization measures, the failure to mobilize our mass base, or concerns about the growing bureaucratization and the influence of an emerging black bourgeois stratum on policy."

These are not small points and, coming from one so close to the scene as Cronin, tend to reinforce my confidence in my own negative reading of the neo-liberal socio-economic project embraced by the present ANC leadership. Moreover, the further articulation of that project since my writing of the original article in 2000 has merely confirmed this reading, with further major adaptations to the neo-liberal paradigm surfacing domestically: accelerated privatization; an apparent indifference to rising structural unemployment; the marketization of service delivery that makes such delivery unattainable to so many; and so on. Moreover, at least equally telling is the extent to which South Africa has emerged ever more clearly as point-man for global capital on the continent, as, it would appear, that system's sub-imperial power there. Though Thabo Mbeki, Trevor Manuel, and Alec Erwin profess to have an agenda for reform of the global market system in mind (even as they embrace it wholeheartedly), in practice their actions both undercut more serious challenges to that system from the Third World (as at the WTO meetings earlier this year in Doha)[2] and mask, as novel and daring departures, entirely submissive and market-friendly initiatives from the continent that are of their own devising (such as NEPAD, the so-called New Economic Partnership for Africa's Development).[3] Meanwhile, the chief goal of ANC free-marketeers seems to be to batter down barriers to South African-based capital's own ambitious plans for expansion into the rest of Africa.

Would Cronin disagree with this further extension of my argument?[4] Certainly such qualifications as he makes to this aspect of my original presentation are relatively minor — save for his extremely strained attempt, in his concluding paragraphs, to extract some scintilla of anti-imperialist consciousness and activism from Mbeki's frankly bizarre handling of the HIV/AIDS controversy in South Africa. Of course, one might then have hoped for some further explanation from Cronin as to why this kind of progression of the ANC project has occurred. The ANC leadership's own favourite excuse, at least for its economic policies, is that the structure of the global economy simply permits no other choice. By suggesting that the ANC has "erred seriously" in this sphere (he also speaks, with reference to GEAR, of "mistakes" having been made) Cronin does at least acknowledge that other options were indeed feasible. But does "erred seriously" really capture the dynamic of crystallizing class interest and preoccupation with consolidating its own power that has driven the ANC elite into both forging the alliance it has with global capitalist players and disempowering its ostensible mass base? More clarity regarding these processes — how structural they are and what room for manoeuvre they leave open — is required before taking seriously Cronin's favoured political remedies for what ails post-apartheid South Africa.

For whatever the degree of Cronin's agreement with me as regards my socioeconomic analysis (and regardless of the silences he also permits himself regarding that analysis), it is on the political front that he stakes his central critique of my position. Unfortunately, in stating his disagreements with me, he manages — whatever may be considered to be the merits of his own position — to wilfully distort my own, doing so by means of three distinct (albeit linked) moves. His first, and broadest, move is to claim that my approach is "cynical" (he identifies "a problematic cynicism of the will," said to be negatively twinned to my "healthy pessimism of the intellect") — a claim reinforced by his emphasis on my deployment of the term

"tragedy" and his suggestion that this too frames an almost entirely negative outlook on prospects for humane outcomes in South Africa.[5] Thus, owing to my "imposition of this tragic reading onto what is . . . still a relatively open-ended, complex
and highly contested reality," I am compelled (this is, in fact, his second move in
misrepresenting my argument) both to overstate the degree to which neo-liberal
capitalist hegemony has been established and to denigrate the "programmatic perspectives and achievements of progressive forces" in the country.

As it happens, I now rather regret deploying the term "tragedy" (although, in
truth, I only did so twice in over fifty pages) since, apparently, it can be taken to
imply that I regard as ineluctable a certain downward spiral in South Africa. But
the fact is that I neither evoke any such denouement elsewhere in the article nor
do I believe that it accurately characterizes the situation on the ground. Indeed,
Cronin knows perfectly well (as will any reader of the article — now chapter 9
here) that I have neither a grimly determinist view regarding the irreversibility of
global capitalism's hold upon South Africa nor a pessimistic view regarding the viability of resistance to it in that country. His first two points are, then, merely rather
seedy ploys designed to set up the third and most crucial point that he wants to
make against me: my "deep pessimism about the wisdom of progressive forces in
South Africa sticking with the ANC." Note, please, that this third point would make
no sense at all if I did not think that there are deep contradictions, economic, social,
and political, within South African capitalism that make resistance possible (even
inevitable) and did not think, as well, that there are genuine and vibrant "progressive forces" in South Africa capable of fighting that system. Can anyone read my
article and honestly argue that I do not present South Africa as offering "a relatively
open-ended, complex and highly contested reality"?

No, the real debate is not about my "cynicism," "pessimism," or "tragic" reading of the South African prospect. Really, for Cronin, it is about the judgment he
imputes to me that "there is no longer a radical transformational potential within
the ANC." Indeed, he continues, "Nothing short of leading the 'left' out of 'bondage'
to the ANC will, one suspects, begin to satisfy Saul." Note again, however, that on
this now much more substantive ground of presumed difference of opinion there
is also little evidence in my article to support Cronin's reading of my position. I
did argue that the stark contradiction between the ANC leadership's chosen socio-
economic priorities and the felt needs of the masses is giving rise to real tensions
that have begun to stoke the fires of a new mass resistance (to neo-liberalism) in
South Africa. But I left open the question of whether such energies would ultimately find their most effective expression within the ANC and its (capital "A")
Alliance — altering, even overthrowing, the current project of the ANC's leadership
from within — or would, instead, have to be mounted from outside that project.
Of course, Cronin is ultimately forced to acknowledge this too of my argument,
finally reduced to suggesting only that I have all too rudely underestimated just
how much opportunity still exists to advance an effective left project from within.

Nonetheless, we have now been permitted to reach the bedrock of Cronin's actual argument: his defence of the virtually exclusive primacy of the ANC and the Alliance as the terrain for meaningful left assertion.

What is one to make of this? To begin with, it is worth noting several illuminating "footnotes" that cast further light on the position taken by Cronin in his response. One surfaces from a reading of the now famous interview given (about the time of his fashioning his response to me) by Cronin to Irish journalist Helena Sheehan.[6] As it happens, Sheehan was moved to interview Cronin by having read my original article and some part of the interview is directed towards evoking his reactions to that piece. What is especially interesting is that, in this and other sections of the Sheehan interview, Cronin has much franker things to say about the actual room for manoeuvre offered within the ANC family than he concedes in his *Monthly Review* version. In this interview, for example, he speaks of tendencies towards "the Zanufication of the ANC" and of "a bureaucratisation of the struggle" and concedes that "the neo-liberals" represent "a powerful force inside the ANC" (though this group, he insists, "has its own weakness"). He also acknowledges that there are, in ANC practices, "elements of a brutal [and] very dictatorial dealing with the left." Noting in this regard the publication of an National Executive Committee (NEC) Bulletin denouncing an "ultra-left conspiracy" within the movement, he admits that he and others on the left "have been through a tough couple of years in the NEC. We've been marginalised, shouted down, subjected to heavy presidential attacks on us. . . . We've stood our ground but it's been hard." Perhaps, in light of these admissions, Cronin himself might be "less impolite," to use his phrase, to those (Cronin is quite willing to apply the term "ultra-leftists" to them in his interview and other writings) who begin to argue that the more assiduous pursuit of left alternatives outside the ANC/Alliance is becoming both viable and necessary. For, even if is arguable, it is far from "obvious" (once again, Cronin's word) that progressive endeavour in South Africa "requires on ongoing commitment to and engagement with and within the ANC."

And then there are the most recent of developments within the ANC, developments that have directly affected Cronin himself and that can also be considered to cast doubts on the adequacy of Cronin's *Monthly Review* argument: how available can the ANC be considered to be for progressive assertion in light of what has befallen Cronin personally in the wake of the Sheehan interview? For he was soon under heavy fire within the ANC for the effrontery of his criticisms, and the whipping boy at a highly publicized meeting of the ANC's NEC that ended with his abject apology for the remarks he had made in this interview. There has since been much debate in South Africa as to how best to situate this incident. The initial attack on Cronin (coming from the notorious right-wing demagogue, prominent KwaZulu-Natal-based ANC politician Dumisane Makhaye) had a racist, black-nationalist edge,[7] but there was much more to it than that. Was it, observers asked, primarily about disciplining heterodoxy, even of the mildest kind, within the ANC itself or was it about bringing to heel the SACP within the Alliance? Something of both perhaps, although the most immediate drama was a more personal one. For Cronin followed up his in-camera NEC recantation with the release of an extraordinary public statement:

> The unqualified apology that I made to the ANC National Executive meeting over the past weekend, for the contents of the interview I gave to Dr. Helena Sheehan, was neither coerced nor tactical. It has been made sincerely and as a matter of principle. In its approach, tone, and in the discussion of many internal matters outside of our organisations the interview was a mistake. What I most regret about the interview is that the undisciplined handling of serious issues can, precisely, undermine the fostering of robust debate, criticism, self-criticism and unity within our movement, not least between communist and non-communist ANC members. In the context of my own apology, the unambiguous reaffirmation by the ANC NEC of its commitment to the right of every member to raise and debate issues with and within the structures of the movement is one I welcome and remain dedicated to fostering.[8]

My own reaction (circulated widely on the Debate e-list in South Africa) was immediate, and I reproduce it here only because it is germane to developing in the present article my response to Cronin's overall position:

> Very sad — surely one thing the often sorry record of left endeavor during the twentieth century might have purged us of is this kind of 'correct-line' bull-shit — undisciplined be damned: I've read few more depressing paragraphs in recent years (in fact, it seems to confirm all my worst fears re. the ANC, the Alliance, and much else, as expressed in the original article that Jeremy critiqued in his interview!).

Similarly aghast was Sheehan herself, agreeing with me that she too had "read few more depressing paragraphs in recent years. I thought that the 21st century would be different, at least in that way. It reads as if it is Lukacs and the Comintern."[9]

Even more telling were voices raised by South Africans themselves. The distinguished journalist William Gumede in the *Sunday Times* urged his readers (in an article suggestively entitled: "Silence isn't golden in a true democracy: The ANC is doing South Africa no favours by lashing at anyone who dares to criticise it") to:

> Be worried, very worried, about SACP deputy general secretary Jeremy Cronin's grovelling apology for "uncomradely" public criticism of the ANC. Be equally worried when two enforcers of the party line, ANC Youth League leader Malusi Gigaba and ANC Kwazulu-Natal leader Dumisani Makhaye, rage against those who criticize the government "under the auspices of freedom of expression and debate" and get the party bosses' approval. . . . This kind of "disciplining"

by the ANC party bosses underlines the great pressure in South African society to conform and to defer criticism for the sake of "unity" and "patriotism."[10]

As Gumede continues: "The problem is that in the ANC the exile culture predominates. It is one of excessive control, centralisation of power, absolute loyalty and the discouragement of open electoral contexts." Moreover, "a loss of internal debate in the ANC has important implications for open debate in society. Quashing debate internally will inevitably lead to a muzzling of debate in broader society."

Interestingly, this interpretation echoes themes raised in a number of letters I myself received in reaction to my original article, notably one from the (now late) Lionel "Rusty" Bernstein, for over fifty years a key ANC/SACP activist. In that letter he thanks me for encouraging him to think further about "what is now happening to confound our hopes," about what, in short, "went wrong?" His answer: "Somewhere in the transition of the movement from 'home' to 'abroad,' that movement's leading cadre began to view liberation as meaning [merely] the acquisition of state power" and this "drive towards 'power' has corrupted the political equation in various ways." He added:

In the late 1980s, when mass popular resistance led by the United Democratic Front (UDF) "revived again inside the country," this drive led the ANC to see the UDF as an undesirable factor in the struggle for power, and to fatally undermine it as a rival focus for mass mobilization. It had undermined the ANC's adherence to the path [of] mass resistance as the way to liberation, and substituted instead a reliance on manipulation of the levers of administrative power. It has paved the way to a steady decline of a mass-membership ANC as an organiser of the people, and turned it into a career opening to public sector employment and the administrative "gravy train." It has reduced the tripartite ANC-COSATU-CP alliance from the centrifugal force of national political mobilisation to an electoral pact between parties who are constantly constrained to subordinate their constituents' fundamental interests to the overriding purpose of holding on to administrative power. It has impoverished the soil in which ideas leaning towards socialist solutions once flourished, and allowed the weed of "free market" ideology to take hold.[11]

My point here is not to debate the wisdom of Cronin's own choices in this affair or to score easy debating points off him, for purposes of the present exchange, in the wake of his personal discomfiture.[12] We can note, in passing, that he himself seems to have learned his lesson well, announcing, in the first of his interventions made public since the events — and against almost all evidence — that "by and large, the ANC and the government have maintained consistent anti-neo-liberal positions on all of the key issues of the day."[13] But, in any case, it is more important for present purposes to suggest that Cronin's own fate further underscores the likelihood that he has distinctly overstated, in his reply to me, the space for left manoeuvre that the ANC as now directed and institutionalized makes available. Moreover, this is a point reinforced by several documents released since the Cronin affair but bearing the marks of that event. First a leaked internal document from the ANC Political Education Unit fulminated against all those (especially various unnamed "foreigners")[14] who charge the ANC with "neo-liberalism," these "anti-neo-liberals" said, rather bizarrely, to now be in an "unholy alliance" with the neo-liberals themselves to "carry out a counter-revolutionary offensive against the democratic revolution."[15] Equally ominous was the tone-setting statement made by President Thabo Mbeki to the ANC's Policy Conference of September 27, 2002, which attacked the "ultra-left" without but also within the ANC. Noting that this ultra-left (pretty much defined as anyone who criticizes the leadership's policies from the left) "works to implant itself within our ranks" and "hopes to capture control of our movement and transform it into an instrument for the realisation of its [socialist] objectives," Mbeki then advances the proposition, as regards ANC membership, that "I am now convinced that we must also pay particular attention to the principle — better fewer, but better"![16]

I might add here that, in a much more modest way, I myself experienced something of this same high-handed ANC/SACP treatment of critics during a recent visit to South Africa. I was there to participate in several of the counter-conferences organized to contest the World Summit on Sustainable Development (WSSD), but at a moment that, coincidentally, also stood in the immediate shadow of Cronin's recantation. In Johannesburg I chose to give a university seminar designed to promote a discussion of my original argument in Monthly Review and of Cronin's response, the better to frame, on the ground, the present reply to it. The discussant was Raymond Suttner, like Cronin an ANC and SACP stalwart and also, like him, a heroic figure in the pantheon of those who had put their bodies on the line in the struggle against apartheid.[17] Unfortunately, Suttner seemed uninterested in engaging with the substance of my argument, choosing instead to caricature it and, with three or four other rather senior ANC and SACP personnel who had come to the seminar, to lend his voice to an attempt to carry out some kind of ritual humiliation of me. Fortunately, other South Africans at the well-attended seminar joined in helping me turn back this verbal assault. But, by the end of the meeting, nothing like enlightenment had occurred nor had any real airing of alternative views been encouraged to transpire. As one veteran of South African debate, long used to being on the receiving end of such tactics, said to me afterwards, now I knew what it was like to be "panga-packed" by the ANC/SACP.[18]

This kind of encounter was discouraging, but a second indication of ANC closure that I witnessed at first-hand in South Africa that same week was far more dramatic. On Saturday, August 24, an all-day meeting of the Anti-Globalization Forum, a counter-conference to the WSSD, addressed by such luminaries as Vandana Shiva, Maude Barlow, and Naomi Klein and attended by hundreds of South Africans, wound down. Those in the hall were now to set out on a peaceful candlelight march from the University of the Witwatersrand campus, where we had been in session, to the main police station in downtown Johannesburg in order to highlight the fact that the right to protest was being rolled back in the days leading up to the WSSD. (Substantial numbers of activists from each of three separate movements — Sowetans demonstrating against service cutoffs, landless people, and aggrieved former ANC soldiers — had been rounded up and detained in a manner reminiscent of the bad old days.)[19] However, only a few yards off the campus we were met by a strong police line and, almost immediately, by a brace of percussion bombs fired into the crowd. A young Canadian comrade (Karen Cocq) marching near me in the crowd was hit, suffering severe burns to her legs. The marchers did boldly rally and an impromptu meeting was held, anchored by the always impressive South African township activist Trevor Ngwane, before dispersing. For me, however, the event — and not least the scalding of Karen Cocq — served as a grim wakeup call as to just what the post-apartheid state and its "Zanufied" ANC leadership might be prepared to do, now and in future, to defend its turf.

But if this was how that week in Johannesburg began it was to close on a quite different note seven days later: with a large and spirited march (well over twenty thousand people), on August 31, on the WSSD Summit. This demonstration had been called in opposition to the "official" march sponsored by the ANC, and only a week of tense negotiations with the authorities had encouraged the latter to yield in anticipation to the alternative march's growing size and scope and declare it to be "legal." Setting out from the impoverished township of Alexandra it covered, over a number of hours, the ten-kilometres passage — from one world to another! — to the wealthy centre of Sandton where the summit was being held. Meanwhile, the ANC's own march drew only a few thousand people and quickly aborted, to be correctly described the next day as "a massive flop" by one South African newspaper.

It was impossible not to be caught up in the excitement. En route I was stopped for a television interview by the well-known Canadian writer and activist Naomi Klein. She immediately asked the most probing of questions, one I had myself been puzzling over in the week leading up to the event. "As a long-time anti-apartheid activist in Canada," she asked, "are you surprised to find yourself now participating in a march against the ANC?" Many of us had suspected all along, I answered Klein, that it might prove easier to lay formal apartheid to rest than to tackle the capitalist-induced inequalities that were also part of the old order. But, I continued, it was hard not to see in the energies of the thousands surging forward on this day precisely the same spirit of resistance to inequality and injustice that those of us in the anti-apartheid movement abroad had been privileged to associate ourselves with in the 1970s and the 1980s. Moreover, it was no accident, I reflected to myself later, that such energies had come into focus against the ANC and its neo-liberal policies.

For the chief protagonists of the unofficial march, both the leaders and rank-and-file of the "Social Movements' Indaba" central to its success, were drawn from a range of increasingly well-organized grassroots initiatives that have surfaced in the past few years to focus the involvement of people in active resistance to their own government's bankrupt policies. Indeed, it is the groups driving such initiatives that have begun to redefine the South African political landscape. They include, amongst others, the Anti-Privatization Forum, the Soweto Electricity Crisis Committee, the Treatment Action Campaign, the Western Cape Anti-Eviction Campaign, the Concerned Citizens' Forum in Durban, and the Landless People's Movement, and much of their spirit and thrust is captured in Ashwin Desai's recent book from Monthly Review Press, *We Are the Poors: Community Struggles in Post-Apartheid South Africa*, which can be recommended confidently to all present readers.[20] But the mainstream press has also had to take note of such developments, a fascinating *Washington Post* article of a year ago focusing on the activities of the Soweto Electricity Crisis Committee whose guerrilla electricians illegally reconnect those in the township whose supply has been shut off by the authorities for non-payment. Moreover, the article gives voice to the likes of Soweto-resident Agnes Mohapi:

"We shouldn't have to resort to this," Mohapi, 58, said as she stood cross-armed and remorseless in front of the home as the repairmen hot-wired her electricity. Nothing, she said, could compare to life under apartheid, the system of racial separation that herded blacks into poor townships such as Soweto. But for all its wretchedness, apartheid never did this: it did not lay her off from her job, jack up her utility bill, then disconnect her service when she inevitably could not pay. "Privatization did that," she said, her cadence quickening in disgust. "And all this globalization garbage our new black government had forced upon us has done nothing but make things worse. . . . But we will unite and we will fight this government with the same fury that we fought the whites in their day."[21]

For all Cronin's deep sense of commitment I fear that, in the end, the anger and urgency in Mohapi's voice simply find too little echo in his response. Equally instructive is the fact that Cronin makes no mention of the "social movements" just cited in his reply to me, even though their increased saliency was there for him to see by the time he wrote his reply. Of course, such is the volatility of developments in South Africa that it is not easy to keep abreast of their cutting edge. Take my own original article. In it I marked the beginnings of what I saw to be a sea change in South African politics — while noting (*pace* Cronin) both that the process of building an alternative politics was only then beginning and that it was far from certain whether the fresh stirrings of popular discontent already visible would find their most effective expression within or without the ANC and its Alliance. Still, I did argue the importance of an emerging (small "a") alliance capable of drawing the trade unions into common cause with other actors in "civil society" (the churches, SANGOCO, and the like) to bring genuine pressure to bear on the ANC-controlled state (and, beyond that, on capital, worldwide and local) in order to realize more humane and economically effective developmental possibilities in South Africa. Ironically, the groups I had then identified were the very groups that found themselves lured by the ANC into endorsing its own abortive march on the WSSD instead of linking up with the stirring demonstration of strength mounted by the Social Movements' Indaba.[22] In short, since I wrote in 2000, it is the other groups mentioned above that have stepped forward to give real substance to the radical promise of "working-class civil society." It begins to appear that COSATU and the NGOs will have to run to keep up with their sometime constituency as that constituency now turns left.

In light of this experience it has become easier to embrace the possible wisdom of those South African activists who do indeed seek to "lead the 'left' out of 'bondage' to the ANC" than it was when I wrote my earlier article. For, in fact, the ANC as now directed and constituted has little to say to such people and to such groupings. Nor can one have any great confidence that, in this respect, the SACP will overcome the inevitable ambiguities of its ties to the ANC: in but not of it, without electoral purchase, and, although abused and disempowered within the Alliance, offering nonetheless — in the very fact of its existence — a convenient excuse for the ANC leadership to dodge any leftist vocation of its own by consigning that remit to its ostensible ally.[23] One might expect the bulk of the trade union leadership to be even more promising potential tribunes for the people, but for them too entanglement in the Alliance increasingly seems to be at least as much snare as opportunity, a certain (valuable) recognition of union rights traded off against far too little leverage to affect progressive outcomes in most macro-policy spheres. Can one not then suspect, more strongly than ever, that the ANC project, the Alliance project, is — as one South African friend suggested to me — "exhausted"?

Perhaps, but, at the same time, I must refuse to be bullied by Cronin into accepting the mantle of "ultra-leftism" which he proffers me, or into seeing the situation as being less complicated than it really is. It would be foolish, for example, to underestimate the strength of the ANC's own continuing legitimacy, as the party of liberation, in many quarters, and the extent to which it still focuses the positive energies of numerous people who would nonetheless wish it were much more progressive than it has become. As one senior ANC official insisted in a letter to me in response to my *Monthly Review* article, the danger exists "of the left (defined in this case as the labor unions, the SACP and independent Marxists of various stripes and hues) isolating themselves on the left fringes of society" and thereby "handing the movement over to the right to do within it what it pleases": "If, as I imply, the ANC is itself a site of class struggles, would it be the smart option to move out of it and by default hand it to the rising waBenzis, or would it be smarter to contest their thrust?" And a recent news article brings a report that, in the run-up to the ANC's national conference of December 2002, "leftists" are indeed lobbying to place many more "left sympathizers" on the NEC — although this same article suggests that President Mbeki's most recent attacks on the "ultra-left" and the COSATU leadership are designed at least in part to help pre-empt any such outcome.[24] And there is also the fact that the process of "starting from scratch," if that is what is now required, will be uneven, more pronounced in Gauteng (the province housing Johannesburg and Pretoria), say, than in the Eastern Cape, where ANC hegemony is especially strong.

Similarly, it would be naive to overestimate the strength and unity of the new social movements, the breadth of their reach and of their alliances, the clarity of their strategies,[25] and the current level of their organizational capacity. There is, without doubt, a great deal of work to be done in order to seal the promise of a more progressive and appropriate politics in South Africa along novel lines, whatever these may prove to be. It is true, for example, that many workers begin to sense that wearing the political hat of their township and "social movement" identities rather than that of their unions promises to give them more effective leverage on power. Beyond this, some on the left may wish to argue that — in addition to the pull on many trade union leaders to identify upwards in the power game — organized workers more generally are often just too well sited socio-economically within the increasingly impoverished and polarized society that is today's South Africa to readily identify downwards and outwards with the country's vast army of the unemployed and the landless. And yet it would be foolish for radicals to ignore the South African "working class" and the formidable trade unions it has created: these unions' size, their organizational and financial capacities, their long history of militant struggle. Vulnerability to the assault of neo-liberal policies in post-apartheid South Africa is widely shared, as many unionized workers have found out for themselves in recent years. Finding a way more effectively to link trade unions and social movements (in a "structured movement"? a political party?) for progressive purposes is just one of the many challenges, barbed and unpredictable, that must be on the agenda of the ANC leadership's critics.

The issues thus raised are much too vast to explore in a mere "reply," of course. Let me conclude by simply stating that I feel, even more strongly than I did in writing my original article, that we are now entering novel and complex political terrain in South Africa, terrain that is extremely dangerous but also marked by genuine promise. Certainly, it is far too early to say that "the tide is turning," as one of the leaders of the August 31st march from Alex to Sandton enthusiastically shouted out to me along the route. Nonetheless, it was difficult to be on that march and not sense that it served as a significant signpost on the road to a post-neo-liberal and post-nationalist politics in South Africa — and as an impressive rallying point for those forces from below that might yet get things back on track in their country.

# A Reply to Suttner

*A subsequent issue of Monthly Review (June 2003)²⁶ brought a response to my reply to Cronin (and also to my characterization, mentioned in passing, of Raymond Suttner's own rather negative role in a seminar presentation of some of my interpretations of South Africa's recent development) from Suttner himself. I replied, briefly, as follows.*

The Johannesburg seminar is a pretty unimportant footnote to the broader struggle being waged in South Africa and, in any case, you probably had to be there, but many in attendance other than myself had a reading exactly like my own of the exchange in question. More generally, Suttner's derisive characterization here of the inadequacy of my scholarship and of the shortfalls in my intellectual and political integrity gives a good idea of the level at which he pitched his critique of my argument at that seminar. He'd do better to discuss substance (while providing some evidence of his own) and to note, as well, that I'm very far from being alone in my strong conviction as to the inappropriateness of the ANC's post-apartheid project (demonstrated even in the thinness of its service delivery accomplishments!) and in my growing suspicion that effective resistance to South Africa's neo-liberal project will have to come primarily from without the ANC and its vaunted Alliance. Moreover, most such critics are activists inside South Africa itself where, in any case, this "debate" will have ultimately to be settled. Nor, to repeat to Suttner what I said to Cronin, am I pessimistic ("tragically" or otherwise) about the prospect that a revival of resistance will occur; indeed, as I strove to establish, such a revival already is underway.

Meanwhile, the same week that brings Suttner's reply to my computer screen brings, amongst other sobering reports from South Africa, two items of particular interest. One finds South Africa's foreign minister lauding, against all the evidence, the progress that Mugabe's merciless authoritarian regime in Zimbabwe is making in moving towards democracy (this being part of a more general recent attempt by Mbeki and his team to run interference, within the Commonwealth and the Non-Aligned Movement, for Mugabe). Recall that Jeremy Cronin had his wrists slapped for suggesting that a "Zanufication" of the ANC was well underway. But what is one to think about Zanufication in light of this recent trend in ANC policy: indeed, the embrace of Mugabe is just one more reason for concern about the ANC's likely response to meaningful popular resistance to its own project at home as it continues to mount, I would have thought. And then there's the news that the ANC is seeking to breathe new life, from the top down, into SANCO, the until recently moribund central organization of South African civics, while setting it running against a "disloyal" COSATU — and, by implication, against the various popularly based organizations whose promising activities I underscored in my reply to Cronin. Of course, this represents a tacit acknowledgement on the part of the ANC leadership both of the growing strength of these latter movements and of the growing pull on many trade unions and their members to themselves begin to contemplate the embrace of a new kind of politics. But it also exemplifies, on the part of the ANC, a worrying, but consistent, strategy of attempted co-optation and control by increasingly dominant elites, black and white, rather than one of popular empowerment.

Indeed, one is left to ask just how far right the ANC under Thabo Mbeki's leadership would have to move before comrades like Suttner could begin to concede that this is not quite the outcome they had in mind when they sacrificed (as in Suttner's own case) many years in jail to overthrow the apartheid state? Meanwhile, for the record and for better or worse, I am not now and never have been a Trotskyist, if Suttner is seeking to imply otherwise with his "ice-pick" aside. Since he raises the point, however, I would guess that a long history of Stalinist politics within both the ANC and the SACP is one of several reasons why many cadres of these parties have difficulty in acknowledging the present strength of left, post-nationalist critique and accepting an invitation to substantive debate. But surely we must move beyond the practices both of studied disdain and mere name-calling if any such debate is to be truly open.

CHAPTER 11

# THE HARES, THE HOUNDS, AND THE ANC: ON JOINING THE THIRD WORLD IN POST-APARTHEID SOUTH AFRICA

The utility of framing questions of global inequality in relation to a "First World" and a "Third World," a North and a South, of developed countries and developing (or underdeveloped) countries has been debated since the end of the Cold War. This chapter addresses in general terms the issue of the perceived weaknesses and possible continued strengths of the notion of the Third World, and then grounds such a discussion through an analysis of how the African National Congress government in post-apartheid South Africa has approached the question of global inequality. Since its election in 1994, and more particularly since Thabo Mbeki succeeded Nelson Mandela as president, the ANC has presented itself as having an especially important leadership role on behalf of the Third World.

Yet the profound contradictions inherent in the ANC's effort both to retain its Third Worldist credentials and to present itself a reliable client to the Bretton Woods institutions and foreign investors provide insights into how to design alternative strategies for overcoming worldwide poverty, strategies that might be more effective than those chosen by the ANC. Since the ANC was elected to government in 1994 it has pursued a brand of deeply compromised reformism that serves primarily to deflect consideration away from the options presented by other much more meaningfully radical international and South African labour organizations, environmental groups, and social movements. At the present juncture a range of increasingly well-organized grassroots movements in South Africa find that they have no choice but to mobilize in active resistance to the bankrupt policies of the ANC. The increasing significance of these efforts points to the possibility that they might eventually push South Africa — either through the transformation of the ANC itself or through the creation of some new, potentially hegemonic political project in that country — back into the ranks of those governments and groups that seek to use innovative and appropriately revolutionary approaches to challenge the geographical, racial, and class-based hierarchies of global inequality.

Analytically, the value of conceptualizations that cast the issue of global inequality in terms of geographically defined hierarchies and binaries (First World vs. Third World; developed vs. underdeveloped or developing countries; "North" vs. "South") have come into some disrepute in recent years — even if, in political circles, these dichotomies continue to retain considerable resonance. In South Africa the government, particularly under the stewardship of President Thabo Mbeki, has presented itself as having an especially important leadership role to play in mediating and reconciling the gaps and tensions that such binaries evoke. There are, however, severe and quite revealing contradictions inherent in the ANC's attempt to articulate such a role for itself. Indeed, the peculiar difficulties of a government that has, simultaneously, professed to run with the hares of the Third World poor while also aspiring to hunt with the hounds of global capitalist power-wielders are themselves particularly revealing when it comes time for others to define alternative strategies that might prove more effective in overcoming worldwide poverty.

## What Is the Third World?

What, first, of geographically defined hierarchies?[1] As we mark, with a straight face, the twenty-fifth anniversary of the Third World Quarterly it is tempting to note the irony that Mark Berger seemed to have laid to rest with the very notion of "the Third World" almost a decade ago — and in this same journal. "The idea of a 'Third World,'" Berger wrote, "now serves primarily to generate both a dubious homogeneity within its shifting boundaries and an irrelevant distinction between the 'Third World' (developing) and the 'First World' (developed) on the other."[2] In thus critiquing the commonsensical understanding of the existence of a straightforward causal connection between the co-existence of a wealthy North and an impoverished South that once structured many analyses in both left and liberal development circles, he and others have sought to inter both "Third Worldist" conceptualizations and those suggested by the other often-used binaries. Such formulations, they believe, have lost much of whatever usefulness they might originally have had both for analyzing the (increasingly diverse) fates of the economies of the formerly colonized countries of the global South and for focusing the struggle against grinding poverty and the existing manifestations of extreme material inequality in an ever more globalized socio-economic environment.

Of course, the concept of Third World has seemed especially questionable to such writers, not least when considered with reference to the once rather more convincing logic of its original coinage: the disappearance — with the crumbling of the Eastern so-called socialist states, of anything that might once have been considered a "Second World" — has underscored the most self-evident of difficulties in this regard. More important is the problem (also thought to bedevil the other parallel binaries) of the increasing lack of clear referent for the concept even in its own terms. After all, South Africa is not the only country said to have both First World and Third World conditions (that is, extremes of wealth and poverty) within its own borders: this is true within the most advanced of capitalist societies as well.

Small wonder that, more recently, a writer such as Ankie Hoogvelt can suggest global inequality to be now much more "social" than "geographical" in its co-ordinates. "The familiar pyramid of the core-periphery hierarchy is no longer a geographical but a social division of the world economy," she writes.[3] For her, a global division of labour, more centrally than ever defined along lines of class and (often) socio-economic exclusion that cut across national frontiers, has created both a dominant transnational capitalist class and vast outer circles of less privileged people, both North and South. Such a model helps, she suggests, to comprehend growing inequalities within countries. But it also helps us to incorporate into our approach a much clearer acknowledgement of the dramatic diversity to be found among the countries of the so-called Third World itself: a spectrum that stretches all the way from the material accomplishment of the newly industrialized countries to the desperate situation to be found in the countries of the most impoverished zones of Africa.

But if the truth value of such tropes is so limited, what is to account for the fact that their continued deployment "has legs," surfacing as they still do not only in the common-sense discourse of prevalent political and journalistic shorthand but also in more scholarly publications and debates? A number of negative reasons have been adduced as to why this usage has occurred. Thus Berger approvingly cited Arturo Escobar to the effect that "to represent the Third World as 'underdeveloped' is less a statement about 'facts' than the setting up of a regime of truth through which the Third World is inevitably known, intervened on and managed." Berger's own conclusion: this is a crucial means by which key Western players can "homogenize" the experience of the very "particularity of social formations on the so-called 'periphery,'" the better to control them in the name of a universalizing "modernization theory."[4]

In addition, the attendant emphasis on the "original" nature of the "backwardness" of such social formations serves to shift attention away from a focus on the less than benign workings of "international market relations" and of global capitalist power that explain more adequately the problems they confront. As Berger specifies this point, "Economic development in the 'Third World' is seen primarily as a technical or policy problem . . . that can be overcome by the right mix of advice, investment, aid and liberal reforms . . . rather than [seen as] a historico-political problem."[5]

There is also the fact that tropes that emphasize the continued centrality of geographical hierarchy to the reality of global poverty have been subject to the most self-interested kind of manipulation by Southern leaders of often highly dubious provenance. Once again Berger makes the pertinent point: "'Third World' elites have emerged in the international arena claiming to speak for the 'Third World' at the same time as they are deeply implicated in the prevailing international discourses and structures which work to manage the "Third World.'"[6] As Brian Smith adds:

> There is thus the risk that the expression "Third World" might obscure the heterogeneity of social classes, each with its own political objective. The concept of the Third World has consequently been denounced . . . as mystification designed to conceal dependency and exploitation, as well as a device allowing rulers of Third World countries to present a common interest between themselves and the masses to disguise their own alliance with metropolitan interests.[7]

Here such points have general implications. For the ANC leadership in post-apartheid South Africa, however, there could scarcely be better shorthand descriptions of the role chosen for itself — albeit rather against the hopes and expectations that had arisen for it during the anti-apartheid struggle.

That said, there are a number of more positive reasons as to why conceptualizations of the Third World/First World and developed/underdeveloped type continue to have positive resonance. To begin with, it is not actually quite as easy as Hoogvelt and others imply to ignore the geographical co-ordinates of inequality. For, as Giovanni Arrighi and others have continued to document tirelessly over many years, there is still a great deal about the global hierarchy that remains spatially defined, and along lines that are also "largely a legacy of Western territorial and industrial expansion since about 1800." Thus, in a 1992 article on "the increasing inequality of the global distribution of incomes," Arrighi demonstrated "a major widening of the already large income gap that fifty years ago separated the peoples of the South from the peoples of the organic core of the capitalist world-economy." His conclusion: "The nations of the world . . . are differentially situated in a rigid hierarchy of wealth in which the occasional ascent of a nation or two leaves all the others more firmly entrenched than ever they were before."[8] This finding exemplifies for him a "seemingly 'iron law' of a global hierarchy that stays in place no matter what governments on the lower rungs of the hierarchy do or do not do." For in the absence of self-conscious correctives, the "oligarchic wealth" achieved by the West always tends to draw the bulk of capitalist activity towards it, hence widening the gap. Arrighi, updating his argument in 2003, also emphasizes the extent to which aggressive Northern neo-liberal policies deliberately reinforced this hierarchy when, in the 1970s, things seemed set to shift slightly in the South's favour.[9] He thus comes to precisely the same conclusion that he had a decade earlier as to the persistence of a North/South hierarchy of income — and this even though (and even because) some degree of industrial convergence has indeed occurred.[10]

There is, then, something important about the nature of the geographically defined material realities of the global hierarchy that must be kept on the table.[11]

As people in the Third World seek to improve their lot they do confront a global system of power, in economic and political terms (think: the militarized U.S. state and its complex interface with global capital), that — whatever else it may be — is also asymmetrical in spatial terms. Moreover, if a global movement to overcome inequality is to be built, one that seeks to unite struggles in both North and South, it cannot ignore the extent to which many in the North, and well beyond the ranks of the most wealthy, have come to share in one way or another in the North's "oligarchic wealth." In consequence, if the legitimate claims of Southern peoples to global income redistribution, equitable environmental controls, rights of migration, and freedom from high-handed military incursions are to be grasped and supported by potential allies of the South in the North, those Northern allies will have to understand more clearly the conditions surrounding both the creation and the persistence of the existing global hierarchy.

There is a cultural dimension to this challenge — and to a reconsideration of the potentially positive charge of the conceptual binaries. For the imperialist history that spawned global economic and political hierarchy also has a strongly racist dimension that helps to lock into place complacency in the North regarding the legitimacy both of its enjoyment of "oligarchic wealth" and of its often unilateral actions, economic and military, to ensure that wealth. Small wonder that the global hierarchy has recently been defined as a kind of "global apartheid"[12] or that Robert Biel could write of "the racial capitalism that exists between the North and the South" and the need to confront the racist premises of the system's functioning head on and in their own right.[13] Small wonder, too, that Southern intellectuals have sought to complement concrete struggles for material equality carried out by the poorest of the poor with cultural assertions that claim, vis-à-vis Western cultural hegemony, the right to be heard in their own voices. Most recently this has taken the form, in the academy, of a preoccupation with "post-colonialism," producing a post-colonial school of thought that claims not merely to expose Eurocentric biases within the global centres of cultural production but also to listen afresh to those diverse voices of the South that would otherwise be squeezed out of the canon and global public discourse.

While suggestive, this kind of preoccupation with "identity" and voice can also, its critics suggest, be misleading. As Arif Dirlik argues, "Postcolonial critics have been largely silent on the relationship of the idea of Postcolonialism to its context in contemporary capitalism; indeed, they have suppressed the necessity of considering such a possible relationship by repudiating a possible 'foundational' role to capitalism in history."[14] It need come as no surprise, therefore, that Ella Shohat can cap her own critique of the post-colonial approach in a manner quite germane to the development of my own argument here:

> The circulation of "post-colonial" as a theoretical framework tends to suggest a supercession of neo-colonialism and the Third World and Fourth World as

unfashionable, even irrelevant categories. Yet, with all its problems, the term "Third World" does still retain heuristic value. . . . At this point in time, replacing the term "Third World" with the "post-colonial" is a liability. Despite differences and contradictions among and within Third World countries, the term "Third World" contains a common project of (linked) resistances to neo-colonialisms [and] implies a belief that the shared history of neo/colonialism and internal racism form sufficient common ground for alliances among such diverse peoples.[15]

This formulation also provides an additional reason for validating, up to a point, Third Worldist, left-developmentalist, and Southern-focused problematics: the potential they retain for both enlivening and focusing radical projects of redress of grievances by the poorest of the global poor.[16] Shohat herself is circumspect here: "The term 'Third World' is most meaningful in broad political-economic terms, and becomes blurred when one addresses the differently modulated politics in the realm of culture, the overlapping spaces of inter-mingling identities." For this reason, she writes, the concept of Third World, while "schematically productive," must itself be "placed under erasure, as it were, seen as provisional and ultimately inadequate."[17] Nonetheless, the thrust of her argument links to that of others who have sought to validate such notions as part of a language in terms of which global claims are staked vis-à-vis global capitalism and progressive mobilization is advanced in both the South and the North: "Third Worldism is in part about reminding people that poverty is still a problem, and that in general there are widening gaps between the developed and the developing countries."[18] Indeed, what Fred Cooper and Randall Packard write of the "marvellous ambiguity" of the concept "development" might also be said of the concept "Third World": "What at one level seemed like a discourse of control is at another a discourse of entitlement, a way of capturing the imagination of a cross-national public around demands for decency and equity."[19] Not "After the Third World" then (as the title of a special issue of *Third World Quarterly* would have it). Better put, what is at issue is how notions of "the Third World," "the developing world," "the global South," "global apartheid," and even "the post-colonial" are linked to a simultaneous consideration of the realities of the global class structure and the imperatives of the global class struggle. This is what determines, in context, both their accuracy and their efficacy.

# Where Is South Africa?

The ANC government in South Africa came to power with the strongest of Third Worldist credentials; the battle against apartheid was amongst the most salient of twentieth-century liberation struggles. And while it is true that ANC spokespersons once in power have not tended to use the term "Third World" very often, they have, nonetheless, sought in many of their pronouncements to build on their

struggle credentials in order to present themselves, both domestically and internationally, as key representatives, interpreters, and defenders of the countries of the
Southern poor. The litany is impressive, up to a point. Consider, for example,
Mandela's own statement at the 1999 Davos forum that brought together heads of
state and of multinational corporations to discuss the question "Is global capitalism
delivering the goods?" Mandela was prepared to ask some questions of his own:
"Is globalization only to benefit the powerful and the speculators? Does it offer
nothing to men, women and children who are ravaged by poverty?"[20] But it is
Mandela's successor, Thabo Mbeki, who has taken the initiative most vigorously in
a number of his speeches both before and after his ascending to the presidency. In
1998 he made a pronouncement to the effect that South Africans "must be in the
forefront in challenging the notion of 'the market' as a modern God, a supernatural
phenomenon to whose dictates everything human must bow in a spirit of helpless-
ness."[21] An important speech to the twelfth heads of state meeting of the
Non-Aligned Movement included the statement that "the 'free market' path of
development . . . has failed to live up to the expectations of the people of the
South."[22] As Rok Ajalu epitomized the occasion:

> What then is President Mbeki's solution to the problem of market fundamen-
> talism? He concluded his speech by urging the Non-Aligned Movement to go
> back to basics, to demand a new world order — "to turn itself into an effec-
> tive organ for the creation of the new political, economic and security world
> order which will succeed actually to assist in the life and death matter that the
> aspirations of the weak and the poor become an integral part of the actual
> agenda of the entirety of our world."[23]

Statements like these, and Mbeki's attendant evocation of the fact of "global
apartheid" (explicitly so named) have led so astute a commentator on developments
in Africa as Rok Ajalu to embrace their authors' progressive credentials with unbridled enthusiasm — this being true, in particular, of Mbeki's much-trumpeted presentation of the need for what he calls an "African Renaissance." This is said by
Ajalu to represent a potential rebirth of African self-respect, sense of efficacy, and
"rebellion" — even to the point of seeming "to imply a subtle and sophisticated
challenge to globalisation."[24] In fact, Ajalu is so agog at Mbeki's various rhetorical
flourishes that he comes to a most startling conclusion:

> It would seem, therefore, that those who have assumed the pinnacle of Mbeki's
> African renaissance to be the drive for the virtues and dictates of the free mar-
> ket, making Africa safe for the overseas multi-national investments and private
> capital, are grossly mistaken. Mbeki's African renaissance represents a much
> more nuanced and a subtler critique of the contemporary world order than such
> interpretations allow. It is indeed a call to take up an anti-imperialist stance![25]

Yet one is left to wonder at the precise provenance of such a bizarre and overstated testimonial. It is not merely that Mbeki tends to switch the tenor of his rhetoric markedly from one audience to another that might have given Ajalu some pause here. More importantly, the bulk of the evidence regarding Mbeki and company's actual practice ("Talk left, act right," as domestic critics of the ANC have come to epitomize such flights of Mbekian fancy-talk) suggests a quite opposite conclusion. For the ANC in action has dedicated itself to a version of neo-liberalism that is baldly market-driven and premised on a kind of "one-worldist" celebration of the more or less unqualified hegemony of capital, worldwide and local. This tendency is most evident, as most commentators of both the left and right widely acknowledge, in domestic policies, but it also underpins the initiatives that post-apartheid South Africa has taken on the world stage — as distinct from what it is given to saying that it is doing.

The best proof of the counter-argument to Ajalu's case is offered by the deeply conservative cast of post-apartheid South Africa's policies at home. The process by which the ANC came to embrace a starkly neo-liberal domestic project was capped dramatically by then-vice-president Mbeki's pugnacious comment, "Just call me a Thatcherite" at the launching of GEAR in 1996 (see chapter 9).[26] True, many of the ANC's pre-liberation formulations had emphasized the need to impose a much stronger measure of social control over the workings of the market and a capitalist economy that was very much more developed in South Africa than elsewhere on the continent. Much was heard of the prospects for nationalizations and, of special interest, of economic strategies designed to facilitate "growth through redistribution." Linked implicitly to a radical notion of "structural reform" that seemed to have as a goal a progressive closing in on the prerogatives of capital by movement and state, such strategies would have sought to press capital to slowly but surely gear an increasingly high proportion of its productive energies to meeting popular needs (rather than permitting capital freely to pursue the logic of its own global ambitions).

And yet the transition would instead produce a development project premised primarily on "global competitiveness," the centrality of foreign investment, the rule of the market and, more specifically, accelerated privatization, an apparent indifference to rising structural unemployment, and the marketization of service delivery that makes such services unattainable to so many.[27] The esteemed Indian writer Arundhati Roy has written, both poignantly and accurately, of this sad denouement to the anti-apartheid struggle:

And what of Mandela's South Africa? Otherwise known as the Small Miracle, the Rainbow Nation of God? South Africans say that the only miracle they know of is how quickly the rainbow has been privatised, sectioned off and auctioned to the highest bidders. Within two years of taking office in 1994, the African National Congress genuflected with hardly a caveat to the Market

God. In its rush to replace Argentina as neo-liberalism's poster boy, it has insti-
tuted a massive programme of privatisation and structural adjustment. The government's promise to re-distribute agricultural land to 26 million landless people has remained in the realm of dark humour. While 60 per cent of the population remains landless, almost all agricultural land is owned by 60,000 white
farmers. Post-apartheid, the income of 40 per cent of the poorest black families has diminished by about 20 per cent. Two million have been evicted from
their homes. Six hundred die of AIDS every day. Forty per cent of the population is unemployed and that number is rising sharply. The corporatisation of
basic services has meant that millions have been disconnected from water and
electricity.[28]

And so, for the mass of the population, doomed in practice to increasingly high
levels of unemployment during the period of "rationalization" of the South African
economy in line with global "imperatives," their jobs as well as their welfare needs
were to be provided for — mostly in the much longer run — by the trickle-down
effects that a beneficent and expansive market-driven capitalism is said to be poised
to deliver. Unfortunately, that this aggressively capitalist project has so far proven
to be such a dismal failure at home does not seem to have dampened the ANC leadership's enthusiasm for it.

Nor has it dissuaded the ANC from pushing such "solutions" upon others: the
ANC's global and continental strategies have become, in practice (if not always in the
terms of the rhetoric that accompanies them), merely an extension of its domestic
approach. Thus, even while advancing a case for some measure of "reform" (debt
relief, increased aid, the lowering of Northern trade barriers, and, not least,
increased investment) within such bastions of global power as the international
financial institutions and the WTO, South Africa's moderate approach has (in the
words of senior government minister Alec Erwin) been premised on "attempting to
break with a conception of contestation by stressing partnership" and by avoiding
(in the words of a core ANC document) the temptation "to elaborate solutions that
are in discord with the rest of the world" or that represent "a voluntarist South
African experiment of a special type."[29] Yet how relevant can a "non-discordant"
practice of global reformism — a projected "partnership" between hares and hounds
— really be when global capitalism offers so little by way of positive promise for
the kind of reformist strategies that the ANC says it is striving to achieve? The case
for Africa is clear, at least — as Colin Leys and I argued earlier (chapter 1): in Africa,
a continent relegated to the margins of the global economy, "the dream of a transformative capitalism in Africa remains just that: a dream".[30]

The meagre returns to Africa for the reformist entreaties of South African and
other continental leaders at sites where Northern powers meet to consider the present and future — most notably at G8 Summits at Kananaskis in 2001 and Evian in
2003 — give additional pause. For Africans who seek significant development for

their continent will have to become participants in global and continental initiatives that proceed on the basis of a much more profoundly anti-capitalist perspective than the one that the ANC leadership is prepared to countenance.

Moreover, the situation as regards the ANC's global program may actually represent something rather more negative than merely the almost inevitably failed practice of a naive reformism. For recent analyses of the ANC's record in international negotiations suggest more sinister possibilities. Thus Dot Keet, in a scrupulous analysis of South Africa's role (and particularly that played by Minister of Trade Erwin) within the WTO, notes the claim (made by Erwin) that South Africa, as a "major player" on the global stage, acts as "a bridge between the developed and the developed countries."[31] A close tracking of Erwin's role in WTO assemblies both in Seattle (1999) and Doha (2001) provides a very different picture. When not denouncing the demonstrators in the street in Seattle, Erwin was found to be eschewing any close contact with other African delegations and, much to the consternation of those representatives, concentrating instead on the opportunity given him to enter the "inner circle" of "Green Room" discussions by the global heavy hitters (European Union, United States, Canada, Japan) and their occasional invitees.

As Keet documents in even more telling detail for Doha, Erwin and his delegation were once again deemed to have run principally with the hounds of global capital in seeking to push African (and other Third World) delegations towards making, in the name of "realism" and its own "broad agenda," various "trade-offs" that would have compromised those delegations' demands on a wide range of fronts. Not surprisingly Keet found that "many developing countries, especially in Africa," were noting "with wry comments that, while South Africa keeps its distance from the more active and effective developing countries in the WTO, there is a contrasting readiness of South Africa to engage actively with the governments of the more powerful countries, separately and together." Hence Keet's hard-edged but entirely convincing conclusion as to "the South African government's highly questionable role" in such a context:

> Following the logic inherent in its own strategic choices, and independently of Pretoria's self-defined "good intentions" and declared "tactical" aims, South Africa played and plays an increasingly questionable WTO role within Africa and internationally. As events unfolded, in the past three years, Pretoria's strategic positioning in the WTO and tactical interventions in international negotiations have lead to the widely held conclusion that South Africa is playing a role not so much as a bridge between the developed and developing countries but rather as a bridge for the transmission of influences from the developed countries for the promotion of their economic interests and global aims throughout the world.[32]

Moreover, as Patrick Bond and others have tirelessly demonstrated in their volumi-nous writings on related themes, much the same could be said of the role that the South African minister of finance, Trevor Manuel, and other South African repre-sentatives have played from the lofty positions to which they have ascended within the halls of the World Bank and IMF.[33]

As for the much heralded African Renaissance, it seems to have been narrowed in its terms of reference to the horizons encompassed by the New Economic Partnership for African Development proposals — drafted, it would seem, primarily by Mbeki and his advisors and then shepherded through various pan-African bodies by the troika of Mbeki and presidents Olusegun Obasanjo of Algeria and Abdelaziz Bouteflika of Nigeria. These leaders pushed hard to see that NEPAD was on the agen-da of the G8 Summit to be held in Kananaskis, Canada, in 1999 and that the pro-posals were also central to the premises that underpinned the recasting of the Organization of African Unity into the African Union. It is, of course, tempting to hail an initiative that has sought to bring Africa and its plight to the attention of the globally powerful. Moreover, NEPAD does have useful things to say about the extent to which trade in African products is blocked by the protectionist economic policies of Northern countries, while also including a measure of self-criticism regarding the undemocratic practices of the African regimes themselves.

Nonetheless, at core, NEPAD seems a sad, defeated document, evidencing the ever-deepening subservience of the African leaders who authored it to the "com-mon sense" of a neo-liberalizing, structural-adjusting global capitalism; while writ-ten by African leaders, it reads as though it could just as easily have been framed in the offices of the World Bank and IMF.[34] Absolutely central to it, certainly, is a very familiar (and very damaging) premise: that African countries must continue to "adjust" their economies in order to provide the enabling conditions for their ever deeper penetration by global capital — with increased foreign investment pre-sented as the primary key to progress. Not just at Seattle and at Doha, but also on the African continent itself, South Africa emerges ever more clearly as point-man for global capital. And not only for global capital. For there is also a growing sus-picion in some continental quarters that the kind of further freeing up of African markets that NEPAD envisions may also serve the desire of ANC free-marketeers to bat-ter down barriers to South African-based capital's own ambitious plans for the fur-ther penetration of the rest of Africa. Not South Africa as "anti-imperialist," then, but as "sub-imperialist."

Patrick Bond traces such policies, at least in part, to their grounding in a "defeatist — and highly questionable — attitude" towards globalization that he suggests is held by Mbeki and his closest colleagues in South Africa (Trevor Manuel, his minister of finance, and Alec Erwin, his minister of trade, being amongst the most prominent of them). In Mbeki's own words, "The process of globalization is an objective outcome of the development of the productive forces that create wealth, including their continuous improvement through the impact on them of advances in science, technology and engineering." Hence Bond's conclusion that "the driving force of globalization boils down, in Mbeki's neutral story, to little more than technological determinism."[35] True, the likes of Rok Ajalu can attempt to put a bold face on this, praising Mbeki for realistically urging his fellow African heads of state not to react to globalization like "King Canute striving to wish the waves away."[36] And yet the mild reformism that Mbeki's approach gives rise to is very far removed from a necessary understanding that the existing market-dominated global order — driven by "a minority class that draws its wealth and power from a historically specific form of production" — is, to repeat Greg Albo's words, "contingent, imbalanced, exploitative and replaceable."[37] Very far indeed, that is, from the kind of genuinely "anti-imperialist stance" that we have seen Ajalu erroneously take it to be. Yet it is such a stance — real not rhetorical — that can alone guarantee progress for the poorest of the poor in today's global economy.

South Africa: running, however ineffectively, with the hares? Or — as one increasingly suspects to be the case — hunting, however guardedly, with the hounds? Either way, what remains is that the ANC's brand of deeply compromised quasi-reformism serves primarily to deflect consideration of other, much more significant, radical alternatives, both globally and locally. As Bond writes, the exercise of a more meaningful "Third Worldism" by the South African government would involve something very different from an approach that "excludes (indeed most often rejects) alliances with increasingly radical local and international social, labour and environmental movements who in reality are the main agents of progressive global change."[38] Moreover, the ANC government also has chosen in its own country to turn its back coldly on those forces that might begin to provide the social and political base for any more meaningful "anti-imperialist" project. Indeed, in South Africa today a range of increasingly well-organized grassroots initiatives has surfaced — organizations that find they have no choice but to mobilize people in active resistance to their own government's bankrupt policies. Included on the list would be, amongst other initiatives, the Anti-Privatization Forum, the Soweto Electricity Crisis Committee, the Treatment Action Campaign, the Western Cape Anti-Eviction Campaign, the Concerned Citizens' Forum in Durban, the Landless People's Movement, and unions, churches, and women's organizations.[39] The further growth of such initiatives could eventually produce the political will necessary to draw South Africa back into the ranks of those who challenge in significant ways the geographical, racial, and class-based hierarchies of global inequality.

PART IV

# CONCLUSION

# CHAPTER 12

# AFRICA: THE NEXT LIBERATION STRUGGLE?

This book has evoked, then, the history of both failed nationalism and bankrupt capitalism in Africa, with its focus most prominently upon the fate of that "radical nationalism" born of the liberation struggles in Southern Africa from which so much more was once hoped. Yet beyond the success and the very real achievement of overthrowing white minority rule there remain the various morbid economic and political symptoms produced by the failures of post-colonial regimes across the continent. And yet another element to consider — or reconsider — is the tainted record of various socialist experiments, and the distinct need to extract lessons from both the economic policy-making and the political practices of progressive forces once in power in Africa — not least by critiquing their too often imbalanced and overweening emphasis on technology, largeness of scale, and regimentation in the economic sphere and their invariably authoritarian tendencies in the political.

These are lessons that could become relevant if, as, and when regimes of more progressive, counter-capitalist intent once again assume power — even if it is also true that the terrain, both local and international, upon which they mount their projects will differ substantially from that of the 1960s and 1970s when those earlier experiments were in their fullest flower. Nonetheless, the immediate challenge facing progressives is a different one: that of once again seeking to forge social and political initiatives that can expect, eventually, to attain such power. My primary focus here, then, is upon "liberation" itself, and upon the terms of any renewed struggle to obtain it in Africa.

## The Contradictory Present

Liberation? I began this book by arguing for the continuing necessity of a revolutionary, even socialist, emancipation in Africa. The need both to conceptualize and to attain a more effective revolutionary practice is all the more important given the extremity of the African crisis itself. For, as we have seen, international-financial-institution-sponsored "economic fundamentalism"[1] has served merely to magnify the weakness of African economies and forced them to "compete" ever more nakedly in a game they cannot possibly win. As Fantu Cheru writes:

In the context of economic globalisation and onerous debt accompanied by disciplinary neoliberalism . . . economic adjustment and liberalisation have been forced down the throats of African people against the background of depressed commodity prices, declining foreign assistance, withdrawal of private lending, increased Northern protectionism and unsustainable levels of debt [with the result that] few African countries have achieved creditably in terms of any of the indicators that measure real, sustainable development. Instead, most have slid backwards into growing inequality, ecological degradation, de-industrialisation and poverty.[2]

In such a context there is really little or no prospect of merely "reforming" present-day Africa.

It is true that by the 1990s even the IFIS themselves had begun to manifest rather greater concern than previously regarding the costs of unqualified structural adjustment and to place a greater emphasis on the need for a marginally more assertive "enabling state" (this problem being phrased in terms of the challenge of "governance"[3] and the need for "poverty reduction" and even, albeit on a very modest scale indeed, for debt reduction). Nonetheless, the very modesty of such assertions serves merely to underline, as Harry Shutt puts it, "the central weakness in the global economic structure which is preventing any effective moves to avert disaster: the remorseless demand to sacrifice all other objectives to that of meeting the ever more voracious demand for profit from the continuously swelling and increasingly redundant mass of capital."[4] Small wonder that Africa appears merely to have been "redlined" by many elements of capital, with the continent still viewed primarily as a "resource cow" — a field for extractive activities in the spheres of oil, minerals (including, notably, diamonds) and agricultural production (and for debt recovery and arms sales as well), with only limited interest being expressed in the likely growth of markets and investment opportunities beyond those limits.[5]

And yet, despite this, there are also Africans who seek not revolution but reform, from within and in Africa's favour, of the global capitalist system — the Lagos Plan of Action and the "African Alternative Framework" perhaps being early markers of this tendency. More recently, the post-apartheid regime in South Africa (led by Thabo Mbeki and his ruling ANC) seems to have nominated itself as principal bearer of such a "dream" — seeking to balance its markedly uncritical embrace of a neo-liberal economic strategy within its borders by presentation of a case for equity, for "partnership," and, in the words of Trade and Industry Minister Alec Erwin, for "solutions that are [not] in discord with the rest of the world" within the IFIS and the WTO. In doing so, as Patrick Bond points out, it has chosen, quite self-consciously, to "exclude (indeed most often reject) alliances with increasingly radical local and international social, labour and environmental movements who in reality are the main agents of progressive global change."[6]

Moreover, even though the ANC's preferred capitalist development strategy has generated little return, the South African government has not been dissuaded from this approach — as witness its championing of the New Economic Partnership for Africa in international circles (see chapter 11). More interesting, perhaps, is the second NEPAD foundation-stone: the promise that African states will seek to recast their political systems to conform more closely to the liberal, quasi-democratic structures of the West. Of course, the existence of more democratically responsive states in Africa would indeed be cause for celebration. And yet the enthusiasm of Mbeki and his colleagues for democratic outcomes — a momentary enthusiasm, as events like that of their support for Mugabe in Zimbabwe would quickly prove — seemed to speak primarily to the reality that Western interests have been pushing "democracy of a sort" on Third World countries as a means of pursuing their own goals.[7] Still, in playing, however opportunistically, to this audience, African leaders are also being forced to some extent to connect to a more positive political development: a wave of democratic reform that swept across Africa, especially at the turn of the 1990s, characterized by some changes of government, the emergence of official oppositions, greater media freedom, and the opening up of further space for groups in civil society to practise politics.[8]

Such space, once pried open, may indeed render more viable the assertion of popular interests in the long run. Still, in the short run such developments have tended to be of a far more limited middle-class provenance rather than marking the genuine empowerment of broader social forces — at best merely a "liberal democracy" rather than a genuinely "popular democracy." Moreover, the (limited) ground of democratic advance that has been gained has been extremely difficult to hold. The NEPAD document itself premises its "hope" for Africa on the belief that "democratic regimes . . . committed to the protection of human rights, people-centred development and market-oriented economies are on the increase on the continent." Yet, as activists in Africa argue, these three terms are not mutually compatible: under African conditions, the third, "market-oriented economics," easily negates the other two. In a related manner, Rita Abrahamsen draws on the experiences of Zambia, Ghana, Ivory Coast, and Kenya to demonstrate how certain external pressures dovetailed with popular resistance to globally driven austerity in Africa to drive demands (relatively successful in the short run) for greater democracy in those countries. And yet, as she also points out, the waning of the original domestic thrust towards such a democratic outcome has seemed even more ineluctable:

There are few signs of a mutually reinforcing relationship between democracy and economic liberalism in Africa's new democracies. The rapid deterioration of democratic standards in many countries has in large part . . . been caused by the pressures arising from the continuation of structural adjustment. These programmes threaten the consolidation of democracy by exacerbating social conflict and differentiation, while at the same time undermining the state's capacity to respond to domestic demands. . . . Although external pressure may have secured the survival of certain structures and procedures of democracy in Africa, the demand for economic liberalisation has at the same time impeded the consolidation of democracy. Instead of consolidation, the result has been a fragile democracy, often little more than a facade, and this seems an almost inevitable outcome of the pursuit of simultaneous economic and political liberalisation in conditions of poverty and underdevelopment.[9]

In short, the arrival of quasi-liberal democracy has not been readily sustainable in its own limited terms, let alone genuinely empowering of most ordinary Africans. And this has been particularly true, it would seem, in rural Africa, where most Africans live and where, as Mahmood Mamdani vividly argues, the "subject" (as distinct from "citizen") status of ordinary rural-dwellers has almost never been successfully transcended.[10]

We return by this route to consider once again the challenge presented by the building of movements of resistance, potential bearers of a "popular democracy," that can actually take power in Africa. If nationalism, even in its liberation movement phase, can now be judged to have failed in producing the radical outcomes so necessary to address the requirements of the vast majority of Africans, what next? Are we not indeed driven back to starting, more or less, "from scratch"? If so, we must acknowledge that this re-engagement will have to be carried out under bleak circumstances given the global imbalance of power — and will certainly have to take place in conjunction with others struggling elsewhere to repeal the writ of unfettered global capital. At the same time, the moment can also be perceived, paradoxically, as being one of opportunity. For in Africa many of the left illusions of the past have also been smashed: any notion that nationalist movements, whether spawned by active liberation struggles or other more pacific means, could merely shift gears and deliver "socialist transformation" to the masses by "benevolent" leaders acting from above, for example; and any sense that Stalinist practices, political or economic, had anything to teach us (a misconception that scarred so much of what was done in the name of socialism in Mozambique, for example, as I myself had occasion to witness at first-hand). In this context we may even want to conceive, as I do, that Africa is standing on the brink of a crucial new phase of its history — a moment akin to that of 1945, when few could have anticipated the speed with which African nationalist movements would win independence for their territories from colonial rule (or, for that matter, the speed with which that independence would in turn be translated into neo-colonial domination).

# The Radically Possible?

We must now explore the boundaries of this moment, this threshold of renewal for liberation, more closely. First, to summarize: what we have in Africa is a mode of incorporation into the global capitalist system that seems unlikely to produce a significant measure of material and humane advance for the majority of people. It is also a situation in which the road to significant reform within the system and to the advantage of the impoverished seems largely closed. Reinforced by the failure/defeat of socialism, a system has been established that, in the view of observers such as Robert Biel and David Plank, has stepped beyond both colonialism and neo-colonialism and towards the establishment of the ever more unmediated rule of global capital and its operative imperatives of capital accumulation (a circumstance Plank terms, writing of the African case, "recolonization").[11] This is a system in which policy has been downgraded merely to "a question of 'adapting' a country in the South to fit into the system by creating local conditions (for example, reducing interference from local bureaucrats) so that capital could find its way without hindrance to the most promising sectors."[12]

But let us further note, with Biel, that this new system is also one that has created a fundamental problem for "the North" and not merely in economic terms: "The 'national economy' is one of capitalism's best inventions because it provides a good basis for social control. . . . The new form of direct rule which I am calling 'post-neo-colonial' would be very risky." As he then further focuses the point:

> The new vision may appear plausible to elites, since it presents the North and South as united within a single free-market economic model (in contrast to the division between Keynesianism for the North and development economics for the South which was characteristic of the post-war regime). But in reality the free market is an expression of profoundly unequal power relations, and the practical consequences of this are all too obvious to the masses: to give only one example, it leads to a virtual monopoly by the North of mass consumption.[13]

"All too obvious to the masses": would that things were so simple! But the formulation does have the virtue of leading us back to the question of the "historically possible": the question as to how, if at all, the system of "capitalism in Africa" might come to be radically challenged from below by those popular forces that are most disadvantaged by it.

We need not be too categorical about the precise components, sociological and ideological, of any such challenge. After all, as Ken Post and Phil Wright argued some years ago — in more general terms admittedly but ones that nonetheless have applicability to Africa — grassroots oppositions on the periphery form to prepare for socialist solutions, "even though the political manifestation of this may not initially take the form of a socialist movement."[14] Indeed, it is from a range of "disparate forces" (although the catholicity of their inclusion within the camp of potential agents of change who could come to see liberation from capitalism to be "their only salvation" would not have been alien to the expansive perspective of a "revolutionary nationalist" like Amilcar Cabral) that new movements of more radical provenance could yet be built in Africa.

As we've seen — particularly in chapter 1 but also throughout this book — outcries of pain have been clearly heard in Africa — from those both angry at existing conditions and sceptical about prospects for significant reform — stirrings linked at least in part to the "collective insubordination" of Africa (to again use Célestin Monga's term) and directed against not only parasitic governments but also IFI-induced austerity. For all the rather anomic form that this more radical amplification of "insubordination" can sometimes take (the so-called "IMF riots," for example), it nonetheless serves to bear out Riley and Parfitt's conclusion about the great diversity of strategies adopted in active response to the oppressions of a system and way of life that are not of the masses' own choosing.[15] These diverse initiatives are more or less well-organized, and are also highly ambiguous as to just how readily they can move people beyond (entirely laudable) resistances to authoritarianism and towards more counter-hegemonic perspectives on the global capitalist system that feeds and nurtures autocracy.[16] Nonetheless, such initiatives do dramatize the importance, real and potential, of "street-level democracy" and "political settings at the margins of global power." As Jonathan Barker focuses these phrases in his book on the subject:

> The fragmentation of political space and the impact of global power on national institutions do not form the whole story. There has been a marked increase in the number, range, and energy of non-state, non-family, and non-business voluntary associations — a trend noted in Asia, Africa, and Latin America. On a general level this trend is a social response to the expansion of market logic into social relationships that have more than economic meaning to people. . . . Societies react against the reduction of land and labour and money to the status of commodities.[17]

Fantu Cheru has also written with particular eloquence of such developments in Africa, which he characterizes as a virtual "renaissance" of "popular resistance from below":

> The flag-bearers of this new renaissance are based in the church, the informal sector, human rights movements, grassroots ecology movements and development NGOs that have sprung up all across Africa in the last decade to articulate alternative visions of survival and democratic governance. They employ both overt and hidden forms of resistance, thus pressing demands on the state

through the "politics of claims," non-payment of taxes and open insurrections. These new social movements advance the idea that development is a human right, and that its achievement requires popular participation and control.[18]

And, certainly, the range of information on such initiatives is impressive, revealed in diverse scholarly accounts as well as websites located in, and reporting on, a wide array of such undertakings across a wide range of African countries. Writers such as Graham Harrison and others[19] have highlighted an additional range of such emanations elsewhere on the continent, running through varied resistances by youth, unions, and women in Mali, Burkina Faso, Cameroon, Zambia, Zimbabwe, Nigeria, and elsewhere and including the pinpointing of specific assertions like that of the Movement for the Survival of the Ogoni People (MOSOP) and the successful campaign against the World Bank's policy on cashew-nut processing in Mozambique.

True, Cheru also sees dangers for some of the most organized of such undertakings in their dependency on financing from Western sources. But he does go on to emphasize, on other grounds, the importance of a "North-South popular alliance" — judging that "in the context of the considerable power held by elites and firms that underpin the globalisation process . . . local-level resistance [in Africa] in isolation from potential allies in other countries and regions will have limited impact." For Cheru is frank about the difficulties of building from below:

> In the specific case of Africa, the vibrancy of the new institutions of civil society contrasts with the paucity of their strategic power and resources. Organizing around daily subsistence increasingly consumes much of people's energy and meagre resources, thus making the task of developing a counter-project exceptionally difficult and slow.

Still, the African experience has taught Cheru and others that when it comes to mounting a bottom-up hegemonic project there are no shortcuts via nationalist organizations, liberation movements, or vanguard parties (the chimeras of an earlier moment of African struggles): "Instead of focusing on a unifying conception of society and transformation, we must look for a workable sense of cohesion to emerge out of seemingly irreconcilable modes of resistance waged from below."[20]

Interestingly, Barker also notes that observers "frequently see . . . a dispersed series of piecemeal actions and only rarely observe the revolutionary overthrow of governing institutions."[21] This is a reflection of what he calls the "scale mismatch" between "hopeful localisms" and the more negative impact of global determinations. The question remains, then: how might the playing field of this mismatch be levelled and the further crystallization of a "workable sense of cohesion" be facilitated? One response to this can be seen, perhaps, in those continental activities (meetings, information exchanges, and intellectual endeavours ranging from

Jubilee 2000 to the African Social Forum to CODESRIA) that seek to link actors, initiatives, and ideas from across the continent. Thus Bond cites such high-water marks in this respect as the Lusaka Declaration of 1999, drafted by "leading African social movements and church organisations working on debt" (and the beginnings of its attendant "African People's Consensus" movement), the Yaounde conference and the Dakar Summit of civil-society-based organizations in 2001, and the ongoing work of the Accra-based African Trade Network and the Southern African People's Solidarity Network (the latter having embraced, in turn, the Jubilee debt cancellation movement, amongst other initiatives).[22]

In more general terms, Colin Leys (in an interesting debate with Barker) has also underlined the importance of complementing Barker's (and, in effect, Cheru's) focus on the centrality of local initiatives with a sensibility that continues to emphasize at least equally the age-old imperatives of ideological coherence and political organization as building blocks for effective struggle. Here he speaks of the required emergence of "unified" and hegemonic projects:

> Looked at in one way it will necessarily be a multiplicity of projects, in different sectors, nations and regions, the aspirations of different groups, movements and peoples. Yet unless these unite to confront the political and economic power of the transnationals and the states that back them, they will ultimately fail. . . . As a minimum it will require nation-wide movements and/or parties capable of exercising state power, and making it felt in supra-national institutions.[23]

For, as Cheru himself acknowledges:

> A comprehensive development alternative cannot go far without a basic change in power structures. Until this happens the popular sector can only pressure government for some policy changes and accumulate little victories here and there. This implies that the popular sector has to come up with a state agenda of its own and suggests entering the terrain of the nation-state: national politics.[24]

Fortunately, there have been signs in Africa's recent practice of precisely such developments. The emergence of an effective opposition party to Robert Mugabe's wretched rule in Zimbabwe out of a dense array of resistances within civil society there could be seen, at least briefly, as one particularly promising example. Indeed, Bond was moved momentarily to write of this new Movement for Democratic Change (MDC), in its early years, as representing the birth in Africa of the first "post-nationalist and post-neo-liberal" political party.[25] In practice, the pull on the MDC in turn to conform to neo-liberal premises proved to be very strong (as had been true in the case of Frederick Chiluba's Movement for Multiparty Democracy [MMD] in Zambia before it), and in any case Mugabe has proven to be ruthless in his ability to command violence and demagogy in his ability to hold power (while also manipulating the outstanding land issue to effect). Nonetheless, Bond and his co-authors Darlene Miller and Greg Ruiters have made a strong case for hailing the stirring of such co-ordinated resistances (keyed by trade unions but very far from being confined to their assertions) across the Southern African region.[26]

In South Africa, the site of my own most immediate exposure to such novel developments, the costs of the post-apartheid neo-liberal apostasy of the ANC and of its abandonment (in practice) of the basic needs of the mass of the South African population have been particularly high — even if the continuing (if somewhat fraying) legitimacy that the ANC enjoys means that any move towards establishment of a new party to challenge it directly seems unlikely for the foreseeable future. And yet, as we've seen, oppositional activities of a somewhat different sort do exist: a range of actors and organizations in what some South African writers have come to term "working-class civil society," all of them critical of the direction that post-apartheid South Africa has come to take. They speak of the necessity of beginning to co-ordinate their critical outlooks and activities to exert far more pressure on the ANC than they have up to now.

For a time it appeared that established organisations such as COSATU and SANGO-CO were possible bearers of this new politics; but my more recent visits to South Africa have also impressed upon me the salience of a whole new range of grass-roots initiatives (see chapter 10).[27] While it remains far too early to speak with grand confidence of the attempt by various forces in South African civil society to link up more self-consciously, within and across sectors, in a popular alliance from below, those groupings have begun to take strength from each other and find an encouragement to think beyond the frameworks of their separate and more specific assertions. They may also take further steps towards the effective institutionalization of a (heretofore often only implicitly) shared theory and practice of struggle. Despite the setbacks that have undermined parallel efforts in Zambia and Zimbabwe, the signs of the first stages of building what I have termed, following Canadian trade union activist Sam Gindin, a "structured movement" in South Africa are present.[28] This initiative might also begin to find echo in other African countries, notably in Nigeria.[29]

Pan-African generalizations are dangerous, of course, not least because of the continent's great diversity. Especially in the most marginalized of countries and/or countries of absolute crisis, near-collapse, or firmly positioned authoritarianism, the pace of change may be very different from that in the most developed of countries. As with the original post-1945 pattern of successful nationalisms across Africa, the pace of radical change — if, as, and when it comes — will be uneven, accelerating and decelerating erratically and spilling over borders both by example and in more direct ways. Since the progress of "the next liberation struggle" will most likely prove complex in its detail, we desperately require a more fine-grained mapping of socio-political contradictions and revolutionary prospects across the continent — something comparable, that is to say, to Chris Allen's brilliant cataloguing of diverse African polities a decade ago.[30] Nonetheless, such movements-in-the-making demand to be taken seriously, for they are amongst the most important harbingers of an alternative future for the continent.

## Socialism?

What we have, then, are movements, parties, tendencies a-borning — albeit ones diverse in terms of the sites of struggle at which they erupt and the kinds of socio-political agency they embody.[31] There is an additional question to ask of such initiatives, however: what "imaginary," what sense of projected future, do they, will they, manifest? I return by this route to the point at which, in my introduction, I began this book: the evocation of Arrighi's and my original argument that, with actually existing capitalism, worldwide and local, being so central to defining the problem in post-colonial Africa, "socialism" will have to be part of the solution. While taking seriously Cheru's warning that there may be "no single formula for how individuals and communities go about 'decoding' the ideology of developmentalism or globalisation,"[32] I continue to think this to be the case. To so argue is, of course, to court not so much scholarly opprobrium as scholarly ridicule. James Krugman in his book *The Return of Depression Economics*, filled though it is with criticisms of the functioning of the global capitalist system, nonetheless inquires sneeringly as to "who can now use the word socialism with a straight face," concluding that "the heart has gone out of the opposition to capitalism."[33] Writers such as Richard Sklar have made latter-day careers out of claiming to have gone "Beyond Capitalism and Socialism in Africa" and seeking to carry the North American Africanist establishment with them to the right on such questions.[34]

Even more disturbing is the mood on the continent itself. The wholesale move of the ANC leadership — after its great victory over apartheid in South Africa — into the camp of neo-liberalism has been sobering enough. But what is one to make of how even Julius Nyerere, who did contest until his death the irrational outcomes produced by global capitalism's cruel grip on Africa, could nonetheless find himself uttering his sarcastic message about tossing out his country's "ideas about socialism."[35]

Indeed, even Arrighi, in his bleak update of the plight of Africa within the capitalist world system, now finds none of the promise of a socialist future there but merely hankers for some mild reformism to temper the winds that buffet residents of the continent.[36] Meanwhile, the liberal/neo-liberal "common sense" of the moment has also found its way deep inside the African academy. As Issa Shivji points out, even the "intellectual proponents" of a genuinely "popular perspective" are now timid when it comes to stepping forward and speaking out, so that much "remains unsaid."[37]

Still, as Bond emphasizes, significant centres of intellectual resistance do exist on the continent, and they are contesting an ascendant, if spiritually and economically bankrupt, capitalism in Africa.[38] The pronouncements of South African activists and progressive commentators provide an example, as do those of others, continent-wide, who have grouped behind the undertakings of the African Social Forum and the like. This is not surprising since, speaking more generally, even Krugman assumes that the current situation "will not last forever," that "surely there will be other ideologies, other dreams" — and that these may even "emerge sooner rather than later" under present global circumstances. In this context it seems to me plausible to argue that we are standing on the brink of a crucial new phase of African history. As I have suggested, the present can best be seen as a moment akin to that of 1945. Of course, it is no easier now than it was then to divine the range of the likely struggle against "post-neo-colonial" domination. Or to answer the variety of questions that this moment will throw up: as Africans forge more effective organizations for resistance, for example, how will their new movements balance the rival claims to centrality of local, national, regional, continental, and global sites of struggle in the focusing of their efforts? How will the actors handle the trade-off of the relative priorities of plausible short-term reform against the necessary claims of long-term structural transformation? And (perhaps most importantly of all) in terms of what counter-hegemonic imaginary, or imaginaries, will this "post-nationalist, post-neo-liberal" project be cast?

African activists themselves will have to be in the front lines in answering such questions, of course. But the undertakings of a new generation of researchers and writers focusing critically, if also supportively, on the kinds of resistances I have begun to sketch out here will be important — as was once the work of "the Dar es Salaam generation" and its counterparts elsewhere on the continent in interpreting and amplifying earlier rounds of struggle. Certainly, we must continue to ask ourselves whether the relatively upbeat picture of contemporary resistance that I have presented here might again be too much the reflection of an "optimism of the will," even if it does mesh with activities that are indeed visible and marked with genuine potential. Would a "realism" that dictated a more "pessimistic" response of "the intellect" to the severe difficulties of building and sustaining resistance under current African circumstances be more appropriate? Let me merely conclude by saying that, whatever may prove to be the case in this respect, the reported evidence of resistance is still too fragmentary; and the resistance itself is also both relatively understudied and undertheorized. There can be little doubt that we must both engage with and know a great deal more about the immediate scope and long-term resonance of the various counter-hegemonic activities evoked both in the writings I have cited above and elsewhere.[39]

At the same time we also need to ask ourselves what "realism" actually connotes in the African context. Not a retreat to passivity, or even to mere "reform," surely. For, in concluding, I stand by my hunch that it will prove neither possible nor wise for Africans to avoid, in the long run, the claims of "realistic socialism" that Canadian political economist Greg Albo has juxtaposed self-consciously to the claims of "utopian capitalism" in his discussion of the characteristics of the global political economy. True, any such program of "realistic socialism" (Albo himself suggests the need for "more inward-oriented economic strategies" and the devaluation of "scale of production as the central economic objective") must be specified for Africa by such social forces as mobilize themselves to place a more progressive agenda on the table. Nonetheless, Albo's broader premise — that positive outcomes "can only be realized through re-embedding financial capital and production relations in democratically organized national and local economic spaces sustained through international solidarity and fora of democratic co-operation" — seems a good place to start. But this will only happen when Africans, with others, move to better comprehend the reality that the existing market-dominated global order — driven by "a minority class that draws its wealth and power from a historically specific form of production" — is (once again, in Albo's words) "contingent, imbalanced, exploitative and replaceable."[40] That struggle continues, in Africa as elsewhere.

# A CLASS ACT: CANADA'S ANTI-APARTHEID RECORD

*Included here is my review of Linda Freeman's The Ambiguous Champion: Canada and South Africa in the Trudeau and Mulroney Years (Toronto: University of Toronto Press, 1998), from the pages of Southern Africa Report, 14, 2 (March 1999), a journal, linked to the Toronto Committee for Southern Africa, that several of us edited in Toronto for many years. This article may stand as a reminder of the considerable volume of written work, by myself and many others (including Freeman), to be found in SAR. In its substance, however, it can also serve as a reminder of a different sort: of how the struggle for the liberation of Africa takes place not just on the continent itself but also in those countries, like Canada, that are much closer to the "centre" of the global system and whose structural position within the system and self-conscious actions have helped to define so many of the problems that the continent must face.*

Diplomacy is the art of going abroad to lie politely for one's country. So the wags would have it. And whatever else one might say about Nelson Mandela's otherwise very moving visit to Canada late last year there was quite a lot of lying going on. How else to categorize the constant references to Canada's grand and glorious record in the anti-apartheid struggle?

Not that Mandela was the main perpetrator of such fabrications. As often as not he spoke about the record of Canadians in general rather than that of the Canadian government in particular when handing out kudos (although even he trotted out the heroic litany of "Diefenbaker, Trudeau and Mulroney" during his remarkable SkyDome appearance and elsewhere). Veterans of the anti-apartheid struggle in this country could take some solace from the possibility that, most often, he was really speaking about us rather than about the Canadian politicians and businessmen with whom he was in fact spending most of his time.

And yet it was just such politicians and businessman — now basking in the glory of Mandela's presence — who seemed most smugly engaged in facilitating the pretence that Canada had been in Mandela's corner all along. Difficult, it is true, to put on too many airs in the presence of someone who spent twenty-seven years in prison for his belief in racial equality and human dignity and then emerged to embrace his captors in a spirit of reconciliation. Nonetheless, there was a distinct atmosphere of self-congratulation all round about the visit, and, needless to say, not a hint of apology from "official Canada" about the role Canada had actually played in the anti-apartheid struggle.

# No Apology

Still, apology would have been the most appropriate response. It is the great strength of Linda Freeman's new book, The Ambiguous Champion: Canada and South Africa in the Trudeau and Mulroney Years, that it permits of no other conclusion about Canada's record. Moreover, it makes its case with such a wealth of documentation and careful argument that it should stand as the essential touchstone for all future discussion of the topic.

Freeman has come by her expertise honestly. The bibliography reveals that she earned her Ph.D. on the topic of "The Nature of Canadian Interests in Black Southern Africa" as far back as 1978. And readers of SAR will recall her relentless tracking of Canada's Southern Africa policy through over a decade of annual surveys in these pages (indeed, her very short list of acknowledgements includes gracious thanks to "the Southern Africa Report collective"). This is a book long in the making, then, but worth the wait since the scholarship it represents is thorough and formidable (the footnotes and bibliography run to 130 pages, for example, almost a third the book's length!) and the argument important.

What she does is demonstrate convincingly how compromised Canada's official policy towards white minority rule in Southern Africa was over the decades. For example, she usefully debunks the overblown legend of Diefenbaker as scourge of South Africa within the Commonwealth in the early 1960s. And she neatly documents Lester Pearson's role, later in the decade, both in rationalizing for a wider audience Britain's half-hearted response (through the weakest of sanctions packages) to Rhodesia's UDI and in himself resisting any economic measures whatsoever against South Africa.

However, Freeman saves her main fire for Trudeau and Joe Clark. Trudeau remains a great enigma for the progressively minded in Canada, along the lines of: he's so smart, why didn't he do a lot better? In fact, on Southern Africa he did worse, as Freeman clearly documents. His was a callous failure of humane principle made all the more galling by his infamous statement of the time that "we should either stop trading or we should stop condemning." But, of course, he continued to do both. A smug prisoner of Canada's presumed capitalist imperatives, Trudeau idly allowed Canada's economic links to apartheid to deepen on his watch and, as Freeman scrupulously documents, permitted the likes of Hedley Bull and his Space Research Institute to bolster South Africa's military arsenal — this despite the UN's mandatory arms embargo of 1977. Nor, as one might anticipate, were things carried out in any more principled a manner during Joe Clark's brief interregnum as prime minister.

## Theoretical Interlude

Of course SAR readers, accustomed to Freeman's trenchant articles in our pages over the years, will need little persuading as to the merits of her book, in terms both of the comprehensiveness of the data she provides and of the general accuracy of the analysis she presents. No doubt many of you will already have read the book for yourselves. Rather than gild the lily, then, let me seek instead to engage critically with several of the book's more controversial dimensions — in terms both of its approach and some of its substantive interpretations — that are likely to be of particular interest to those for whom the experience of the anti-apartheid struggle remains an active legacy.

To a considerable degree Freeman allows her careful documentation to drive her argument on these matters. But she is too good a social scientist to pretend that it is really possible for "the facts" merely to speak for themselves. Some theoretical perspective is necessary and here, in the first instance, she chooses to emphasize the importance to the definition of Canada's policy of structural determinations, these defined principally by the logic of Canada's capitalist economy and the vested interests, corporate and bureaucratic, linked to that logic. This proves to be a powerful entry point, as a *Globe and Mail* staffer felt forced to acknowledge of her book when first reviewing it last year (Sean Fine, "How Canada failed South Africa," *G&M*, April 11, 1998). Fine concedes Freeman's case that the "politics of balance" (social justice vs. economics) claimed by decision-makers as driving Canada's South African policy was largely "illusory": "The guiding philosophy was that the state should not interfere with the private sector."

Still, Freeman is unwilling to advocate any straightforward brand of economic determinism, emphasizing — as a means both of defending herself against such a charge and of enriching her analysis — the simultaneous importance of certain "autonomous variables." In this regard she makes much of the impact of "discourse," the extent to which the common-sense premises of establishment discussion of South African issues become a factor in their own right in determining outcomes, especially within the foreign policy-making bureaucracy. And yet what Freeman presents as evidence in this regard is the operation of pretty unmediated capitalist ideology: the reduction of national interests to the unquestioned pursuit of profit.

More convincingly, she notes the impact of the discourse of "non-violence," much trumpeted by "official Canada" to justify its not taking sides more unequivocally — although here too she shows any such preoccupation to have been pretty opportunistically and selectively defined, not least in Cold War terms. Still, if Freeman had pressed her search for intervening variables a little harder she might also have made much more than she does in this book of our pattern of institutionalized racism that made it all too easy for Canadians to deny to Africans the necessary means of their liberation that (for example) we had been more than willing to grant to the maquis of Europe during the Second World War.

Even more important for Freeman as an "autonomous variable," however, is something she calls "politics," this latter said to qualify the impact on policy of established economic interests that seem otherwise to define so much about the supine role of Canada towards apartheid South Africa that she describes. Here the shift in Canadian policy undertaken by Brian Mulroney, the other key player focused on in Freeman's book, becomes a critical test case for her. If structural/economic determination serves to explain so much about most phases of Canadian policy towards South Africa, why, Freeman asks, was Mulroney able to go further than any other Prime Minister in acting, rather than merely speaking, tough towards South Africa? For Mulroney did, as Freeman scrupulously documents, carry Canada's sanctions' policy and some related anti-apartheid initiatives to a high-water mark.

## The Mulroney Moment

The issue may be less complicated than Freeman supposes. One other possible intervening variable (somewhere between economic structure and "politics") she rather surprisingly downplays is class, a factor never systematically embraced in a book that otherwise seeks to stake out radical ground in the study of Canadian foreign policy. And yet what binds businessmen, politicians, and higher-level civil servants is the privileged position they share in the upper reaches of the class hierarchy in this society and the (hegemonic) outlook — "discourse"! — they are encouraged to share. Against this kind of analysis, however, Freeman chooses to frame her radical critique by highlighting what she calls the "structured representation of interests," an approach that risks functioning as a kind of left variant of pluralist theory. Thus, under normal circumstances, some voices — notably those linked to capital — are argued to sound more loudly in the pluralist chorus that drives our politics than others. But when they don't, at least in any very straightforward manner, the reason must be "politics," this term implying, apparently, the impact on policy of a much wider range of political interests. What we were witnessing in the Mulroney case, she argues, is "a response at the political level to the dramatically new conjuncture at home in Canada and abroad in South Africa. In this way, the new policy demonstrated the relative autonomy of the Canadian state from key forces wedded to the policy of the past" (p.134 — this and later page references are to Freeman's original book).

No doubt developments in South Africa itself did change the terrain of decision-making considerably and demanded fresh thinking about appropriate Canadian policies. But how far does the invocation of "the political level" and "relative autonomy" take us in explaining Mulroney's own response? Not far enough, I fear, if Freeman is suggesting that forces from beyond the sphere of ruling class interests had suddenly become central to Canada's policy-making vis-à-vis South Africa. For the fact remains that "key forces" from the past — the hegemonic Canadian capitalist class — dictated outcomes even during this period.

Of course, the terms of such ruling class hegemony cannot be read crudely off the presumption that some entirely straightforward "logic of capital" is at work; class analysis of a far more shrewd and supple kind is required. Political assertions from below do have some impact, for example: but this is primarily because an effectively hegemonic class will be at its most successful when it is able to co-opt and contain such oppositional demands rather than merely seek to repress them. This point is particularly important to our discussion, below, of Freeman's analysis of the Canadian anti-apartheid movement. More central here is the fact that struggles within that hegemonic class (struggles between factions and fractions shaped by differing interests and differing levels of craft and understanding) to define its strategies are often as intense as any struggle between classes. Indeed, in seeking to understand the apparent anomalies of the "Mulroney moment," it is precisely by focusing upon such intra-class struggles that we learn far more than through any insights provided by "radical pluralist theory."

## Saving the Baby

Thus capital in South Africa itself had long profited from the cheap labour made available by a parallel system of racial oppression. However, what seems evident is that, by the mid-1980s, a profound debate had emerged within the capitalist class, worldwide and local, over how best to deal with the problem that a near-revolutionary South Africa now posed. Cooler heads within that class had begun to have some pretty daring thoughts, in effect echoing the earlier insight of Anglo-American executive Zac de Beer that "we all understand how years of apartheid have caused many blacks to reject the economic as well as the political system. . . . We dare not allow the baby of free enterprise to be thrown out with the bathwater of apartheid."

Particularly important in advancing this point of view was Malcolm Fraser, the Conservative former Prime Minister of Australia, who was an extremely vocal member of the Eminent Persons' Group assigned by the Commonwealth in the mid-1980s to investigate the South African situation. Echoing the EPG's call for sanctions to force apartheid South Africa to its senses before the confrontation there escalated out of control, Fraser (as cited by Freeman), argued that an escalating conflict would mean that "moderation would be swept aside. . . . The government that emerged from all this would be extremely radical, probably Marxist, and would nationalize all western business interests." As I wrote at the time (in my article "Mysteries of the Dark Cabinet: What Is behind the Mulroney Government's Surprising Stand on South Africa?" This Magazine, August-September 1988), "It seems clear that Mulroney responded to this reading of the South African situation. To the goal of ingratiating himself with the black Commonwealth was now added the role of spearheading the forces of enlightened capitalism!" From such a perspective much of the mystery attached to the explanation of Mulroney's anti-apartheid initiative falls away.

To be fair, Freeman does allude to much of this evidence and it is also true that some of the other variables she introduces did have pertinent effects: for example, it probably did make some difference to Mulroney's ability to embrace the side of the intra-capitalist strategic debate he did that he was not a racist like Reagan and Thatcher. Still, Freeman at times seems so intent upon looking elsewhere for additional "political" explanations of Mulroney's choice that she tends to blur the central insight offered by a more firmly grounded class analysis of that choice. Moreover, this latter way of understanding Canadian policy-making is further verified by what happened next: when the South African government seemed to have succeeded at least momentarily in crushing domestic resistance through its Emergencies of the later 1980s, its apparent success suggested the possibility of a return to "business-as usual" on the old racist terms — and reinforced the less adventurous perspectives both of other capitalist actors in Canada and of other, larger, capitalist powers, notably Britain and the United States.

At this point Mulroney's own enthusiasm waned (p.165), further solidifying a context within which the forces in Canada supportive of a more conventional capitalist approach to South Africa (their lineup usefully itemized by Freeman here) waxed strong once again, and the malignant Clark could emerge as Cabinet point man for reining in what was now thought to have been too forward a policy. This is not too surprising. After all, even in acknowledging the uniqueness of the Mulroney moment Freeman demonstrates just how short-lived and shallow the high-water mark of Mulroney's anti-apartheid initiative actually was. Now, as that moment faded, she can link her evaluation of Mulroney that much more firmly to her earlier discussion of the likes of Diefenbaker and Trudeau and emphasize the flimsy nature of Mulroney's own claim to the legendary status that has begun to accrue to him on this front (p.256).

And yet, at the same time, it is interesting to note the number of members of the capitalist class who would come to see Mulroney as having been right the first time. Indeed, it was precisely during the late 1980s period of Mulroney's retreat from his advanced thinking regarding apartheid that certain similarly inclined capitalists in South Africa itself were beginning to press forward successfully the logic of a very similar containment strategy for pre-empting and taming black aspirations.

## The Anti-Apartheid Movement

What, while all this was going on, of the Canadian anti-apartheid movement? It bears emphasizing that in her concern to allow "politics" to matter Freeman is led to study carefully the role — one that another writer might have ignored — played by various forces in Canadian society that swam against the current of establishment interest and orthodoxy as regards South Africa. In her book this encourages an important acknowledgement of the often impressive efforts of a wide range of churches, unions, NGOs, and liberation support organizations linked to the Canadian anti-apartheid movement, broadly defined. And yet, as hinted earlier, in her search for the "political" explanation for the rise of Mulroney's own anti-apartheid policy — one that, given her approach, must emphasize the broadening and diversifying of the range of relevant political forces in order to explain outcomes — she may give the movement far more credit for producing that enlightened policy than it deserves. Even more clearly, she places far too much blame upon the movement for permitting the subsequent weakening of Mulroney's commitments (she speaks, in this respect, of the negative impact of "the splintering of the movement" in the late 1980s, of the "rut into which [it] seemed to have fallen," and of extent to which its self-destructive tendencies "removed a key irritant from within civil society" [pp.232-33]).

For starters, in documenting the range of organizations and individuals involved in anti-apartheid work in Canada Freeman misreads the nature of the movement in important ways. Thus her main point of reference in measuring movement success seems to be the degree of its institutionalization as a national movement. Yet this is not a particularly illuminating angle of vision. True, as she demonstrates, the movement was pulled forward, briefly, towards a more integrated national focus during the heyday of Mulroney's policies. But most anti-apartheid activists had never been naive about what could be accomplished at that level, choosing instead to prioritize efforts in their own diverse constituencies, social and geographical.

After all, the alternative model was the British Anti-Apartheid Movement, its measure of unity facilitated by the compact geography of the UK but also by a degree of enforced policy conformity (uncritical support of the ANC, for example) that many anti-apartheid activists in Canada would not (quite rightly, in my opinion) countenance. As for the fact that some left-liberal campaigners fell for Clark's venal attempt in the late 1980s to substitute various feel-good gimmicks (his focus on the media question, for example) for any substantial deepening of sanctions, or were co-opted by monies momentarily made available by the government for certain kinds of anti-apartheid activities, this was perfectly predictable. Nonetheless, in my experience and in sharp contradiction to the elegiac tone adopted by Freeman about such matters, there was no slackening off of anti-apartheid work in Toronto itself and in many Toronto-based institutions (but this was also true elsewhere in the country) as the 1980s wore on, whatever the decay of the soft unity that had momentarily surfaced nationally amongst very diverse constituencies, regionally, politically, and ideologically.

But what about the impact of this movement, however interpreted, on policy? No doubt, in its very diversity, it did make some difference: ironically, Freeman herself — only several pages (p.248) after her pronouncement of the movement's self-destruction — is to be found hailing the extent to which forces in civil society (churches, unions, and the like) stayed the Mulroney government from merely dumping such sanctions as were in place at the point when the negotiations process began in South Africa in 1990! But in the 1980s phase Freeman focuses upon most centrally, the movement's fate was to flow most strongly with the opportunity offered (largely for reasons beyond the movement's own control) by the Mulroney moment and to appear to ebb somewhat when that moment passed. To interpret events otherwise — to "blame the movement" for Mulroney's backsliding, for example — is to miss the main point to be gleaned from an alternative reading of the history of the anti-apartheid movement in Canada.

For the one thing that a structural-cum-class analysis of Canadian policy-making should underscore is just how limited in its impact a reformist approach (including the attempt to reform one particular aspect of Canada's foreign policy) must inevitably be without a far more fundamental transformation of Canadian society and polity. This is the hard lesson that radical anti-apartheid activists kept learning during the years of their activity as they were confronted constantly with the economic-cum-class logic of our country's link to racial capitalism in South Africa. This is not to say that they — we — were wasting our time, nor is it to say that we couldn't have worked both harder and more effectively. It is to suggest, however, that Freeman's pluralistic/"political" qualifications of her main argument risk blurring the very strength of the case (about the overbearing impact on policy of the untransformed socio-economic structures in this country) she makes most effectively . . . and usefully.

## The Struggle Continues?

In the end, interestingly, these latter structures reclaim centrality in her argument about Canadian policy-making. Not the least of the virtues of this important book is Freeman's insistence on carrying her story through, however briefly, to the post-apartheid present — a sign of her welcome insistence throughout on wedding careful scholarship to social and political concern. Moreover, her "Conclusion and Epilogue" demonstrate, once again, the strengths of the structural emphasis within her overall argument. For she reveals unerringly the narrow and selfishly market-driven character of Canada's continuing outreach (trade, aid, and the rest) to post-apartheid South Africa, making this chapter of far more than historical interest and indeed required reading. Her conclusion is powerful: "In the current conjuncture of neo-liberal fundamentalism, dominant forces in Canada and the West seem even more indifferent to the interests of the vast majority [in South Africa] than they were in the long battle to end apartheid" (p.304).

Good stuff. Yet even in this last chapter there must be nagging doubts as to the efficacy of the overall framework (marked by its downplaying of class analysis) that Freeman adopts. The South African state under ANC leadership has proven to be a willing recipient of such market-defined, post-apartheid Canadian outreach. Why? Special attention must be paid, in this regard, to the embourgeoisement of a stratum of Africans, within and without the ANC, and the very considerable evidence that this development has contributed mightily to the movement's leadership accepting, in Freeman's words, "policies at odds with the principles of the ANC Freedom Charter" and adopting a brand of "neo-liberal fundamentalism." Was not this precisely the outcome that the deep thinkers within the capitalist class had begun to consider possible in the late 1980s (if not, perhaps, Mulroney himself:

whatever the cunning of his broader strategic views, his government crudely down-graded the claims to centrality of the ANC until quite late in the day)? Yet, as Freeman analyzes the ANC (p.301), first and foremost this "drift to the right in discourse and the approach towards economic policy of senior ministers in the Mandela government, although not entirely uncontested, indicates how narrow the options are"!

This is, at best, only half right. The structural constraints imposed on the ANC by the power of capitalist interests, worldwide and local, are real enough. But the ANC itself has also become part of the problem in many ways, the constraints generated by class formation and class polarization (and by the proto-hegemonic quality of its chosen "discourse") beginning to cut across it just as surely and as sharply as they do across Canadian society and the Canadian political system.

# NOTES

## Introduction: Liberation, and After

1.  Lionel Cliffe and John S. Saul, eds., *Socialism in Tanzania: Politics and Policies*, 2 vols. (Nairobi: East African Publishing House, 1972-1973); and Giovanni Arrighi and John S. Saul, *Essays on the Political Economy of Africa* (New York: Monthly Review Press, 1973).

2.  It is worth recalling Perry Anderson's evocation of these terms, posing as it still does a very considerable analytical challenge: "Any study of imperialism faces one of the key dilemmas of the social sciences: how can a diachronic and a synchronic perspective be combined? The reconciliation is easy enough in principle, but extremely hard in practice. It will be remembered that de Saussure defined a diachronic order as one in which each 'moment' can only be understood in terms of all those that have preceded it: thus in a bridge game, the meaning of any trick depends on all the tricks before it and cannot be understood without knowledge of them. In contrast, a synchronic moment is one in which every moment is visible in the present; it is coextensive with the relationship of all the existing data to each other. Thus, at any move, a game of chess is always comprehensible without any knowledge of the previous moves. It is clear that any society has both of these dimensions: it is at once a *structure* which can only be understood in terms of the interrelationship of its parts, and a *process* which can only be understood in terms of the cumulative weight of its past. The difficulty is to synthesize the two aspects in any actual study." See Anderson, "Portugal and the End of Ultra-Colonialism," *New Left Review*, 15-17 (1962), p.113.

3.  For this introductory survey of Southern Africa's recent history I draw on my brief overview article, "The Thirty Years' War for Southern African Liberation (1960-1990)," in *Encyclopedia of African History*, vol. 1, ed. Kevin Shillington (London: Fitzroy and Dearborn, 2005). See also John S. Saul, "The Southern African Revolution," ch.1 in Saul, *Recolonization and Resistance: Southern Africa in the 1990s* (Trenton, N.J.: Africa World Press, 1993).

4.  For historical background on the Zimbabwean case, see John S. Saul, "Zimbabwe: The Next Round," ch.4 in Saul, *Socialist Ideology and the Struggle for Southern Africa* (Trenton, N.J.: Africa World Press, 1990); and also the appropriate sections in "The Southern African Revolution" in the same book. There is a host of more recent material, including Patrick Bond and Masimba Manyanya, *Zimbabwe's Plunge: Exhausted Nationalism, Neoliberalism and the Search for Social Justice* (Durban and London: University of Natal Press and Merlin, 2003).

5.  See, for example, the wealth of materials collected in Cliffe and Saul, eds., *Socialism in Tanzania*, 2 vols.

6.  Roger Murray, "Second Thoughts on Ghana," *New Left Review*, 42 (1967). This was a formulation that Arrighi and I cited on several occasions in *Essays on the Political Economy of Africa*. As we further argued (*Essays*, pp.22-23), "It may be . . .

that the changes in surplus utilization, which we see to be necessary for real development, are not possible under present historical conditions, particularly in view of the short-term losses in economic growth and, quite possibly, in political stability that would ensue from any serious attempt at disengagement from international capitalism or reform of the power base of the African governments involved. This question, however, by no means invalidates the historical necessity of the change itself, which should therefore be of central importance in socialist debate."

7.  Adam Przeworski, *Capitalism and the Market* (Cambridge: Cambridge University Press, 1991), p.122.

8.  Arrighi and Saul, *Essays on the Political Economy of Africa*, pp.53, 86.

9.  As we further situated this reality in Arrighi and Saul, *Essays on the Political Economy of Africa* (p.68), "The decisive fact about contemporary independent Africa is the continuance of its subservient economic position vis-à-vis the industrial centers of the West. This subordination originated, as is well known, in the pattern of trade and investment of colonial times, whereby Africa came to play, within the international division of labour, a role of supplier of raw materials and outlet for the manufactures of centers of accumulation. It is important to reemphasize that, as compared with other areas of the underdeveloped world, this 'classic' pattern of extractive imperialism has remained relatively untransformed in Africa."

10. Manfred Bienefeld, "Dependency Theory and the Political Economy of Africa's Crisis," *Review of African Political Economy*, 43 (1988), pp.85-86.

11. But see Colin Leys and John S. Saul, "Dependency," in *The Elgar Companion to Development Studies*, ed. David A. Clark (Cheltenham: Edward Elgar Publishing, 2005).

12. Arrighi and Saul, *Essays on the Political Economy of Africa*, p.86.

13. Ibid., pp.86, 84, 23-24.

14. Ibid., p.87. Something of the flavour of the times can be gleaned from our further comment (p.87): "Much more important, a successful socialist revolution in Southern Africa would radically restructure neocolonialist relationships on the whole continent since, after a necessary (and admittedly difficult) period of reconstruction, it would act as a powerful pole of politico-economic attraction for the less developed and less wealthy nations of Tropical Africa. Our discussions should have dispelled any illusions concerning the nature and short-term prospects of the struggle in Southern Africa. Yet, at the present historical moment, this provides the main, if not the only, leverage for revolutionary change in sub-Saharan Africa."

15. Indeed, this is the conclusion to which Arrighi himself seems to have come. See Giovanni Arrighi, "The African Crisis: World Systemic and Regional Aspects," *New Left Review*, 15 (2002).

16. See also, on this theme, John S. Saul, "Globalizing African Studies: Political Science Fiction and the North American Africanist," and "Afterword: The

Radical Africanist and the Socialist Alternative," in Saul, *Millennial Africa: Capitalism, Socialism, Democracy* (Trenton: Africa World Press, 2001).

## PART I CONTINENTAL CONSIDERATIONS

## Capitalism, Socialism, Democracy

1. Richard Sklar, "Beyond Capitalism and Socialism in Africa," *The Journal of Modern African Studies*, 26, 1 (1988).

2. Giovanni Arrighi and John S. Saul, "Socialism and Economic Development in Tropical Africa" and "Nationalism and Revolution in Sub-Saharan Africa," chs.1 and 2 in *Essays on the Political Economy of Africa*.

3. See, as an example of more broad-gauged writing, John S. Saul, "The Role of Ideology in the Transition to Socialism," in *Transition and Development: Problems of Third World Socialism*, ed. Richard R. Fagan, Carmen Diana Deere, and José Luis Coraggio (New York: Monthly Review Press, 1986), republished with other related essays, including "Ideology in Africa: Decomposition and Recomposition," in Saul, *Socialist Ideology and the Struggle for Southern Africa*.

4. See, for example, John S. Saul, *Development after Globalization: Theory and Practice for an Embattled South in a New Imperial Age* (Delhi and London: Three Essays Press and Zed Books, 2005), for example. See also John S. Saul, "Identifying Class, Classifying Difference," in *Fighting Identities: Race, Region and Ethnic Nationalism: Socialist Register 2003*, ed. Leo Panitch and Colin Leys (London: The Merlin Press, 2002); and Saul, "Globalization, Imperialism, Development: False Binaries and Radical Resolutions," in *The New Imperial Challenge: Socialist Register 2004*, ed. Leo Panitch and Colin Leys (London: The Merlin Press, 2003); both of these essays are included in *Development after Globalization*.

## 1. Sub-Saharan Africa in Global Capitalism (with Colin Leys)

This chapter was originally co-authored with Colin Leys and appeared, in much the same form, in *Monthly Review*, Special Summer Issue on "Global Capitalism," July-August 1999. I am grateful to Colin Leys for his permission to publish it here; the co-authors also wish to thank Jane Borges and Pablo Idahosa for assistance and advice during the preparation of the original article.

1. World Bank, *World Development Report 1996* (Washington: World Bank, 1996).

2. Economic Commission for Africa (ECA), *Economic Report on Africa 1996* (Addis Ababa: ECA, 1996).

3. World Bank, *Global Development Prospects 2004: Realizing the Development Promise of the Doha Agenda* (Washington: International Bank for Reconstruction and Development, 2003).

4. African Development Bank (ADB), *African Development Report* (Oxford: Oxford University Press, 1998), pp.33, 47-48, and later documents.

5. Ibid., pp.51-52.

6. See, for example, Economic Commission for Africa (ECA), *African Economic Report 1998* (Addis Ababa: ECA, 1998; available at <http:// www.un.org/deptseca>).

7. The figure of forty-eight states includes a number of island states and statelets that are more or less near Africa and conventionally included in it, but whose history, resource endowment, present economic structures, and cultures distinguish them in various ways from Africa proper. These are Cape Verde (pop. 0.4 m.), Madagascar (pop. 15.8 m.), Mauritius (pop. 1.1 m.), São Tomé and Principe (pop. less than 100,000), and Seychelles (pop. 100,000). Seychelles and Mauritius have relatively high per capita incomes, based on tourism and also, in the case of Mauritius, on clothing exports.

8. In the eight years to 1997, thirty African countries had per capita income growth of over 1.5 per cent, while only twenty-three had less, or declining incomes (ADB, *African Development Report*, p.3). This was markedly better than the 1980s, but starting from a lower base: many countries had still to get back to the per capita income levels of 1980, and, in any case, counting countries rather than populations distorts the picture because many of the better-performing economies were small.

9. ECA, *African Economic Report 1998*.

10. United Nations Integrated Regional Information Networks (IRIN), *IRIN News*, "'Africa's Poverty Rose by 43 Percent in Last Decade' — UN Economic Commission for Africa," 2004 (available at <http://www.irinnews.org>), presented with the following heading: "SUMMARY & COMMENT: Poverty in Africa has increased by a whopping 43 per cent in the last ten years. And despite being informed of this, a meeting of economists and academicians gave an age old prescription: Increase trade in Africa. But will it work?"

11. *IRIN News*. As ECA Executive Secretary Amoako also stated at the same conference: "Noting that African populations are growing much faster than the continent's economies, Amaoku said the number of Africa's poor is likely to rise from 315 million in 1999 to 404m in 2015." As the Africa Union's trade commissioner Elizabeth Tankeu added, "Africa has been on the losing side of the globalization process and that trade had not served as an instrument of growth and rising prosperity, as in other developing regions," although her proposed solution to this was a familiar if unconvincing one: "Becoming more competitive." Both are quoted in "Amaoku Calls for Action on African Unemployment, Poverty," ECA, Press Release no.12, 2004.

12. Quoted in *IRIN News* "'Africa's Poverty Rose.'"

13. ECA, *African Economic Report 1998*.

14. Geoffrey Kay, *Development and Underdevelopment: A Marxist Analysis* (London: Macmillan, 1975), p.x.

15. In 1997 the whole of Africa (including North Africa) attracted less than 3 per cent of all the world's foreign direct investment, and sub-Saharan Africa excluding South Africa, barely half of that — i.e. $2.7 billion; and slightly over half of this went to the half-dozen oil-exporting countries. IRIN News, "'Africa's Poverty Rose.'"

16. Manuel Castells, The Information Age, vol.3, End of Millennium (Oxford: Blackwell Publishers, 1998), "The Dehumanization of Africa," pp.88-90.

17. As we will see, there was a rough, if misleading, plausibility to all of this. African states were not, by and large, "developmental" in any meaningful sense of the word, but had instead become predatory excrescences, parasitic upon the peasantry certainly and with little residual popular legitimacy. It was therefore that much easier for outside actors to present Africa's problems as being exclusively internal and as largely state-inspired.

18. This is the title Bill Freund gives to the last chapter — on Africa's most recent period — of the new edition of his definitive short history of the continent, The Making of Contemporary Africa (Boulder, Col.: Lynne Rienner Publishers, 1998).

19. Eboe Hutchful, "From 'Revolution' to Monetarism: The Economics and Politics of the Adjustment Programme in Ghana," in Structural Adjustment in Africa, ed. Bonnie Campbell and John Loxley (London: Macmillan, 1989), pp.122-23.

20. John Ravenhill, "A Second Decade of Adjustment: Greater Complexity, Greater Uncertainty," in Hemmed In: Responses to Africa's Decline, ed. Thomas Callaghy and John Ravenhill (New York: Columbia University Press, 1993), p.47.

21. ECA, African Economic Report 1998.

22. As quoted in Ashley Seager, "U.N. Trade Rise Is Hurting the Poorest," The Guardian, May 28, 2004.

23. In his book, A Future for Africa: Beyond the Politics of Adjustment (London: Earthscan, 1992), Bade Onimode mounts a powerful case against structural adjustment, capping the point we have quoted here with the observation (p.1) that "a generation of Africans has been lost and a second is under serious threat, while the marginalization of Africa has accelerated alarmingly in most spheres."

24. David Plank, "Aid, Debt and the End of Sovereignty: Mozambique and Its Donors," Journal of Modern African Studies, 31, 3 (1993), pp.429-30.

25. A notorious example is Robert D. Kaplan, "The Coming Anarchy," The Atlantic Monthly, February 1994, pp.44-76.

26. Perry Anderson, Lineages of the Absolutist State (London: New Left Books, 1974), pp.549.

27. Chris Allen, "Understanding African Politics," Review of African Political Economy, 65 (1993), pp.301-20. The account given here draws heavily on Allen's important analysis.

28. Catherine Boone, "States and Ruling Classes in Post-Colonial Africa: The Enduring Contradictions of Power," in State Power and Social Forces, ed. Joel S. Migdal, Atul Kohli, and Vivienne Shue (Cambridge: Cambridge University Press, 1994), pp.108-40.

29. Catherine Boone, "'Empirical Statehood' and Reconfigurations of Political Order," in The African State at a Critical Juncture, ed. Leonardo A. Villalon and Philip A. Huxtable (Boulder, Col.: Lynne Rienner Publishers, 1998), pp.129-41.

30. Dale Grant, "Canadians Cry 'Havoc' and Let Slip the Dogs of War," Toronto Star, March 9, 1999.

31. Ankie Hoogevelt, Globalization and the Postcolonial World (Baltimore: Johns Hopkins University Press, 1997), pp.180-81.

32. Allen, "Understanding African Politics", subsection "Guerilla War and Socialist States," pp.315-16.

33. Harry Magdoff and Paul Sweezy, "The Stakes in South Africa," editorial, Monthly Review, 37, 11 (April 1986).

34. On the taming of the South African transition see, among other things, chs.2, 3, 8, and 9 here.

35. Castells, Information Age, subsection "Africa's Hope? The South African Connection," p.122.

36. See Hein Marais, South Africa: Limits to Change: The Political Economy of Transition (London: Zed Books, 1998).

37. Castells, Information Age, p.127.

38. "Even after successfully implementing most of the broad elements of this [the World Bank's] agenda . . . the incidence of poverty will still rise in both absolute and relative terms. Dependence on foreign assistance will continue unabated. There should be no illusions," writes Israt Husain in "Structural Adjustment and the Long-term Development of Sub-Saharan Africa," in Structural Adjustment and Beyond in Sub-Saharan Africa, ed. R. Van der Hoeven and Fred Van der Kraaij (The Hague/London: Ministry of Foreign Affairs/James Currey, 1994), p.170.

39. For an analysis of such initiatives in the 1980s, see Onimode, Future for Africa.

40. Jonathan Barker, "Debating Globalization: Critique of Colin Leys," Southern Africa Report, 12, 4 (September 1997), p.21; see, however, in the same issue of Southern African Report, Leys's response to Barker ("Colin Leys Replies"), which empha-sizes the parallel need for "nation-wide movements and/or parties" through which such local groups and initiatives can ultimately "unite to confront the political and economic power of the transnationals and the states that back them" (pp.22-23).

41. Stephen P. Riley and Trevor W. Parfitt, "Economic Adjustment and Democratization in Africa," in Free Markets and Food Riots, ed. John Walton and David Seddon (Oxford: Blackwell, 1994), p.167.

42. Célestin Monga, The Anthropology of Anger: Civil Society and Democracy in Africa (Boulder, Col.: Lynne Reinner, 1996).

43. Riley and Parfitt, "Economic Adjustment and Democratization," p.170; they, in turn, are quoting P.H. Smith, "Crisis and Democracy in Latin America," World Politics, 43, 4 (1991).

44. Patrick Bond, "Post-Nationalist Politics for Zimbabwe?" *Red Pepper*, April 1999; for the very great difficulties that have arisen in seeking to realize the kind of "post-nationalist and post-neoliberal" future for Zimbabwe envisaged by Bond, see, however, ch.6 here.

45. On the importance of the distinction between "liberal democracy" and "popular democracy" in Africa see ch.3 here.

46. Mahmood Mamdani, *Citizen and Subject* (Princeton, N.J.: Princeton University Press, 1996).

47. See, for example, Paul Tiyambe Zeleza and M.C. Diop, "Report of Codesria Eighth General Assembly," *Codesria Bulletin*, 4 (1995).

48. Quoted from Bundy, "Problems and Prospects for South African Socialists," paper presented at Political Science Seminar, York University, Toronto, October 1991.

## 2. "What Is to Be Learned?" The Failure of African Socialisms and Their Future

This chapter was first presented in draft to "Beyond Market and Plan: Toward New Socialisms," a workshop held at York University, March 23-24, 2002, and there I benefited in particular from the formal commentaries on the draft presented by Pamela Leach and George Niksic, and also from subsequent observations on the text by Colin Leys; in addition, a shortened version of this chapter was published in Rob Albritton et al., eds., *New Socialisms: Futures beyond Globalization* (London: Routledge, 2004).

1. Murray, "Second Thoughts on Ghana," p.39.

2. I draw here on my overview article "Socialism in Postcolonial Africa," in *Encyclopedia of African History*, ed. Shillington.

3. For a more sympathetic account of "African Socialism" see the relevant chapters of Robert Young, *Postcolonialism: An Historical Introduction* (Oxford: Blackwell, 2001).

4. There is a vast literature on Tanzania's socialist experiment, to which I also contributed at the time: see, for example, Cliffe and Saul, eds., *Socialism in Tanzania*; and "Tanzania: African Socialism in One Country," in Arrighi and Saul, *Essays on the Political Economy of Africa*. More recently I have returned to such themes in two articles that I have drawn on here: "Poverty Alleviation and the Revolutionary-Socialist Imperative: Learning from Nyerere's Tanzania," *International Journal*, 62, 2 (Spring 2002); and "Julius Nyerere: The Theory and Practice of (Un)Democratic Socialism in Africa," in *The Legacies Of Julius Nyerere: Influences on Development Discourse and Practice*, ed. David M. McDonald and Eunice Njeri Sahle (Trenton, N.J.: Africa World Press, 2002); see also ch.7 in this book.

5. Julius K. Nyerere, "Ujamaa — The Basis of African Socialism" (1962), in Julius K. Nyerere, Freedom and Unity/Uhuru Na Umoja: A Selection from Writings and Speeches, 1962-1965 (Dar es Salaam: Oxford University Press, 1966), pp.162, 170.

6. Julius K. Nyerere, as summarized in The Nationalist (Dar es Salaam), Sept. 5, 1967. On another occasion Nyerere was reported as saying: "African leaders have their price these days. The moment one becomes a minister, his price also gets determined. The prices are not even big; some are bought for only £500, or a simple house." The report went on to say: "Mwalimu also said that although it was possible to buy ministers, there was one section of Africa that could not be bought. 'The people,' he said, 'cannot be bought.'" The Standard, July 8, 1967.

7. Julius K. Nyerere, "Economic Nationalism," speech, Feb. 28, 1967, in Nyerere, Freedom and Socialism (London: Oxford University Press, 1968). Nyerere completed the argument by adding: "To Tanzanians this inevitable choice is not unwelcome. We are committed to the creation of a classless society in which every able-bodied citizen is contributing to the economy through work, and we believe that this can only be obtained when the major means of production are publicly owned and controlled. But the fact remains that our recent socialist measures were not taken out of blind adherence to dogma. They are intended to serve the society."

8. Manfred Bienefeld, "Tanzania: Model or Anti-Model," in The Struggle for Development: National Strategies in an International Context, ed. Manfred Bienefeld and Martin Godfrey (Clichester: John Wiley, 1982), p.300. As Bienefeld continues, "Of course, there can be no guarantee that this change would produce long-term benefits for Tanzania's people. This would depend on the actual use made of these possibilities and, no doubt, this too would fall short of the ideal."

9. Once again, there has been a strong literature on Mozambican themes; my own contributions, which inform the writing here, include John S. Saul, ed., A Difficult Road: The Transition to Socialism in Mozambique (New York: Monthly Review Press, 1985); and "Rethinking the Frelimo State," in Real Problems, False Solutions: Socialist Register 1993, ed. Ralph Miliband and Leo Panitch (London: The Merlin Press, 1993).

10. Quoted, from my translation of an interview with Eduardo Mondlane (in Portuguese) conducted by Aquino da Bragança, in my introduction to Eduardo Mondlane, The Struggle for Mozambique, 2nd ed. (London: Zed Books, 1983). As Mondlane continued in the same interview, it would be "impossible to create a capitalist Mozambique" because "it would be ridiculous to struggle — for the people to struggle — to destroy the economic structure of the enemy and then reconstitute it in such a way as to serve the enemy." And he also stressed the importance of learning from the "concrete experience, including the errors, of the socialist countries which since 1917 have worked and lived the socialist experience."

11. Note, however, that the most important "mistake" Frelimo made during this period was its fateful decision to commit itself to the continuing struggle to

liberate the rest of Southern Africa, for which noble decision, a clear by-product of its overall level of revolutionary commitment, it was to pay dearly.

12. See William Minter, *Apartheid's Contras: An Inquiry into the Roots of War in Angola and Mozambique* (London: Zed Books, 1994).

13. See Plank, "Aid, Debt and the End of Sovereignty."

14. Magdoff and Sweezy, "Stakes in South Africa.".

15. On this and other points relevant to this section see, among others, Marais, *South Africa*; Patrick Bond, *Elite Transition: From Apartheid to Neoliberalism in South Africa* (London: Pluto Press, 2000); John S. Saul, "Cry for the Beloved Country: The Post-Apartheid Denouement," *Monthly Review*, 52, 8 (January 2001); and ch.9 here.

16. See the section "Starting from Scratch?" in Saul, "Cry for the Beloved Country," pp.33ff.

17. Gavin Kitching, *Rethinking Socialism* (London and New York: Methuen, 1983), pp.2-3.

18. Gavin Kitching, *Development and Underdevelopment in Historical Perspective* (London: Methuen, 1982).

19. Ken Post and Phil Wright, *Socialism and Underdevelopment* (London and New York: Routledge, 1989), pp.151-52.

20. Ibid., p.178.

21. Ralph Miliband, *Socialism for a Sceptical Age* (London: Verso, 1994), pp.190-91.

22. See Plank, "Aid, Debt and the End of Sovereignty."

23. Quoted in Fantu Cheru, *The Silent Revolution in Africa: Debt, Development and Democracy* (London: Zed Books, 1989), ch.3, "Tanzania: Suffering with Bitterness," pp.56-57.

24. Colin Leys, *The Rise and Fall of Development Theory* (Bloomington and London: Indiana University Press and James Currey, 1996), especially ch.9, "Development Theory and the African Tragedy."

25. Bond, "Post-Nationalist Politics for Zimbabwe?"

26. Amilcar Cabral, *Revolution in Guinea: An African People's Struggle* (London: Stage 1, 1969); Mahmmod Mamdani argues vividly, in his *Citizen and Subject* (Princeton: Princeton University Press, 1996), that in rural Africa, where most Africans live, the "subject" (as distinct from "citizen") status of ordinary rural-dwellers is not easily transcended.

27. See John S. Saul, "Rot, Reform and the Revival of Resistance in Postcolonial Africa," paper presented at workshop on "The Political Economy of Africa Revisited," John Hopkins University, April 22-23, 2002; and see also my "Conclusion," ch.12 here.

28. Monga, *Anthropology of Anger*.

29. Fantu Cheru, "The Local Dimensions of Global Reform," in *Global Futures: Shaping*

*Globalization*, ed. Jan Nederveen Pieterse (London: Zed, 2000), p.124.

30. Riley and Parfitt, "Economic Adjustment and Democratization in Africa," p.167.

31. Jonathan Barker, *Street-Level Democracy: Political Settings at the Margins of Global Power* (Toronto and West Hartford: Between the Lines and Kumarian Press, 1999), p.13.

32. Cheru, "Local Dimensions of Global Reform," p.119.

33. Colin Leys, "Colin Leys Replies," a reply to Jonathan Barker, "Debating Globalization: Critique of Colin Leys," *Southern African Report*, 12, 4 (September 1997).

34. Graham Harrison, "Bringing Political Struggle Back In: African Politics, Power and Resistance," *Review of African Political Economy*, 89 (September 2001); see also Leo Zeilig, ed., *Class Struggle and Resistance in Africa* (Gretton, U.K.: New Clarion Press, 2002).

35. I draw for these paragraphs on, among other places, Saul, "Role of Ideology in the Transition to Socialism."

36. I have further spelled out this proposed economic model with reference to the Mozambican experience in Saul, ed., Difficult Road, ch.2.

37. See Clive Thomas, *Dependence and Transformation: The Economics of the Transition to Socialism* (New York: Monthly Review Press, 1974); and William Luttrell, *Post-Capitalist Industrialization: Planning Economic Independence in Tanzania* (New York: Praeger, 1986).

38. Leys, *Rise and Fall of Development Theory*, p.131.

## 3. Liberal Democracy vs. Popular Democracy in Sub-Saharan Africa

This chapter was first published, in much the same form, in Kidane Mengisteab and Cyrille Daddieh, eds., *State Building and Democratization in Africa: Faith, Hope and Realities* (Westport, Conn. and London: Praeger, 1999) and, in a different format and in two parts, in *Review of African Political Economy*, 72 and 73 (1997).

1. Issa Shivji, ed., *State and Constitutionalism: An African Debate on Democracy* (Harare: SAPES, 1991); see his chapters "State and Constititonalism: A New Democratic Perspective" (ch.2) and "Contradictory Class Perspectives in the Debate on Democracy" (editor's Epilogue). Shivji also identifies a third, "statist," perspective on democracy.

2. Ibid., p.255.

3. Ibid.

4. Thomas M. Callaghy and John Ravenhill, eds., *Hemmed In: Responses to Africa's Economic Decline* (New York: Columbia University Press, 1993), p.17.

5. Larry Diamond, "Three Paradoxes of Democracy," in *The Global Resurgence of*

*Democracy*, ed. Larry Diamond and Marc F. Plattner (Baltimore: Johns Hopkins University Press, 1993), p.103 (emphasis added); see also Larry Diamond, "The Globalization of Democracy," in *Global Transformation and the Third World*, ed. Robert O. Slater, Barry M. Schutz, and Steven R. Dorr (Boulder, Col.: Lynne Rienner Publishers, 1993).

6. Diamond, "Three Paradoxes of Democracy," pp.104-5. Note the parallel with a much earlier formulation by one of the gurus of the current democratization literature, Samuel Huntington: "Problems of governance in the United States today stem from an 'excess of democracy'. . . . The effective operation of a democratic political system usually requires some measure of apathy and non-involvement on the part of some individuals and groups." This quotation is from Samuel Huntington, "The Democratic Distemper," *The Public Interest*, 41 (Fall 1975), quoted in Benjamin Barber, *Strong Democracy: Participatory Politics for a New Age* (Berkeley and Los Angeles: University of California Press, 1984), p.95 (n.2).

7. Diamond, "Three Paradoxes of Democracy," p.98. This is an extremely one-sided way of presenting the development record in Africa — to go no further afield; Diamond's formulations ignore the catastrophic outcomes of most capitalist development strategies on the continent, as well as the crucial role that the state (authoritarian, interventionist) has played in settings (the Asian newly industrialized countries [NICs], for example) in which capitalism has been more successful. Here, as so often in their "scientific" writings, Diamond and his colleagues in the democracy business are marketing almost pure ideology.

8. Ibid., p.106.

9. Ibid.

10. Not that this is a novel tendency: note, also, Claude Ake's pungent comment that "the history of democracy is a history of resistance to its essence, popular power." Claude Ake, "The New World Order: A View from Africa," in *Whose World Order? Uneven Globalization and the End of the Cold War*, ed. Hans-Henrik Holm and George Sorenson (Boulder, Col.: Westview Press, 1995), pp.19-42.

11. Giuseppe di Palma, *To Craft Democracies: An Essay on Democratic Transitions* (Berkeley and Los Angeles: University of California Press, 1990), pp.22-24.

12. Ibid. Emphasis added.

13. Perry Anderson, *A Zone of Engagement* (London: Verso, 1992), pp 355-56; for an earlier discussion highlighting the distinction between "thin" and "strong" democracy, see Barber, *Strong Democracy*.

14. Barry Gills, Joel Rocamora, and Richard Wilson, eds., *Low Intensity Democracy* (London: Pluto Press, 1993).

15. Colin Leys, "The World, Society and the Individual," *Southern Africa Report*, 11, 3 (1996). p.17. The reference to the Solar Temple is to an incident that occurred on October 5, 1994, when "25 people, members of the Church of the Solar Temple, killed themselves, or were killed by their leaders, in a house belonging to the Church in Switzerland. . . . A community of people had destroyed

itself, or had been destroyed by its leaders, in the name of some far-out utopian ideal. . . . Yet I believe that the self-destruction of the Church of the Solar
Temple is a symbol (for) what is happening on the world's stage."

16. Manfred Bienefeld, "Structural Adjustment and the Prospects for Democracy in
Southern Africa," in *Debating Development Discourse: Institutional and Popular Perspectives*,
ed. David B. Moore and Gerald G. Schmitz (New York: St. Martin's Press,
1995), p.52. In Bienefeld's words, the "new enthusiasm for democracy is con-
ditional. . . . Democracy will lead to good governance, as defined by the IFIs
[international financial institutions], only if electorates 'choose' to support their
neo-liberal policies. Just as Henry Ford once declared his Model-T to be available 'in any colour so long as it is black,' bemused electorates now find they
can choose 'any policy regime, so long as it was the neo-liberal one.' In fact
they can only choose how to deal with the consequences of that regime and
those who demand a wider choice are dismissed as naive, foolish or subversive, on the grounds that 'reasonable' people understand that this regime is
good for them and that there is no alternative in any event."

17. Leys, "World, Society and the Individual," p.19.

18. Diamond, "Three Paradoxes of Democracy," pp.104-5.

19. Perhaps Diamond is also being disingenuous when he extends such qualifications of his arguments to the global level — significantly enough, as a kind of
unproblematic aside — with the thought that "the new democracies will also
need economic assistance, access to Western markets, and debt relief if they are
to show that democracy can work to solve the staggering economic and social
problems they face. The international system can play a crucial role in creating
the economic space for struggling democracies to undertake badly needed economic transformation with a social safety net and a human face, thereby making them politically sustainable." Diamond, "Globalization of Democracy,"
p.61. These kinds of qualifications, if further problematized and shifted from
the margins towards the centre of his analysis, would, of course, totally transform that analysis.

20. Adam Przeworski, *Democracy and the Market* (Cambridge: Cambridge University
Press, 1991), p.122. See also p.8 here.

21. Ibid., p.37.

22. Ibid., p.34. Przeworski seems here to be working with a concept of democracy that Philip Green would probably label mere "pseudodemocracy." Philip
Green, *Retrieving Democracy: In Search of Civil Equality* (London: Methuen, 1989). See
also ch.5 here.

23. Miliband, *Socialism for a Sceptical Age*, pp.190-91. See also p.46 here.

24. John Loxley and David Seddon, "Stranglehold on Africa," *Review of African Political
Economy*, 62 (1994), pp.485-93.

25. See David G. Becker and Richard L. Sklar, "Why Postimperialism?" in
*Postimperialism: International Capitalism and Development in the Late Twentieth Century*, ed.
David G. Becker, Jeff Frieden, Sayre P. Schatz, and Richard L. Sklar (Boulder,

Col. and London: Lynne Rienner Publishers, 1987).

26. Becker and Sklar, "Preface," in *Postimperialism*, ed. Becker, Freiden, Schatz, and Sklar, p.ix. The narrow economic determinism that underlies this approach can sometimes be quite breathtaking. Offered up in the name of "realism" and as evidence of the virtues of "analyzing capitalism holistically, as postimperialism does," Sklar's collaborator Becker ends his concluding essay, "Postimperialism: A First Quarterly Report," by suggesting: "The implication is that socialism in the 'third world' may be achieved after a considerable prior experience of capitalist development" (p.219). But what instructions follow from this kind of sub-Second International Marxism for progressives in the many Third World countries (not least in Africa) in which capitalism merely fails to "develop" their countries to any significant degree?

27. Jean-François Bayart, "Civil Society in Africa," in *Political Domination in Africa: Reflections on the Limits of Power*, ed. Patrick Chabal (Cambridge: Cambridge University Press, 1986), p.125.

28. Colin Leys, "Confronting the African Tragedy," *New Left Review*, 204 (March-April 1994), p.46.

29. Note, for example, the final sentence of Loxley and Seddon's overview article on the IFIs' "stranglehold on Africa." Echoing Leys's point that African governments must have "a bigger voice in their own futures," they nonetheless conclude their (largely economically driven) argument with a challenge to the democratic theorists of Africa: "As to how these governments may be rendered more representative of, and accountable to, the broad mass of their citizens, [that] is another matter." Loxley and Seddon, "Stranglehold on Africa," p.493.

30. See Susan George and Fabrizio Sabelli, *Faith and Credit: The World Bank's Secular Empire* (London: Penguin Books, 1994), especially ch.7, "Governance: The Last Refuge?" from which my quotations in this paragraph are drawn.

31. Gerald Schmitz, "Democratization and Demystification: Deconstructing 'Governance' as Development Discourse," in *Debating Development Discourse*, ed. Moore and Schmitz, p.32.

32. Joan Nelson, "The Politics of Economic Transformation: Is Third World Experience Relevant in Eastern Europe?" in *World Politics*, 45, 3 (April 1993), pp.459-60. For a relevant, and suggestive, African case study, see Marcia Burdette, "Democracy vs. Economic Liberalization: The Zambian Dilemma," *South African Report*, 8, 1 (July 1992).

33. Goran Hyden, "Governance in the Study of Politics," in *Governance and Politics in Africa*, ed. Goran Hyden and Michael Bratton (Boulder: Lynne Rienner Publishers, 1992), p.22.

34. As Schmitz, "Democratization and Demystification," p.41, adds in capping his point (he also refers to Hyden, amongst numerous others): "the 'vision' of governance tries to evade the implications of this because at bottom, even when it speaks of popular participation and 'empowerment of the poor,' it is really not a democratic approach which respects peoples' rights to freely choose

their own modes of development and to decide their own public policies. Participation — which has an obvious appeal for purposes of fund-raising and building public support for development — is seen more restrictively as instrumentally valuable to the success of development projects."

35. Chris Allen, Carolyn Baylies, and Morris Szeftel, "Surviving Democracy?" in *Review of African Political Economy*, 54 (1992), p.6.

36. Jacques-Mariel Nzouankeu, "The African Attitude to Democracy," *International Social Science Journal*, 128 (May 1991), pp.373-85. Not that one can easily escape the conclusion that an embracing of the legitimacy of multi-partyism is a necessary condition for the kind of societal openness necessary to the building of a democratic culture and practice; the point is that it is very far from being a sufficient one. Nonetheless, those who once argued for the possibility of a "democratic one-party state" (the literature on the Tanzanian experience in the 1960s and early 1970s under the leadership of Julius Nyerere provides numerous examples of writers tempted by such a formula, including the present author) have had good reasons to rethink their position.

37. See the various chapters in Shivji, ed., *State and Constitutionalism*.

38. Allen, Baylies, and Szeftel, "Surviving Democracy?" p.10.

39. Sidgi Kaballo, "Human Rights and Democratization in Africa," *Political Studies*, 43 (1995), p.203. This failure is further defined, he suggests, by the inability of the African bourgeoisie "to generate an ideological and intellectual discourse that would rally the masses under its leadership." Compare Shivji's emphasis on the need for "*reconceptualizing* the dominant human rights and constitutionalist ideologies into ideologies of resistance of the oppressed," in Shivji, ed., *State and Constitutionalism*, p.257.

40. Peter Anyang'Nyongo, "Democratization Processes in Africa," *Review of African Political Economy*, 54 (1992), p.97.

41. Ake, "New World Order," pp.39-40.

42. Kaballo, "Human Rights and Democratization in Africa," p.203.

43. Przeworski, *Democracy and the Market*, p.85. Emphasis added.

44. James Dunkerley, *The Pacification of Central America: Political Change in the Isthmus*, 1987-1993 (London: Verso, 1994), p.3.

45. Miliband, *Socialism for a Sceptical Age*, p.192. See also, in this connection, Benjamin Barber, *Jihad vs. McWorld* (New York and Toronto: Random House, 1995); Barber sees fundamentalism, or "jihad" (a word he seeks to use generically) as a comprehensible, if inevitably unhealthy, reaction — "It identifies the self by contrasting it with an alien 'other,' and makes politics an exercise in exclusion and resentment" (p.222) — against the raw and radically desocializing individualism that has been so central a feature of the globalization process ("McWorld"). As Barber summarizes his argument, "In a future world where the only available identity is that of blood brother or solitary consumer, and where these two paltry dispositions engage in a battle for the human soul,

democracy does not seem well placed to share in the victory, to whomsoever
it is delivered. Neither the politics of the commodity nor the politics of resentment promise real liberty" (p.224).

46. Nancy Fraser, "From Redistribution to Recognition? Dilemmas of Justice in a
'Post-Socialist' Age," New Left Review, 212 (July-August 1995). Fraser so argues
even while noting that "the struggle for recognition is fast becoming the par-
adigmatic political conflict of the late twentieth century." As she continues,
"Demands for 'recognition of difference' fuel struggles of groups mobilized
under the banners of nationality, ethnicity, 'race,' gender, and sexuality. In
these 'post-socialist' conflicts, group identity supplants class interest as the chief
medium of political mobilization. And cultural recognition displaces socioeconomic redistribution as the remedy for injustice and the goal of political struggle" (p.68). Her aim, she suggests, "is to connect two political problematics
that are currently dissociated from one another."

47. Joe Slovo, "Negotiations: What Room for Compromise?" The African Communist,
130 (3rd Quarter 1992), pp.36-37. As Slovo adds: "But what could we expect
to achieve in the light of the balance of forces and the historical truism that no
ruling class ever gives up all its power voluntarily? There was certainly never
any prospect of forcing the regime's unconditional surrender across the table."

48. Gender difference might also be mentioned here, although, unfortunately and
despite considerable efforts (and some accomplishments) to the contrary, these
were rather less prominent amongst the "differences" seen to demand recon-
ciliation/resolution during the transition than they should have been.

49. Steven Friedman, "South Africa's Reluctant Transition," Journal of Democracy, 4, 2
(April 1993), p.57.

50. See, for example, Andrew Reynolds, ed., Election '94 South Africa: The Campaign,
Results and Future Prospects (London: James Currey, 1994).

51. Alaister Sparks, Tomorrow Is Another Country: The Inside Story of South Africa's Road to
Change (New York: Hill and Wang, 1995).

52. Steven Friedman, ed., The Long Journey: South Africa's Quest for a Negotiated Settlement
(Braamfontein: Ravan Press, 1993); and Steven Friedman and Doreen Atkinson,
eds., The Small Miracle: South Africa's Negotiated Settlement (Braamfontein: Ravan Press,
1994).

53. Jeremy Cronin, "The Boat, the Tap and the Leipzig Way," The African Communist,
130 (3rd Quarter 1992), pp.182-83.

54. Timothy D. Sisk, Democratization in South Africa: The Elusive Social Contract (Princeton,
N.J.: Princeton University Press, 1995), p.123.

55. See, for example, Joseph Hanlon, "Acceptable — but Was It Fair?" African
Agenda, 1, 4 (1995); and Morris Szeftel, "'Negotiated Elections' in South Africa:
1994," Review of African Political Economy, 61 (1994).

56. See, for example, Frederick Johnstone, "Quebeckers, Mohawks and Zulus:
Liberal Federalism and Free Trade," Telos, 93 (Fall 1992); and Frederick

Johnstone, "New World Disorder: Fear, Freud and Federalism," *Telos*, 100 (Summer 1994).

57. Hermann Giliomee, "Democratization in South Africa," *Political Science Quarterly*, 110, 1 (1995). Giliomee, in support of his misgivings, also cites Marina Ottaway, who from quite early on in the transition had raised doubts about the actual depth of the ANC's democratic commitment. See Giliomee, "Liberation Movements and Transition to Democracy," *Journal of Modern African Studies*, 29 (March 1991). See, in addition, Roger Southall, "The South African Elections of 1994: The Remaking of the Dominant-Party State," *Journal of Modern African Studies*, 32, 4 (1994).

58. Richard Saunders, "Not by Votes Alone," *African Agenda*, 1, 4 (1995), p.6. See also Saunders, "A Hollow Shell: Democracy in Zimbabwe," *Southern Africa Report*, 10, 4 (May 1995).

59. This is not to say that the ANC's historical record suggests it to be innocent of such tendencies within its ranks — although it is also true that the ANC would be hard-pressed to match the kind of overweening and self-conscious arrogance of power that has driven Robert Mugabe and his colleagues in Zimbabwe.

60. Giliomee, "Democratization in South Africa," sensibly enough, sees the absence of broad-based economic development and the continuing existence of deep-seated cultural divisions as, in their own right, qualifying South Africa's democratic prospects. He is less sensitive to the possibility that even a relatively achieved liberal-democratic system may, under African circumstances and in the long run, merely exacerbate such problems.

61. Chris Landsberg, "Directing from the Stalls? The International Community and the South African Negotiation Forum," in Friedman and Atkinson, eds., *Small Miracle*, pp.290-91.

62. Sisk, *Democratization in South Africa*, p.3; emphasis added.

63. Thus he cites in apparent agreement (albeit in a footnote) the notion that, in defining its own negotiations strategies, one of the key things that the National Party learned from the transitions in Zimbabwe and Namibia was that "the opposition [i.e. the ANC] will be hamstrung by world pressures in its attempts to redistribute wealth." Sisk, *Democratization in Africa*, p.180.

64. There are, of course, those who have always been deeply sceptical of the suggestion that the ANC, qua liberation movement, was ever actually the bearer of a radical/socialist project. Such analysts are therefore not surprised when they find evidence of the ANC's leadership failing to press for transformative policies or aggrandizing itself in individual terms. See, for example, Baruch Hirson, "The Election of a Government," and "South Africa: The State of a Nation," in the final issue of *Searchlight South Africa*, 12 (June 1995).

65. Note, for example, an intervention at the time by South African poet and activist Dennis Brutus, who argues: "The struggle within the ANC between TINA and THEMBA — There Is No Alternative, and There Must Be an Alternative — seems to have been won by those who want to push into the world economy

at all cost, even gutting the RDP via the White Paper, accepting IMF condition-
ality, destroying once protected industries, and encouraging arms exports."
Quoted in Patrick Bond, "Under the Microscope: The ANC in Power," *Southern
Africa Report*, 10, 3 (March 1995).

66. "SA: Concern Grows at Apathy over Voter Registration," *Southscan*, 10, 10 (April
14, 1995); see also Judith Matleff, "South African Blacks Ask Why They Should
Vote," *Christian Science Monitor*, Feb. 17, 1995.

67. As quoted in "Widespread Voter Registration Manipulation Alleged," *Southscan*,
10, 34 (Sept. 15, 1995).

68. Thus, another report on the then-upcoming local elections in South Africa
("Ethnic Electioneering as IFP Makes Coloured Pact," *Southscan*, 10, 35 (Sept. 22,
1995) suggested that "racial politics is starting to become the dominant theme
in party electioneering for the upcoming local government poll," adding that
"the IFP and the Pan-Africanist Congress (PAC) are seeking to whip up support
on ethnic lines, estimating that this will be the main way in which they can
glean votes and undercut the African National Congress and National Party
(NP)."

69. Sparks, *Tomorrow Is Another Country*, pp.238-39, where he predicts — however
belatedly in terms of the silences in his earlier discussion of the politics of transition — the growing centrality "of a new class stratification gradually beginning to overlay South Africa's old racial strata, never completely eliminating the
old divisions but blurring them and adding a different dimension."

70. African National Congress, *The Reconstruction and Development Programme*
(Johannesburg: Umanyano Publications, 1994); see also Patrick Bond, "The
RDP: A Site for Socialist Struggle," *The African Communist*, 137 (Second Quarter
1994); and SACP, "Defending and Deepening a Clear Left Strategic Perspective
on the RDP," *The African Communist*, 138 (Third Quarter 1994).

71. Nelson Mandela, quoted in Karl von Holdt, "COSATU Special Congress: The
Uncertain New Era," *South African Labour Bulletin*, 17, 5 (September-October
1993), p.19.

72. Jeremy Cronin, "Sell-Out, or the Culminating Moment? Trying to Make Sense
of the Transition," paper presented at "Democracy: Popular Precedents,
Practice, Culture," History Workshop Conference, University of the
Witwatersrand, Johannesburg, July 1994.

73. Bond, "Under the Microscope," p.7. Note also "anc Will Reassert Self in New
Session of Parliament," *Southscan*, 10, 30 (Aug. 18, 1995), a news story suggesting that "the ANC will use the new session of parliament . . . to assert its
control and seek to restore a sense of direction to its members and supporters." The story also quotes veteran academic observer David Welsh as saying:
"I sense in the African National Congress something akin to desperation. They
feel that they must take a grip on the country that they believe is rightfully
theirs and begin to pass those laws that will alter it. . . . There is mounting
evidence of impatience amongst their own people. . . . They have got to come

to grips with the legislation that will affect the lives of the people . . . who voted for them."

74. Glenn Adler and Eddie Webster, "Challenging Transition Theory: The Labour Movement, Radical Reform, and the Transition to Democracy in South Africa," *Politics and Society*, 23, 1 (March 1995), pp.76-77.

75. See John S. Saul, "The Frelimo State: From Revolution to Recolonization" in Saul, *Southern Africa in the 1990s*, ch.3.

76. See, on this subject, the judicious account of Minter, *Apartheid's Contras*.

77. For a related, and instructive, case study see Carollee Bengelsdorf, *The Problem of Democracy in Cuba: Between Vision and Reality* (New York and Oxford: Oxford University Press, 1994).

78. Plank, "Aid, Debt, and the End of Sovereignty. See also Merle Bowen, "Beyond Reform: Adjustment and Political Power in Contemporary Mozambique," *Journal of Modern African Studies*, 30, 2 (1992); and Judith Marshall, *War, Debt and Structural Adjustment in Mozambique: The Social Impact* (Ottawa: North-South Institute, 1992). Bowen analyzes the head-long process of class formation now afoot in Mozambique, while Marshall discusses the sapping, under the tutelage of the IFIS, of the various social programs that were once Frelimo's proudest accomplishment. The work of Anne Pitcher of Colgate University on the quasi-colonial role of new joint venture companies in northern Mozambique is also extremely revealing of present trends.

79. For detailed analyses of the actual carrying out of the Mozambican elections, see the various papers presented at seminar on "Eleicoes, Democracia e Desenvolvimento" held in Maputo, Mozambique, June 13-15, 1995, notably the contributions from Brazao Mazula (head of the National Elections Commission during the electoral process): "As Eleiçoes Moçambicanas: A Trajectória da Paz e Democracia," and Luis de Brito, "O Comportamento Eleitoral nas Primeiras Eleiçoes Multipartidárias em Moçambique." See also the special issue of *Southern Africa Report*, 10, 2 (December 1994) on the Mozambican election. On the implications of the elections for women, see Ruth Jacobson, *Dancing towards a Better Future? Gender and the 1994 Mozambican Elections*, a report prepared for the Norwegian Agency for Development Cooperation, November 1994.

80. On this subject, see Alex Vines, '*No Democracy without Money': The Road to Peace in Mozambique (1982-1992)* (London: Catholic Institute for International Relations, 1994); Cameron Hume, *Ending Mozambique's War: The Role of Mediation and Good Offices* (Washington: United States Institute for Peace, 1994); and ch.4 here.

81. For a documentary history, from a United Nations' perspective, of the latter stages of the overall transition process up to and including the elections, see United Nations, *The United Nations and Mozambique, 1992-1995*, The United Nations Blue Books Series, vol. 5 (New York: United Nations, 1995).

82. See the cover story, entitled, quite specifically, "Winner Takes All," to *Mozambique Peace Process Bulletin*, 14 (February 1995), a periodical published over

the course of the Mozambican electoral process by AWEPA, the European Parliamentarians for Southern Africa. See also Joseph Hanlon, "A Democratic One-Party State," *African Agenda*, 1, 4 (1995), who argues (controversially) that "Frelimo has used the multi-party electoral system imposed by the West to reinstate the one-party state" (p.11), adding that "the industrialized world has been trying to sell [Africa] a very narrow concept: namely, that democracy is simply holding multi-party elections" regardless of whether or not such a process actually "involves everyone, without significant exclusions, in discussion, policy-formulation and decision-making."

83. Its military capacity had tended to melt away, in any case, as soldiers in their thousands (from both sides, as it happens) voted with their feet for civilian life — while also availing themselves of UN-sponsored demobilization buyouts.

84. Of course, the legacy of the war has continued to make itself felt negatively across a wide range of related fronts; the markedly high level of criminality, for example, is as much a reflection of the wholesale availability of arms and of war-induced lack of moral scruple (on the part of many of the recently demobilized former combatants, amongst others) as it is of the desperate economic situation in which the country finds itself. And land-mines, widely and cavalierly sown across the country during the war, continue to take a deadly toll.

85. It is also true that Frelimo had often been tempted, in its initial modernizing arrogance, to ride roughshod over such sensibilities, thus providing fertile ground for the particular brand of the "politics of recognition" that Renamo has now exploited for its own purposes.

86. Wilson's intervention, in response to an earlier article in *Southern Africa Report*, 10, 4 (May 1995) by a "Special Correspondent" and entitled "After the Count Is Over: Mozambique Now," appears in *Southern Africa Report*, 11, 1 (October 1995).

87. Compare, for example, the approach taken several years earlier by the late Otto Roesch in "Mozambique Unravels? The Retreat to Tradition," *Southern Africa Report*, 7, 5 (May 1992). See also Bridget O'Laughlin, "Interpretations Matter: Debating the War in Mozambique," *Southern Africa Report*, 7, 3 (January 1992).

88. Shivji, ed., *State and Constitutionalism*, p.255; note, too, Shivji's additional observation to the effect that "democracy from a liberal perspective, I argue, is part of the ideology of domination — in Africa essentially a moment in the rationalization and justification of compradorial rule."

89. Issa Shivji, "The Democracy Debate in Africa: Tanzania," *Review of African Political Economy*, 50 (March 1991), p.82.

90. Shivji, *State and Constitutionalism*, p.255.

91. Ellen Meiksins Wood, "The Uses and Abuses of 'Civil Society,'" in *The Retreat of the Intellectuals: Socialist Register 1990*, ed. Ralph Miliband and Leo Panitch (London: The Merlin Press, 1990).

92. Another such thinker is Philip Green. In his important book *Retrieving Democracy*

(see ch.3, n.22), Green labels the vision of this latter group of theorists as "pseudodemocracy": "representative government, ultimately accountable to 'the people' but not really under their control, combined with a fundamentally capitalist economy." As he adds, this kind of democracy is "preferable to most of the immediately available alternative ways of life of the contemporary nation-state. But it is not democracy; not really" (p.3). Colin Leys and I summarize the relevant point in Colin Leys and John S. Saul, *Namibia's Liberation Struggle: The Two-Edged Sword* (London: James Currey, 1994), ch.10, "The Legacy: An Afterword": "In reality . . . liberal democracy does not imply that citizens rule themselves, but that rule by elites is made legitimate by periodic elections, and — very importantly — by various ancillary mechanisms, above all the mediation of political parties." It is along these lines that we discuss the limitations of the "transition to democracy" in Namibia in the wake of that country's liberation from South African colonialism.

93. Barber, *Strong Democracy*, pp xi, 4.

94. In Barber, *Strong Democracy*, p.149, the author writes: "Democracy in the unitary mode resolves conflict . . . through community consensus as defined by the identification of individuals and their interests with a symbolic community and its interests." But this, in turn, throws up "all the grave risks of monism, conformism and coercive consensualism. No wonder that liberal democrats cringe at the prospect of 'benevolent' direct democratic alternatives." As he adds, "the central question for the future of democracy thus becomes: is there an alternative to liberal democracy that does not resort to the subterfuges of unitary democracy?" His answer, as we see, is "strong democracy."

95. Barber, *Jihad vs McWorld*, p.276.

96. Ibid., p.288. For a related analysis that specifies, quite concretely, some of the global political strategies that might help "reverse the race to the bottom," see Jeremy Brecher and Tim Costello, *Global Village or Global Pillage: Economic Reconstruction from the Bottom Up* (Boston: South End Press, 1994).

97. The comparison between Barber and his South African counterparts on the one hand, and the likes of Diamond, Huntington, and Timothy Sisk (whose book on the South African transition, cited above, never rises above a rather crude rational choice model in explaining political interactions) on the other is reminiscent of a comparison that C.B. Macpherson once made between Jeremy Bentham and John Stuart Mill: "Mill must be counted more of a democrat. For he took people not as they were but as he thought them capable of becoming. He revolted against Bentham's material maximizing criterion of the social good . . . and put in its place the maximum development and use of human capacities. . . . This was, we may say, an act of democratic faith." See Macpherson, "Politics: Post-Liberal Democracy?" an important essay reprinted in *Ideology in Social Science*, ed. Robin Blackburn (London: Fontana, 1972), p.21. Unfortunately, there is far too little of such faith in most currently fashionable democratic theory.

98. Barber, *Strong Democracy*, p.252.

99. See John S. Saul, "South Africa: Between 'Barbarism' and 'Structural Reform,'" and Saul, "Structural Reform: A Model for the Revolutionary Transformation of South Africa," chs. 4 and 5 in Saul, *Recolonization and Resistance*. Note, too, that Adler and Webster, "Challenging Transition Theory," link their emphasis on the important ongoing role of "civil society" and "social movements" in South Africa's transition to a project for progressive socio-economic transformation (albeit a somewhat more modest version of that transformation, which they label "radical reform").

100. As presented in the contributions of Godongwana and Jordan to "Social Democracy or Democratic Socialism," a debate featured in *South African Labour Bulletin*, 17, 6 (November-December 1993).

101. Leys, "Confronting the African Tragedy," p.46.

102. Miliband, *Socialism for a Sceptical Age*, pp.194-95.

# PART II  SOUTHERN AFRICA: A RANGE OF VARIATION

## Peace and Reconciliation, Authoritarianism, and "African Socialism"

1. For further background to my approach, over many years, to developments in Mozambique, see, for instance: John S. Saul, "Mozambique: FRELIMO and the War of Liberation, 1962-75" and Saul, "Mozambique: Machel (1933-86) and the FRELIMO Revolution, 1975-86," both in *Encyclopedia of African History*, ed. Shillington; and also Saul, "FRELIMO and the Mozambique Revolution," ch.8 in *Essays on the Political Economy of Africa*, ed. Arrighi and Saul. See also "Mozambique and the Struggle for Southern Africa" and the postscript, "Mozambique: The New Phase," in John S. Saul, *The State and Revolution in Eastern Africa* (New York: Monthly Review Press, 1979); the various essays by myself and diverse authors in *Difficult Road*, ed. Saul; Saul, "Development and Counter-Development Strategies in Mozambique," in Saul, *Socialist Ideology and the Struggle for Southern Africa*; and Saul, "Frelimo State," in Saul, *Recolonization and Resistance*.

2. See John S. Saul, "Inside from the Outside? The Roots and Resolution of Mozambique's Un/Civil War," in *Civil Wars in Africa: Roots and Resolution*, ed. Taisier Ali and Robert O. Matthews (Montreal and Kingston: McGill-Queen's University Press, 1999), and reprinted in much the same form in Saul, *Millennial Africa*.

3. As quoted in "More Doubts about the Mozambican Election Success Story," an information dossier edited and circulated regularly from <jhanlon@open.ac.uk> by Joseph Hanlon (hereafter "Hanlon dossier"), which also includes the full text of Zacharias's interview with Akwe Amosu of the All African News Service. For further criticism of the difficulties of using GDP figures for measuring economic performance, see also Alan Harding's note in the Hanlon-circulated "More Debate on the Mozambican Economic Success Story," July 29, 2002.

4. See Castel-Branco's contribution to "Even More Debate on Inaccurate Numbers and the Mozambican Success Story," Hanlon dossier, Aug. 2, 2002.

5. See "IMF Praises Mozambique but Economists Disagree," Hanlon dossier, July 23, 2003.

6. See Republic of Mozambique, "Poverty Reduction Strategy Paper Progress Report," issued in April 2002, and posted on the IMF website <http://www.imf.org> (July 28, 2002).

7. See (in addition to the notes in chapter 5) Colin Leys and John S. Saul, "Liberation without Democracy? The Swapo Crisis of 1976," *Journal of Southern African Studies*, 20, 1 (March 1994); and Leys and Saul, *Namibia's Liberation Struggle*.

8. Thus, when Sam Nujoma, seemed at last (in 2004) to accept the fact of his retirement as president, the three contenders for the Swapo candidacy (and, in effect, for the presidency, Swapo still being the dominant party in Namibia) were three old hands from Swapo's days in exile (victorious days vis-à-vis apartheid South Africa to be sure, but ones that also saw substantial abuses of power by those who held it, including the three candidates): Lucas Pohamba (the ultimate winner), Hidipo Hamutenya, and Nahas Angula.

9. See, for example, John S. Saul, "Transforming the Struggle in Zimbabwe," in Saul, *State and Revolution in Eastern Africa*; and Saul, "Zimbabwe: The Next Round."

10. Useful here, perhaps, are Cliffe and Saul, eds., *Socialism in Tanzania*; Saul, "Socialism in One Country: Tanzania"; and the several essays in Section 2, "Tanzania and the Resistance to Neocolonialism," in Saul, *State and Revolution in Eastern Africa*.

## 4. On War and Peace in Africa: The Mozambican Case

A much more detailed version of this chapter was originally published under the title "Inside from the Outside? The Roots and Resolution of Mozambique's Un/Civil War," in *Civil Wars in Africa: Roots and Resolution*, ed. Taisier Ali and Robert O. Matthews (Montreal and Kingston: McGill-Queen's University Press, 1999) and as chapter 4 of John S. Saul, *Millennial Africa: Capitalism, Socialism, Democracy* (Trenton: Africa World Press, 2001).

1. See Ali and Matthews, eds., *Civil Wars in Africa*.

2. See John S. Saul, "Writing the Thirty Years' War for Southern African Liberation (1960-1990): What Criteria? What Narrative?" paper presented at 20th Anniversary Conference of the *Journal of Southern African Studies*, University of York, U.K., September 1994.

3. Chester Crocker, "Foreword," in Cameron Hume, *Ending Mozambique's War: The Role of Mediation and Good Offices* (Washington: United States Institute of Peace, 1994), p.ix. See also Crocker, *High Noon in Southern Africa: Making Peace in a Rough Neighborhood* (New York: Norton, 1992).

4. I will not dwell at length here on the extraordinary costs — in human terms (death, displacement of population, and the like) and in terms of the destruc-

tion of socio-economic infrastructure — of the war to Mozambique over the years, but see Africa Watch, *Conspicuous Destruction: War, Famine and the Reform Process in Mozambique* (New York: Human Rights Watch, 1992); Hilary Anderson, *Mozambique: A War against the People* (London: Macmillan, 1992); and Marshall, *War, Debt and Structural Adjustment in Mozambique.*

5. Leys, "Confronting the African Tragedy," p.46; see also Leys, "World, Society and the Individual."

6. By far the best overview of Renamo and its role is to be found in Minter, *Apartheid's Contras.* See also Alex Vines, *Renamo: Terrorism in Mozambique* (London: James Currey, 1992).

7. From an interview that appeared in *Noticias* (Maputo), June 25, 1995.

8. It is the subject of some discussion, for example, as to whether the 1983 Congress of Frelimo heralded, primarily, the beginnings of a wise tempering and refining of socialist intention or the first strong expression of the retreat towards the "recolonization" that was to come. On the ambiguities of Frelimo's project see Saul, *Recolonization and Resistance*, especially ch.3, "The Frelimo State: From Revolution to Recolonization."

9. This interpretation is advanced, most ostentatiously, in Gervase Clarence-Smith, "The Roots of the Mozambican Counter-Revolution," *South African Review of Books* (April/May 1989), and finds echo in Vines, *Renamo.* See also Christian Geffray, *La cause des armes aux Mozambique: Anthropologies d'une guerre civile* (Paris: Éditions Karthala, 1990); for more balanced views, see Dan O'Meara, "The Collapse of Mozambican Socialism," *Transformation* (Durban), 14 (1991); and, crucially, Bridget O'Laughlin, "Interpretations Matter: Evaluating the War in Mozambique," *Southern Africa Report*, 7, 3 (January 1992).

10. Minter, *Apartheid's Contras*, pp.283-84. As Minter adds (p.286), "The fortunes of the internal contenders were decisively influenced by the scale of external intervention. Whatever may have been the grievances or goals of Unita [in Angola] and Renamo leaders, their capacity to build powerful military machines was dependent both on clientship to the apartheid state and on enrollment in the global Cold War crusade. They took advantage of existing social cleavages and regime policy failures. But the fundamental course they and their patrons laid out for the insurgent armies was to weaken the state by destroying the economic and human infrastructure of society and maximizing civilian suffering. The military advantage they gained by fostering insecurity more than made up for the potential popular support they lost by abusing civilians."

11. Minter, *Apartheid's Contras*, p.284.

12. Joseph Hanlon, *Mozambique: Who Calls the Shots?* (London: James Currey, 1991).

13. Plank, "Aid, Debt and the End of Sovereignty." See also Merle Bowen, "Beyond Reform: Adjustment and Political Power in Contemporary Mozambique," *Journal of Modern African Studies*, 30, 2 (1992).

14. Crocker, *High Noon in Southern Africa*, p.237. For Crocker (p.233), Mozambique thus became "one of the first laboratories of Africa's 'new thinking.'"

15. Quoted in John S. Saul, "Mozambique: The Failure of Socialism?" *Southern Africa Report*, 6, 2 (November 1990).

16. Crocker, *High Noon in Southern Africa*, p.249.

17. See Robert Gersony, "Summary of Mozambican Refugee Accounts of Principally Conflict-Related Experience in Mozambique: Report Submitted to Ambassador Jonathan Moore and Dr. Chester A. Crocker," Department of State Bureau for Refugee Programs, Washington, 1988. See also William Minter, "The Mozambican National Resistance (Renamo) as Described by Ex-Participants," research report submitted to the Ford Foundation and Swedish International Development Agency, 1989.

18. The essential sourcebook for tracking the UN role in Mozambique is United Nations, *The United Nations and Mozambique, 1992-1995*, United Nations Blue Books Series, vol.5 (New York: Department of Public Information, United Nations, 1995), pp.17-18, including the important summary introduction by Boutros Boutros-Ghali, then secretary-general.

19. United Nations, *United Nations and Mozambique*, p.69. For an important opposing version of the UN's role, see Joseph Hanlon, "No Even-Handed Policy: The United States Used the UN in Mozambique to Pursue Policies Left over from the Cold War," *African Agenda*, 1, 5 (1995), pp.15-16.

20. See Human Rights Watch, *Still Killing: Landmines in Southern Africa* (London and Washington: Human Rights Watch, 1995); and, for a moving first-hand account by Canadian singer Bruce Cockburn, "The Mines of Mozambique," *Southern Africa Report*, 11, 1 (November 1995).

21. *Mozambique Peace Process Bulletin* (AWEPA, European Parliamentarians for Southern Africa), Dec. 16, 1995.

22. Douglas Patrick Mason, "Mozambique's Democracy One Year On: What Next?" unpublished manuscript, p.1. As Mason continues: "Locked in by the new regional geo-political realities and a donor determined policy environment anchored on multi-party democracy and structural adjustment, little substantive ideological or other differences separate the parties other than history and mutual loathing."

23. See, in this regard, Ken Wilson, "Mozambique Now," *Southern Africa Report*, 11, 1 (October 1995). This point is discussed at greater length in ch.3 here.

24. Leys, "Confronting the African Tragedy," p.46.

## 5. Lubango and After: "Forgotten History" as Politics in Contemporary Namibia (with Colin Leys)

An earlier version of this paper, co-authored with Colin Leys (to whom I owe thanks for his permission to republish it here) was first presented at a workshop on "Public History, Forgotten History," University of Windhoek, Aug. 22-25, 2000. It was first published in *Journal of Southern Africa Studies* 29, 2 (June 2003), a pendant to our earlier related article on Namibia, "Liberation without Democracy?

The Swapo Crisis of 1976," *Journal of Southern Africa Studies*, 20, 1 (March 1994).

1.  These were the issues broached by two (they have been chosen at random merely to make the point) of the many important papers presented at the workshop on "Public History, Forgotten History," University of Windhoek, Aug. 22-25, 2000 — papers that nonetheless focused on issues much more distant in the past than is the issue central to this chapter.

2.  Although professing to draw on first-hand experience in making the claim, this informant — like some others with whom we spoke on such matters and no doubt for good reason under the circumstances — chose anonymity.

3.  See Leys and Saul, *Namibia's Liberation Struggle*; S. Groth, *Namibia: The Wall of Silence* (Peter Hammer Verlag, Wuppertal, 1995); R. Pakleppa, *I Have Seen*, documentary film; an interview with Johannes "Mistake" Gaomab by Susan Brown, first published in *The Independent* (London, 1989); and also several of the memoirs included in C. Leys and S. Brown, eds., *Histories of Namibia: Living through the Liberation Struggle* (London: The Merlin Press, 2005). When they come to deal with such issues, one hopes that future professional historians will do rather better than did the review by Jeremy Silvester of our own book, in "Demons and Democrats," *African History*, 37 (1996), pp.342-43, which sought to trivialize our work on such issues as being merely "a Conradian quest for the 'heroic and horrific' within Swapo's past," one whose chief argument he summarizes dismissively in the sentence: "A new demon stalks the forest."

4.  Lauren Dobell, "Silence in Context: Truth and/or Reconciliation in Namibia," *Journal of Southern African Studies*, 23, 2 (June 1997), pp.372-73.

5.  Quoted in Groth, *Namibia*, p.178.

6.  In our judgment, at the very least, the Swapo leadership has much to answer for. As for the level of responsibility of different elements in the Swapo leadership for what occurred there, this is generally seen as varying. The head of the Swapo Security Service, Solomon ("Jesus") Hawala, clearly bears prime responsibility for everything that happened in the Lubango detention centres (hence his unenviable sobriquet, "Butcher of Lubango"); and those under his command, including those who carried out "interrogations," and others who were in charge of guarding detainees, bear direct responsibility for the torture, unhealthy living conditions, malnutrition, and withholding of medical care that led to all the mental suffering, physical injuries, illnesses, and deaths that occurred. The personal responsibility of individual members of the Swapo executive may be said to vary inasmuch as only some — Moses Garoeb and Hidipo Hamutenya are mentioned specifically by ex-detainees — are said to have been permitted to visit the detention centres; and Sam Nujoma himself is sometimes said not to have been informed about what went on in them, even as one close member of his family, Aaron Mishimba, is said to have been detained and tortured there and his own wife at one point threatened with detention. On the other hand, it is widely agreed that Hawala reported directly to the president; and whatever the formal arrangements under which the

abuses occurred, the president and the entire Swapo executive clearly share responsibility for making and/or accepting them.

7.  We will have to return to the very practical question of whether a TRC-type proceeding would be the most appropriate means for pursuing such questions in Namibia in any case — in light, in particular, of the aforementioned fact that, unlike the South African case, many (though not all) of the chief perpetrators on "the other side" of the battlelines (as functionaries of the South African regime of occupation) had long since left the country. For this reason the ANC's own "internal" but public investigations of its behaviour might be an even more appropriate point of reference for Namibians than the TRC itself.

8.  "African National Congress Statement to the Truth and Reconciliation Commission," of August 1996, especially section 6, "Did the ANC perpetrate any gross violations of human rights?" (ANC website); "Further Submissions and Responses by the ANC to Questions raised by the Commission for Truth and Reconciliation," May 12, 1997 (ANC website); Truth and Reconciliation Commission, Truth and Reconciliation Commission of South Africa Report, Cape Town, 1998, vol. 2, ch.4.

9.  Quoted in Groth, Namibia, p.180.

10. Critics note reports of high-handed and even illegal activities by state security personnel (see Gwen Lister's trenchant "Political Perspective" column on this issue in The Namibian, June 11, 1999, for example), including the rampage in Windhoek by Nujoma's own Special Field Force in beating up men wearing earrings and tearing these earrings off, this in furtherance of the president's shrill campaign against homosexuality. Even more serious have been accounts of the detention and alleged torture of "Caprivi secessionists" and "UNITA supporters" in the north of the country; the pressure exercised upon judges acting in these cases (against their giving bail, for example); and the astonishingly intemperate tirades, over an extended period, of the Swapo minister of home affairs and apparently, with the passing of Moses Garoeb, the party's designated demagogue, Jerry Ekandjo (whose excesses are generally echoed by the Swapo Youth League) against judges, gays, and anyone else who seemed to offer a handy target.

11. This letter is quoted at length in Christo Lombard's important article, "The Role of Religion in the Reconstruction of Namibian Society: The Churches, the New Kairos and Visions of Despair and Hope," Journal of Religion and Theology in Namibia, 1 (1999).

12. Lombard, "Role of Religion," speaks of the considerable impact in this regard of "the press conference of the first group of 153 on July 6, 1989, in Windhoek, where some of them showed their torture scars," suggesting that this forced "the churches and other Swapo allies to break their silence publicly as well" (pp.56-57).

13. The original 1989 document, A Report to the Namibian People: Historical Account of the SWAPO Spy Drama, was republished in 1997 by the Breaking the Wall of Silence (BWS) Movement (Windhoek, 1997). The second source mentioned in this

paragraph is N. Basson and B. Motinga, *Call Them Spies: A Documentary Account of the Namibian Spy Drama* (African Communications Project, Windhoek and Johannesburg, 1989).

14. In 1988 Swapo announced that it was holding two hundred people in detention, and began showing videotaped "confessions" to selected audiences — especially to Swapo students — abroad. Many years later (in November 1996), Reverend Shejavali would confess, apologetically, that he had been misled at this time by these often wildly implausible videos, many of which were by then known to have been extracted under threat of torture.

15. Lombard, "Role of Religion." Two other important sources for tracing the Namibian churches' role during this period are Philip Steenkamp, "The Churches," in Leys and Saul, *Namibia's Liberation Struggle*; and Paul Trewhela, "Swapo and the Churches: An International Scandal," *Searchlight South Africa*, 2, 3, 7 (July 1991), pp.65-88.

16. Lombard, "The Role of Religion," p.59.

17. Ibid., p.58; the quote by Gurirab is from *Times of Namibia*, July 19, 1989.

18. *Debates of the National Assembly*, May 30, 1990, p.331.

19. We have not seen this report; it was summarized by Moses Katjiuonga, MP, in *Debates*, May 30, 1990, p.307.

20. *Debates*, May 30,1990, pp.337-38.

21. As reported by Prime Minister Geingob, in *Debates*, Oct. 13, 1994.

22. Eric Biwa, in *Debates*, July 26, 1994, p.204, in giving notice of his motion.

23. *Debates*, Oct. 6, 1994, p.43.

24. Ibid.

25. Ibid., pp.49-51.

26. *Debates*, Oct. 13, 1994, pp.219, 221. The claim that Swapo was fighting a guerrilla war in quite the sense implied is rather problematic, of course, as is the claim that there were genuine spies in detention, given the methods used by Swapo security to interrogate detainees.

27. *Debates*, Oct. 18, 1994, pp.305, 307.

28. Lauren Dobell, "Namibia's Wall of Silence," *Southern Africa Report*, 11, 4 (July 1996), pp.30-33.

29. Ibid., p.33. In the event, the Oshivambo translation of the book was to take much longer to prepare than originally foreseen; it finally saw the light of day in 2001, with as yet uncertain impact.

30. "Calls for Groth Book To be Burnt," *The Namibian*, March 3, 1999; and "Garoeb Goes Ballistic: Warns SWAPO Is Ready for a 'New War,'" *The Namibian*, March 3, 1996; as the latter newspaper account continues, "According to Garoeb, what had happened to SWAPO detainees was a normal thing which happened in any war situation and should be left alone because of reconciliation." See also Dobell, "Silence in Context."

31. See the press release of his speech, entitled "His Excellency President Sam Nujoma's Response to Pastor Siegfried Groth's book: 'The Wall of Silence,'" which is in our possession; it bears noting that in his speech Nujoma explicitly underscored that he was speaking not only as president of both Swapo and Namibia but also as commander-in-chief of the Namibian armed forces. See also Christo Lombard, "Do You Have No Respect for Truth, Mr. President?" *Windhoek Observer*, March 9, 1996, which was also published as "Open Letter to the President," *The Namibian*, March 11, 1996.

32. Swapo, *Their Blood Waters Our Freedom* (Windhoek, 1996).

33. "Where Is Your List? PM Challenges Opposition to Tell Their 'Truth,'" speech in parliament by Prime Minister Geingob, published in full in *New Era*, 4/6 (October 1996).

34. "UDF's Biwa Slams 'Book of the Dead,'" *The Namibian*, Oct. 9, 1996.

35. See National Society for Human Rights (NSHR), *Critical Analysis: Swapo's "Book of the Dead"* (Windhoek, 1996). The fearless role of Phil ya Nangolah, president of the NSHR and co-editor (with Zen Mnakapa) of this report, in keeping alive the issue of the ex-detainees and of advancing more generally the cause of human rights in Namibia throughout the 1990s bears special mention here. Founded in 1990, the NSHR itself grew out of the Parents' Committee, mentioned earlier; see NSHR, "Media and Issue of 'Missing Persons,'" press clippings, 1990-1998, Windhoek, 1998.

36. NSHR, *Critical Analysis*, p.14.

37. For other alleged "discrepancies" and related critical points see NSHR, *Critical Analysis*, pp.10-11. A moving interview with Hatuikilipi's widow, which underscores the ironies inherent in the manipulation of his memory by Swapo, appears in Pakleppa's film *I Have Seen*.

38. One other feature of Swapo's "Book of the Dead" perhaps deserves mention here, namely the high number (338) of these overwhelmingly young men and women in exile who were said to have died "natural deaths." A majority of these died in Lubango, and they formed a very high proportion of the 140 people who the NSHR said were missing Lubango detainees. Of these 140, 39 were listed as having died "natural deaths," while most of the rest were said to have died from mainly preventable or curable diseases — 23 from beri-beri, 17 from TB or pneumonia, 15 from malaria, and 7 from diarrhea or dysentery — compared with just 27 who were said to have died in combat. At best it appeared that Swapo did not provide elementary medical services for some of the people in its care in Lubango; at worst the figures suggested that people had been allowed to die of illnesses arising from malnutrition (the cause of beri-beri) and cold and unhealthy conditions, if not from torture.

39. Steenkamp, "The Churches," a careful academic survey, once again merely reinforces the point.

40. Ndeikwila was a key figure in the CCN from the time of his appointment there in 1983. He was the first director of the Contextual Theology Cluster, then later

in charge of the Faith, Justice and Society Unit. He was himself a former victim of the Swapo leadership's high-handedness (during the 1960s in Tanzania)
and was soon to be a moving spirit in the BWS as well.

41. See the Resolution of the 10th Annual General Meeting of the CCN, Dec. 7,
1995, in which it was stated that the CCN, "deeply conscious and penitent of
its own failures and shortcomings, will seek amongst other matters to address
the detainee issue during the course of 1996 by sponsoring a meeting with
partners and relatives" (in the authors' possession).

42. See, for example, letters in our possession to Rev. Nakamhela refusing involvement in the launch from Kleopas Dumeni, Presiding Bishop of the Evangelical
Lutheran Church of Namibia (ELCIN) and, it would seem, a major protagonist
in the self-censorship of the churches during this period (letter of Feb. 12,
1996; see also his pronouncement of "ELCIN's Stand-point regarding National
Conference on Reconciliation," Feb. 11, 1996); from P. Dieghaardt, Bishop of
the Evangelical Lutheran Church in the Republic of Namibia, letter of Feb. 15,
1996; and from B. Haushiku, (Roman Catholic) Archbishop of Windhoek, letter of February 1996. Amongst the reasons given by Dumeni for his stance are
that "the book is one-sided on the issue," that it is "even written by an "out-
sider,'" and that "the contents of the book disturb the policy of reconciliation
in our country." In contrast, Haushiku at least acknowledged that "it is a very
good book giving very valuable information about things that happened in
exile during the struggle for the liberation of Namibia." As for the CCN itself,
its Executive Council voted unanimously on Feb. 15, 1996, not to participate
in the launch (a decision described as "disgraceful" by The Windhoek Advertiser,
Feb. 20, 1996, in an editorial that also wondered aloud: "Did or didn't the
Council act on certain recommendations or suggestions by the President?").

43. "CCN to Sponsor Conference on Ex-Detainees," press release, Windhoek, Feb.
19, 1996 (in the authors' possession).

44. See "CCN Member Churches Pulling Out: 'Truth Meeting' Now in Question"
New Era, March 28,1996; Haushiku and Dumeni are amongst those cited (and
quoted) in this article, as is Anglican bishop James Kaulumu. Only Peter Strauss
of the United Reformed Church is presented as holding his ground, stating that
"it will be very wrong for the government to cover, smash or belittle the real
moral issue crying for attention," while adding that no government will "ever
survive the judgment of time when refusing moral responsibility."

45. See "Memorandum: On the Occasion of a Visit with the President of the
Republic of Namibia, Dr. Sam Nujoma, 13 August 1997, State House," signed
by Bishop Kleopas Dumeni, CCN President, and Rev. Ngeno Nakamhela, CCN
General Secretary (in the authors' possession).

46. See the interview with Rev. Ngeno Nakamhela conducted in Windhoek by John
S. Saul, June 11, 1999, as well as subsequent personal communication.

47. Although of some interest the exchanges in such workshops were most often
cast in disappointingly vague and general terms and proved to offer little of
consolation to the ex-detainees themselves. See, for example, the "Working

Document" prepared for the Church Leaders' Workshop: "Reconciliation from a Christian Perspective," Windhoek, March 1997; documents from the "Celebrating Our Unity in Reconciliation," Council of Church Leaders, Windhoek, June 11-12, 1997; and the wide range of documents produced for and by the more ambitious CCN "Conference on Restoration" held at Okahandja, March 5-7, 1998, including the "Report on CNN's Conference of Restoration" written by Rev. Nakamhela (all of these documents are in the authors' possession). Indeed, the BWS annual general meeting in October 1997 would sharply criticize the CCN, "for failing to adequately address the Swapo detainee issue during a year which the church body had declared the 'Year of God's Grace'" (printed in *The Namibian*, Oct. 21, 1997), stating in one of its formal resolutions that "The declaration of 1997 as the 'Year of God's Grace' by the ecumenical body [the CCN] has not borne any fruits and is a fiasco."

48. There was also, during this period, an extremely lively exchange of letters in the correspondence columns of several Namibian newspapers, a revealing source of diverse popular opinion about Swapo's exile record and how it might most appropriately be dealt with.

49. From the report of Dr. Ramashala's speech in the Breaking the Wall of Silence Movement's *BWS Annual Report 1997* (Windhoek, 1997).

50. See Lombard's informative letter, *Windhoek Advertiser*, Feb. 21, 1998, published under the heading "Despicable Death Threats against Emma Kambangula."

51. Lombard's letter, and also the interview with Emma Kambangula in London by Colin Leys, October 2000. It may well have been the announced aim to record testimonies, including those of "perpetrators," in order to disclose "the dark side of Swapo's history" (in Kambangula's words) that was seen to pose the most serious threat.

52. In another attempt of the period to raise the issue publicly, veteran Namibian opposition politician Emil Appolus announced that he had "written to the Secretary General of the United Nations, Kofi Annan, seeking advice on how the perpetrators of atrocities in Swapo camps like Lubango could be brought to justice through the [newly established] International Criminal Tribunal." Mentioning, in particular, the disappearance in Lubango of his young relative, Joseph Pieters, and the beating to death of Swapo official Lukas Stephanus, Appolus added that "the case was not against Swapo as an organization but was aimed at individuals, including Swapo's top leaders." See "Lubango Camp Resurfaces in Nam Appeal to the UN," *The Namibian*, Feb. 18, 1999.

53. The film also contains footage of Henry Boonzaaier's lonely and silently accusatory vigil (as well as an interview with him): until his death in 2000 Boonzaaier was a ubiquitous figure, often to be seen pacing the streets of Windhoek semi-clad and carrying a large cross and placards calling upon President Nujoma to come clean on the detainee issue. Boonzaaier spent over a decade in the dungeons. It was also said that he had been forced to dig most of the dungeons himself.

54. Transcribed by the authors from Pakleppa, *I Have Seen*. Angula adds, "This

should not be a one-sided story. . . . Those who fought for the evils of apartheid should also stand up and say we were wrong." Unfortunately, he gives no hint as to how he envisions the kind of process through which the necessary reflection he has in mind might occur, nor where the leadership he sees to be necessary to undertake such a process might come from. This is no small matter since, as we have seen, the much more typical Swapo response has been silence, bluster, or threat. In the film itself Prime Minister Geingob attempts a more ingenious tack, suggesting the whole matter to be a question of "economic reconciliation": "If we would have our economy working, if people's stomachs were full, the pain they [the ex-detainees] have been feeling because of the past will somehow disappear, they will forget it. If we can achieve [economic reconciliation] we will close the chapter."

55. This summary of Gawanas's remarks is drawn from Pakleppa's own privately circulated report on the screenings (in the authors' possession). He further notes in this report that Pauline Dempers of the BWS "challenged the audience to state if anyone there had not heard of the things told in the film before [and] said that we all know these things, that the ex-detainees are waiting for answers, for people to take [a] position." And he writes movingly of his own experience during the first presentation: "I chose to sit next to Elisabeth Matanga [one of the ex-detainees interviewed in the film] during the screening of the film. As she observed herself speak her first words in the film — "it is unforgettable unto my death" — she broke down crying. One of her fellow ex-detainees and I held her shaking and crying for quite a while before she could recover. I was very struck by this experience. It [was] a vivid reminder of the fact that trauma lives in a timeless space and indicative of the urgency of rehabilitation."

56. Interview with Samson Ndeikwila by John S. Saul, Windhoek, Aug. 25, 2000, and subsequent personal communication.

57. "Ex-Detainees to Mark Dungeons Anniversary," The Namibian, July 1, 1999.

58. As quoted in "We Won't Be Silenced, Vow Former Detainees," The Namibian, July 12, 1999.

59. As quoted in "We Won't Be Silenced."

60. The Namibian, July 9, 1999.

61. As quoted in "We Won't Be Silenced."

62. See "Who Killed Swapo's 700 Missing Detainees?" Mail and Guardian (Johannesburg), May 26, 2000.

63. S. Nujoma, Where Others Wavered: The Autobiography of Sam Nujoma (London: Panaf Books, 2001). Note, as well, that a recently agreed joint Namibian-German Government project on funding an Archives of "anti-colonial resistance and the liberation struggle" takes as its official cutoff date the year 1966. See Professor Peter Katjavivi, "The Preservation of Namibian Heritage," MBEC/GTZ, draft report "Preservation of a Namibian Heritage: The Establishment of a Documentation and Research Centre on the History of the Anti-Colonial Resistance and the

Liberation Struggle of the Namibian People," Windhoek, March 15-16, 2000.

64. Nujoma, *Where Others Wavered*, pp.172, 180.

65. The Zambia story is recounted at length in Leys and Saul, *Namibia's Liberation Struggle*.

66. Leys and Saul, "Liberation without Democracy?" pp.123-47. See also the first-hand account by Keshii Pelao Nathanael in his *A Journey to Exile: The Story of a Namibian Freedom Fighter* (Aberystwyth: Sosiumu Press, 2002).

67. As Nujoma continues: "The South African military intelligence and the Special Branch must have spent millions of rand in bribing such people. They were well-dressed and some arrived with brand new cars. Even if some succeeded in misleading people, the national liberation war was increasingly effective." Nujoma, *Where Others Wavered*, p.246.

68. Nujoma, *Where Others Wavered*, pp.356-57.

69. Presumably this is not the kind and quality of "leadership" that Nahas Angula (in his contribution to Pakleppa, *I Have Seen*) thought to be necessary if there were to be a new, more productive, approach to recovering the history of Lubango.

70. "New Detainee Drama," *The Namibian*, Feb. 6, 2001.

## 6. Mugabe, Gramsci, and Zimbabwe at Twenty-Five (with Richard Saunders)

An earlier version of this chapter was published in David Moore and Todd Leddy, eds., *Zimbabwe: Crisis and Transition* (Durban: University of KwaZulu-Natal Press, 2005) and in a special issue of *International Journal* in honour of Robert Matthews's retirement from the University of Toronto (fall 2005).

1. Saul, "Transforming the Struggle in Zimbabwe" (originally published in *Southern Africa*, February 1977). Indeed, Linda Freeman, "Contradictory Constructions of the Crisis in Zimbabwe," paper delivered to "Africa: The Next Liberation Struggle?" conference, York University, Oct.15-16, 2004, finds this 1977 analysis of "petty-bourgeois politicking" to be "extremely prescient." Thus, she states, "At the time of Zimbabwean independence [Saul could also write] of Mugabe 'guarding his options and seeming deliberately to muddy the ideological waters,' and he [Saul] warned the left . . . against 'waiting for Mugabe'"(p.8).

2. Saul, "Transforming the Struggle in Zimbabwe." See also David Moore, "The Contradictory Construction of Hegemony in Zimbabwe: Politics, Ideology and Class in the Formation of a New Africa State," unpublished doctoral dissertation, York University, 1990. For a far more favourable picture, presented at the time by Terence Ranger, of the revolutionary credentials of "old guard" — and one that is specifically critical of the perspective offered in Saul's 1977 article — there is T.O. Ranger's rather hagiographical "The Changing of the Old Guard: Robert Mugabe and the Revival of ZANU," *Journal of Southern Africa Studies*,

7, 21 (October 1980). But see also, more recently, Ranger's far more critical, and deeply revealing, paper, "Historiography, Patriotic History and the History of the Nation: The Struggle over the Past in Zimbabwe," delivered in Zimbabwe, October 2003, and published in *Journal of Southern African Studies*, 30, 2 (June 2004), pp.215-34.

3.  Quoted in Saul, "Zimbabwe: The Next Round."

4.  John Merrington, "Theory and Practice in Gramsci's Marxism," in *Socialist Register 1968*, ed. Ralph Miliband and John Saville (London: The Merlin Press, 1968), p.157.

5.  Chantal Mouffe, "Introduction: Gramsci Today," in *Gramsci and Marxist Theory*, ed. Chantal Mouffe (London: Routledge and Kegan Paul, 1979), pp.9-10. As Mouffe continues, Gramsci himself was keen to integrate his Marxist preoccupation with "fundamental classes" with an understanding of the simultaneous importance of the "national-popular." Thus she approvingly cites (p.9) Hobsbawm's positive view of Gramsci as "the only Marxist thinker to provide us with the basis for integrating the nation as a historical and social reality within Marxist theory."

6.  Ibbo Mandaza, ed., *Zimbabwe: The Political Economy of Transition, 1980-1986*, in his own chapter, "The State in Post-White Settler Colonial Situations," (Dakar: CODESRIA, 1986), p.51. Mandaza states, "As the African petit bourgeoisie began gradually to find access to the same economic and social status as their white counterparts so, too, did it become increasingly unable to respond effectively to the aspirations of the workers and peasants. . . . There was more than a symbolic commitment to the capitalist order as the members of the African petit bourgeoisie variously bought houses, farms, businesses, etc.; political principles and ideological commitment appeared mortgaged on the alter of private property."

7.  Catholic Commission for Justice and Peace in Zimbabwe and the Legal Resources Foundation, *Breaking the Silence, Building True Peace: A Report on the Disturbances in Matabeleland and the Midlands, 1980 to 1988* (Harare, 2000). See also Richard Saunders, *Never the Same Again: Zimbabwe's Growth towards Democracy, 1980-2000* (Harare: ESP, 2000), pp.24-31; and Iden Wetherall, "The Matabeleland Report: A Lot to Hide," *Southern Africa Report*, 12, 3 (June 1997), who notes (p.21): "Zimbabwe's rulers have reacted defiantly to a report which implicates them in gross human right violations in Matabeleland and Midlands provinces in the 1980s."

8.  See Welshman Ncube, "Constitutionalism, Democracy and Political Practice in Zimbabwe," in *The One Party State and Democracy: The Zimbabwe Debate*, ed. Ibbo Mandaza and Lloyd Sachikonye (Harare: SAPES Books, 1991).

9.  See Saunders, *Never the Same Again*, pp.52-55.

10. See Richard Saunders, *Dancing out of Tune: A History of the Media in Zimbabwe* (Harare: ESP, 1999).

11. Carl Boggs, *Gramsci's Marxism* (London: Pluto Press, 1976), p.39.

12. See both John Makumbe, "The 1990 Zimbabwe Elections: Implications for Democracy," in One Party State and Democracy, ed. Mandaza and Sachikonye; and John Makumbe and Daniel Campagnon, Behind the Smokescreen: The Politics of Zimbabwe's 1995 General Elections (Harare: University of Zimbabwe Publications, 2000), especially ch.9, "Towards an Entrenched Authoritarianism."

13. Lionel Cliffe, "The Politics of Land Reform in Zimbabwe," in Land Reform in Zimbabwe: Contraints and Prospects, ed. T.A.S. Bowyer-Bower and Colin Stoneman (Aldershot, U.K.: Ashgate, 2000).

14. As Mandaza, Zimbabwe, p.51, adds, "There was more than a symbolic commitment to the capitalist order as the members of the African petit bourgeoisie variously bought houses, farms, businesses, etc."

15. Carolyn Jenkins and John Knight, The Economic Decline of Zimbabwe (Houndmills, U.K.: Palgrave, 2002), p.4.

16. Lee Cokorinos, "Zimbabwe Ten Years Later: Prospects for a Popular Politics," Southern Africa Report, 6, 1 (July 1990), pp.29-30.

17. On "the Willowgate scandal," see Saunders, Never the Same Again, p.36.

18. Paradoxically, there was suddenly the possibility of engaging in a critique without running the risk of being put away as a dissident sympathizer; as a result, there was an explosion of critique and debate that emerged quite quickly and publicly.

19. Jenkins and Knight, Economic Decline of Zimbabwe, p.1. Indeed, the situation was to worsen for many Zimbabweans as the period wore on: "The adjustment of the economy to the excess demand generated by large deficits undermined the policy of redistribution to the rural poor, leaving them worse off than they had been at the end of the decade [of the 1980s] than they had been at the beginning. More severe adjustment under ESAP from the end of 1990 and the devastating droughts of the 1990's have exacerbated this trend" (p.9).

20. Richard Saunders (Zimbabwe Correspondent), "Zimbabwe: Economic Crisis and the Politics of Venality," Southern Africa Report, 5, 3 (December 1989). The immediate and harsh state response to the initial public criticism of this shift to liberalization was notable: University of Zimbabwe law professor Kempton Makamure, formerly a vocal supporter of the "socialist" ZANU-PF, was detained under Emergency Powers after offering mild criticisms of liberalization on ZBC public radio in May 1989. The radio producers responsible for the program were first suspended without pay, then transferred out of the current affairs department at the state-controlled national broadcaster.

21. Lionel Cliffe, "Were They Pushed or Did They Jump? Zimbabwe and the World Bank," Southern Africa Report, March 1991.

22. Hevina S. Dashwood, Zimbabwe: The Political Economy of Transformation (Toronto: University of Toronto Press, 2000), pp.189, 193.

23. When, a decade later, certain differences did actually play themselves out within ZANU, however, the disciplinary attack, using the "war vets" and others, on

some party structures by the leadership was aimed not so much at settling differences of opinion regarding the relative merits of liberalizing markets or the reverse but, rather more baldly, at facilitating the reimposition of the ruling party leadership's own power and authority.

24. As quoted in Dashwood, Zimbabwe, p.195. On ESAP see also Patrick Bond, *Uneven Zimbabwe: A Study of Finance, Development and Underdevelopment* (Trenton, N.J.: Africa World Press, 1998), especially ch.12, "Eternal Suffering for the African People (ESAP)."

25. This was pitifully evident, at the time, in the establishment's schizoid public ideological persona; one of us recalls, for example, the difficulties that the national broadcaster, ZBC, had in deciding whether the late Ceaucescu was a "Comrade" or a "deposed dictator," flipping back and forth for some days in its use of these terms. See Richard Saunders, "When Is a Comrade Not a Comrade?" *Moto*, January 1990.

26. Meanwhile, human rights organizations were emerging only slowly. For example, ZIMRIGHTS, which would be important from the mid-1990s, was formed only in 1991-92.

27. On developments in the 1990s and beyond, and especially in the crucial period, 1996-2002, see Ian Phimister and Brian Raftopoulos, "Zimbabwe Now: The Political Economy of Crisis and Coercion," *Historical Materialism*, 12, 4 (2003) and, in a second version, as "Embattled Modernizers: Authoritarian Nationalism and Anti-Imperialism in Zimbabwe," in *Zimbabwe: Crisis and Transition*, ed. David Moore and Todd Leddy (Durban: University of KwaZulu-Natal Press, 2005). See also, usefully, David Moore, "Zimbabwe's Triple Crisis: Primitive Accumulation, Nation State Formation and Democratisation in the Age of Neo-liberal Globalisation," *African Studies Quarterly*, 7, 2-3 (December 2003), and the version in *Zimbabwe*, ed. Moore and Leddy, where "democratisation" is seen as possible "key to Zimbabwe's turn-around." Indeed, Moore suggests, "most Zimbabweans appear to believe this proposition, but have been prevented by force and fraud from participating in its testing" (pp.14-15). See, in addition, Saunders, *Never the Same Again*; and Bond and Manyanya, *Zimbabwe's Plunge*.

28. The most important, perhaps, was the aforementioned overturning of the Private Voluntary Organisations Act in 1985, which would have given government effective control over the whole of the NGO sector. A similar act, sharpened in the form of a new NGO Bill, was reintroduced by ZANU-PF in the last quarter of 2004. This time around ZANU-PF's newly appointed Supreme Court judges allowed it.

29. The NCA's initial aim was to explicitly remove the aspects of the ZANU-PF-doctored constitution that gave President Mugabe extremely strong executive powers and had also allowed ZANU-PF to use its parliamentary super-majority to overturn entrenched constitutional rights.

30. For a collection of analyses on the contemporary national labour movement, see B. Raftopoulos and L. Sachikonye, eds., *Striking Back: The Labour Movement and*

the *Post-Colonial State in Zimbabwe, 1980-2000* (Harare: Weaver, 2001).

31. Richard Saunders, "Striking Ahead: Industrial Action and Labour Movement Development in Zimbabwe," in Raftopoulos and Sachikonye, eds., *Striking Back*.

32. For documentation of these national strikes and analysis of their implications, see the important ZCTU report, "Staying Away to Move Forward: A Report on the March 1998 Stay-Away," June 1998.

33. About one-half of the MDC's first national executive was composed of trade union leaders. In advance of the MDC launch in August 1999 the ZCTU General Council formally endorsed the formation of the MDC and committed the labour movement to assisting in the party's consolidation.

34. See Solidarity Peace Trust, *National Youth Service Training, "Shaping Youths in a Truly Zimbabwean Manner": An Overview of Youth Militia Training and Activities in Zimbabwe* (Bulawayo, 2003).

35. In one case, for example, the provincial administrator — the senior government administrative official at the provincial level — was publicly and unceremoniously chased from office by a mob of "war vets."

36. The extremely negative role — in helping Mugabe "get away with it" — played by Thabo Mbeki and his dispiriting ANC regime in neighbouring South Africa cannot be understated and requires careful explanation; for a good, and suitably jaundiced, start towards such an explanation, see Ian Phimister and Brian Raftopoulos, "Mugabe, Mbeki and the Politics of Anti-Imperialism," *Review of African Political Economy*, 101 (2004); and Linda Freeman, "Unraveling the Contradictions: South Africa's Zimbabwe Policy," unpublished paper, Ottawa, 2004, part of Freeman's indispensable continuing work on the subject.

37. This dispensation is, of course, also guaranteed physically — by the army, police, war vets, and youth militia — and even, to some extent, intellectually: by those intellectuals and professionals who have decided for various reasons, to ride the present gravy train.

38. Richard Saunders, "Zimbabwe: State Militarisation and Civic Responses," paper presented at "10 Years of Democracy in Southern Africa" conference, Queen's University/University of South Africa, Kingston, 2004.

39. Freeman, "Contradictory Constructions of the Crisis in Zimbabwe."

40. See the articles by Iden Wetherall and Marc Epprecht under the general title "Gay Bashing in Zimbabwe," *Southern Africa Report*, 11, 4 (July 1996), an issue with several other important articles on Zimbabwe.

41. Freeman, "Contradictory Constructions of the Crisis in Zimbabwe."

42. Ibid.

43. From Gramsci, *Prison Notebooks*, as quoted in Boggs, *Gramsci's Marxism*, p.27. See also *Selections from the Prison Notebooks of Antonio Gramsci* (London: Lawrence and Wishart, 1971), especially "Notes on Politics," ch.1, "The Modern Prince," pp.123-205, and ch.2, "State and Civil Society," pp.206-76. See also James Joll,

Gramsci (London: Fontana, 1977), esp. Part Two; and Jean-Marc Piotte, *La Pensée Politique de Gramsci* (Montreal: Parti Pris, 1970).

44. The precise role that the MDC and Tsvangirai will have in any such revived progressive vocation for Zimbabwe remains to be seen. A consensus among the array of social interests grouped within the MDC is still in the process of being built under the most difficult of conditions, including an exceptional degree of harassment by government and pressure from regional and international forces for the MDC to fall into line with the principles of global neo-liberalism. At the same time, however, the MDC's leading allied constituencies in civil society have maintained their insistence on pursuing social and economic rights and strengthening popular participation in a future democratized Zimbabwean state. Any detailed assessment of the politics of the MDC, both within Zimbabwe and internal to the movement itself, would therefore require a separate account; here the primary focus is on the current reality of the Mugabe regime and its manifest contradictions.

## 7. Julius Nyerere's Socialism: Learning from Tanzania

The first section of this chapter draws on a paper presented at a memorial workshop held at Queen's University, Kingston, in February 2000 to mark the passing of Julius Nyerere. The paper, "Julius Nyerere: The Theory and Practice of (Un)Democratic Socialism in Africa," was published in *The Legacies Of Julius Nyerere: Influences on Development Discourse and Practice*, ed. David M. McDonald and Eunice Njeri Sahle (Trenton, N.J.: Africa World Press, 2002). The chapter's second section, "Poverty Alleviation and the Revolutionary-Socialist Imperative," is a series of related reconsiderations of the Nyerere years presented at a workshop in Toronto in October 2001, in honour of Cranford Pratt, first principal of the University of Dar es Salaam, with whose own opinions regarding developments in Tanzania I had sparred often over the years. An earlier version of these further thoughts on Tanzania were published in *The International Journal*, 57, 2 (Spring 2002).

1. See Saul, "Globalization, Imperialism, Development."
2. See also chapter 2, p.35. As cited there, this speech was reported in *The Nationalist*, Sept. 5, 1967.
3. Julius K. Nyerere, "Education for Self-Reliance," ch.30 in Nyerere, *Freedom and Socialism/Uhuru na Ujamaa* (Dar es Salaam and London: Oxford University Press, 1968).
4. Nyerere, "Economic Nationalism," pp.5-6.
5. Cranford Pratt, "Julius Kambarage Nyerere, 1922-1999," *Southern Africa Report*, 15, 1 (December 1999).
6. Quoted in Cheru, *Silent Revolution in Africa*, pp.56-57. See ch.2, p.46 here for the full quotation.
7. Hevina S. Dashwood and Cranford Pratt, "Leadership Participation and Conflict

Management: Zimbabwe and Tanzania," in *Civil Wars in Africa*, ed. Ali and Matthews.

8. Jonathan S. Barker and John S. Saul, "The Tanzanian Elections in Post-Arusha Perspective," in *Socialism and Participation: Tanzania's 1970 National Elections*, ed. The Election Study Committee, University of Dar es Salaam (Dar es Salaam: Tanzania Publishing house, 1974).

9. Anonymous informant (by e-mail).

10. The reference is to Michael Cowen and Robert Shenton, *Doctrines of Development* (London: Routledge, 1996).

11. Barker, ed., *Street-Level Democracy*.

12. Andrew Coulson, *Tanzania: A Political Economy* (Oxford: Clarendon Press, 1982), pp.270-71.

13. The focus here is on Nyerere's Tanzania — the Tanzania of the 1960s and 1970s — and also on subsequent developments in Nyerere's own thinking once he had removed himself from power. For sobering accounts of more recent developments in Tanzania (including the brutal repression that occurred in Zanzibar in 2000), see Karim F. Hirji, "Tanzania: The Travails of a Donor Democracy," *ACAS Bulletin* (Association of Concerned African Scholars), 59 (Winter 2000); and Greg Cameron, "Zanzibar Election Update," *Review of African Political Economy*, 88 (June 2001), as well as Cameron, "Zanzibar: The Turbulent Transition," in manuscript for publication in a forthcoming issue of the *Review*.

14. Although this emphasis on Pratt's work reflects in part the original purpose of the paper on which this article is based (the Pratt symposium), I also find, more generally, a critical engagement with Pratt's work to be one useful entry point into the discussion of Nyerere's Tanzania. For the earlier debate referred to here see Cranford Pratt, *The Critical Phase in Tanzania, 1945-1968: Nyerere and the Emergence of a Socialist Strategy* (Cambridge: Cambridge University Press, 1976); Pratt, "Tanzania's Transition to Socialism: Reflections of a Social Democrat," in *Towards Socialism in Tanzania*, ed. Bismarck U. Mwansasu and Cranford Pratt (Toronto: University of Toronto Press, 1979); John S. Saul, "Tanzania's Transition to Socialism," *Canadian Journal of African Studies*, 11, 2 (1977), reprinted as ch.10 in Saul, *State and Revolution in Eastern Africa*; and Cranford Pratt, "Democracy and Socialism in Tanzania: A Reply to John Saul," *Canadian Journal of African Studies*, 12, 3 (1978).

15. Dashwood and Pratt, "Leadership Participation and Conflict Management," in Ali and Matthews, Civil Wars in Africa, pp.240-41.

16. This point will be powerfully reinforced by the richly documented study of the rise and fall of the RDA being prepared by Leander Schneider; this promises to be one of the most revealing works on Tanzanian history produced in recent years.

17. Pratt (writing now with Dashwood, "Leadership Participation and Conflict Management") now presents his case for "one-party democracy" much more circumspectly than in his earlier writings, arguing only that it "may well be

highly useful for a comparatively short, transitional period in states whose unity is fragile but in which there is widely popular nationalist party [viz., Tanzania]." Indeed, he continues, "mounting corruption and increasing oligarchical tendencies will probably soon negate its value" (p.248). Despite this argument, however, he permits himself no criticism of Nyerere's own central role in choking off, undemocratically, precisely those "strong popular forces that can insist on greater answerability" that he (Pratt) professes to deem necessary to counter "self-seeking, oligarchical temptations" (p.247) on the part of the elite.

18. Hirji, "Tanzania."

19. Paul Kaiser, "Structural Adjustment and the Fragile Nation: The Demise of Social Unity in Tanzania," *The Journal of Modern African Studies*, 34, 2 (1996).

20. Pratt, "Julius Kambarage Nyerere."

21. Bienefeld, "Tanzania: Model or Anti-Model," p.300. As Bienefeld continues: "Of course, there can be no guarantee that this change would produce long-term benefits for Tanzania's people. This would depend on the actual use made of these possibilities and, no doubt, this too would fall short of the ideal."

22. This represented no small acknowledgement of democratic imperatives in its own right, of course, given the normal practice of many other rulers in Africa.

23. Mwalimu Julius K. Nyerere, *Africa Today and Tomorrow*, 2nd ed. (Dar es Salaam: Mwalimu Nyerere Foundation, 2000).

24. Ibid., pp.29-30. Nyerere finishes this 1996 speech with the observation that "from what I have been saying, and from what I believe to be the reality, the outlook for Africa as we approach the end of the millennium is thus a gloomy one. Africa's share in the world economy is marginal. Sudden change is unlikely" (p.32). Nonetheless, Nyerere concludes that Africa "cannot afford to acquiesce in its own marginalization" and here and elsewhere in this volume of speeches evokes the possibility of action, national, continental (especially continental, this being a familiar focus of his throughout his career) and global.

25. See ch.2, pp.46, and p.149 in this chapter.

26. Julius K. Nyerere, "Reflections," in *Reflections on Leadership in Africa: Forty Years after Independence: Essays in Honour of Mwalimu Julius K. Nyerere on the Occasion of his 75th Birthday*, ed. Haroub Othman (Dar es Salaam: Institute of Development Studies, University of Dar es Salaam, 2000). Nyerere's apparently uncritical embrace of South African capital as a possible continental saviour is another of the more problematic dimensions of his intervention here. The Swahili term "*Hamna*" means "There is none."

27. Nyerere, "Economic Nationalism."

28. Siba Grovogui, "Dreams and Nightmares," *BBC Focus on Africa* (January-March 2000).

29. See chapter 1, "Sub-Saharan Africa in Global Capitalism," here, where Leys and I summarize the relevant point by observing that "Africa's development and the

dynamics of global capitalism are no longer convergent, if they ever were."

30. Richard Sandbrook, *Closing the Circle: Democratization and Development in Africa* (Toronto and London: Between the Lines and Zed Books, 2000), p.1. Sandbrook, a colleague of Cranford Pratt's over many years, was the chair of the panel at the Pratt symposium at which the earlier version of this article was presented.

31. Ibid., pp.131-32.

32. Leys, "Confronting the African Tragedy," p.46.

33. Read, for those who require the clarification, "*democratic socialism*" (but not "social democracy").

34. Drawing on the work of Issa Shivji and others, I have both spelled out this distinction and sought to make the case for prioritizing "popular democracy" in Africa; see ch.3 here.

35. See Sandbrook, *Closing the Circle*, pp.5-6, which critiques the positions of both Shivji and myself.

36. Shivji, ed., *State and Constitutionalism*, especially ch.2 and the "Epilogue," by Shivji.

37. Robert Cox as quoted in Leo Panitch, "Globalisation and the State," in *Between Globalism and Nationalism: Socialist Register 1994*, ed. Ralph Miliband and Leo Panitch (London: The Merlin Press, 1994), pp.90-91.

38. On South Africa, see Part III here; for an extended discussion of the appropriateness of the concept of "structural reform" (a concept that seeks to navigate between the twin dangers of mere reformism on the one hand and romanticized revolutionary posturing on the other) in the South African/African context, see Saul, *Recolonization and Resistance*, chs.4, 5.

39. On this concept, see Saul, ed., *Difficult Road*, especially pp.103-36.

# PART III  SOUTH AFRICA: DEBATING THE TRANSITION

## South Africa in Transition

1. For an outline of my early work and experience in this regard, see the Introduction. It bears noting that this work was as much about Canadian foreign policy and its (largely) negative workings vis-à-vis Southern Africa as it was about Southern Africa itself, and it also led to a series of writings that I helped to focus on these Canadian (and more broadly international) dimensions of what remained, nonetheless, a primarily African-sited struggle. See, for example, John S. Saul, "Both Sides of the Street," *The Canadian Forum*, March 1973, republished in John S. Saul, *Canada and Mozambique* (Toronto: DEC/TCLPAC, 1974) and also TCLSAC, *Words and Deeds: Canada, Portugal and Africa* (Toronto, 1976). It was also a major theme of the magazine we produced for fifteen years through TCLSAC, *Southern Africa Report* (1985-2000); here the various contributions over the years of Linda Freeman were particularly illuminating, but see also,

included as an appendix to the present volume, my review of her book *The Ambiguous Champion: Canada and South Africa in the Trudeau and Mulroney Years* (Toronto: University of Toronto Press, 1998) on the subject: "Canada's Anti-Apartheid Record: A Class Act," *Southern Africa Report*, 14, 2 (March 1999).

2.  John S. Saul, "In the Belly of the Beast: John Saul in South Africa," *This Magazine*, 13, 5&6 (November-December 1979), p.53.

3.  John S. Saul and Stephen Gelb, *The Crisis in South Africa* (New York: Monthly Review Press, 1981).

4.  John S. Saul and Stephen Gelb, *The Crisis in South Africa*, rev. ed. (New York and London: Monthly Review Press and Heinemann, 1986).

5.  John S. Saul, "Without Proper Papers: Inside South Africa," *Monthly Review*, 40, 8 (January 1989), reproduced under that same title in *History As It Happened*, ed. Bobbye Ortiz (New York: Monthly Review Press, 1990).

6.  Neville Alexander is to be found speaking these words in Robin Benger's excellent film, *Madiba: The Life and Times of Nelson Mandela*; Alexander's words are echoed in that film by a number of other South Africans. See Alexander, who is also author of *An Ordinary Country: Issues in the Transition from Apartheid to Democracy in South Africa* (Pietermaritzburg: University of Natal Press, 2002), as interviewed by Robin Benger in the latter's CBC-TV documentary, aired May 26, 2004 (interview available at <http/www.cbc.ca/lifeandtimes/mandela/alexander.pdf>).

7.  See my own enthusiastic first-hand account of the 1994 electoral moment: John S. Saul, "Now For the Hard Part" *Southern Africa Report*, 9&10, 5&21 (July 1994).

8.  Dale McKinley, "A Disillusioned Democracy: South African Elections Ten Years On" (sent out on the Internet, April 21, 2004).

9.  From a version of the McKinley's paper, which was subsequently published in *Mail and Guardian*, May 16, 2004.

10. Trevor Ngwane, "Militancy and Class Struggle: The Ideological and Strategic Questions Facing the New Social Movements in the New South Africa" (sent out on Internet, June 29, 2004).

11. Quoted in Ngwane, "Militancy and Class Struggle."

12. Dennis Davis, "The Real State of the Nation," *Interfund Development Update*, 4, 3 (2003), as cited extensively in Ngwane, "Militancy and Class Struggle"; here Davis is referring, contemptuously, to the SACP's notorious "two-stage theory of revolution."

13. Ngwane, "Militancy and Class Struggle."

## 8. The Transition

An earlier version of this chapter was published under the same title in *Between Globalism and Nationalism: Socialist Register 1994*, ed. Ralph Miliband and Leo Panitch (London: The Merlin Press, 1994).

1.  Magdoff and Sweezy, "Stakes in South Africa." See also pp.26-27 here.

2.  Michael Burowoy, "The Capitalist State in South Africa: Marxist and Sociological Perspectives on Race and Class," *Political Power and Social Theory*, 2 (1981), p.326.

3.  Some of these complexities are discussed in Saul, "South Africa: Between 'Barbarism' and 'Structural Reform,'" which, before being reprinted in Saul, *Recolonization and Resistance in Southern Africa in the 1990s*, was published in its original form in *New Left Review*, 188 (July-August 1991); and in an exchange with Alex Callinicos, *New Left Review*, 195 (September/October 1992).

4.  Larry Diamond and Mark Plattner, "Introduction," in *The Global Resurgence of Democracy*, ed. Larry Diamond and Mark Plattner (Baltimore: Johns Hopkins, 1993), p.ix.

5.  Larry Diamond, "Three Paradoxes of Democracy," in *Global Resurgence of Democracy*, ed. Diamond and Plattner, p.103. The rebirth of modernization theory has also produced the startling result that many once familiar figures from the netherworld of U.S. political science have resurfaced astride the current "global resurgence of democracy" — Samuel Huntington, for example, and, *mirabile dictu*, the likes of Almond and Verba. Note, for example, the larger frame within which Diamond immediately casts the point quoted here: "This is why Gabriel Almond and Sidney Verba, in their classic book *The Civic Culture*, call the democratic political culture 'mixed.' It balances the citizen's role as participant (as agent of political competition and conflict) with his or her role as subject (obeyer of state authority) and as 'parochial' member of family, social and community networks outside politics. *The subject role serves governability while the parochial role tempers political conflict by limiting the politicization of social life*" (emphasis added).

6.  Green, *Retrieving Democracy*, p.3. On the "pluralist" analysis (and endorsement) of liberal democracy, see also David Held, *Political Theory and the Modern State* (Cambridge: Polity Press, 1989), ch.2.

7.  Philip Green, "Introduction: Democracy as a Contested Idea," in *Democracy*, ed. Philip Green (Atlantic Highlands, N.J.: Humanities Press, 1993), pp.14-15. See also Rick Salutin, *Waiting for Democracy: A Citizen's Journal* (Markham, Ont.: Viking/Penguin, 1989).

8.  Shivji, "Democracy Debate in Africa: Tanzania," pp.81-82.

9.  Perhaps too easy: it could be argued that, in the South African insurrection, the favoured rallying cry of "ungovernability" (as in: "making the townships ungovernable") substituted all too readily for the more firmly grounded and organizationally developed politics that might have borne even greater long-term promise.

10. See also our citations, in ch.3 here, of writings by both Joe Slovo and Stephen Friedman in support of this interpretation of the transition in South Africa. For Przeworski, see p.59 here.

11. Joe Slovo, "The Negotiations Victory: A Political Overview," *The African Communist*, 135 (Fourth Quarter 1993).

12. Joe Slovo, "Negotiations: What Room for Compromise?" in *The African Communist*, 130 (Third Quarter 1992), p.36. Moreover, he continued, "the negotiating table is neither the sole terrain of the struggle for power nor the place where it will reach its culminating point. In other words, negotiations are only a part, and not the whole, of the struggle for real people's power."

13. Perhaps this is why one will look in vain in the pages of a book of the time that drew together Nelson Mandela's various public pronouncements since his release from prison in 1990 — *Nelson Mandela Speaks: Forging a Democratic, Nonracial South Africa* (New York: Pathfinder, 1993) — for the making of any real connection between the process of ensuring democratization (much discussed) and the prospect, near or afar, of socialism (virtually unmentioned).

14. It is such actors who are most ready to avail themselves of the ANC's "discursive practice" in order to breathe new life into the movement's time-honoured distinction between the "national democratic" and the "socialist" phases/moments of struggle. In fact, they seemed quite happy to cede to the union movement and the SACP the role of safeguarding that socialist moment in the struggle — the better to insulate the ANC from any such requirement. For background on this subject see John S. Saul, "South Africa: The Question of Strategy," *New Left Review*, 160 (November/December 1986).

15. Pallo Jordan, "Strategic Debate in the ANC," mimeo, October 1992; an abbreviated version of this paper appeared as "Committing Suicide by Concession," *The Weekly Mail*, Nov. 13, 1992.

16. Jeremy Cronin, "Nothing to Gain from All-or-Nothing Tactics," *The Weekly Mail*, Nov. 13, 1992, p.9. In Cronin's view, "Slovo reminds us we are dealing with a chastened, crisis-ridden but still powerful opponent. Both sides find themselves locked in a reciprocal siege. From our side the objective remains the total dismantling of apartheid. But we simply cannot will this objective into being. So how do we move from here to our longer term goals? Slovo suggests principled compromises . . ."

17. See Cronin, "Boat, the Tap and the Leipzig Way." See also p.69 here. Note also Joe Slovo's own acknowledgement of this "shortcoming" of the negotiations process: "The balance between negotiations and mass struggle was not always perfect. We were not always clear of what we were trying to achieve with mass action. Remember the debate about the 'tap,' our tendency to turn mass action on and off in a very instrumentalist way?" Slovo, "Negotiations Victory," p.10.

18. Jeremy Cronin, "In Search of a Relevant Strategy," *Work in Progress*, 84 (September 1992), p.20.

19. Suttner's comment appeared as part of the account of the "Central Committee Discussion of Joe Slovo's Presentation," The African Communist, 135 (Fourth Quarter 1993), p.14.

20. Henry Bernstein, "South Africa: Agrarian Questions," Southern Africa Report, 9, 3 (January 1994), p.7.

21. Slovo, "Negotiations Victory," p.7.

22. There were also grounds for viewing this effort critically, however; thus Roger Etkind and Suzanna Harvey, two organizers with the National Union of Metal Workers of South Africa, were particularly scathing about the moderate terms in which the Accord was being cast, suggesting that "the roles and interests of COSATU and the ANC are clearly opposed" and that the workers "must not adapt to a 'realism' dictated by leadership." See Roger Etkind and Suzanna Harvey, "The Workers Cease Fire," South African Labour Bulletin, 17, 5 (September-October 1993), p.85.

23. For a particularly effective statement of such concerns, see Adrienne Bird and Geoff Schreiner, "COSATU at the Crossroads: Towards Tripartite Corporatism or Democratic Socialism," South African Labour Bulletin, 16, 6 (July/August 1992). It has been difficult, nonetheless, to avoid the conclusion that the trade unions have remained, at least potentially, the most progressive of actors within the new South Africa in the making.

24. For a closely related account of the positioning of gender-related struggles within an overall process of "democratization," see Linzi Manicom, "Women for Democracy, Democracy for Women? Gender and Political Transition in South Africa," paper presented at annual meeting of the (American) African Studies Association, Boston, December 1993. See also Shireen Hassim, "The Gender Agenda: Transforming the ANC," Southern Africa Report, 7, 5 (May 1992); and Sheila Meintjes, "Chartering Women's Future," Southern Africa Report, 9, 2 (November 1993).

25. Nelson Mandela, quoted in Karl von Holdt, "COSATU Special Congress: The Uncertain New Era," South African Labour Bulletin, 17, 5 (September-October 1993), p.19. Mandela is further quoted there as stating that "the SA Communist Party must also not be complacent. With our background I do not think it would be possible for the ANC to betray the SACP. But it would be foolhardy for the SACP to be complacent and rely on the goodwill of the ANC." See also p.73 here for the Mandela statement.

26. Steven Friedman, "South Africa's Reluctant Transition," Journal of Democracy, 4, 82 (April 1993), p.58.

27. Karl Marx, "On the Jewish Question," in The Marx-Engels Reader, ed. Robert Tucker (New York: Norton, 1978), pp.26-46. See also the remarkable introduction by Lucio Colletti in Marx: Early Writings (Harmondsworth, U.K.: Penguin, 1975), an edition that includes a different translation of "On the Jewish Question."

28. John Keane, "Democracy and the Idea of the Left," in Socialism and Democracy, ed. David McLellan and Sean Sayers (London: Macmillan, 1991), pp.16-17.

29. Andrew Gamble, "Socialism, Radical Democracy and Class Politics," in Socialism and Democracy, ed. McLellan and Sayers, p.29. Of course, it is also true (as Gamble concludes) that "socialists cannot assume any longer that socialism and democracy go hand in hand. It has to be demonstrated. The really testing time for the relevance of socialism to the modern world may only just be beginning."

30. Perry Anderson, Zone of Engagement, pp.361-63.

31. Ibid., pp.366-67. This is suggestively phrased, although one might wonder about the pertinence to the efforts of South African socialists on their own turf of a vision of struggle cast so exclusively in terms of contestation at the global level (whatever that might mean).

32. Przeworski, Democracy and the Market, p.122.

33. See, however, ch.3, note 19.

34. From an interview with Mbeki, Mayibuye (ANC journal), March 1991, p.2.

35. Business Day, Jan. 13, 1993.

36. Thus, in a speech of the time delivered at the University of the North, Jan. 20, 1994, Mandela spoke in praise of Investec's sponsorship of a new business school there, citing "the skilling of Black prospective business-persons . . . [as] a solid investment in the future of our country": "Up until now Black business persons have been restricted to the role of taxi owners, shebeeners, tuckshop owners and the like. Notwithstanding, they have performed with remarkable aplomb. [But now] we can have the kinds of candidates for senior position in South Africa's financial and industrial world. Now we can begin to talk about empowerment far more convincingly" (emphasis added). As it happened — as part of a process that is not problematized by Mandela here — the speed with which this "financial and industrial world" was snapping up such "candidates for senior position" was already, by 1994, one of the most crucial processes redefining the South African class structure.

37. I have sought to specify this kind of revolutionary practice, to be distinguished both from "mere reformism" on the one hand and from "abstract revolutionism" on the other, in Saul, "South Africa: Between 'Barbarism' and 'Structural Reform,'" and Saul, "Structural Reform." See also André Gorz, "Reform and Revolution," in Socialist Register 1968 (London: The Merlin Press, 1968); and Boris Kagarlitsky, The Dialectic of Change (London: Verso, 1990).

38. See, for example, Eddie Webster and Karl von Holdt, "Towards a Socialist Theory of Radical Reform: From Resistance to Reconstruction in the Labor Movement," paper presented at Ruth First Memorial Colloquium, University of the Western Cape, August 1992; and also the thoughtful evocation of related themes by Jeremy Cronin, "South African Socialists Respond," South African Labour Bulletin, 17, 6 (November-December 1993).

39. Patti Waldmeir, "Mandela Warns of Need for Change," *Financial Times*, Feb. 15, 1994. Note, too, that even Archbishop Tutu is quoted to the effect that "after sanctions are lifted, it must not be business as usual. There has got to be a code of conduct for business in South Africa for a kind of investment that seeks to turn around the dispossession of power and empower the dispossessed." Quoted in Linda Freeman, "The New Rules of the Game," *Southern Africa Report*, 9, 4 (March-April 1994).

40. From Lewis's contribution to the "Social Democracy or Democratic Socialism" debate, *South African Labour Bulletin*, 17, 6 (November-December 1993), pp.86-87. But see also Avril Joffe, David Kaplan, Raphael Kaplinsky, and David Lewis (ISP Co-Directors), "Meeting the Global Challenge: A Framework for Industrial Revival in South Africa," presentation at the IDASA meeting on South Africa's International Economic Relations in the 1990s, April 27-30, 1993.

41. From Cronin's own contribution to the "Social Democracy or Democratic Socialism" debate, *South African Labour Bulletin*, p.94.

42. "'Mutually searching': Trade Union Strategies, South Africa and Canada," an interview with Sam Gindin, *Southern Africa Report*, 8, 5 (May 1, 1993); and "Trade Union Strategies: The Debate Continues," an exchange between Gindin and the ISP's Avril Joffe, *Southern Africa Report*, 9, 3 (January 1994). At a workshop held in Toronto this debate also surfaced provocatively between delegations of South African and Canadian unionists; for a report on this workshop see "Workers of the World, Debate," *Southern Africa Report*, 9, 1 (July 1993).

43. See, for example, Stephen Gelb, "Democratizing Economic Growth: Alternative Growth Models for the Future," *Transformation*, 12 (1990), and subsequent writings by the same author.

44. Etkind and Harvey, "Workers Cease Fire," pp.86-87. Compare, however, the rather more modest, though still critical, tone in a second article, "COSATU and Its Reconstruction Accord with the ANC," *South African Labour Bulletin*, 17, 5 (September-October 1993). Thus, for Jenny Cargill, COSATU's "challenge is how to tailor strategies to political and economic realities on the one hand, but avoid abdicating to the status quo on the other."

45. See Lawrence Harris, "Building the Mixed Economy," and "How Are We Going to Pay for Economic Reconstruction?," papers presented to a seminar, ANC Department of Economic Planning, Harare, April-May 1990.

46. Lawrence Harris, "South Africa's Economic and Social Transformation: From 'No Middle Road' to 'No Alternative,'" *Review of African Political Economy*, 57 (1993), pp.91-103.

47. I have noted some of Harris's distortions of my own position in Saul, *Recolonization and Resistance*, pp.183-84.

48. Nicoli Nattrass, "Economic Restructuring in South Africa: What It Is and How Can It Be Managed," paper presented to Annual Research Workshop, Canadian Research Consortium on Southern Africa, Kingston, Ont., Jan. 23, 1994.

49. As it happens, Nattrass cannot quite decide whether authoritarian or democrat-

ic structures are more conducive to capitalist development. She is, in any case, even more preoccupied with the likely capacities of the South African bureaucracy to play the "rational" role required of it by capital than she is with the class character of the state itself.

50. The danger of such an outcome was amongst the possibilities discussed in Stephen Gelb, "Democracy and Development in South Africa," a paper presented at "Political Economy Seminar" series, York University, Toronto, Feb. 14, 1994.

51. Colin Bundy, "Problems and Prospects for South African Socialists," paper presented at Political Science Seminar, York University, Toronto, October 1991, p.20. That, by the end of the decade, Bundy would find himself, as vicechancellor of the University of the Witwatersrand, entrapped in the very worst kinds of neo-liberal delusions about how to run a university need not detract from the strength of the positions he argued earlier.

52. Robert D. Kaplan, "The Coming Anarchy," The Atlantic Monthly, February 1994.

53. Gamble, "Socialism, Radical Democracy and Class Politics," pp.29-30.

54. Thus Winnie Mandela, so deeply compromised by the excesses of her own political practice, nonetheless struck a potentially powerful note — one that may well be heard again — when in the wake of the circulation of the ANC's "Strategic Perspective" document she criticized the "so-called power sharing deal between the elite of the oppressed and the oppressors" and spoke of the "looming disaster in this country which will result from the distortion of a noble goal in favor of a shortcut to parliament by a handful of individuals." Winnie Mandela, quoted in "Swinging Attack by Winnie Indicates Populist Dissent," Southscan, 8, 2 (Jan.15, 1993).

55. Roger Murray, "Second Thoughts on Ghana," New Left Review, 42 (March-April 1967), p.39.

## 9. The Post-Apartheid Denouement

A version of this chapter, under the title "Cry for the Beloved Country: The Post-Apartheid Denouement," was first published in Monthly Review, 52, 8 (January 2001) and reprinted in Review of African Political Economy, 89 (September 2001).

1. John S. Saul, "Magic Market Realism," Transformation, 38 (1999); I have also adapted some paragraphs of this text in writing this chapter.

2. Saul, "South Africa: Between 'Barbarism' and Structural Reform." The original source of the Magdoff and Sweezy quotations is Magdoff and Sweezy, "Stakes in South Africa."

3. Paul Hirst and Grahame Thompson, Globalization in Question (London: Polity Press, 1999), p.189.

4. Saul, "South Africa: Between 'Barbarism' and Structural Reform."

5. See Jonathan Hyslop, "Why Was the White Right Unable to Stop South Africa's

Democratic Transition?" in *Africa Today: A Multi-Disciplinary Snapshot of the Continent in 1995*, ed. Peter Alexander, Ruth Hutchinson, and Deryck Schreuder (Canberra, Aust.: Humanities Research Centre/ANC, 1996), pp.145-65.

6.  In this context it has been possible, for example, to register strong pronouncements in the public realm as to the necessity of advancing women's demands within the new South Africa-in-the-making.

7.  See Cronin. "Boat, the Tap and the Leipzig Way." See also Cronin, "In Search of a Relevant Strategy," p.28, where he writes: "It is critical that in the present we coordinate our principal weapon — mass support — so that we bring it to bear effectively upon the constitutional negotiations process. . . . Democracy is self-empowerment of the people. Unless the broad masses are actively and continually engaged in struggle, we will achieve only the empty shell of a limited democracy."

8.  Quoted in "Central Committee Discussion of Joe Slovo's Presentation," p.14.

9.  David Howarth, "Paradigms Gained? A Critique of Theories and Explanations of Democratic Transitions in South Africa," in *South Africa in Transition: New Theoretical Perspectives*, ed. D. Howarth and A. Norval (New York: St Martin's Press, 1998), p.203.

10.  Mamdani, *Citizen and Subject*.

11.  Gerhard Maré, "Makin' Nice with Buthelezi," *Southern Africa Report*, 14, 3 (May 1999), p.10.

12.  Quoted in Asghar Adelzadeh, "Loosening the Brakes on Economic Growth," *Ngqo!* 1, 2 (February 2000). For further evidence of these trends, see Eddie Webster and Andries Bezuidenhout, "Globalization, Vulnerability and Population," report prepared for the National Population Unit, South Africa, November 1999.

13.  Landsberg, "Directing from the Stalls?" pp.290-91.

14.  Centre for Development and Enterprise (CDE), *Policy-Making in a New Democracy: South Africa's Challenges for the 21st Century* (Johannesburg: CDE, 1999), a report funded by South African Breweries and written by Ann Bernstein, p.83.

15.  Marais, *South Africa*, p.156. As Marais (p.147) quotes Anglo-American executive Clem Sunter: "Negotiations work. Rhetoric is dropped, reality prevails and in the end the companies concerned go on producing the minerals, goods and services."

16.  Quoted in *Financial Times*, June 10, 1986.

17.  See Dan O'Meara, *Forty Lost Years: The Apartheid State and the Politics of the National Party, 1948-1994* (Randberg, South Africa and Athens: Ravan Press and Ohio University Press: 1998).

18.  See Marais, *South Africa*, p.153.

19.  Cited in Andrew Nash, "Mandela's Democracy," *Monthly Review*, 50, 11 (April 1999), p.26. Mandela's reversal of ground on the nationalization question was

actually quite rapid after 1990, such that by 1994 he could assure *Sunday Times* readers: "In our economic policies . . . there is not a single reference to things like nationalization, and this is not accidental. There is not a single slogan that will connect us with any Marxist ideology" (quoted in Marais, *South Africa*, p.146). Patrick Bond (private communication) suggests that the early decision taken (in April 1990) by Mandela and other ANC leaders to abandon any thought of a program of nationalizations was already the key marker of the left's defeat. Instead, accelerated "privatization" was to become a central component of the post-apartheid government's strategy.

20. ANC Department of Economic Policy, "Discussion Document on Economic Policy," 1990.

21. Tito Mboweni, "Growth through Redistribution," in *Transforming the Economy: Policy Options for South Africa*, ed. G. Howe and P. le Roux (Natal: Indicator Project SA, University of Natal Institute for Social Development, 1992).

22. T. Moll, "Growth through Redistribution: A Dangerous Fantasy?" *The South African Journal of Economics*, 59, 3 (1991).

23. As described in Patrick Bond, "Social Contract Scenarios," ch.2 in Bond, *Elite Transition*.

24. Bill Freund and Vishnu Padayachee, "Post-Apartheid South Africa: The Key Patterns Emerge," *Economic and Political Weekly*, May 16, 1998, p.1175.

25. Quoted in Marais, *South Africa*, p.154.

26. As arch neo-liberal columnist Howard Barrell wrote in the *Mail and Guardian*, June 18, 2000, at the time of Mbeki's announcement of his new cabinet: "Both [Erwin and Manuel] have won the confidence of the markets and their presence in their current portfolios is seen as a measure of the government's determination to stick to its current economic course."

27. John S. Saul, ". . . or Half Empty? Review of the RDP," *Southern Africa Report*, 9, 5 (July 1994), p.40. Both Marais, *South Africa*, ch.6, "The RDP: A Programme for Transformation," and Bond, *Elite Transition*, ch.3, "Rumours, Dreams and Promises," provide excellent accounts of the rise and fall of the RDP.

28. Asgar Adelzadeh, "From the RDP to GEAR: The Gradual Embracing of Neo-Liberalism in Economic Policy," *Transformation*, 31 (1996).

29. Marais, *South Africa*, p.171.

30. Adelzadeh, "From the RDP to GEAR," p.67. As Bond, *Elite Transition*, p.216, summarizes this pattern: "Much of South Africa's national sovereignty continued to be offered up on a plate to impetuous and whimsical local and international financial markets."

31. Bond, *Elite Transition*, p.200. Once again, the accounts by Bond and by Marais, *South Africa*, provide essential points of reference on such developments in the economic sphere, but see also Charles Millward and Vella Pillay, "The Economic Battle for South Africa's Future," in *Transformation in South Africa? Policy Debates in the 1990s*, ed. E. Maganya and R. Koughton (Braamfontein: IFAA, 1996).

32. This point has been underscored for me most forcefully by South African econ- omist Oupa Lehulere in private communications.

33. The point is convincingly argued, and linked to the extreme inequalities of eco- nomic power and income that exist in South Africa, by Adelzadeh, "Loosening the Brakes on Economic Growth."

34. Castells, *Information Age*, the subsection "Africa's Hope? The South African Connection," p.122.

35. Bond, *Elite Transition*, pp.193ff. For a further detailed critique of GEAR's perform- ance, see Asghar Adelzadeh, "The Costs of Staying the Course," in *Ngqo!* 1, 1 (June 1999). *Ngqo!* is the economic bulletin of the National Institute for Economic Policy (NIEP), a successor organization to MERG.

36. Lucien van der Walt, unpublished communication, July 2000.

37. See pp.31, 192.

38. See Greg Albo, "A World Market of Opportunities? Capitalist Obstacles and Left Economic Policies," in *Socialist Register 1997: Ruthless Criticism of All That Exists*, ed. Leo Panitch (London: The Merlin Press, 1997), pp.28-30, 41.

39. CDE, *Policy-Making in a New Democracy*, p.145; Gordon Smith, an economist with Deutsche Morgan Grenfell Bank, quoted in Norm Dixon, "ANC Reassures Big Business after Win," *Green Left Weekly*, e-mail edition, n.d. (July 1999?).

40. Ben Fine and Zavareh Rustomjee, *The Political Economy of South Africa: From Minerals- Energy Complex to Industrialization* (Boulder, Col.: Westview Press, 1996). On this and other related points, see also Carolyn Bassett, "Negotiating South Africa's Economic Future: COSATU and Strategic Unionism," Ph.D. dissertation, York University, Toronto, June 2000.

41. See Frantz Fanon, *The Wretched of the Earth* (Harmondsworth, England: Penguin, 1967).

42. As quoted in *Star* (Johannesburg), Sept. 15, 1992.

43. "South Africa: How Wrong Is It Going?" *The Economist*, Oct. 12, 1996, p.23.

44. Mark Gevisser, "Ending Economic Apartheid: South Africa's New Captains of Industry," *The Nation*, Sept. 29, 1997, p.24. The general thrust of this quotation remains suggestive despite Ramaphosa's own shifting fortunes in his business ventures. See "Ramaphosa's Departure Raises Key Black Empowerment Issues," *Southscan*, 14, 5 (March 1999).

45. Freund and Padayachee, "Post-Apartheid South Africa," p.1179. As they con- tinue: "If there was a phrase that captured the imagination of South Africans black and white within a year of the ANC taking power it was that of 'the gravy train.'"

46. The speeches are included in the final section of Adrian Hasland and Jovial Rantao, *The Life and Times of Thabo Mbeki* (Rivonia: Zebra Press, 1999).

47. Thabo Mbeki, "Speech at the Annual National Conference of the Black Management Forum," Kempton Park, Nov. 11, 1999 (ANC website).

48. Closer to the truth may be the frank and quite unequivocal statement of a brash emergent African entrepreneur, Tumi Modise, as quoted in David Goodman, *Fault Lines: Journeys into the New South Africa* (Berkeley: University of California Press, 1999), p.270: "Race is not the issue anymore," she told Goodman, "It's class."

49. Dale McKinley, *The ANC and the Liberation Struggle: A Critical Political Biography* (London: Pluto Press, 1997).

50. I have cited this statement (from 1984) and other questions posed in seeking to divine the historical character of the ANC in Saul, "South Africa: The Question of Strategy."

51. *Washington Post*, June 6, 1999.

52. Hasland and Rantao, *Life and Times of Thabo Mbeki*, ch.7.

53. Quoted in Bond, *Elite Transition*, p.83.

54. Nash, "Mandela's Democracy."

55. As quoted in "Mandela Poses Hard Questions about Reach of Globalization," *The Globe and Mail* (Toronto), Jan. 30, 1999, p.A19.

56. Thabo Mbeki, speaking at the twelfth heads of state meeting of the Non-Aligned Movement in South Africa, Sept. 3, 1998; quoted in Robert Wade and Frank Venerosa, "The Gathering World Slump and the Battle over Capital Controls," *New Left Review*, 231 (September-October 1998), p.20.

57. "Statement by Deputy President Mbeki at the African Renaissance Conference," Johannesburg, Sept. 28, 1998 (ANC website).

58. Albeit not too much responsibility: on balance, Mbeki's South Africa seems quite content to propose itself for the role of the U.S. and global capital's tribune (and gendarme) on the African continent; for the way this role has begun to play itself out in Southern Africa, for example, see Larry Swatuk, "Bully on the Block?" *Southern Africa Report*, 15, 3 (Third Quarter 2000). Recall also the warm tone adopted by Mandela during his presidency towards dictators in Indonesia, Malaysia, and Saudi Arabia who were often not only key targets for South African arms sales but also to become important contributors to the ANC's electoral war-chest in 1999.

59. Hein Marais, "Topping up the Tank: How the ANC Has Reproduced Its Power since 1994," *Development Update*, 3, 1 (October 1999), from which the quotations in the next two paragraphs are drawn; these themes are further elaborated upon in a new and revised edition of Marais, *South Africa: Limits to Change* (London: Zed Books, 2001).

60. It is in the sphere of the spreading of (still rather minimal) welfare benefits to Africans that one finds the one clear post-apartheid contribution to poverty alleviation, perhaps.

61. For a parallel argument see Sipho Seepe, "How Mbeki Is Hampering the Renaissance," *Mail and Guardian*, June 9, 2000, in which Seepe, an educator, describes Mbeki (p.28) as "a president who is ultra-sensitive, unable to accommodate others and who is impatient with differing opinions. . . . A president

who is unable to accept that he could be mistaken, and has conveniently surrounded himself with sycophants."

62. "SACP Reeling from Mandela, Mbeki Attacks," Southscan, 13, 14 (July 10,
1998), pp.107-8.

63. Quoted in Salim Vally, "Education on Trial: The Poor Speak Out," Southern Africa
Report, 14, 1 (December 1998), p.27. It is Vally who suggests that the reader
note "the disarming use of the associative 'we,' Mbeki apparently seeking in
this way to signal his affinity with the teachers even while mercilessly castigat-
ing them." As for the "toyi-toyi," it is a vigorous dance step engaged in collectively and associated with demonstrations.

64. William Marvin Gumede, "The Presidency: Losing Patience: COSATU, SACP
Irksome," Financial Mail, May 19, 2000, p.39.

65. Cited in Vally, "Education on Trial," p.27.

66. "Outspoken Government Attacks on Unions as Strike Action Spreads," Southscan,
14, 17 (Aug. 20, 1999), p.130.

67. Glenn Adler and Eddie Webster, "Toward a Class Compromise in South Africa's
'Double Transition': Bargained Liberalization and the Consolidation of
Democracy," Politics and Society, 27, 3 (September 1999). For a convincing refu-
tation of this line of argument, see Carolyn Bassett and Marlea Clarke, "South
Africa: (Class Compromise) . . . Class Struggle," Southern Africa Report, 15, 2 (2nd
Quarter 2000); and also Carolyn Bassett and Marlea Clarke, "Alliance Woes:
COSATU Pays the Price," Southern Africa Report, 15, 1 (December 1999). For a
critique of NEDLAC as a possible terrain for successful labour struggle, see also
Bassett, "Negotiating South Africa's Economic Future."

68. Howard Barrell, "Mbeki: Talking Left and Doing Right," Mail and Guardian, Jan.
21, 2000. By May, however, the Financial Mail report by Gumede, "The
Presidency: Losing Patience," could suggest that Mbeki might actually be
preparing himself for a showdown: "Even though COSATU is a key cog in the
ANC's voting machine, Mbeki is considering bringing this Alliance partner into
line regardless of the consequences this might have for the upcoming local
elections."

69. As quoted in Dixon, "ANC Reassures Big Business after Win."

70. Gumede, "The Presidency: Losing Patience."

71. Right-wing commentators, and even some erstwhile left-wing ones, continue
to attack the organized labour movement as representative of a "labour aristocracy," for example. This charge has generally been advanced in the most
opportunist manner against a vulnerable working class; nonetheless, the sting
of that charge may be providing one additional incentive for trade unions to
reach out more actively to the rest of impoverished South African society,
including the vast army of the unemployed.

72. September Commission Report, presented to the 6th National Congress of COSATU,
Sept. 16-19, 1997, pp.49-50.

73. Shamim Meer, "The Demobilization of Civil Society: Struggling with New Questions," *Development Update*, 3, 1 (1999).

74. For the quotations in this paragraph, see Wonder Hlongwa, "Church Asked to Fight Gear from the Trenches," *Mail and Guardian*, July 10, 1998. See also "Unemployment and Retrenchments: What is the Role for the Church in SA?" a discussion paper prepared jointly by a range of important church organizations, August 1999; it includes sections on "Neoliberalism: The Rich Get Richer" and "The Church and Neoliberalism."

75. For early reflections on this trend, see Patrick Bond and Mzwanele Mayekiso, "Developing Resistance, Resisting 'Development': Reflections from the South African Struggle," in *Socialist Register 1996: Are There Alternatives?* ed. Leo Panitch (London: The Merlin Press, 1996).

76. William Marvin Gumede, "New Seeds of Opposition," *Financial Mail*, May 19, 2000.

77. Sam Gindin, "The Party's Over," *This Magazine* (November-December 1998), p.15.

78. More recently Gindin has defined this as a politics that differs from the practices of established political parties in Canada (but also, we might add, from the practices of the ANC in South Africa) in terms of "how it organizes, educates and mobilizes; the depth of its challenge to the status quo; the emphasis it puts on developing a counterculture; its faith in the potential of ordinary people." Gindin, letter to the editor, *This Magazine*, July/August 2000, pp.10-11.

79. See, for example, Blade Nzimande, "Towards a Socialist South Africa," *Mail and Guardian*, Feb. 18-24, 2000, p.39, and Nzimande, "State Should Drive the Economy," *Business Day*, May 29, 2000, p.10.

80. ANC, "The State, Property Relations and Social Transformation: A Discussion Paper towards the Alliance Summit," October 1998 (available on the ANC website).

81. See "ANC's Drift to Right Comes under Challenge from Mbeki Loyalist," *Southscan*, 13, 19 (Sept. 18, 1998), which identifies the author as Joel Netshitenzhe, deputy-director of communications in the office of President Mandela. The article also speculates interestingly as to some of the inter-party politicking that may have given rise to such a document, asking, among other questions, "How accurate is Netshitenzhe's presumed reading that the ANC's leadership has become heterodox and rebellious enough to challenge Mbeki's intellectual and strategic authority?" Unfortunately, the apparent answer to that question has been not encouraging.

82. Ferial Haffajee, "Jobs Summit Will Clarify GEAR Shift," *Mail and Guardian*, Oct. 23, 1998.

83. Jaspret Kindra, "'Cuba, China Models for SA,'" *Mail and Guardian*, May 12-18, 2000, p.14. The article title is a quotation from the secretary general.

84. As reported in *Mail and Guardian*, May 19, 2000.

85. Note, however, the terms in which such criticism is sometimes cast on the centre-left of the party. Emphasizing that encouragement by the ANC leadership of the ever deeper penetration of monopoly capital in South Africa may actually contradict that leadership's claim to be expanding the scope of a nascent black bourgeoisie, such critics suggest that the least compradorial elements of this bourgeoisie might therefore be recruitable to a class alliance capable of redirecting the party to the left. See Z. Pallo Jordan, "Ruth First Memorial Lecture," Witwatersrand University, Aug. 28, 2000, for a particularly clear statement of this position. The temptation visible here to merely recycle the ANC's old "national-democratic revolution" concept at the expense of a more working-class-centred definition of ongoing revolutionary struggle illustrates once again the difficulties of conceptualizing a left-project from within the ideological universe of the ANC.

86. Marais, "Topping up the Tank," p.27.

87. See "Mbeki Champions Poor against Black and White Elites," Southscan, June 12, 1998.

## 10. Starting from Scratch? A Debate

The Cronin critique ("Post-Apartheid South Africa: A Reply to John S. Saul") of my original Monthly Review article (see Chapter 9) and my response ("Starting from Scratch? A Reply to Jeremy Cronin," reprinted here as chapter 10), were originally published in Monthly Review, 54, 7 (December 2002).

1. See, for example, John S. Saul, "South Africa's Tragic Leap to the Right," Mail and Guardian, June 23-29, 2000.

2. A case made scrupulously in Dot Keet, South Africa's Official Position and Role in Promoting the World Trade (Cape Town: Alternative Information and Development Centre [AIDC], 2002).

3. See Trevor Ngwane, "Should African Social Movements Be Part of the New Partnership for Africa's Development (NEPAD)?" speech presented to the African Social Forum's African Seminar, World Social Forum, Porto Alegre, Brazil, Feb. 2, 2002. See also Patrick Bond, Fanon's Warning: A Civil Society Reader on the New Partnership for Africa's Development (Trenton, N.J. and Cape Town: Africa World Press and AIDC, 2002) <http://www.aidc.org.za>.

4. Perhaps now he would. In one of his first interventions after his dramatic disciplining by the ANC Cronin made an astonishing, even fawning, claim: "Through Nepad and through a wide range of other multinational forums the ANC has been playing a role in redefining global priorities, In doing so they have been challenging the core assumptions of neo-liberalism." Jeremy Cronin, "No One Is Infallible: Jeremy Cronin Argues That the ANC Should Be Leading the Anti-neo-liberal Coalition," Mail and Guardian, Oct. 10, 2002.

5. In his related interview with Helena Sheehan he, regrettably, even plays a

crypto-racist card, suggesting my intervention to have been characterized by "a kind of northern scepticism, a northern left scepticism, about the left project in general, not least left project in the south" — this a rather odd and disturbing charge given my own long history of advocacy of socialist efforts in Tanzania, Mozambique, and elsewhere. Odd, but also ironic given that he himself was to be "white-baited" in the wake of the Sheehan interview.

6. Helena Sheehan, interview with Jeremy Cronin, Jan. 24, 2002.

7. In a speech Makhaye referred dismissively to Cronin as "a white messiah and a factory fault," stating more generally (with reference, some observers reported, to the SACP) that "there are dogs who are biting the ANC and these dogs are calling themselves our friends. The ANC would not be defeated, the ANC is strong. Some of us are prepared to die for the ANC and to kill for the ANC." *The Mercury*, Aug. 18, 2002.

8. Jeremy Cronin, SACP Deputy General Secretary and ANC NEC member, statement issued Aug. 19, 2002.

9. Personal Communication, Aug. 20, 2002. But see also the front-page report of Sheehan's response to Cronin: "'No Apology Was Needed: Irish Academic Disappointed in Jeremy Cronin for Having Apologised to the ANC," *The Sowetan*, Aug. 28, 2002.

10. William Mervin Gumede, "Silence Isn't Golden in a True Democracy: The ANC Is Doing South Africa No Favours by Lashing at Anyone Who Dares to Criticise It," *Sunday Times*, Aug. 25, 2002. A much more demagogic critique of Cronin's action was undertaken, from the right, by (then) *Mail and Guardian* editor Howard Barrell, who suggested that Cronin's "craven capitulation" indicated that he had "merely turned tail and fled the battlefield onto which he had led others . . . And you, comrade Jeremy? We shall see what magnanimity awaits you once you've said a dozen 'Hail Thabos.'" *Mail and Guardian*, Aug. 23-29, 2002.

11. Personal communication, June 8, 2001.

12. Some have recalled, however, the active role that Cronin himself played, several years ago, in the expulsion of left author and activist Dale McKinley from the SACP, and suggested that Cronin, in that instance, may merely have helped to sharpen the knife which, more recently, has been pressed to his own throat. For McKinley's own pungent take on Cronin's Sheehan interview, see his "A Polemical Reply to Cronin," May 1, 2002.

13. See Ngwane, "Should African Social Movements Be Part of the New Partnership for Africa's Development?" Moreover, Cronin was quickly to claim that this statement was an internal document, leaked, without his knowledge, to the press.

14. "In time," the document threatens, "we will explain who these South African-based foreign enemies of the ANC are." This seems a particularly tasteless nationalist smear in light of the absolutely central roles played by activists, South African and black, such as Trevor Ngwane, Virginia Setshedi, John

Appolis, and Oupa Lehulere, amongst many others and alongside ageless veterans such as MP Giyose and Dennis Brutus, in mounting the resistance, both intellectual and practical, that found one of its most dramatic expressions in the August 31 Alex-to-Sandton march.

15. ANC Political Education Unit, "Contribution to the NEC/NWC Response to the 'Cronin Interviews' on the Issue of Neo-Liberalism," widely circulated on the web but eventually published in edited form as "Unholy Coalition Will Not Win: The ANC's Policy Education Unit Charges That the Left Is Waging a Counter-revolutionary Campaign against the Government," Mail and Guardian, Oct. 11, 2002. The document concludes by claiming that in order to achieve its nefarious end ("a victorious socialist revolution") "the anti-neo-liberal coalition is ready to treat the forces of neo-liberalism as its ally." It is difficult to attach any rational meaning to this and many other assertions in the document. See also Christelle Terreblanche, "Secret ANC Paper Slams 'Unholy Alliance': 'Anti-neo-liberal Left' and 'Pro-liberal Right' Have Joined Forces against Ruling Party, Venomous Document Claims," The Star, Oct. 3, 2002.

16. Thabo Mbeki, "Statement of the President of the African National Congress, Thabo Mbeki, at the ANC Policy Conference, Kempton Park, Sept. 27, 2002.

17. See Raymond Suttner, Inside Apartheid's Prison: Notes and Letters of Struggle (Melbourne and Pietermaritzburg: Ocean Press and University of Natal Press, 2001).

18. "Panga" is an African word for "machete." To be fair, in a subsequent private chat during my visit Suttner proved to be a much more open and sympathetic interlocutor. Indeed, one begins to feel that if the term "tragic" applies at all in contemporary South Africa it is to the plight of the Cronins, the Suttners, and other uneasy ANC loyalists who are increasingly caught between a rock and a hard place as the ANC moves right and as the contradictions inherent in the SACP's posture of fellow-traveller vis-à-vis the ANC intensify.

19. On events leading up to the August 24 abortive march, see Sarah Duguid, "ANC 'Behaving like Nat Regime': The Government's Crackdown on World Summit Protests Has Raised Unsavoury Comparisons," Mail and Guardian, Aug. 23-29, 2002.

20. Ashwin Desai, We Are the Poors: Community Struggles in Post-Apartheid South Africa (New York: Monthly Review Press, 2002). See also the important recent contributions of Neville Alexander, Issues in the Transition from Apartheid to Democracy in South Africa (Pietermaritzburg: University of Natal Press, 2002); and Gillian Hart, Disabling Globalization: Places of Power in Post-Apartheid South Africa (Pietermaritzburg and Berkeley/Los Angeles: University of Natal Press and University of California Press, 2002).

21. Washington Post, Nov. 6, 2001, p.A1.

22. To its credit, SANGOCO (the South African NGO Coalition) actually dropped out of the ANC rally and march at the very last moment, deeming these events to be too uncritically pro-government.

23. This is an oft-repeated ploy, recycled in almost exactly these terms in Mbeki,

"Statement of the President of the African National Congress." There, categorically rejecting any possible socialist tainting of the ANC's "national democratic
revolution," he also makes the improbable claim that "our movement, like all
other national liberation movements throughout the world, is, inherently and by definition,
not a movement whose mission is to fight for the victory of socialism"
(emphasis added).

24. Jaspreet Kindra, "Left Seeks Soul of ANC: Leftists Are Pushing for the Inclusion
in the NEC of Party Members with Strong Activist Credentials," Mail and Guardian,
Oct. 11, 2002.

25. Local, national, regional, global? Elections, demonstrations and representations,
symbolic acts of defiance, more dramatic forms of confrontation?

26. See Suttner's further brief commentary, "Saul — Opening or Closing Debate?"
Monthly Review, 55, 2 (June 2003), together with my response, "Reply to
Suttner," (which is included in this chapter).

## 11. The Hares, the Hounds, and the ANC: On Joining the Third World in Post-Apartheid South Africa

A version of this chapter was originally published as an article in Third World
Quarterly: Journal of Emerging Areas, Special 25th Anniversary Issue, 25, 1 (2004).

1. I have advanced more detailed versions of some of the general arguments in
this first section in two related articles: John S. Saul, "Globalization,
Imperialism, Development: False Binaries and Radical Resolutions," in Socialist
Register 2004, ed. Leo Panitch and Colin Leys (London: The Merlin Press, 2003);
and Saul, "Identifying Class, Classifying Difference," in Socialist Register 2003, ed.
Leo Panitch and Colin Leys (London: The Merlin Press, 2002), both of which
are reproduced in Saul, Development after Globalization. I draw on certain of the formulations to be found in those articles here.

2. Mark Berger, "The End of the 'Third World'?" Third World Quarterly, 15, 2
(1994), p.258.

3. Hoogvelt, Globalization and the Post-Colonial World: The New Political Economy of
Development, 2nd ed. (London: Palgrave, 2001), p.xiv. As Arrighi and Silver have
correctly pointed out — see Beverley J. Silver and Giovanni Arrighi, "Workers
North and South," in Socialist Register 2001: Working Classes, Global Realities, ed. Leo
Panitch and Colin Leys (London: The Merlin Press, 2000), pp.56-57 —
Hoogvelt's use of the term "social" is misleading: the geographical hierarchy
of nations that they themselves continue to emphasize is, of course, also a
social relationship. Nonetheless, what Hoogvelt is here seeking to underscore
is important, if highly controversial.

4. Berger, "End of the 'Third World'?" p.260. This is also true in some of its variants of neo-liberalism, that now ubiquitous "ultra-modernist" take on development — as Fred Cooper and Randall Packer term it. See Fred Cooper and
Randall Packard, eds., International Development and the Social Scientists (Berkeley and

Los Angeles: University of California Press, 1997), p.2. But note that some of the crustier architects of the neo-liberal counter-revolution in development studies (Peter Bauer, for example) have turned this argument inside out: they also profess to see "the Third World" as being a Western artifact, but this time as the artifact of "'Western guilt' and the politics of foreign aid" — which holds, erroneously in their view, that "the West is responsible for the poverty of most of Asia, Africa and Latin America." See the summary of this position in John Toye, Dilemmas of Development: Reflections on the Counter-Revolution in Development Economics, 2nd ed. (Oxford: Blackwell Publishers, 1993), ch.1, "Is the Third World Still There?" pp.25-26.

5. Berger, "End of the 'Third World'?" p.270.

6. Ibid., p.258.

7. Brian S. Smith, Understanding Third World Politics (Bloomington: Indiana University Press, 1996), ch.1, "The Idea of the 'Third World,'" p.29.

8. Giovanni Arrighi, "World Income Inequalities and the Future of Socialism," New Left Review," 189 (September-October 1991).

9. Giovanni Arrighi, Beverley J. Silver, and Benjamin D. Brewer, "Industrial Convergence, Globalization and the Persistence of the North-South Divide," Studies in Comparative International Development, 38, 1 (Spring 2003).

10. In the same issue of Studies in Comparative International Development, 38, 1 (Spring 2003), that carries the Arrighi, Silver, and Brewer article, there is also a critique of their position by Alice Amsden, "Good-bye Dependency Theory, Hello Dependency Theory," as well as a response to her by the original authors. This stimulating exchange merely serves to reinforce the latter's case, in my opinion.

11. As Toye, Dilemmas of Development, p.31, writes, "The Third World is not . . . a figment of our imagination ready to vanish when we blink."

12. Salih Booker and William Minter, "Global Apartheid," The Nation, July 9, 2001.

13. Robert Biel, The New Imperialism: Crisis and Contradiction in North/South Relations (London: Zed Books, 2000), pp.131-32.

14. Arif Dirlik, "The Postcolonial Aura: Third World Criticism in the Age of Global Capitalism," in Dangerous Liaisons: Gender, Nation and Postcolonial Perspectives, ed. Anne McClintock, Amir Mufti, and Ella Shohat (Minneapolis: University of Minnesota Press, 1997), p.502. In sharp contrast, Robert Young, Postcolonialism: An Historical Introduction (Oxford: Blackwell, 2001), p.57, attempts to defend post-colonial theory from these kinds of criticisms: "Many of the problems raised can be resolved if the postcolonial is defined as coming after colonialism and imperialism, in their original meaning of direct-rule domination, but still positioned within imperialism in its later sense of the global system of hegemonic economic power." This may be somewhat disingenuous, for even Young professes his own unease with the term, suggesting his actual preference for the notion of "tricontinentalism" as capturing even more directly "a theoretical and political position which embodies an active concept of intervention within such

oppressive circumstances." Nonetheless, he claims that "postcolonialism" as he defines it can still serve the purposes he has in mind, capturing the "tricontinental" nature of Southern resistance to imperialism while remaining sensitive to the sheer diversity of the settings in which such resistance occurs.

15. Ella Shohat, "Notes on the 'Post-Colonial,'" Social Text, 31/32 (1992), pp.111. As she adds, "The 'neo-colonial,' like the 'post-colonial' also suggests continuities and discontinuities, but its emphasis is on the new modes of and forms of old colonialist practices, not on a 'beyond'" (p.106). See also, in the same issue of Social Text, Anne McClintock, "The Angel of Progress: Pitfalls of the Term 'Post-Colonial.'"

16. Berger, "End of the 'Third World'?" p.258, cites several related arguments.

17. Shohat, "Notes on the 'Post-Colonial'" p.110. As she further suggests, "A celebration of syncretism and hybridity per se, if not articulated in conjunction with questions of hegemony and neo-colonial power relations, runs the risk of appearing to sanctify the fait accompli of colonial violence" (p.109).

18. Smith, Understanding Third World Politics, p.24.

19. Cooper and Packer, eds., International Development and the Social Scientists, "Introduction," p.4.

20. As quoted in "Mandela Poses Hard Questions about Reach of Globalization," The Globe and Mail, Jan. 30, 1999, p.A19. Of course, this statement must be compared with his 1994 affirmation to the U.S. Joint Houses of Congress that the free market was a "magic elixir" that would produce freedom and equality for all." Quoted in Nash, "Mandela's Democracy," p.26.

21. From a speech by Mbeki at the opening of the ministerial meeting of the Non-Aligned Movement, Durban, August 1998.

22. Thabo Mbeki, speaking at the twelfth heads of state meeting of the Non-Aligned Movement, South Africa, Sept. 3, 1998; quoted in Robert Wade and Frank Venerosa, "The Gathering World Slump and the Battle over Capital Controls," New Left Review, 231 (September-October 1998), p.20.

23. Rok Ajalu, "Thabo Mbeki's African Renaissance in a Globalising World Economy: The Struggle for the Soul of a Continent," Review of African Political Economy, 87 (March 2001), p.36.

24. Ibid., p.35. In an alternative reading, I have described the domestic collapse of the notion of an "African Renaissance" into a rationale for the self-aggrandizement of a black petty bourgeoisie in Saul, "Cry for the Beloved Country" (see ch.9 here).

25. Ajalu, "Thabo Mbeki's African Renaissance in a Globalising World Economy," p.37. Ajalu is also referencing an Mbeki speech to the Non-Aligned Summit when he cites him as stating that the process of globalization "ineluctably results in the reduction of the sovereignty of states, with the weakest, being ourselves, being the biggest losers — those who are already the worst off suffer losses of the first order as a result of a marginal adjustment by another" (p.35).

26. See ch.9, "The Post-Apartheid Denouement," here, but also, inter alia, Marais, South Africa; and Bond, Elite Transition. See also Thabo Mbeki, "The Fatton Thesis: A Rejoinder," Canadian Journal of African Studies, 18, 3 (1984), p.609.

27. See, amongst other of his numerous writings on these matters, Patrick Bond, Against Global Apartheid: South Africa Meets the World Bank, IMF and International Finance, 2nd ed. (London: Zed Press, 2003).

28. Arundhati Roy, "When the Saints Go Marching Out," ZNet (www.zmag.org), Sept. 2, 2003.

29. These quotes are cited in Patrick Bond, "South Africa's Agenda in 21st Century Global Governance," in Review of African Political Economy, 89 (September 2001), p.416.

30. See ch.1, "Capitalism: Sub-Saharan Africa in Global Capitalism," here.

31. As cited in Keet, South Africa's Official Position and Role in Promoting the World Trade.

32. Ibid., p.4. See also Patrick Bond, Sustaining Global Apartheid: South Africa's Frustrated International Reforms (in manuscript: forthcoming), ch.5, "The Doha Trade 'Agenda': Splitting Africa to Launch a New Round."

33. Here, too, one of Bond's chapters, "Washington Renamed: A 'Monterrey Consensus' on Finance," in Sustaining Global Apartheid, is particularly useful; more generally, in this book and its predecessor (Against Global Apartheid) Bond provides much the richest and broadest analysis of South Africa's deeply compromised post-apartheid global positioning.

34. For a critique, detailed and powerful, of NEPAD along these lines see Bond, ed., Fanon's Warning. As Bond documents, a wide range of organizations drawn from South African civil society, as well as from elsewhere in Africa, have been amongst the most articulate and assertive critics of NEPAD. See also, in this regard, Ngwane, "Should African Social Movements Be Part of the New Partnership for Africa's Development?"

35. For Bond's argument, with several useful citations from Mbeki, see his Against Global Apartheid, p.139.

36. Thabo Mbeki, "Statement at the 35th Ordinary Session of the OAU Assembly of Heads of State and Government," Algiers, Aug. 13, 1999, cited in Ajalu, "Thabo Mbeki's African Renaissance in a Globalising World Economy."

37. Albo, "World Market of Opportunities?" p.30; as Albo continues, more positive outcomes "can only be realized through re-embedding financial capital and production relations in democratically organized national and local economic spaces sustained through international solidarity and fora of democratic co-operation."

38. Bond, "South Africa's Agenda," p.416.

39. Much of the spirit and thrust of such initiatives is captured in Desai, We Are the Poors. See also the important contributions of Neville Alexander, Issues in the Transition from Apartheid to Democracy in South Africa (Pietermaritzburg: University of Natal Press, 2002); and Gillian Hart, Disabling Globalization: Places of Power in Post-

*Apartheid South Africa* (Pietermaritzburg and Berkeley/Los Angeles: University of Natal Press and University of California Press, 2002).

# PART IV CONCLUSION

## 12. Africa: The Next Liberation Struggle?

This concluding chapter draws on a paper first presented to "Peasants, Liberation and Socialism in Africa," a conference held to mark Lionel Cliffe's retirement at Leeds University, May 2002; it was subsequently published, in revised form, in *Review of Political Economy*, 96 (2003). It also also draws on my paper "Rot, Reform and the Revival of Resistance in Postcolonial Africa," presented to "The Political Economy of Africa Revisited," a conference held at the Institute of Global Studies, Johns Hopkins University, April 2002. I am grateful to Patrick Bond, David Harvey, Colin Leys, Bill Minter, and Pat Saul for comments on various drafts.

1. John Mihevc, *The Market Tells Them So: The World Bank and Economic Fundamentalism in Africa* (Penang/Accra: Third World Network, 1995).

2. Cheru, "Local Dimensions of Global Reform."

3. David Moore, "'Sail on, O Ship of State': Neo-Liberalism, Globalisation and the Governance of Africa," *The Journal of Peasant Studies*, 27, 1 (2000).

4. Harry Shutt, *The Trouble with Capitalism: An Enquiry into the Causes of Global Economic Failure* (London: Zed Books, 1998), p.161.

5. We are registering here the virtual impossibility of the present system — now driven more by the speculative activity of holders of financial capital than by the pursuit of "productive investment" — to act "rationally" at the aggregate level (and thus, for example, to render Africa an additional site for the system's drive to realize itself as a transformative [and, in the long term, ever more profitable] engine of expanded reproduction). True, there are some within the system itself who may bewail that fact. See, for example, the rather heterodox World Bank document prepared in 1994 by Agarwala and Singh, "Sub-Saharan Africa: A Long-Term Perspective Study," a paper commissioned by the World Bank for the Learning Process on Participatory Development, which does evoke (rather against the grain of most other World Bank commentary) the immediate need for the much more subtle "embedding" of the market in the logic of local societies and polities and the much more slow and measured immersing of Africa, unprotected and vulnerable, into the acid-bath of the global marketplace. But, as Biel argues in *New Imperialism*, ch.11, "Permanent Subordination? Structural Adjustment as Control," pp.231-32, structural adjustment programs have been a particularly blunt instrument in this regard, successful in "using the 'debt' as a lever to break resistance to the demands of the new accumulation system." And yet, he continues, however good "SAPs may have been . . . at destroying the old . . . this does not mean they could provide a

basis for a stable self-reproducing set-up even within the confines of the current accumulation regime."

6. Bond, "South Africa's Agenda."

7. Bond, in "South Africa's Agenda," underscores the shallowness, in practice, of the African elite's commitment on this front, as they have backed away from any meaningful implementation of the "peer-review" mechanism promised under NEPAD and, in Mbeki's case, refrained from giving any significant support to democratic forces opposing the authoritarian practices of Mugabe in neighbouring Zimbabwe.

8. J.A. Weisman, ed., *Democracy and Political Change in Sub-Saharan Africa* (London: Routledge, 1995).

9. Rita Abrahamsen, *Disciplining Democracy: Development Discourse and Good Governance in Africa* (London and New York: Zed Books, 2000), pp.135-36.

10. Mamdani, *Citizen and Subject*.

11. Plank, "Aid, Debt and the End of Sovereignty."

12. Biel, *New Imperialism*, pp.232-33.

13. Ibid., pp.242-43.

14. Post and Wright, *Socialism and Underdevelopment*, pp.151-52; and ch.2 here.

15. Cf. ch.1 here; amongst the texts deployed there were Riley and Parfitt, "Economic Adjustment and Democratization in Africa." Recall, as well, that Riley and Parfitt identified an impressive range of (primarily urban) actors — "lawyers, students, copper miners, organisations of rural women, urban workers and the unemployed, journalists, clergymen and others" — whose direct action in recent years has shaken numerous African governments.

16. The grim denouement to Chiluba's project in Zambia provides a case in point here of the limits and ambiguities of "merely" anti-authoritarian mobilization; the transition from Moi to Kibaki in Kenya (greeted, understandably enough, with considerable euphoria) will also have to be tracked with close attention in this respect.

17. Barker, *Street-Level Democracy*, p.13.

18. Cheru, "Local Dimensions of Global Reform," p.124.

19. Harrison, "Bringing Political Struggle Back In."

20. Cheru, "Local Dimensions of Global Reform," p.119.

21. Barker, *Street-Level Democracy*, p.13.

22. Patrick Bond, "Cultivating African Anti-Capitalism," draft manuscript.

23. Colin Leys, "Colin Leys Replies" (a reply to Jonathan Barker, "Debating Globalization: Critique of Colin Leys"), *Southern African Report*, 12, 4 (1997).

24. As Cheru, "Local Dimensions of Global Reform," p.128, adds, however: "Here lies the dilemma of the people's organizations. . . . They will have to find the appropriate combination of strategies to handle effectively the contradictory

trajectories of state politics, which is integrative or centralizing, and social politics, which is horizontal or centrifugal."

25. Patrick Bond, "Post-Nationalist Politics for Zimbabwe?" *Red Pepper* (April 1999); for his further considered reflections on the Zimbabwean case, see, however, Bond and Manyanya, *Zimbabwe's Plunge.*

26. Patrick Bond, Darlene Miller, and Greg Ruiters, "The Southern African Working-Class: Production, Reproduction and Politics," in *Working Classes, Global Realities*, ed. Panitch and Leys; see also Harrison, "Bringing Political Struggle Back In."

27. Desai, *We are the Poors.*

28. Gindin, "Party's Over."

29. See Harrison, "Bringing Political Struggle Back In."

30. See Allen, "Understanding African Politics."

31. For a more general discussion of site, agency, and imaginary as relevant criteria for interrogating and guiding radical practice in Third World settings, see Saul, "Globalization, Imperialism, Development."

32. Cheru, "Local Dimensions of Global Reform," p.121.

33. James Krugman, *The Return of Depression Economics* (New York: Norton, 1999), p.5.

34. See Saul, *Millennial Africa*, pp.1-3 and ch.2.

35. Nyerere, "Reflections." See p.160 here.

36. Arrighi, "African Crisis."

37. See p.54 here.

38. See Patrick Bond on, precisely, "African anti-capitalism" in his "Cultivating African Anti-Capitalism"; see also Bond, "Potentials for African Anti-Capitalism: Uneven Development and Popular Resistance," *Policy Paper* 1/2003 (Berlin: Rosa Luxemburg-Foundation, 2001).

39. For a perspective on the brand of unity of theory and practice that might be expected to guide effective scientific work in the service of African transformation in the present conjuncture, see Saul, *Millennial Africa*, "Afterword: The Radical Africanist and the Socialist Alternative."

40. Albo, "World Market of Opportunities?" pp.28-30, 41.

# INDEX

Abrahamsen, Rita 259
abstract revolutionism 323(n.37)
accountability 62
accumulation 43, 45, 48, 50-51
activism 29, 138
Adelzadeh, Asghar 207
Adler, Glenn 74
African Alternative Framework 258
African Development Bank 19
African National Congress (ANC) 27, 31, 34,
    46, 48, 51, 82, 110-11, 126, 163, 167-
    72, 229-41, 258-59, 265, 266, 275,
    276-77, 294(nn.57, 59, 63-65),
    295(nn.68, 73), 314(n.36), 321(n.14),
    322(n.25), 329(n.58), 331(nn.78, 85),
    332(n.4), 334(n.23)
  Department of Economic Policy (DEP)
    205
  Freedom Charter 204, 276
  GEAR strategy 207, 209, 214, 217, 220-
    22, 229, 230, 249
  liberal democracy and 68-73
  Macro-Economic Research Group
    (MERG) 189-91, 205
  National Executive Committee (NEC)
    232-33
  National Growth and Development
    Strategy 207
  Political Education Unit 235
  post-apartheid state and 197-228, 242-
    53
  Reconstruction and Development
    Programme (RDP) 73, 206
  socialism in South Africa and 41-42
  South African transition (1994) and
    173-74, 178-84, 188, 190, 192,
    194
  "Strategic Perspective" document 180,
    325(n.54)
  Thirty Years War and 3-6
  Truth and Reconciliation Committee, see
    South Africa
  "Zanufication" of 232, 236, 240
African Party for the Liberation of Guinea and
    Cape Verde (PAIGC) 4
African People's Consensus 264
African Renaissance 212-13, 248, 252,
    337(n.24)
African Social Forum 264, 267
African Socialism 26, 33-35, 38, 93, 146-47
African Trade Network 264

African Union 252
Africanization 132
Afrikaner Weerstands Beweging (AWB) 198
agriculture 19-22, 142, 158, 258
Ahtissaari, Martti 115
AIDS 6, 28, 217, 226, 230
Ailonga, Salatiel 113
Ajalu, Rok 248-49, 253
Ake, Claude 65, 289(n.10)
Albo, Greg 209, 253, 267-68, 338(n.37)
Alexander, Neville 170, 319(n.6)
Algeria 38
All-African Alternative Framework 28
Allen, Chris 26, 265
alternative politics 227
Amin, Samir 31
Amosu, Akwe 299(n.3)
Amsden, Alice 336(n.10)
Anderson, Perry 24, 58, 186-87, 279(n.2)
Angola 2-6, 25, 26, 34, 40, 90-91, 116, 151
  Lubango detention centre 107-28,
    303(n.6), 306(n.38), 308(n.52),
    310(n.69)
Angula, Nahas 116-17, 122-23, 126,
    310(n.69)
Annan, Kofi 308(n.52)
anti-apartheid movement 48
  in Canada 269-77
anti-colonialism/anti-imperialism 4, 10, 33,
    48, 87, 162, 252-53
  in Mozambique 95, 97
  in Zimbabwe 142, 145, 146
Anti-Globalization Forum 235
Anti-Privatization Forum 237, 253
anti-racism 146
Anyang'Nyongo, Peter 65
apartheid, see also post-apartheid state
  in Namibia 111
  in South Africa 3, 5, 6, 26, 41-42, 46,
    75, 87, 94, 100, 111, 138, 167-69,
    173, 177, 197, 198, 266
Appolis, John 333(n.14)
Appolus, Emil 308(n.52)
Arrighi, Giovanni 8, 245, 266
Arusha Declaration 10, 36, 158-59
Association of Women's Clubs (AWC)
    (Zimbabwe) 139
Auala, Bishop 113
authoritarianism 27, 45, 48, 70, 87, 91, 92,
    180, 184, 196, 257, 262, 265
  democratization and 59, 66

in Mozambique 39, 98-99
in Tanzania 151
in Zimbabwe 132, 138, 142-43
racial 197
autocracy 262
auto-determination 38

Babu, Mohamed 151
Banda, 76
Bantustan governments, independent 198
bantustanization 90
barbarism, socialism or 228
Barber, Benjamin 80-82, 292(n.45),
    298(nn.94, 97)
Barker, Jonathan 29, 49, 149, 152, 262-64,
    284(n.40)
Barlow, Maude 235
Barrell, Howard 219-20, 327(n.26),
    333(n.10)
barriers, removal of 22
Basson, Wouter 107, 125, 128
Becker, David 60, 84, 291(n.26)
Bentham, Jeremy 298(n.97)
Berg Report 22
Berger, Mark 243, 244
Bernstein, Ann 210
Bernstein, Henry 181-82, 183
Bernstein, Lionel "Rusty" 234
Biel, Robert 246, 261
Bienefeld, Manfred 8, 36, 58, 158-59, 163,
    286(n.8), 290(n.16)
binaries, geographically defined 242-45
Biwa, Eric 116, 117-18, 119, 126
black bourgeoisie 213, 229
black capitalism 212
black elite 227
black empowerment 188, 212-13
black liberation 215
black markets 28
Blair, Tony 210, 215
Boggs, Carol 134
Boipatong massacre 200
Bond, Patrick 30, 49, 208, 252-53, 258, 265,
    266, 285(n.44), 326(n.19), 338(nn.33-
    34)
Boonzaaier, Henry 308(n.53)
Boputhatswana 198
Botha, P.W. 100, 178
Botswana 3, 18, 96, 116
bourgeoisie 131, 137, 211, 213, 229,
    292(n.39)
Bouteflika, Abdelaziz 252
Boutros-Ghali, Boutros 102-03, 105
Bowen, Merle 296(n.78)
Brazil 201

Breaking the Wall of Silence (BWS) 107, 108,
    118, 120, 121, 124-25, 128
Bretton Woods 242
British Anti-Apartheid Movement 275
Brutus, Dennis 294(n.65), 333(n.14)
Bull, Hedley 270
Bundy, Colin 31, 192, 209, 325(n.50)
Burkina Faso 19, 34, 64, 263
Burowoy, Michael 173
Burundi 119
Buthelezi, Gatsha 68, 70, 198-99, 201-02,
    226

Cabral, Amilcar 34, 49, 262
Cameroon 18, 263
Canada 223, 251, 331(n.78)
    anti-apartheid record of 269-77,
    318(n.1)
Cape Verde 282(n.7)
capitalism 16, 61, 67, 137, 195, 262, 266
    free-market 72
    global, see global capitalism
    hegemony of international 96
    liberation of, in South Africa 203-09
    political economy of 87
    utopian 267
    vs. socialism 7-10
Cargill, Jenny 324(n.44)
Castel-Franco Carlos Nunes 88
Castells, Manuel 27, 208, 226
Catholic Church 77
Central Intelligence Organization (Zimbabwe)
    134
centralized bureaucracy 24-25
Centre for Development and Enterprise (CDE)
    (South Africa) 203, 210
Cheru, Fantu 49, 257-58, 264, 266
Chidzero, Bernard 137
Chiluba, Frederick 30, 264
Chissano, Alberto Joaquim 77, 101-02
church, role of
    in Namibia 113, 118, 120, 305(n.15)
    in South Africa 238, 253
Churchill, Winston 146
Ciskei 198, 200
citizen and subject 201
civil society 49, 79-83, 104, 107, 265, 275,
    299(n.99), 315(n.44), 338(n.34)
    in South Africa 178, 185-86, 221, 223,
    238
    in Zimbabwe 134, 136, 139-40
Clark, Joe 270, 274-75
class
    in Mozambique 39
    in South Africa 189, 191, 203, 211,

215, 230, 242, 244, 247
  in Tanzania 34, 35, 147, 156, 162
  in Zimbabwe 132-33
  ZANU and 136-38
clientelism 24
Cliffe, Lionel 137
Clinton, Bill 215
Cocq, Karen 236
Codesria 31, 264
Cokorinos, Lee 135
Cold War 4, 5, 91, 271
  Mozambique and 94, 95
  socialism and 39, 42, 46-47
  South Africa and 175, 185, 242
collective insubordination 49, 262
collectivization 36-38, 51
colonialism 1, 3, 17, 23, 33, 39, 75, see also
  imperialism
  overthrow of 3
Compagnon, Daniel 134
comparative advantage 22
Concerned Citizens' Forum (Durban) 237,
  253
Congo DRC 18, 25, 140-41
Congo PR 18
Congress of Democrats (COD) 124, 125
Congress of South African Trade Unions
  (COSATU) 42, 73, 182-83, 200, 206,
  218-24, 238-40, 265, 322(n.23),
  324(n.44)
Conservative Party (South Africa) 198
Convention for a Democratic South Africa
  (CODESA) 182, 203
Cooper, Fred 247, 335(n.4)
cooperativistas 104
co-operativization 51
corruption 20, 37, 136
Côte d'Ivoire 18, 19, 259
Coulson, Andrew 152
Council for Namibia 89
Council of Churches of Namibia (CCN) 113,
  118, 120
counter-capitalism 257
counter-hegemony 26, 50, 75, 145, 193, 267
counter-socialism 5
Cox, Robert 162
Crocker, Chester 96, 101-02, 105
Cronin, Jeremy 73, 170, 180-81, 189, 200,
  240-41, 332(n.4), 333(n.13)
  response to 229-39
cultural nationalist triumvirate 149
Cunningham, Grif 153

Dakar Summit 264
Dashwood, Hevina 137, 155

Davis, Dennis 171
Davos forum 214, 248
De Beer, Zac 203-04, 273
de Klerk, F.W. 167, 178, 197-98, 199, 204
decentralization 78
decolonization 3, 9
  false 9, 211
deindustrialization 209
democracy 15-16, 29, 44, 136, 259,
  289(n.6), 298(n.94)
  in South Africa 174, 175-87, 193-94,
  196-202
  in Tanzania 154-57
  liberal 29, 42, 68-79, 92, 175-76, 196,
  213, 259-60, 297(n.92)
  liberal capitalist 56, 59, 193-94
  liberal vs. popular 54-84
  low intensity 58-59
  neo-liberalism and 55, 59, 61, 71-72,
  76, 82, 83
  peace, development and 102-06
  popular 42, 61, 77, 79-83, 162-63,
  176-77, 180, 184, 193, 259-60
  pseudo vs. substantive 175-77
  radical 186
  social 144, 161
  street-level 262
  strong 80-82
Democratic Alliance (South Africa) 201, 219-
  21, 224, 231-33, 237-38, 240
democratic elitism 56, 80, 175
democratic empowerment 181
Democratic Party (South Africa) 199, 201
democratic substitutionism 156
democratic transformation 201
democratic transition 201
democratization 24, 29, 51, 55, 294(n.60),
  321(n.13), 322(n.24)
  in Mozambique 78
  in South Africa 70-71, 175, 182-84,
  187, 215
  political economy of 55-61
  political science of 61-67, 81
Dempers, Pauline 108, 128, 309(n.55)
deracialization 215
Desai, Ashwin 237
destabilization 4-5, 138
  Mozambique and 39, 75, 94, 96, 98,
  105
development, peace, democracy and 102-06
development theory 47
developmental state 21-22, 24, 33, 225
developmentalism 76
Dhlakama, Afonso 77
di Palma, Giuseppe 57, 59-60, 62, 66

Diamond, Larry 175, 289(n.7), 290(n.19), 298(n.97)
on democratization 55-56, 59, 62, 66, 81
diamond industry 20, 25, 258
Diefenbaker, John 269-70, 274
Dirlik, Arif 246
disenfranchisement 139
disinformation 113
dissident activity 136
Dithlake, Albie 222, 226
Dobell, Lauren 109, 110-11, 118
domestic dynamics, in Zimbabwe 137
drug trafficking 20
Du Bois, W.E.B. 3
Dumeni, Kleopas 307(n.45)
Dunkerley, James 66
dynamizing groups 40

Eastern Europe 39, 47, 75, 95-96, 98, 100, 138, 180
Economic Commission for Africa (ECA) 18, 19
Economic Community of West African States (ECOWAS) 28
economic decline 24
in Zimbabwe 136
economic dependency 89
economic fundamentalism 257
economic inequality 199
economic liberalization 55
economic liberation 159
economic nationalism 160
economic planning, in South Africa 189-90
Economic Structural Adjustment Program (ESAP) (Zimbabwe) 136-40
economy 17-18, 19-24, 27, 28-29, 35
agrarian 17-18
in South Africa 202-03, 203-09
intervention in 21-24
education 19, 35, 132, 139, 222
Ekandjo, Jerry 304(n.10)
El Salvador 66
elections
in Mozambique 41, 55, 76-79, 88, 103-05, 296(nn.79, 82)
in South Africa 55, 68-69, 167, 170-71, 173-74, 197, 200, 206, 210, 219, 242
in Tanzania 149
in Zimbabwe 134, 139
elite-pacting vs. popular mobilization, in South Africa 177-85
elites 9, 133, 135, 227, 241, 244, 263
aggrandizement of 36
black 227

political 56
Eminent Persons' Group 273
enabling state 258
Eritrea 34
Erwin, Alec 206, 226, 230, 250-52, 258, 327(n.26)
Escobar, Arturo 244
Ethiopia 18, 34
ethnic chauvinism 132
ethnic hostility 87, 157
ethnic politics, mobilization of 37, 155
ethnicity 66, 130, 133
ethnie 6
Etkind, Roger 322(n.22)
Eurocentrism 33, 147
European Union 251
exchange controls, removal of 22
exploitation vs. marginalization 20-21
export production 24-25

faith-based movements 140
Fanon, Frantz 146, 211
fetishization of the market 58
Fifth Brigade (Zimbabwe) 134
Fine, Ben 210
First World 242
vs. Third World 243, 245
Fraser, Malcolm 273
Fraser, Nancy 67, 293(n.46)
Fraser-Moleketi, Geraldine 219
free markets 22, 72, 99, 205-06
Freeman, Linda 143-45, 318(n.1)
review of 269-77, 318(n.1)
Frelimo (Front for the Liberation of Mozambique) 2, 4, 5-6, 34, 38-41, 75-79, 87-89, 95-105, 130, 149, 153, 156, 286(n.11), 296(n.78), 297(n.85)
Congress of (1983) 301(n.8)
Freund, Bill 283(n.18)
Friedman, Steven 69, 184-85, 321(n.10)
Front Line States 101
fundamentalism 292(n.45)

G8 Summit
Evian (2003) 250
Kananaskis (2001) 250, 252
Gabon 18
Gamble, Andrew 186, 193
Garoeb, Justus 116
Garoeb, Moses 115-16, 118, 303(n.6), 304(n.10), 305(n.30)
Gauteng province 226, 239
Gawanas, Bience 112, 123, 309(n.55)
Geingob, Hage 110, 115, 117, 119, 122, 125, 308(n.54)

Gelb, Stephen 168
General Agreement on Tariffs and Trade (GATT) 208
geographically defined hierarchies 242-45
George, Susan 62
Gersony, Robert 102
Ghana 10, 22, 24, 26, 32, 33, 64, 259
Gigaba, Malusi 233
Giliomee, Herman 70, 294(nn.57,60)
Gills, Barry 58
Gindin, Sam 189, 223-24, 265, 331(n.78)
global apartheid 246-48
global capitalism 8-9, 15, 18-21, 26, 41, 47, 60, 72, 74, 258, 261-62, 266
    IFIs and 22, 28-30
    IMF and 20, 22-23, 27
    in South Africa 193-94, 195, 230-31, 244, 248
    in Tanzania 154, 159, 160
    sub-Saharan Africa in 17-31
    World Bank and 17, 20, 22-23, 27
global competitiveness 249
global deregulation 28
global division of labour 244
global hierarchy 245-46
global inequality 242-44, 253
global poverty 244
global South 247
globalism, "new" 173-74, 194
globalization 46-47, 60, 81, 159, 174, 195, 196, 248, 253, 263
Godongwana, Enoch 82, 188, 190
Gono, Gideon 143
Gorz, André 188
governance 62-63, 258, 289(n.6), 290(n.16), 291(n.34)
Government of National Unity (GNU) 77, 178-79, 199
Graham, Paul 72
Gramsci, Antonio 129, 131-34, 145, 168, 311(n.5)
grand narratives 61
Grant, Dale 25
Great Britain, empire of 129, 135, 146
Green, Philip 175-77, 290(n.22), 297(n.92)
Groth, Siegfried 109, 118-19, 120, 124
Grovogui, Siba 160
Growth, Employment and Redistribution (GEAR) strategy, see ANC
growth through redistribution 209, 249
Guatemala 201
Guiné 10
Guinea 33
Guinea-Bissau 4, 34
Gumede, William 233-34

gun-running 20
Gurirab, Theo-Ben 114-15

Hamutenya, Hidipo 115, 303(n.6)
Hanlon, Joseph 100, 103
Hannekom, Derek 218
Harris, Lawrence 190, 192, 205
Harrison, Graham 50, 263
Hartzenberg, Ferdy 198
Harvey, Suzanna 322(n.22)
Hatuikilipi, Tauno 120, 306(n.37)
Hawala, Solomon "Jesus" 128, 303(n.6)
health 19, 132, 139, 222
hegemony 10, 28, 46, 49, 96, 134, 264, 272-73
    nationalism as 130-33
    South Africa and 170, 172, 198, 217, 239
Herero Chiefs Council 89
High Commission Territories 3
Highly Indebted Poor Countries initiative 28
Hirji, Karim 157
Hirst, Paul 196
history, forgotten, in Namibia 107-28
Honwana, Fernando 101
Hoogvelt, Ankie 244, 335(n.3)
human rights 108, 136, 140, 199, 306(n.35), 313(n.26)
humanitarianism 100
Huntington, Samuel 81, 289(n.6), 298(n.97), 320(n.5)
Husain, Israt 284(n.38)
Hutchful, Eboe 22
Hyden, Goran 63, 291(n.34)
Hyslop, Jonathan 198

identity politics 16, 66, 71
imperialism 33, 60, 61, 94, 162, see also colonialism
industrial production 50
industrialization 21-22, 40
Inkatha Freedom Party (IFP) 68, 70, 198-99, 201-02, 295(n.68)
Institute for Democracy in South Africa 72
Institutional Revolutionary Party (PRI) (Mexico) 42, 227
institutionalization 37, 40
International Committee of the Red Cross (ICRC) 115-16, 126
international financial institutions (IFIs) 46, 49, 60, 76, 257-58, 262
    global capitalism and 22, 28-30
international market relations 244
International Monetary Fund (IMF) 46, 49, 83, 88, 100, 262

global capitalism and 20, 22-23, 27
South Africa and 180, 188, 215, 252
Tanzania and 148, 159
Ivory Coast, see Côte d'Ivoire

Japan 251
Jenkins, Carolyn 135
jihad 292(n.45)
Jordan, Pallo 82, 180, 188, 190
Jubilee 2000 - 28, 148, 222, 264

Kaballo, Sidgi 65-66
Kabila, Laurent 25
Kagarlitsky, Boris 188
Kaiser, Paul 157
Kambangula, Emma 122, 308(n.51)
Kaplan, Robert 192-93
Kathindi, Nagula 123
Katjiuonga, Moses 126
Kaulumu, James 307(n.44)
Kaunda, Kenneth 30, 34, 90
Kay, Geoffrey 21
Keane, John 186, 193
Keet, Dot 251
Kempton Park negotiations 182, 203
Kenya 18, 24, 30, 33-34, 259
Kenyatta, 24
Keynesianism 21-22, 205, 261
Keys, Derek 188
Kitching, Gavin 43-44, 45, 50, 51
Klein, Naomi 235-36
Knight, John 135
Koch, Eddie 76
Krugman, James 266-67
KwaZulu-Natal province 198-99, 200, 202, 221

labour aristocracy 183, 330(n.71)
labour movement 139, 140
Labour Relations Act (Zimbabwe) 138
Laclau, Ernesto 186
Lagos Plan of Action 28, 258
land, struggle for in Zimbabwe 132, 139, 142-43
land reform 136
Landless People's Movement 237, 253
Landsberg, Chris 71
Leadership Code (Tanzania) 37, 155
left developmental dictatorship 40, 75, 105, 247
left-populism 33
Lehulere, Oupa 328(n.32), 333(n.14)
Lekota, Terror 219
Lenin, V.I. 150, 219
Lesotho 3

Lewis, Dave 189-90
Leys, Colin 47, 53, 105, 250, 264, 284(n.40), 291(n.29), 308(n.51)
on socialism 58, 61, 67, 84
on Tanzania 151, 160-61
liberal capitalist democracy 56, 59
high costs of, in South Africa 193-94
liberal democracy 29, 42, 68-79, 92, 175-76, 196, 213, 259-60, 297(n.92)
ANC and 68-73
in Mozambique 74-79
in South Africa 68-74, 175
liberal vs. popular democracy 54-84
liberalism 54, 70, 79, 157
liberalization 78, 138, 229, 312(n.20)
economic 55
Liberation Committee (of OAU) 5
liberation movements 2-6, 48, 49
Liberia 25
limited federalism 199
Lombard, Cristo 113, 118-19, 122
low intensity democracy 58-59
Loxley, John 60, 291(n.29)
Lubango detention centre 107-28, 303(n.6), 306(n.38), 308(n.52), 310(n.69)
Lusaka Declaration 264
Luttrell, William 51

Machel, Graça 78-79, 100
Machel, Samora 38-39, 78, 98, 101, 132, 149
Macozoma, Saki 220
Macpherson, C.B. 298(n.97)
Madagascar 282(n.7)
Magdoff, Harry 26-27, 41, 173, 196-97
Maharaj, Mac 206
Makamure, Kempton 312(n.20)
Makhaye, Dumisane 232, 233, 333(n.7)
Makumbe, John 134
Malawi 76, 96
Mali 263
Mamdani, Mahmood 30, 49, 201, 260
Mandaza, Ibbo 132, 135
Mandela, Nelson 3, 4, 6, 69, 73, 100, 132, 167, 169, 171, 242, 248, 269, 277, 321(n.13), 322(n.25), 323(n.36), 326(n.19), 329(n.58)
and post-apartheid dénouement 197, 204, 214-15, 217-18, 221
and South African transition 173-74, 178, 184, 187-88
Mandela, Winnie 72, 194, 227, 325(n.54), 331(n.81)
Mangope, Lucas 198
Manuel, Trevor 206, 225-26, 230, 252,

327(n.26)
Maputo regime 102
Marais, Hein 203, 215-16, 226
Maré, Gerry 202
marginalization
    of state politics 136
    politics of 24-26
    vs. exploitation 20-21
market economy 92, 137
market imperatives 173-74
market liberalism 27
market-oriented economics 259
market socialism 51
marketization 230, 249
Marshall, Judith 296(n.78)
Marxism 26, 311(n.5), 326(n.19)
    African socialism and 33, 34, 38, 43, 51
    South Africa and 173, 185, 238
Marxism-Leninism 98, 135, 137, 154
    African socialism and 39, 40, 45, 47, 52
Mason, Douglas Patrick 103
mass action 177-85, 187, 200
Mass Democratic Movement (South Africa) 178, 206
Matabeleland 133
Mauritius 282(n.7)
Maxuilili, Nathaniel 118
Mbeki, Thabo 41, 126, 230, 235, 239, 241, 258-59, 314(n.36), 327(n.26), 329(n.58), 330(nn.63, 68), 337(n.25)
    and post-apartheid dénouement 197, 204, 210, 212-15, 217-20, 225-27
    and South African transition 167, 171, 187
    and Third World in post-apartheid South Africa 242-43, 248-49, 252-53
Mboweni, Tito 205, 226
McKinley, Dale 170-71, 333(n.12)
McMenamin, Vic 206
McWorld 81, 292(n.45)
media, in Zimbabwe 134, 136, 138
Meer, Shamim 221
"mere reformism" 323(n.37)
middle class 211
middle-class opportunism 213
Miliband, Ralph 46, 60, 67, 84
militarization, in Zimbabwe 141-43
Mill, John Stuart 298(n.97)
Miller, Darlene 265
Mineral-Energy Complex (MEC) 210
mineral exports 18-20, 21, 25, 258
mining industry 20
Minter, William 40, 98-99, 301(n.10)
Minus Four 123
Mishimba, Aaron 303(n.6)

Mnakapa, Zen 306(n.35)
mobilization, popular 176-85, 187, 194, 200, 203
Mobutu, 24
modernization theory 175, 244, 320(n.5)
Modise, Tumi 329(n.48)
Mofokeng, Takatso 222
Mohapi, Agnes 237
Moi, 24, 30
Moll, Terence 206
Mondlane, Eduardo 38, 149, 286(n.10)
Monga, Célestin 49, 262
Mont Fleur proposals 206
Moosa, Valli 219
Motlanthe, Kgalema 226
Motseunyanye Commission 111
Mouffe, Chantal 186
Mount Carmel Rubber Factory 37, 151-52, 155
Movement for Democratic Change (MDC) (Zimbabwe) 50, 141, 144, 264, 315(n.44)
Movement for Multiparty Democracy (MMD) 264
Movement for the Survival of the Ogoni People (MOSOP) 263
Mozambican National Resistance, see Renamo
Mozambique 1, 2, 4, 5, 23, 55, 87-89, 130, 156, 212, 214, 263, 296(n.78), 299(n.1), 300(n.4), 332(n.5)
    anti-colonialism in 95, 97
    authoritarianism in 39, 98-99
    civil war in 94-96, 105
    Cold War and 94, 95
    democracy in 67, 74-79, 80, 83
    elections in 41, 55, 76-79, 88, 103-05, 296(nn.79, 82)
    peacemaking in 96-97, 100, 103, 105
    socialism in 26, 33, 34, 38-41, 46, 48, 52, 95-97, 260
    South Africa and 94, 95, 97, 100, 102
    trade unions in 78, 104
    war and peace in 94-106
    women's organizations in 78, 104
    World Bank and 100, 105
    UN role in 302(n.18)
MPLA, see Popular Movement for the Liberation of Angola
Mugabe, Robert 6, 30, 92, 240, 259, 264, 294(n.59), 313(n.29), 314(n.26), 315(n.44)
    and consolidation of power in 1980s 133-36
    Gramsci and 129-33, 137, 141, 143-45
Mulroney, Brian, anti-apartheid record of

269, 272-76
multi-party system 64, 157, 292(n.36),
    296(n.82)
Murray, Roger 7, 32, 194

Nakamhela, Ngeno 120-21, 307(nn.42, 45-
    47)
Namibia (see also South-West Africa) 2-6, 87,
    89-92, 212, 294(n.63), 297(n.92),
    300(n.8), 306(nn.31, 35)
    churches, role of in 113-14, 118, 120,
        121, 305(n.15)
    forgotten history as politics in 107-28
    independence of 113
    Lubango detention centre and 107-28
    Truth and Reconciliation Committee
        model 121, 126, 304(n.7)
Namises, Rosa 125
Namoloh, Ndaxu "Ho Chi Minh" 128
Nash, Andrew 214
Nathanael, Keshii Pelao 310(n.66)
National Constitutional Assembly (NCA)
    (Zimbabwe) 140
National Economic Development and Labour
    Council (NEDLAC) (South Africa) 183,
    219
National Economic Forum (South Africa) 183
National Education Conference (South Africa)
    183
National Land Commission (South Africa)
    218, 222
National Liberation Movement (NLM) (South
    Africa) 224-25
National Party (South Africa) 167, 187, 199,
    201, 204, 294(n.63), 295(n.68)
national purpose 132
National Society for Human Rights (NSHR)
    119, 125, 306(n.38)
National Union of Mine-Workers of South
    Africa 31
nationalism 4, 9, 10, 48, 49, 64, 257, 260,
    263, 265
    as hegemony 130-33
    in South Africa 173, 180, 213, 215
    in Tanzania 146-47, 149
    in Zimbabwe 130, 138, 145
nationalization 249
nation-building 64, 67, 132, 133, 156
NATO 88
Nattrass, Nicoli 191, 192, 324(n.49)
natural gas industry 19
Naudé, Beyers 221
Ndebele 130
Ndeikwila, Samson 120, 128
Ndungane, Njongonkulu 221

Nedcor/Old Mutual "Professional Economists'
    Panel" 206
Nelson, Joan 62
neo-colonialism 159, 260-61, 337(n.15)
neo-imperialism 20, 89
neo-liberalism 4, 22, 27, 99, 167, 258, 265-
    66, 276, 290(n.16), 315(n.44),
    335(n.4)
    African socialism and 41, 42, 46-47, 53
    and post-apartheid dénouement 195,
        197, 201, 204, 206, 207-10, 221, 225,
        227
    democracy and 55, 59, 61, 71-72, 76,
        82, 83
    in South Africa 174, 229-32, 235, 239-
        40, 245, 249
    in Tanzania 154, 161, 163
Netshitenzhe, Joel 331(n.81)
New Democratic Party (Canada) 223
New Economic Partnership for Africa's
    Development (NEPAD) 230, 252, 259,
    338(n.34)
Ngwane, Trevor 171, 217, 236, 333(n.14)
Nicaragua 66
Nigeria 18, 24, 30, 50, 263, 265
Nkrumah, Kwame 10, 32, 33, 34, 38, 47
Non-Aligned Movement 215, 240, 248
Non-Aligned Summit 337(n.25)
non-governmental organizations (NGOs) 100,
    138, 222, 313(n.28)
Normative Economic Model (NEM) 204, 208
North vs. South 242-47, 261, 263
Nove, Alex 51
NRM (Uganda) 64
Nujoma, Sam 89, 91, 118, 120, 121-22,
    124, 127-28, 300(n.8), 304(n.10),
    306(n.31), 308(n.53)
Nuns, Mzwandile 221
Nyerere, Julius 7, 24, 34-37, 44, 46, 51, 90,
    92, 266, 286(n.6), 292(n.36),
    317(n.24)
    socialism of 146-63
Nyerere, Rose 148
Nzimande, Blade 224
Nzongola-Ntalaja 65

Obasanjo, Olusegun 252
Odendaal Plan 90
Ogoniland 30
oil industry 19, 25, 258
oligarchic wealth 246
One-Party Democracy 37, 151
one-party dominant system 19
one-party state 138, 149, 154, 156,
    292(n.36), 296(n.82)

Onimode, Bade 23, 283(n.23)
ONUMOZ (United Nations Operation in
	Mozambique) 102
Operation Production 104
Organization of African Unity (OAU) 5, 89,
	252
	Liberation Committee of 89, 146
Ottaway, Marina 294(n.57)
Ovamboland People's Organization (OPO) 89

Packard, Randall 247, 335(n.4)
PAIGC, see African Party for the Liberation of
	Guinea and Cape Verde
Pakleppa, Richard 109, 122, 309(n.55)
Pan-African Movement of East, Central and
	Southern Africa (PAFMECSA) 5, 146
Pan-Africanism 5, 9
Pan-Africanist Congress (PAC) 3, 295(n.68)
Parents' Committee 113, 114, 306(n.35)
Parfitt, Trevor 49, 262
Patriotic Unity Movement (PUM) 116
patronage 24-26
peace, democracy, development and 102-06
peacemaking
	in Mozambique 96-97, 100, 103, 105
	in South Africa 201-02
Pearson, Lester B. 270
peasantry 9, 44, 51, 52, 104, 105, 156-57,
	222
people's wars 4
Phosa, Mathews 212
Pieters, Joseph 308(n.52)
Pitcher, Anne 296(n.78)
Plank, David 23, 76, 100, 261
Plattner, Mark 175
pluralistic democracy 64, 175
Political Consultative Committee 113
political democratization 55
political economy 64
	of capitalism 87
	of democratization 55-61
political economy vs. political science 55-67,
	70, 95-97
political elites 56
political emancipation 185
political science of democratization 61-67, 81
polyarchy 55, 80, 175, 179
popular democracy 42, 61, 77, 79-83, 259-
	60
	in South Africa 176-77, 180, 184, 193
	in Tanzania 162-63
	vs. liberal democracy 54-84
popular democratization 183
popular empowerment 200
popular mobilization 26, 139

	in South Africa 176-85, 194, 200, 203
Popular Movement for the Liberation of
	Angola (MPLA) 4, 90
popular movements, South African 167
popular resistance 262
populism 133, 135
	peasant-centric 44
populist revolts 64
Portugal 3, 4, 38, 39, 75, 88, 95
Post, Ken 44-45, 48, 50, 261
post-apartheid state 167, 174, 180, 190, 230,
	258-59, 265
	dénouement of 195-228
	Nelson Mandela and 197, 204, 214-15,
	217-18, 221
	Thabo Mbeki and 197, 204, 210, 212-
	15, 217-20, 225-37
	neo-liberalism and 195, 197, 201, 204,
	206, 207-10, 221, 225, 227
	Third World and 242-53
post-colonialism 246-47, 266, 336(n.14),
	337(n.15)
postimperialism 291(n.26)
postmodernism 61, 147
post-nationalism 285(n.44)
post-neo-colonialism 267
post-neoliberalism 285(n.44)
poverty 6, 144, 202-03, 215, 258, 329(n.60)
	alleviation of, in Tanzania 154-63
Pratt, Cranford 148, 154-58, 160, 316(n.14)
Private Voluntary Organizations (PVO) Act
	(Zimbabwe) 139, 313(n.28)
privatization 229-30, 249, 326(n.19)
Project for the Study of Violence and
	Reconciliation 122
proletarianization 39
Przeworski, Adam 8, 290(n.22), 321(n.10)
	on liberal/popular democracy 59-60, 62,
	66, 68, 74
	on South Africa 177, 187, 192, 194,
	195
pseudodemocracy 175, 290(n.22), 297(n.92)
public choice 62
public ownership, removal of 22

race 64, 66, 132
	in South Africa 196, 204, 215, 242
racial authoritarianism 197
racial capitalism, crisis of 168
racial equality 39, 227
racism 3, 135, 274
radical democracy 186
radical nationalism 257
radical pluralist theory 273
radical reform, in South Africa 188,

299(n.99)
radical/socialist dimension 66
radicalization 133
Ramaphosa, Cyril 211-12, 3?8(n.44)
Ramashala, Mapule 121-22
Ranger, Terence 310(n.2)
rationalization 250
Ravenhill, John 22-23
Reagan, Ronald 5, 26, 39, 46, 96, 102, 274
realism, in South Africa 188, 195, 251
Rebelo, Jorge 97-98
recolonization 23, 46, 76, 100-02, 261,
    301(n.8)
reconciliation 107, 109-10
Reconstruction Accord 182-83
redistribution 71
    growth through 209, 249
regionalism 66
regulatory manipulation 138
relative autonomy 272
religion 64, 66, 157
Renamo (Mozambican National Resistance) 5,
    40-41, 75-78, 95-104, 297(n.85),
    301(n.6)
Reserve Bank 207
revolutionary reform, in South Africa 188,
    192, 257
revolutionary-socialist imperative, in Tanzania
    154-63
Rhodesia (see also Zimbabwe) 2, 4, 39, 76,
    95, 97, 129, 270
right developmental dictatorship 75
Riley, Stephen 49, 262
Rocamora, Joel 58
Roesch, Otto 297(n.87)
Roy, Arundhati 249
Ruiters, Greg 265
Rural Development Services Network 222
Rustomjee, Zavareh 210
Ruvuma Development Association (RDA) 37,
    152, 155-56
Rwanda 66, 119, 195

Sabelli, Fabrizio 62
Sandbrook, Richard 160
Sankara, Thomas 34
Sanlam 206, 212
São Tome and Principe 282(n.7)
Saunders, Richard 70, 92
Schmitz, Gerald 62, 63, 291(n.34)
Schneider, Leander 316(n.16)
Schroeder, Gerhard 215
Schumpeter, Joseph 55
Second World 243
securocratic vision 133, 143

Seddon, David 60, 291(n.29)
self-reliance, socialism and, in Tanzania 157-
    62
Senegal 18, 33
Senghor, Léopold 33, 34, 147
Sessional Paper no.10 - 33
Setshedi, Virginia 333(n.14)
Sexwale, Tokyo 212
Seychelles 282(n.7)
Shaw, George Bernard 150
Sheehan, Helena 232-33
Shell Oil 30
Shipanga, Andreas 127
Shiva, Vandana 235
Shivji, Issa 162, 176-77, 266, 292(n.39),
    318(n.34)
    on liberal/popular democracy 54-55, 64,
    65, 75, 79, 80, 82
Shohat, Ella 246-47
Shona 130, 133
Shutt, Harry 258
Shuuya, Leonard Philemon ("Castro") 127
Sierra Leone 24, 25
Simango, Uria 149
single party system 64
Sirimanne, Shamika 19
Sisk, Timothy 69, 71, 72, 298(n.97)
Sklar, Richard 15, 60, 84, 266
Skweyiya Commission 111
Slovo, Joe 68, 206, 293(n.47), 321(nn.10,
    17)
    on South African transition 179, 181-82,
    188, 190-91
Smith, Brian 245
Smith, Ian 97, 129-30
social cohesion 226
social democracy 144, 161
social-democratization 161
social equity 136
Social Movements' Indaba 237-38
socialism 4, 15-16, 32-53, 61, 144, 260,
    261, 266-68, 321(n.13)
    Cold War and 39, 42, 46-47
    continental perspectives on 33-34
    Mozambique and 26, 33, 34, 38-41, 46,
    48, 52, 95-97, 260
    objective conditions for 43
    or barbarism 228
    realistic 267-68
    self-reliance and 157-62
    South Africa and 26-27, 33, 34, 41-42,
    46-48, 51, 52, 167, 174, 195, 213-14
    stigmatization of, in South Africa 185-93
    Tanzania and 26, 33, 34-38, 46, 48, 52,
    92, 146-63

Third World 43, 45
vs. capitalism 7-10
socialist transformation 260
socio-economic inequality 6, 201, 244
Somalia 24, 34, 66
South Africa 1-6, 10, 17, 18, 39, 78, 79, 80,
    81, 83, 89-91, 138, 160, 163, 265,
    266, 297(n.92), 299(n.99), 300(n.8),
    314(n.36)
ANC, see African National Congress
and Mozambique 94, 95, 97, 100, 102
and Namibia 114, 121, 126
citizens' movements in 177-78
civil society and 178, 185-86, 221, 223,
    238
class in 189, 191, 203, 211, 215, 230,
    242, 244, 247
Cold War and 175, 185, 242
debating the transition of 167-253
democracy in 174, 175-87, 193-94,
    196-202
democratization in 175, 182-84, 187,
    215
dual transition in 196-203
elections in 55, 68-69, 167, 170-71,
    173-74, 197, 200, 206, 210, 219, 242
elite-pacting vs. popular mobilization in
    177-85
global capitalism and 193-94, 195, 230-
    31, 244, 248
hegemony and 170, 172, 198, 217, 239
IMF and 180, 188, 215, 252
liberal-capitalist-democratic ideology in
    193-94
liberal democracy in 55, 67, 68-74, 76
liberating capitalism in 203-09
market and socialism in 185-93
Marxism and 173, 185, 238
nationalism in 173, 180, 213, 215
neo-liberalism and 174, 229-32, 235,
    239-40, 245, 249
peacemaking in 201-02
popular democracy in 176, 180, 184,
    193
popular mobilization in 176-85, 194,
    200, 203
post-apartheid state in 195-228, 242-53,
    258-59, 265
race in 196, 204, 215, 242
reform, types of, in 188-93, 299(n.99)
socialism in 26-27, 33, 34, 41-42, 46-
    48, 51, 52, 167, 174, 195, 213-14
Stalinism and 173, 180, 199, 213, 241
starting from scratch in 217-28, 229-41
stigmatization of socialism in 185-93

Thatcherism in 209-17
Third World and 242-53
trade unions in 177, 183, 220, 223,
    238-39, 241, 253
transition of (1994) 173-94
Truth and Reconciliation Committee of
    87, 107, 110-11, 121, 126, 199, 217,
    304(n.7)
underdevelopment in 242-43, 245
women's organizations in 177-78, 222-
    23, 253
World Bank and 180, 188, 215, 252
South Africa National Non-Governmental
    Organizations Coalition (SANGOCO)
    222, 238, 265, 334(n.22)
South African Committee for Higher
    Education 183
South African Communist Party (SACP) 42,
    68, 218-19, 224, 233, 235, 238, 241,
    321(n.14), 322(n.25), 333(n.12)
South African Council of Churches 221
South African Defence Force 90
South African Democratic Teachers' Union
    (SADTU) 218
South African Municipal Workers' Union
    (SAMWU) 219
South African National Civics Organization
    (SANCO) 222, 240
South vs. North 242-47, 261, 263
Southern Africa Report 269
Southern African Development Community
    (SADC) 28
Southern African Development Coordination
    Conference (SADCC) 5
Southern African People's Solidarity Network
    264
Southern Rhodesia 3
South-West Africa (see also Namibia) 2, 3, 89
South-West Africa People's Organization, see
    Swapo
South-West African National Union (SWANU)
    89
Soviet Union 102, 214
Soweto Electricity Crisis Committee 237, 253
Space Research Institute 270
Sparks, Alaister 69, 295(n.69)
spoils politics 25
stabilization of capitalist relations 196
Stalinism 50-51, 76, 150, 260
    South Africa and 173, 180, 199, 213,
    241
state-civic conflict, in Zimbabwe 139
statecraft 67
statism 75
Stephanus, Lukas 308(n.52)

Strauss, Peter 307(n.44)
street-level democracy 262
strong democracy 80-82
structural adjustment 22, 24, 46, 55, 135, 258
Structural Adjustment Programs (SAPs) 22
structural reform, in South Africa 188, 190-91, 209, 249-50, 318(n.38)
Stuart Commission 111
student groups 134, 136, 139, 156
sub-Saharan Africa
  in global capitalism 17-31
  liberal vs. popular democracy in 54-84
substantive democracy 175-77
Sudan 18, 25
Sunter, Clem 326(n.15)
surplus extraction 43
Suttner, Raymond 170, 181, 200, 235
  response to 240-41
Swapo (South-West Africa People's Organization) 89-92, 151, 300(n.8), 303(n.6), 304(n.10), 305(nn.14, 26, 30), 306(nn.31, 37, 38, 40), 308(nn.48, 51-52, 54)
  Central Committee 114
  Lubango detention centre and 107-28
Swaziland 3, 18
Sweezy, Paul 26-27, 41, 173, 196-97

Tankeu, Elizabeth 282(n.11)
Tanzania 1, 5, 7, 10, 18, 24, 87, 90, 92, 93, 128, 332(n.5)
  authoritarianism in 151
  class in 34, 35, 147, 156, 162
  democracy in 154-57
  democratization in 160-61
  elections in 149
  global capitalism and 154, 159, 160
  IMF and 148, 159
  Julius Nyerere and 146-63
  nationalism in 146-47, 149
  neo-liberalism and 154, 161, 163
  popular democracy in 162-63
  poverty alleviation in 154-63
  revolutionary-socialist imperative in 154-63
  socialism in 26, 33, 34-38, 46, 48, 52, 92, 146-63
  women's organizations in 156-57
Tanzanian African National Union (TANU) 34, 36-37, 149, 151-52, 154-55, 158
Tanzanian Field Force Unit 37, 155
tariffs, removal of 22
Temu, Arnold 150, 155-56
Terreblanche, Eugene 198

Thatcher, Margaret 197, 274
Thatcherism 209-17
THEMBA (There Must Be an Alternative) 294(n.65)
Third World 43, 45-46, 55, 59, 230
  definition of 243-47
  post-apartheid South Africa and 242-53
  vs. First World 243, 245
Thirty Years War for Southern African Liberation (1960-90) 2-6, 39, 87, 146
Thomas, Clive 51
Thompson, Grahame 196
TINA (There Is No Alternative) 195, 209, 294(n.65)
Toronto Committee for the Liberation of Portugal's African Colonies (TCLPAC) 2
Toronto Committee for the Liberation of Southern Africa (TCLSAC) 2
Touré, Sekou 10, 33
trade liberalization 137
trade unions 52, 134, 138, 157, 167, 263, 322(n.23), 330(n.71)
  in Mozambique 78, 104
  in South Africa 69, 177, 183, 220, 223, 238-39, 241, 253
  in Zimbabwe 134, 138
transition, South African 173-94
  Nelson Mandela and 173-74, 178, 184, 187-88
  Thabo Mbeki and 167, 171, 187
Transitional Executive Council 207
transparency 62
Treatment Action Committee 237, 253
Trudeau, Pierre 269-70, 274
Truth and Reconciliation Committee (TRC), see South Africa
Tsvangirai, Morgan 135, 140, 315(n.44)
Turnhalle process 90
Tutu, Desmond 324(n.39)

Uganda 18, 24, 25, 64
ujamaa 34, 35, 37, 93, 152, 154-55
Ulenga, Ben 124
ultra-leftism 195, 219, 232, 238-39
ultra-modernism 335(n.4)
underdevelopment 67, 144
  and socialism 44-45, 48
  in South Africa 242-43, 245
unemployment 19, 230
Unilateral Declaration of Independence (UDI) (Rhodesia) 3, 129-30, 270
Union for the Total Independence of Angola (UNITA) 5, 103
United Democratic Front (UDF) 116, 234
United Nations 23, 77, 89, 91, 270,

297(n.83), 302(n.18)
Security Council Resolution 385 - 91,
    114
United Nations Operation in Mozambique, see
    ONUMOZ
United States 4, 5, 20, 27-28, 91, 95, 246,
    251
University of Zimbabwe Act 138
urban food subsidies, abolition of 22

vanguard parties 40, 49, 263
Vavi, Zwelinzima 220
Viljoen, Constand 198
villagization 26, 37, 40, 153
voluntarism 98

warlordism 25, 87
war-weariness 100
Webster, Eddie 74
Western Cape Anti-Eviction Campaign 237,
    253
white minority rule 1-3, 87, 95, 130
Willers, David 131, 145
Willowgate scandal 136
Wilson, Ken 78
Wilson, Richard 58
women's organizations 40, 52, 263
    in Mozambique 78, 104
    in South Africa 177-78, 222-23, 253
    in Tanzania 156-57
    in Zimbabwe 134, 139, 140
Wood, Ellen 80
workers' organizations 40, 156, 183
Workers' Party (Brazil) 52
World Bank, 62, 83, 88, 263, 284(n.38)
    global capitalism and 17, 20, 22-23, 27
    Mozambique and 100, 105
    South Africa and 180, 188, 215, 252
World Summit on Sustainable Development
    (WSSD) 235-36
World Trade Organization (WTO) 215, 230,
    251, 258
    Doha assembly (2001) 251-52
    Seattle assembly (1999) 251-52
Wright, Phil 44-45, 48, 50, 261

ya Nangolah, Phil 306(n.35)
Yaounde conference 264
youth brigades, Zimbabwean 134, 141
Yugoslavia (former) 66, 195

Zacarias, Felicio 88
Zaire 24, 65
Zambia 5, 30, 34, 90, 151, 259, 263, 264,
    265

and Namibia 113, 116, 127-28
ZANU 92, 95, 132-33, 137, 141, 144
    in 1980s 133-36
    in 1990s 136-38
    merger with ZAPU 134, 136
    Youth Brigades 134, 141
ZANU-Patriotic Front (ZANU-PF) 70, 129,
    131, 133-39, 141-43, 312(n.20),
    313(nn.28-29)
Zanufication of the ANC 232, 236, 240
ZCTU (Zimbabwean trade unions) 134, 136,
    139, 140
Zimbabwe (see also Rhodesia) 2-4, 6, 10, 18,
    30, 34, 49, 50, 70, 87, 92, 116, 212,
    222, 241, 259, 263, 264, 265,
    285(n.44), 294(nn.59, 63), 315(n.44)
    anti-colonialism in 142, 145, 146
    authoritarianism in 132, 138, 142-43
    citizens' movements in 134, 140
    civil society and 134, 136, 139-40
    economic decline of 136
    Economic Structural Adjustment Program
        (ESAP) in 136-40
    elections/electoral processes in 134, 139
    future prospects for 143-45
    in 1980s 133-36
    in 1990s 136-41
    land in 132, 142-43
    media in 134, 136, 138
    militarization in 141-43
    Mugabe, Gramsci, and 129-45
    nationalism as hegemony in 130-33
    nationalism in 130, 138, 145
    securocratic vision of state politics in
        133, 143
    trade unions in 134, 138
    war veterans in 141-43
    women's organizations in 134, 139, 140
Zimbabwe People's Army (ZIPA) 130
Zimbabwean African People's Union (ZAPU)
    4, 130-34, 136
ZIMRIGHTS 313(n.26)